# TERRY TRUCCO'S
# WHERE TO
# FIND IT

*The Essential Guide to
Hard-to-Locate
Goods and Services
from A to Z*

## Terry Trucco

**A FIRESIDE BOOK**

Published by Simon & Schuster

New York · London · Toronto

Sydney · Tokyo · Singapore

FIRESIDE
Rockefeller Center
1230 Avenue of the Americas
New York, NY 10020

Many of the entries in *Terry Trucco's Where to
Find It* have been previously published in
*The New York Times*.

FIRESIDE and colophon are registered trademarks
of Simon & Schuster Inc.

Designed by Amy Hill

Manufactured in the United States of America

10   9   8   7   6   5   4   3   2   1

Library of Congress Cataloging-in-Publication Data
Trucco, Terry.
Terry Trucco's where to find it : the essential guide to hard-to-
locate goods and services from A to Z / Terry Trucco.
p.   cm.
"A Fireside Book."
Includes Index.
1. Shopping—United States—Directories.   2. Consumer goods—
United States—Directories.   3. Consumer education—United States—
Directories.   I. Title.
TX336.T78   1996
380.1'45'0002573—dc20        95-26079
CIP

ISBN 0-684-80165-5

# Contents

# Contents

# G

# H

# I

# J

# K

# L

# Contents

# Q

# R

# S

# Contents

# Introduction

ANYONE WHO HAS EVER TRIED to accomplish such mundane tasks as getting a necktie cleaned, having a camera repaired or locating someone to smooth out a crystal goblet's chipped rim eventually learns there are people who do these things and do them well—the hard part is finding them.

There are, in fact, people who can repair, resuscitate or replace just about anything, from the broken zipper on a sleeping bag to worn-out tin linings in copper pots, from an antique teapot's shattered spout to the leather handbag strap the dog chewed.

If a wine spill mars a snowy silk blouse, a skilled craftsperson can dye the fabric to mask or match the stain. If the shoe doesn't fit the foot or the fashion, the right repair person can transform plain old pumps into platforms or sling-backs—and make them a half size larger. And if no shop sells the picture frame, floor lamp, belt buckle, photo album or even doghouse of your dreams, there's an artisan out there who can make it from scratch.

On the following pages you'll find dozens of people who can accomplish these and more than 150 other obscure but vital tasks. There are people who make repairs, from modest to museum quality; artisans who create or copy intriguing objects, from hand-made tiles to Victorian-style wallpaper; people who provide unusual services, like kid-proofing a house or finishing a sweater a bored knitter forgot; and purveyors of less-than-obvious supplies, like acid-free tissue paper, antique bed linens, rebuilt three-speed bikes or a Monopoly game from the 1930s. People who clean delicate items—bridal gowns, hats, gloves—are featured as well.

All of these sources are listed alphabetically, by subject, from Air conditioners, cleaned and repaired, to Zippers (hard-to-find).

I received a first-hand introduction to the wizards who make, fix and sell just about anything when I started writing "Where to Find It," a fortnightly column in *The New York Times* devoted to sussing out goods and services that are notoriously difficult to locate. And during the nearly six years I've done the column, I've been continually amazed and delighted by the superb crafts, skills and services readily available in an era when people routinely complain that things just aren't produced—or patched up—the way they used to be.

To zero in on hard-to-find sources, I've consulted countless experts—architects, interior designers, craftspeople, college professors, shopping fanatics, savvy homeowners and source books galore. Whenever possible, I've interviewed the people mentioned here in person, which has meant hundreds of excursions throughout metropolitan New York—to studios in SoHo, warehouses in Queens, factories in Brooklyn, workshops in the Bronx and even the occasional suburban garage. Inevitably, these visits are informative, fascinating and fun.

Indeed, even today the New York City area is oddly reminiscent of Dickens's London, with its abundance of small businesses and skilled artisans, many laboring at handcrafts, like stained-glass making or blacksmithing, rooted in the Middle Ages. New York is also a city of professional hoarders, people who have devoted a lifetime to saving—and selling—almost everything, from ribbons for manual typewriters to obsolete patterns of Tiffany flatware.

I've also come across equally extraordinary artisans and business people across the country and beyond, from Chicago to San Francisco,

Philadelphia to Atlanta, Mobile, Alabama, to the village of Fawley in rural England. And in an era of high-speed postal and delivery service, savvy business people happily accept mail orders. Close to three quarters of the more than 700 sources listed in this book dispatch new or repaired items via Federal Express, United Parcel, the U.S. Post Office or other services. (For sources that ship, look for the icon after each address.)

Despite the best intentions, it is impossible to conduct product tests with every single business I've mentioned. When possible, I've consulted the Better Business Bureau and the local business licensing office. I've also used recommendations from knowledgeable authorities in each field. And, finally, I've asked myself a simple question about each source I investigated: Would I want to do business with this person or company? If you see it here, the answer was yes.

Since these columns were written over several years, I've updated the addresses, telephone numbers and basic information for every source you see. Unless otherwise indicated, firms and addresses mentioned are in Manhattan. Prices are also as up-to-the-moment as possible, though, inevitably, some may have risen a bit by the time you read them. For these and any other quibbles that may crop up, I apologize.

That said, I hope you enjoy using this book as much as I enjoyed writing it. Knowing where to find the right repair person, artisan or shopkeeper can be a pleasure.

## AIR CONDITIONERS, CLEANED AND REPAIRED

W<small>HEN AN AIR CONDITIONER</small> breathes warm air instead of cold or cools less effectively than it did the previous summer, it may just be in need of a good professional cleaning.

Indeed, a dirty condenser is the culprit about 85 percent of the time when an air conditioner doesn't cool properly, according to Rich Piaia, service manager for AA Kold Air, a Bronx concern that repairs and sells air conditioners.

Other things can go wrong, of course. The unit may need a new fan motor or thermostat, or a dose of refrigerant. But before investing in a cleaning or repair, air conditioner owners should consider the age and energy efficiency rating of the machine and decide whether a repair or a replacement is ultimately the smarter buy.

"Machines that are fifteen or twenty years old are relics," said Harold McShane, manager of energy services for the Con Edison Conservation Center in Manhattan. "The new models are up to twice as energy efficient as the old. You're probably paying almost double for energy with an old machine." The center, at 405 Lexington Avenue, (800) 343-4646, offers free advice on anything from whether it is cheaper to replace an old air conditioner to the right size unit to buy.

An energy efficiency rating of 9.5 or above is considered good, while a rating of 5 or 6 is poor. To determine the rating, divide the machine's BTUs by its wattage.

Cleanliness is a big part of keeping an air conditioner humming at top capacity. During air conditioner season, filters should be cleaned once a month when the machine is in use. (Rubber mesh filters can be washed in cold water; paper filters should be replaced.) And condensers should be cleaned every other year, according to Myra Hern, a spokeswoman for Northeast Utilities, the largest utility in New England.

Unlike filters, condensers require a professional cleaning, which is done in a service shop instead of the owner's home. During a complete cleaning at Advantage Air Conditioning, the machine is dismantled, steam cleaned and given a chemical bath with high-pressurized water. The innards are oiled and refrigerant is added if necessary. A complete cleaning runs from $85 to $400, depending on size of machine. Service calls cost $35, from Canal Street to 42nd Street, higher elsewhere in Manhattan.

Advantage, in business since 1982, also sells new and reconditioned air conditioners. The latter are usually two to five years old and come with EERs, according to owner Rahav Segev. **ADVANTAGE AIR CONDITIONING,** 327 East 12th Street, New York, NY 10003; (212) 598-0016.

THE MORE OFTEN a window-unit air conditioner is used, the dirtier it gets, according to Mr. Piaia of AA Kold Air, a more than 30-year-old company that makes service calls in Manhattan and parts of the Bronx. Units suspended over busy Manhattan streets get dirtier than those on quiet side streets.

Mr. Piaia cautions against covering the outside of window air conditioners during the winter. "Covers trap moisture in the unit," he said. To keep cold air out during winter, he suggests taking the front cover off the machine, securing a piece of plastic over the interior and replacing the front.

And while removing a unit during the colder months may make the window look better, it is not necessary for the health of the machine. AA KOLD AIR, INC., P.O. Box 1784, Bronx, NY 10451; (718) 402-9400. Service calls are $48.71.

BESIDES SELLING, cleaning and repairing window air conditioners, Elgot Sales services wall-unit air conditioners. "The sleeve has to be tipped properly so water doesn't leak onto the outside wall or seep into the apartment," explained Elgot a vice-president Ellen Elias, whose father started the business in 1945.

Window air conditioners in Manhattan buildings often require special care from installers, particularly those in landmark buildings, she added. "In some buildings, air conditioners must have the same grills or colors." Service calls cost $65. ELGOT SALES CORP., 937 Lexington Avenue (near 68th Street), New York, NY 10021; (212) 879-1200. The service department is at (718) 617-2222.

# ANIMAL HABITATS

AS ANYONE IN THE MARKET for animal habitats knows, there is no shortage of generic birdcages, dog beds and birdhouses. The hard part is finding something unusual.

Al Fenech, a former fireman from San Francisco, began making decorative birdcages more than 15 years ago, when he couldn't find a cage he liked for his pet parakeet. These days, he designs cages for all types of birds. And his parakeet roosts in a six-foot-tall brass and copper cage. "He's got a real eagle complex," Mr. Fenech said.

Using copper-coated steel rods welded with brass, Mr. Fenech fashions cages that evoke San Francisco's flamboyant Victorian houses, with domes, gables, bay windows and angled corners.

Doors either slide or pull down, moat-style, held by copper chains. "Some birds like to hang out on the door when it's down," said Mr. Fenech, whose grandfather raised birds.

For a dash of color, each cage is outfitted with a three-inch strip of stained glass at the base and top.

Mr. Fenech, whose company is called Victorian Impressions, sells ready-made cages and takes orders for commissioned cages at Mabel's, a pet-motif specialty shop in New York. Customers can choose the size (from 12 inches by 12 inches to over 24 inches by 24 inches), shape and stained-glass color. For a pair of love birds that kept fighting, Mr. Fenech devised a pair of separate but similar cages. Cages cost from $350 to $4,000.

Mr. Fenech says he can build a cage for just about any bird except large parrots, which require wrought-iron bars. "Parrots need to chew," he explained. "These cages are strong, but not that strong." MABEL'S, 849 Madison Avenue (near East 70th Street), New York, NY 10021; (212) 734-3263. ✉

A WHILE BACK, Joseph Biunno saw pictures of a doghouse built as a miniature replica of the owner's house. So Mr. Biunno, who owns a custom woodworking shop in New York, decided to adapt the idea to beds. The result is a line of hand-crafted wood dog beds that resemble people beds.

The line's showpiece is a four-poster 18-by-16-inch mahogany bed, 24 inches tall, carved to resemble bamboo (from $900). Outfitted with a cushion, it can be stained, painted or covered with gold leaf. Mr. Biunno also makes a scaled-down Chippendale four-poster, a rustic wood bed carved to look like twigs and a classic brass bed.

An oval bed with a dome formed from four curved wood posts is a bit less intricate—and cheaper (from $350). A gilded curtain finial, elaborately carved, sits at the top.

Though the beds are designed for small dogs, like poodles and Yorkshire terriers, Mr. Biunno can rescale the beds for middle-size dogs or even larger dogs. "I can make a bed for a doberman, but usually a doberman sleeps wherever it wants to," he said.

Mr. Biunno also works with a dressmaker who creates draperies for the dog bed. JOSEPH BIUNNO, 129 West 29th Street (near Sixth Avenue), New York, NY 10001; (212) 629-5630. ✉

WHENEVER HE VISITS a new town, Pea Ridge Purties stops by the junkyard and forages for old license plates. "Bend it in half, and a license plate makes a great roof for a birdhouse," he explained. Mr. Purties's birdhouses, 7 inches wide, 5½ inches high and 6 inches deep, feature wood bodies, painted in bright colors, with a hole under the gable and a perch, ideal for small birds, like the tufted titmouse.

While many of his license plates are from his native Tennessee, Mr. Purties is partial to the Alabama ("it's a super yellow") and Colorado ("I like the mountains on it") plates. Birdhouses cost $37 at the Museum of American Folk Art's two New York shops.

Also at the museum's shops are pine birdhouses by J. R. Bird & Co, each with a cedar shingle roof and copper cupola and weathervane ($79). The houses, 6 inches wide, 7½ inches long and 20 inches high, can accommodate small songbirds like sparrows and wrens.   MUSEUM OF AMERICAN FOLK ART SHOP, 2 Lincoln Square (Columbus Avenue near 65th Street), New York, NY 10023; (212) 496-2966, and 62 West 50th Street, New York, NY 10112; (212) 247-5611.   ⊠

WHEN AURELIO BARRETO decided to design a house for his dog several years ago, he had no trouble choosing the style. "The igloo is an energy-efficient shape," he said. "It also gives the dog a nice turning radius."

So Mr. Barreto came up with the Dogloo, a dome-shaped doghouse fashioned from structural foam, a tough, nontoxic substance Mr. Barreto worked with during his days as an engineer for Xerox.

Mr. Barreto, president of Dogloo Inc. in Corona, California, said structural foam is harder than wood, will not splinter if the dog chews it and insulates better than plastic or wood. It is formed by injecting nitrogen gas into plastic.

Dogloos, which are patented, are available in blue or tan and come in two sizes, with a 26-inch radius for dogs up to 30 pounds and a 40-inch radius for larger pets. The Dogloo, available with a vinyl door, can be ordered at most pet stores. C & K Distributors in Rego Park, Queens, also has Dogloos in stock, from $90 for a large model.   C & K DISTRIBUTORS, 89-50 Metropolitan Avenue, Rego Park, Queens, NY 11374; (718) 275-5719.

## APPLIANCES, REPAIRS TO SMALL

BUSINESS HAS BEEN GOOD lately at Riverside Housewares, and owner Stanley Stern can't decide whether ecology or the economy is the reason. Mr. Stern, in business over 45 years, repairs small appliances—toasters, percolators, hair dryers, blenders, vacuum cleaners and fans, among others.

"I think the use-it-and-throw-it-away philosophy is changing," he said, standing by a shelf of rehabilitated waffle irons from the 1940s and '50s. "People are more willing to have old things repaired."

By old things, Mr. Stern can mean *really* old things. His specialty is finding and restoring kitchen gadgets that date from the 1930s. Sometimes the touches are cosmetic—new pot handles, new tea kettle whistles, fresh suction cups for an old meat grinder. He also removes asbestos wiring in older appliances.

It doesn't pay to fix all home appliances, Mr. Stern added. "If the motor goes on a can opener, we don't bother." But a $10 or $15 repair can often be worthwhile for a $50 or even $30 item, particularly if the customer is fond of it.

Appliances made of metal, like fans or canister-style vacuum cleaners, are almost always worth fixing. Most old motors were built to last longer than the newer ones, he said, patting a rehabilitated metal table fan. "I'll sell this for $100."

Typical repairs entail new switches or new wiring. Mr. Stern has an inventory of parts, including glass tops for percolators. The store also features a selection of vintage Pyrex glassware, harvested from flea markets. **RIVERSIDE HOUSEWARES,** 2315 Broadway (near 84th Street), New York, NY 10024; (212) 873-7837.

"A LOT OF PEOPLE DON'T REALIZE they can get their appliances repaired," said Stan Benson, an assistant manager at Solomon's Appliance Repair, a mega-repair center in Brooklyn. In business for over 40 years, Solomon's is an authorized factory service center for about 100 companies, including Black & Decker, Braun, Dirt Devil, Kitchen-Aid, Norelco and Waring. Besides obvious products, like shavers, vacuum cleaners and toaster ovens, the company repairs unusual items, like contact lens sterilizers and mobility carts for the elderly. There's also a knife sharpener on staff.

Items need repairs for all sorts of reasons. "The owners put coffee in the water compartment of the coffeemaker, or they immerse the entire coffeemaker in water to clean it," Mr. Benson says, shaking his head. People also drop appliances. And some items just wear out.

For products under warranty, there's no repair charge if the customer   provides a receipt. Other repairs depend on parts and labor. SOLOMON'S APPLIANCE REPAIR, 1701 86th Street (at 17th Avenue), Bensonhurst, Brooklyn, NY, 11214; (718) 236-5065.   ⊠

## APPRAISERS

Ask AN APPRAISER what he or she is most likely to hear when a client describes a cherished heirloom, and the answer is almost always the same: "It's very old."

Unfortunately, age is not synonymous with value. "You can get a work of ancient art for $200," said Barry Leo Delaney, an appraiser with O'Toole-Ewald Art Associates.

Many people are only vaguely aware of what their household effects are worth, from the table that might be a Stickley to Grandma's ruby necklace.

Enter the appraiser. Occasionally, people hire an appraiser simply to satisfy their curiosity about what they own. But most people take action when it becomes necessary to put personal property in order, whether for insurance, estate or tax purposes, or in the case of a divorce settlement.

Choosing a qualified appraiser can be a challenge. A good place to start is with a professional appraisal organization, like the 89-year-old American Society of Appraisers, P.O. Box 17265, Washington, DC 10041; (703) 478-2228, or the 46-year-old Appraisers Association of America, 386 Park Avenue South, New York, NY 10016; (212) 889-5404. Both have strict membership requirements and encourage members to follow guidelines set by the Appraisal Foundation in Washington, D.C., a government agency.

They also provide names of appraisers in specialties from fine art and antiques to gems and general property.

Before hiring an appraiser, Alex Rosenberg, president of the Appraisers Association of America, suggests asking for references and information on educational background, teaching experience or writing.

Ask for a sample appraisal and expect to see a plump document with detailed descriptions and photographs. (Appraisals are legal documents and *must* be in writing.) And hire only an appraiser who charges by the hour instead of by the value of the items being appraised.

Objectivity is also important, because some appraisers are affiliated with auction houses or galleries. "An appraiser may be more objective if he or she is not connected with the sale of works of art or jewelry," said Victor Wiener, executive director of the Appraisers Association.

Two methods of evaluation are generally applied. For insurance purposes, the appraiser usually lists replacement value, which tends to be higher than fair market value, the average amount a buyer will pay a seller. Fair market value is applied to appraisals done for estates, divorces and charitable contributions.

When necessary, the appraiser can supply both sets of valuations. "Often a person who has an appraisal done for insurance purposes will want to sell or donate an item later," said Gayle M. Skluzacek, president of Abigail Hartmann Associates, a six-person fine art appraisal firm that also evaluates general contents of estates.

Appraisals involving divorce settlements can be prickly, she said, recalling an angry husband in Florida who locked all the silver in a closet, then swallowed the key when Ms. Skluzacek arrived for the appraisal. "We had to call the police," she said. In divorce appraisals, it is imperative that each appraiser agree to use the same valuation, whether fair market or replacement. Abigail Hartmann charges $100 an hour plus expenses per appraiser. ABIGAIL HARTMANN ASSOCIATES, 415 Central Park West (at 101st Street), New York, NY 10025; (212) 316-5406.

FOR ELIN LAKE EWALD, whose company, O'Toole-Ewald Art Associates, specializes in damage, loss and fraud appraisals, natural disasters and flooded basements mean business. The 12 appraisers in Ms. Ewald's 60-year-old firm, which handles high-end fine art, often research appraisals using photographs when objects are seriously damaged or destroyed. "We can reconstruct entire houses from family photographs," Ms. Ewald said.

The firm has also dealt with objects damaged in transit, from a Mark Rothko painting slashed by a baling hook to a shrunken head from Colombia that turned up in three pieces after a photo shoot. With damaged objects, the appraiser must determine prior condition, restoration costs and the object's postrestoration value. O'Toole-Ewald charges from $125 to $300 an hour per appraiser.   O'TOOLE-EWALD ART ASSOCI-ATES, INC., 1133 Broadway (at 26th Street), New York, NY 10010; (212) 989-5151.

IN YEARS PAST, appraisals were often vague, with no mention of an object's measurements or condition. But such appraisals are unacceptable these days, said Elizabeth von Habsburg, a partner in Masterson, Gurr, Johns, a 55-year-old Manhattan firm. With estates, Ms. von Habsburg asks questions about the contents and consults old insurance records "to see what's there," she said. If a generalist from her firm discovers an important painting in an estate, a paintings specialist is called in for the appraisal, she said. The firm charges $200 an hour per appraiser.   MAS-TERSON, GURR, JOHNS, INC., 122 East 55th Street, New York, NY 10022; (212) 486-7373.

SOMETIMES AN APPRAISER discovers a happy surprise. Asked to evaluate a house full of sterling silver, Jane H. Willis, of Tenafly, New Jersey, noticed a handsome tea set the owner didn't want appraised. "She assumed it was silver plate because the word sterling wasn't engraved in the silver," Ms. Willis said. But the tea set, by Gorham, was from a brief era at the turn of the century when the firm didn't label its sterling. "It was worth $40,000," said Ms. Willis. Ms. Willis charges $200 an hour. JANE H. WILLIS APPRAISAL SERVICE; (201) 569-6669.

APPRAISAL SERVICES ASSOCIATES, a four-person art and general contents appraisal firm headed by Charles Rosoff, specializes in litigation disputes of all types, including damage/loss claims, bankruptcy and divorce. Liquidity is a key factor in equitable distribution in a divorce, noted Mr. Rosoff. "While a $100,000 painting may be easy to sell, $100,000 in household contents may prove much harder," he said. The

firm charges $100 an hour, plus expenses.   APPRAISAL SERVICES ASSO-
CIATES, 270 Lafayette Street (near Prince Street), New York, NY 10012;
(212) 226-7200.

CLIENTS OFTEN BRING new engagement rings to Robert C. Aretz, Jr., at
Gem Appraisers' Laboratory "for a double check," as he puts it. If the
price is unusually low, the gem may be less valuable than the jeweler
claims. "But the price may be right for the lower quality," he said. Jewelry appraisals vary within a range of about 20 percent. "So if I say
something is worth $1,000 and someone charges $1,050, you're not being overcharged," he said. Since lost gems cannot be appraised from
photographs, jewelry should always be insured. Mr. Aretz charges $200
an hour or from $50 to $100 an item.   GEM APPRAISERS' LABORATORY,
608 Fifth Avenue (near 49th Street), New York, NY 10020; (212) 333-
3122.

HOMEOWNERS WHO SIMPLY WANT a record of what they own, sans valuation, often videotape the contents of their house. A more time-consuming
alternative is to individually photograph and describe each item. Or
you can hire a pro. Ronald Troy, owner of Troy Documentation, documents residences and businesses, photographing contents room by
room.

   He prefers still photography to videotape because "it's easier to
make changes if something is lost or moved," he said. Descriptions and
3½-by-5-inch color photographs are compiled in large three-ring
binders. Mr. Troy charges $50 an hour or about $800 to document a
one-bedroom apartment.   TROY DOCUMENTATION, (212) 353-3883.

## ARCHITECTURAL ORNAMENTS
## (COLUMNS, BRACKETS, PEDESTALS)

IN THE 1960S AND EARLY 1970S, almost no one wanted the ornamental
carved wood columns, brackets, turnings and moldings made by American Wood Column Corp., a Brooklyn concern in business for over 60
years. "You couldn't give them away," says Thomas Lupo, an owner.

All that has changed. In addition to a renewed enthusiasm for restoring historic properties, postmodern buildings often display the occasional classical column or pedestal. Column capitals and pedestals turn up as coffee table bases. And the carved wood fireplaces the Victorians loved are popular once again.

American Wood Column Corp., which created the paneled courtroom for the film *The Verdict,* keeps a large supply of classical columns, capitals and pedestals in stock, priced from around $300. But much of their work is customized. "We can follow a classical architectural detail to the letter," said Mr. Lupo. Or the company can mix, match or create something new. A Corinthian capital can go on any kind of base. And a column can be plain, fluted, twisted or grooved.

The company, which does repairs, also makes ornamental ceiling roundels and wall ornaments, including garlands and cupids, similar to those fashioned from plaster. Wood ornaments are molded from a composition of glue, wood and sawdust, and can be more versatile than plaster as molds are smaller, and it is easier to change details, Mr. Lupo said. AMERICAN WOOD COLUMN CORP., 913 Grand Street, Brooklyn, NY 11211; (718) 782-3163.

BAREWOOD ARCHITECTURAL WOODWORKING in Brooklyn will make almost anything out of wood, says owner Leslie Neilson. But most of their work is customized replications of 18th- and 19th-century woodwork, including columns, handrails, cornices, fireplace mantles, cabinets and furniture. The company also does repairs.

A big part of their business is what Mr. Neilson calls odd jobs. The 16-year-old company recently expanded a 19th-century double bed into a queen-size model. And they modified a carved Victorian fireplace to fit the client's house. Barewood Architectural Woodworking charges $55 an hour. BAREWOOD ARCHITECTURAL WOODWORKING, 106 Ferris Street, Brooklyn, NY 11231; (718) 875-9037.

BASIL WALTER OF SWEENY WALTER ASSOCIATES trained as an architect and once owned a cabinet-making company in New York. So five years ago he combined his skills to become a designer and technical consultant, specializing in architectural woodwork. "We offer someone to control the whole project," Mr. Walter said.

Mr. Walter draws plans for the woodwork, selects and supervises the craftsmen and even chooses the wood. "A lot of Cuban mahogany was used 100 years ago, and the wrong piece of African or Honduran mahogany can look awful next to it," he said.

Much of his work has been for apartments in the Dakota, where much of the original woodwork was removed. Using his knowledge of the period and remaining examples from the building, Mr. Walter, who charges $60 an hour, designed reproductions. SWEENY WALTER ASSOCI- ATES, 601 Broadway, Room 301, New York, NY 10012; (212) 505-1955.

## ARCHITECTURE SALVAGE SPECIALISTS

REMEMBER THE GLAMOROUS old elevator cabs with domed ceilings, gilded mirror frames and paneled walls at the Fifth Avenue outpost of Lord & Taylor? Ever wonder what happened to them?

Evan Blum knows. His firm, Irreplaceable Artifacts, dismantled the eight elevator interiors when new ones were installed, carted them off to his Lower Manhattan showroom and, recently, sold the last one. One is now a ceiling centerpiece in the master bathroom of a private home. Another is in an entrance foyer. "They have endless uses," Mr. Blum said.

Mr. Blum is in the architectural salvage business, or ornamental re- cycling, as he puts it. Every year his workers visit historic buildings be- ing gutted, demolished or remodeled and harvest vast quantities of doors, grates, windows, cornices, finials, fountains, mantelpieces, ban- isters, bathroom fixtures, lighting fixtures, pews and other old col- lectibles.

The proper architectural ornament can be a handsome, even provocative grace note for a house, apartment or garden. And for an old house in the throes of restoration, architectural salvage companies, like Mr. Blum's, are a useful source for doorknobs, hinges, stained-glass windows and similar hard-to-get accoutrements for buildings from a bygone era.

Often an antique ornament needs a little work before it can go into the living room. Columns and capitals can make table bases. Elevator door grates can become room partitions. One customer recently bought a church's Gothic-style wood paneling to use as wainscotting, Mr. Blum said.

A lively history often embellishes the appeal of certain ornaments. Mr. Blum's inventory has included a 1904 walnut-paneled room from the St. Regis Hotel, a two-faced clock that hung in New York's Commodore Hotel and two cast stone cats, over seven feet tall, from Palisades Amusement Park in New Jersey. Mr. Blum also sells bits of the Brooklyn Bridge, namely hand-made railing ($250 for a one-foot-long section).

Mr. Blum got into the antique business at age 12, selling old phonographs. But dealing in grand-scale objects was natural, he added. "I hate to see old things get wasted."

Irreplaceable Artifacts also owns Victorian foundry patterns and reproduces statues, furniture, fountains, urns and other garden enhancements, starting from $75 for a cast-iron dolphin, 14 inches tall. A $4 mail order catalog is available.  **IRREPLACEABLE ARTIFACTS,** 14 Second Avenue (at Houston Street), New York, NY 10003; (212) 777-2900, and 326 South County Road, Palm Beach, FL 33480; (407) 833-4742.  ✉

MARK CHARRY, WHO OWNS Architectural Antiques Exchange, got into the architectural salvage business more than 25 years ago as a Temple University student. "They were demolishing thousands of homes around the university," he recalled. Mr. Charry contacted the wreckers, bought all he could, stored it in garages and has been dealing in oldies but goodies ever since.

Most objects in his 30,000-square-foot Philadelphia showroom are big—doors, mantels, pedestal sinks, wood paneling. But his specialty is Victorian built-in wardrobes, found in Philadelphia houses built between 1870 and 1895. The classic wardrobe, in elaborately carved walnut, chestnut or oak, consists of closets and drawers, with a dressing table and mirror in the middle.

Some customers polish up the wood and put them in bedrooms. Others have Mr. Charry convert them into home entertainment centers or bars. Philadelphia closets range from about $700 to $2,500. Conversions start at around $4,000, closet included. A free brochure is available.  **ARCHITECTURAL ANTIQUES EXCHANGE,** 715 North Second Street, Philadelphia, PA 19123; (215) 922-3669.  ✉

URBAN ARCHAEOLOGY STOCKS numerous doors, closets, mantels and other wood objects, including a handsomely polished shoeshine stand for $17,500. But the cavernous shop, near SoHo, also has a selection of Victorian sinks and tubs. Bathroom soap holders, towel bars and other hardware are another specialty, with old examples as well as copies made from old hardware from New York's Plaza Hotel. Hardware reproductions start at around $100.  **URBAN ARCHAEOLOGY,** 285 Lafayette Street (near Houston Street), New York, NY 10012; (212) 431-6969.

SINCE 1959, BRIMFIELD, MASSACHUSETTS, a tiny hamlet about 30 miles from Hartford, Connecticut, has hosted the enormous Brimfield Outdoor Antique Shows for three six-day stretches every summer. The show attracts hundreds of dealers from all over the country, including many specializing in architectural salvage. For information call (413) 283-6149.

## ART CONSERVATORS

*F*OR MOST ART CONSERVATORS, the big occupational thrill is working on art objects of museum quality. But less significant items can be exciting, too, particularly when they pose interesting problems, says Harriet Irgang, a partner in Rustin Levinson Art Conservation, which conserves, restores and repairs paintings.

Ms. Irgang once worked on a landscape painted on oilcloth by a client's grandmother. It had been nailed to a wall, and the client wanted it cleaned, repaired and framed. Flaking paint needed to be set down. And the disintegration of the unconventional canvas, held together mainly by the paint, had to be halted. "This was a challenge because it was so unusual," said Ms. Irgang, a painting conservator since 1984.

A more common job is repairing enormous contemporary paintings torn and damaged in transit. "People who collect contemporary paintings rarely think about conservation problems, but big paintings need special care when they're moved," Ms. Irgang explained, standing over a huge, ripped canvas.

The Manhattan conservation studio, which has a branch in Miami, Florida, has six conservators and cleans paintings from old masters to the present. They remove discolored varnish and do structural work, which includes creating linings, stretchers and supports, on all sorts of canvases, from cotton to burlap.

Clients include the Whitney Museum, the Forbes Gallery and the AT&T collection. For private clients without museum budgets, work can be done in phases, starting with efforts to prevent the painting from further disintegrating. Cosmetic touches, such as removing discolored varnish, can come later. Rustin Levinson Art Conservation charges $100 an hour. **RUSTIN LEVINSON ART CONSERVATION;** (212) 594-8862.

CLIFFORD CRAINE, OWNER OF DAEDALUS, INC., recently restored a pitcher and basin that belonged to John Hancock. He removed the old restoration, took the objects apart, cleaned them and reassembled everything with a modern adhesive. "About 50 percent of our work is redoing old restorations," says Mr. Craine, a conservator for over 20 years. Early adhesives often lose stability, and paints can yellow and darken.

Daedalus, with studios in Manhattan and Cambridge, has three conservators and works on sculpture from ancient to modern times, as well as archeological and decorative objects. Clients include the Whitney Museum and the Baltimore Museum sculpture gardens. Daedalus charges $85 an hour. **DAEDALUS, INC.;** (800) 252-0368 or (617) 497-4027.

VERY OFTEN AN ARTWORK on paper becomes damaged simply because it was framed improperly, says Daria Keynan, a paper conservator. Mattings not made from 100 percent ragboard can contain acid, which destroys paper. And tape can leave stains and tears. "Half of the damage I see in works on paper from private collection is avoidable," said Ms. Keynan.

Many paper problems can be solved. Darkening and discoloration can often be removed with good quality water or bleaches. Brown spots are also removable. But fading is usually permanent. Daria Keynan charges $75 an hour. **DARIA KEYNAN;** (212) 645-5245.

## AUCTIONS, STORAGE

THEY'RE A POPULAR RESOURCE for people who traffic in things second-hand, such as used furniture sellers, people with booths at flea markets and, occasionally, antiques dealers. But anyone can attend the auctions held periodically by moving and storage companies to clear out unclaimed or impounded goods.

For the sharp-eyed, or the lucky, the right auction can be a treasure hunt, of sorts, yielding items, anything from the welcome to the worthless.

"A lot of what we auction off is stored records of bankrupt companies," said Jack Fuchs, owner of Whitehall Storage, a ministorage concern in Manhattan. But interesting items occasionally turn up, such as good secondhand furniture, boxes of CDs and electronic equipment, from near-new televisions to computers.

Moving and storage company auctions can be attractive for anyone looking for functional houshold items at a modest cost. A box of old appliances needing a cleaning can go for $15 or $20, for example.

But auction shopping is a far cry from visiting a department store or even a flea market. Lots, for example, tend to be enormous—and bulky.

Though moving companies sometimes sell matched items, such as bedroom sets, in single lots, more often the bidding is for the complete contents of 250-cubic-foot container. And at ministorage companies, where customers rent partitioned "rooms" the size of a walk-in closet or larger, bids are for the room's entire contents.

Sales are almost always in cash. And successful bidders must pick up their purchases quickly, usually within five days.

Taking possession, in fact, can be something of a shock, since bidders often buy a portion of their goods without seeing them.

When bidding for a room at a ministorage concern, for example, interested buyers receive an inventory sheet of the room's items. But as they are not allowed to enter the room or touch anything until after the auction, often all they see are items visible near the room's door.

Legal considerations determine the rules and rituals of most moving and storage company auctions. After dispatching warnings to delinquent clients through certified mail and in local newspapers, moving and storage companies can sell the client's goods to help defray unpaid bills.

Auctions occur when a company winds up with sufficient inventory to warrant a sale. For some companies, that can be every two or three months. On the other hand, Bolliger, a moving company, recently held its first sale in six years.

The best way to learn of sales is through the auction listings in *The New York Times* Sunday classified ad section as well as the legal listings in such newspapers as *Newsday* and the *Daily News*. Trade papers, such as the *Arts & Antiques Weekly* in Newtown, Connecticut, also publish auction notices.

Though some sales are held on the moving or storage company's premises, others take place at auction houses, such as Country Auctions, an eight-year-old concern in Long Island City. Much of Country Auctions' inventory comes from moving and storage companies, including Whitehall Storage. But items are sold in single or small lots, and visitors can view them an hour before sale.

"You never know what will be at an auction," said owner Ray Brachfeld, an auctioneer for 30 years. He numbers a carousel horse in a ministorage room that sold for $2,000 and a player piano ($50 for the room) among his more interesting sales.

"But those are the exceptions," he added. "It's usually abused used furniture or clean used furniture." A chair in need of new upholstery can sell for as little as $10.

Call for times and dates of sales.  COUNTRY AUCTIONS, 9-11 43rd Avenue (Vernon Blvd.), Long Island City, NY 11101; (718) 482-1500.

THOUGH IT MAY NOT BE POSSIBLE to see all of the contents in a ministorage room, the price may be right. Rooms start for as little as $10 and can go to few thousand dollars, according to Nick Sprayregen, owner of Tuck-It-Away, a 15-year-old ministorage company. Average room price is $100 to $300. "Bidding usually lasts 60 seconds," he added.

With warehouses in New York, New Jersey and Connecticut, Tuck-It-Away usually has a sale every month.  TUCK-IT-AWAY; (212) 368-1717.

"THE ROOMS ARE BASICALLY FOR HOUSEHOLD GOODS, nothing exotic like cars or motorcycles," said Louis Long, manager of New York Security Mini-Storage. Auctions, usually held every six weeks, are postponed if there are not enough rooms to sell. Rooms routinely start at $10 and can go into the thousands. NEW YORK SECURITY MINI-STORAGE, 28 Laight Street (at Varick Street), New York, NY 10013; (212) 966-9777.

WHEN LIBERTY MOVING AND STORAGE, an agent of Allied Van Lines, holds it annual auction each summer in its two Long Island warehouses, most of the goods are in closed containers. (Bidders can consult inventory sheets made by the movers when they packed the goods.)

Containers usually sell for $500 to $600, said Madeline Connelly, accounts receivable manager. But they can go into the thousands of dollars.

Occasionally, containers are broken up, with large items of furniture, such as bedroom sets, sold separately. But most sales include mystery boxes. "A lot may consist of six or seven boxes with just the top of the boxes open," she explained. "So you see dishes in the top box but can't see the contents below." LIBERTY MOVING AND STORAGE; (212) 223-6440 or (516) 234-3000.

"THE SPACE IS MORE VALUABLE than the stuff," said Richard Siegler of his cluttered Greenwich Village warehouse. A moving company since 1895, when Mr. Siegler's grandfather started it, Siegler Bros. stocks old furniture, electronic equipment and computers. "Often, when you move someone they ask you to take things away," Mr. Siegler said. "And we wind up with it."

Instead of auctions, Siegler Bros. sells secondhand goods outright. Recent sales have included a turquoise and white laminate file cabinet from an office they moved ($60), a sturdy white parson-style desk ($100) and a country-style oak table with modestly carved legs ($200). SIEGLER BROS., INC., 264 West 11th Street, New York, NY 10014; (212) 675-2333.

## AWNINGS

IN THE DAYS BEFORE AIR CONDITIONING, awnings were a popular device to keep houses and apartment buildings cool. And with the current concern for energy conservation, a growing number of well-dressed windows, sundecks and patios are displaying awnings, the brighter the better.

For years, residential awnings looked pretty much alike, with raked tops and scalloped edges. But homeowners can now choose from a variety of styles, colors and even gadgets.

"Awnings have grown increasingly decorative," said Eddy Dee, Sr., who opened Awnings by Dee, 43 years ago when he got out of the army. Woven acrylics, which greatly expanded the palette of color choices, are particularly popular because they let in light but not sun. Oddly enough, white is still the favorite with most customers, Mr. Dee said.

Fabric awnings, which consist of a metal frame hooded in canvas, vinyl or woven acrylic, can be either stationary or retractable. The latter can be motorized to fold with the flick of a switch. Available for more than a decade, motorized awnings have become increasingly sophisticated. Among the innovations is a special sun and wind control; the awning automatically opens when the sun gets hot and closes either at sunset or if the wind reaches 15 miles per hour.

Fabric has improved as well. Acrylic fabrics, for example, won't mildew or rot. The downside: Unlike canvas, which contracts with water, acrylic fabric stretches when it gets wet.

Awnings by Dee, which does repairs, also removes and stores awnings at the season's end. Awnings start at around $450. AWNINGS BY DEE, 249-13 Northern Boulevard, Little Neck, NY 11363; (718) 224-6669.

IN THE LATE 1980s, the most stylish business awnings were burgundy or gray. But today's hot hues are greens and blues, according to Jay LoIacono, a vice-president of Acme Awning Company, makers of customized awnings for businesses and residences since 1921.

For homes, gadgets are increasingly popular, particularly motorized awnings outfitted with remote controls. "We get customers who say, 'I want to lie on my deck chair and watch the awning go up and down,'" Mr. LoIacono said.

Customized awnings at Acme, which also does repairs, start at around $600. ACME AWNING COMPANY, 435 Van Nest Avenue (near East Tremont Avenue), Bronx, NY 10460; (718) 409-1881.

## BEADWORK, REPAIRED AND SOLD

People have used beads to decorate clothing, objects and themselves for thousands of years. "Beads are compelling," said Lois Sher Dubin, author of *The History of Beads, from 30,000 B.C. to the Present* (Abrams, 1987). "They feel good to touch, and your eyes are attracted because light bounces off of them."

The earliest beads were things like bear teeth, bits of shell and water-worn pebbles with natural holes. They were usually talismanic, believed "to give you that extra measure of help out on the hunt," Ms. Dubin said. Countless cultures have devised their own style of beading, right up to the beadwork found on modern evening dresses and wedding gowns.

But what is strung can come unstrung. And finding someone to re-bead an object—whether it's a West African headdress or a 1920's handbag—can be a challenge. Beadwork is slow, tedious and repetitious. It requires sharp eyesight and skillful hands. And matching beads can be difficult, particularly on very old objects.

"These beads were hard to find," said Mary Jo Meade, a Manhattan textile conservator, holding a colorful Sioux shoulderbag covered with minuscule glass beads. "They have to be the right color and size. Obviously, I can't use plastic beads."

Like most bead specialists, Ms. Meade collects old beaded objects as a source of beads for future projects. And she has favorite suppliers, such as Beader's Paradise in Blackfoot, Idaho, which carries Native American beads.

Ms. Meade learned about beading while working in the textile conservation department at the Museum of Natural History. She has worked on Victorian beading, beadwork from the 1920s and more recent wedding gowns. But much of her effort today is on American Indian and West African beadwork. This usually consists of large areas that are completely covered in beads.

"On the Native American pieces, it can be a challenge just to see the beads," she explained. Victorian beads are usually a bit bigger.

Often a little water is all that's needed to clean up a heavily beaded object that looks dirty or dull. "Beads don't fade like textiles," Ms. Meade pointed out. "They just get a little scuffed up sometimes."

Ms. Meade charges $55 an hour.    MARY JO MEADE; (212) 223-0231. ✉

"THERE'S SOMETHING VERY RESTFUL and soothing about working with beads," said Ita Aber, another textile conservator. Mrs. Aber once restored a beaded footstool for the Theodore Roosevelt birthplace in Manhattan. She has also worked on a number of beaded Victorian textiles, including bellpulls and decorative table covers.

Eighteenth-century textiles are considerably more difficult to work with, she said, adding, "They used hand-made threads and even hair to sew on their beads."

Mrs. Aber, who organized the textile study room at the Jewish Museum, charges a $100 consulting fee, which is usually deducted from the cost of the project if the client decides to have the work done. She also decorates cloth-covered sunglasses with pearls, coral and other beading material; they are sold at the Eclectic Collector, 215 Katonah Avenue, Katonah, New York. Prices start at about $125.   ITA ABER, 20 West 72nd Street, New York, NY 10023; (212) 877-6400.  ✉

SHERU IS ONE OF THE OLDEST and biggest bead shops in the garment district. Thousands of beads are on display, including European glass beads in huge bins ($1 a dozen, $9 a gross) and large ceramic beads, shaped like owls or elephants. Some beads are sold on strings, some by weight. And some come in plastic bags ($1 for a dozen colorful corn-row beads). **SHERU,** 49 West 38th Street, New York, NY 10018; (212) 730-0766.

SHIPWRECK BEADS, a shop and mail order house in Olympia, Washington, carries beads in a variety of sizes, colors and materials, from wood to glass. A catalog is $4. **SHIPWRECK BEADS,** 2727 Westmoor Court, SW Olympia, WA 98502; (360) 754-2323. ✉

# BIKES (THREE-SPEEDS AND OTHER HARD-TO-FIND MODELS)

To MOST CYCLISTS, the three-speed bicycle is at best a pleasant memory. But to a core of devotees, the three-speed is easy and uncomplicated, with none of the weird brake systems or confusing gears found on more sophisticated bicycles.

Three-speeds are particularly popular in New York City, with its flat terrain. Some riders, including messengers, choose three-speeds for durability and comfort (rear metal fenders, standard on three-speeds, help to keep puddles from splashing on riders). And many consider three-speeds a less obvious target for thieves than flashier bikes.

Winter, a slow season for most bike shops, is an ideal time to buy a new bike or have an old one reconditioned. That said, finding a three-speed can be challenging. Many shops, well-stocked with more fashionable models, like mountain bikes, don't carry them. And among those that do, the debate rages over whether new three-speeds are as good as those built between the 1950s and the 1970s.

Emey Hoffmann, owner of Emey's Bike Shop, deals mainly in re-conditioned models. "The older bikes were usually stronger, with better gears, better materials, better steel," he said. With a stash of vintage frames and parts, he rebuilds three-speeds to customer specifications, noting the rider's height and biking needs. His rebuilt bikes, with old and new parts, cost $125 to $250.

A good place to find vintage three-speeds is at garage sales, he added. "Then get them reconditioned."

Three-speed bikes, originally known as English racers, became popular in England in the 1930s and 1940s. "They were lighter, faster and more comfortable than the old one-gear American bikes," Mr. Hoffmann said. Highly regarded English makers through the 1970s included Raleigh, Rudge and Humber.

Mr. Hoffmann suggests city riders paint bikes black to deter thefts and use two locks: a U-lock on the front wheel and frame and a chain to attach the back wheel to a pole. "And always wear a helmet," he added. EMEY'S BIKE SHOP, 141 East 17th Street (near Third Avenue), New York, NY 10003; (212) 475-7409.

A GOOD VINTAGE THREE-SPEED will probably cost as much as a new one, according to Frank Arroyo, owner of Frank's Bike Shop. But the Sturmey Archer gear found on older English bikes "lasts forever," Mr. Arroyo said. New three-speeds appeal to customers who want to break in the bike themselves. Unlike bikes with more than five gears, all three-speed gear is hidden in the hub, protecting it in bad weather.

As long as the frame is not cracked, old bikes can usually be overhauled, added Mr. Arroyo. His reconditioned bikes start at $100. Mr. Arroyo also sells new three-speeds by Schwinn, Ross and Giant. FRANK'S BIKE SHOP, 553 Grand Street (near Lewis Street), New York, NY 10002; (212) 533-6332.

THOUGH THREE-SPEEDS are not exactly hot bikes, the six Manhattan Metro Bicycle stores carry new models by Ross, Giant, Raleigh, Specialized and Metro, the company's line. Most new three-speeds, including Raleigh, are made in Taiwan or China and sell for between $200 and $230. But with a steel frame and retro appearance, the Globe 3 by Specialized, a mountain bike maker, costs $300. Metro also sells three-speed folding tricycles. METRO BICYCLE STORES, 1311 Lexington Avenue (88th Street), New York, NY 10128, (212) 427-4450; 360 West 47th Street, New York, NY 10036, (212) 581-4500; 231 West 96th

Street, New York, NY 10025, (212) 663-7531; 332 East 14th Street, New York, NY 10003, (212) 228-4344; 546 Sixth Avenue, New York, NY 10011, (212) 255-5100; 417 Canal Street, New York, NY 10013, (212) 334-8000.

BESIDES SELLING new three-speeds by Raleigh and Schwinn, Roger Bergman's 32-year-old Pedal Pusher Bike Shop rents vintage three-speeds, mainly from the 1970s. Most are English—Raleigh, Rudge, Humber Sport, Robin Hood, Hercules and BSA. "We've got more three-speeds than anything else to rent, so there's always something available," said Russell Blackwell, the manager. Three-speed bikes rent for $3.93 an hour or $9.93 a day.   PEDAL PUSHER BIKE SHOP, 1306 Second Avenue (near 69th Street), New York, NY 10021; (212) 288-5592.

## BILLIARD TABLES, REPAIRED AND CUSTOM-MADE

WHETHER IT WAS THE FILM *The Color of Money* or the drowsy economy, interest in pool enjoyed a renaissance of sorts in the early 1990s, both in homes and in pool halls. And that interest has continued well into the decade.

"Playing pool is cheap entertainment," said Ron Blatt, owner of Blatt Billiards, which sells, moves and repairs new and antique pool tables. To insure a good game, a billiard table must be properly maintained. Regular tune-ups aren't in order. But cloth coverings can wear out, usually after five or six years. Rubber bumpers dry out and harden. And rails, which edge the table, often get scratched and nicked, usually by cue sticks.

The wooden legs of older pool tables may also require restoration, particularly if frustrated players have kicked them over the years. Mr. Blatt's company, founded by his grandfather in 1923, recently repaired the intricate marquetry legs of a handsome 1920s table for a men's club.

Like a piano, a pool table is a precision instrument as well as a piece of furniture. "The structure and frame assembly must be rock solid," said Mr. Blatt, pointing to the wooden buttresses on an unfinished custom table in his upstairs workroom.

The construction of the rail, type of rubber used and way in which the rubber is attached to the rail help determine the speed of the table. Since it can be hard to control the cue ball on a fast table, most people play best on a medium-speed table.

But appearance is important, too; by sheer size the pool table usually becomes a room's dominant decorative object. Most home tables measure 4 feet by 8 feet, compared to the 4½-by-9-foot regulation table; 6-by-12-foot English snooker tables are particularly hard to ignore.

"That's a lot of color for a room," said Mr. Blatt, who offers cloths in 30 different hues. Eighty percent of his customers choose green, which comes in four shades. Re-covering starts at $350.

Besides repairs, Blatt Billiards makes custom tables in everything from carved wood to chrome and sells antique tables dating as early as the 1850s. One 19th-century cast-iron monster weighs 3,000 pounds. BLATT BILLIARDS, 809 Broadway (near 12th Street), New York, NY 10003; (212) 674-8855.

YEARS AGO, POOL TABLES were covered in 100 percent wool, which was pretty but delicate. A bad move with a cue stick could rip the cloth, which can't be patched. Today's coverings are usually of blended wool and nylon. And, fortunately, they're a lot more durable, according to Vernon Loria, a partner in V. Loria & Sons, which has sold and repaired billiard equipment since 1912.

Besides standard green, hot colors for pool tables include teal blue, rose and lavender. Mr. Loria likes banker's gray on chrome tables. His slowest sellers are gold and purple. Mr. Loria charges from $350 to recover a table in green, $25 extra for other colors.

His company, with stores in Manhattan and Yonkers, also moves pool tables (from $450), replaces rubber bumpers (from $175) and repairs cue sticks. V. LORIA & SONS, 178 Bowery near Delancey, New York, NY 10012, (212) 925-0300; 1876 Central Park Avenue, Yonkers, NY 10710, (914) 779-3377.

MOVING BILLIARD TABLES can be hazardous, according to Pete Rossi, manager of the Game Room, a 20-year-old New Jersey concern that sells, makes and repairs pool tables. "Some weigh a ton, literally, and a leg may drag," he said. And side rails, which are more decorative than functional, can pull off. The table also needs to be picked up from its base, not an edge. "Otherwise it's like towing a car from a fender," Mr. Rossi said.

The best way to move a table is to disassemble it, move the parts and reassemble it at its new site, even if the table is simply being moved from one room to another. Tables improperly moved may need to be releveled.

The table's weight comes from its heavy slate playing surface. Unlike plywood, slate won't warp. And a heavy surface insures a better play, Mr. Rossi adds.

A new cloth costs approximately $350, moving starts at around $350. THE GAME ROOM, 461 Route 46 West, Fairfield, NJ 07004, (201) 227-2245; Woodbridge Center Mall, Woodbridge, NJ 07095, (908) 636-1111; 2029 Route 88 East, Brick, NJ 08723, (908) 206-0323.

## BINOCULARS

BINOCULARS PLAYED A LEADING ROLE in the old Alfred Hitchcock movie *Rear Window,* in which a convalescing photographer spies on a neighbor whom he suspects of murder.

But most people use binoculars for more conventional pursuits, such as looking at birds, football games and even stars. "You can actually see nebulae with binoculars if you know how to use them," said Lloyd Malsin, owner of Clairmont-Nichols, an optician specializing in binocular and telescope repairs.

But you won't see much of anything if your binoculars are misaligned or in need of a cleaning, two of the biggest problems owners can have with binoculars.

Binoculars usually lose their collimation—the alignment of the lenses—when they are dropped. "Binoculars have two sets of optics," Mr. Malsin explained. "The brain needs to receive an image equal in size and height through each eye." If the binoculars' interior prisms are disturbed, misalignment occurs.

Cleaning is necessary for a variety of reasons. Dust and moisture can seep into binoculars. Even fungus thrives. "We see binoculars with seeds and spores growing inside," Mr. Malsin said. You can often spot dust and fungus by looking into binoculars the wrong way.

Clairmont-Nichols, opened by Mr. Malsin's great-grandfather in 1885, replaces and realigns prisms, custom-grinds lenses and cleans binoculars. The company also repairs housing parts, replacing old leather and fixing dented cases. Cleanings start at $30; recollimation ranges from $40 to $60.

Telescopes present a different and costlier set of repairs. The worst that can happen is that the front objective lens, which is farthest from the eye, breaks. This usually occurs when the telescope is dropped. Mechanical defects can also hamper the focusing mechanism. Telescope repairs start at around $80.

Occasionally, however, the problem is with the viewer. "It takes the average person between three and six months to learn to use a telescope," said Mr. Malsin, a member of the Amateur Astronomers' Association of New York. He suggests inexperienced stargazers invest in a modest telescope, moving on to a top-flight model once they learn to scan the heavens. CLAIRMONT-NICHOLS INC., 1016 First Avenue (near East 56th Street), New York, NY 10022; (212) 758-2346. ✉

BOTH BINOCULARS AND TODAY'S TELESCOPES descended from Galileo's telescope. But the oldest binoculars to come in for repairs at F. C. Meichsner, a 76-year-old binocular and telescope repair company in Boston, usually date from around World War I. "They won't perform as well as contemporary instruments, but they still work," said Syd Smith, a staff member.

Older telescopes also tend to be more troublesome than new ones, often because they have been incorrectly repaired in the past. Mr. Smith once dealt with a 40-year-old British telescope that had been soldered in the wrong place during a previous modification.

Binocular repairs and alignment start at around $35. Telescope repairs start at $50. F. C. MEICHSNER COMPANY, 182 Lincoln Street, Boston, MA 02111; (800) 321-8439 or (617) 426-7092. ✉

## BOOK BACKS (FAKE)

$E$VERY DAY PHILIP BRADBURN, managing director of the Manor Bindery, makes books no one will ever read. Fashioned from leather, wood and gold, his books are judged solely by their covers. In short, they are fakes.

"The best compliment I can have is for people to try to take one of these off the shelf," Mr. Bradburn said, standing by a cabinet of false books in his shop in Fawley, England.

False book backs, which have been used as room decorations for centuries, are often seen in stately homes, usually masking library doors. They can front cabinets for televisions or bars and are occasionally used to line the bottom of Murphy beds. "They go absolutely anywhere," Mr. Bradburn said. "I don't think there's anything I haven't hidden."

Leather books from the Manor Bindery, set in an old blacksmith's shop just south of Southampton, are made from wood sticks, which are covered with leather, then decorated with gold. Customers can choose from 124 classic titles, including all of Charles Dickens's works. Mr. Bradburn will also age a customer's book backs on request, using dyes and, in drastic cases, sandpaper.

The 21-year-old bindery also makes what Mr. Bradburn calls replica books. From a foot of antique books, a silicon cast is made. Wood and resin are applied, and the resulting books, which come out in panels, "look like leather," Mr. Bradburn said. And at £35 a foot ($57 using an exchange rate of $1.62 to the pound), they are half the price of leather fakes.

The Manor Bindery also makes display books in gold-embossed imitation leather and a variety of book-decorated goods, including video covers and CD covers. THE MANOR BINDERY, Fawley, Hampshire, England SO4 1BB; 011-44-1-703-894-488. ✉

THE FROELICH LEATHER CRAFT COMPANY in Rego Park, Queens, has made dummy book backs, as it calls them, for more than 50 years. Specializing in hand-crafted leather bookbindings and leather desk accessories, Froelich got into the false-book business as a way to use up left-over leather.

Though imitation book backs are still looked upon as a curiosity, business has grown in recent years, in part because traditional decor is back.

Froelich will make false book backs in cloth ($65 a foot), combination cloth and leather ($65.50) and all leather ($70). The company offers a choice of 3,000 titles, stamped on the spine in gold. These prices are for a random selection of titles; specific titles are at extra cost. FROELICH LEATHER CRAFT COMPANY INC., 63-20 Austin Street, Rego Park, Queens, NY 11374; (718) 897-7000. ✉

MOST OF THE BOOKS PRODUCED by Distinctive Bookbinding Inc. have words and pages, but the 36-year-old company also makes imitation book backs.

The company, which specializes in custom bookbinding, leather desk sets and portfolios, can make book backs in many kinds of leather, said the manager, Stephen Vance. Titles and colors are chosen by clients.

"Everything we do is very specific, very individual," Mr. Vance said.

The company charges $60 an hour, plus materials, and gives estimates. DISTINCTIVE BOOKBINDING INC., 1020 19th Street (between L and K Streets), Washington, DC 20036; (202) 466-4866. ✉

FAKE BOOKBINDINGS CAN APPEAR on just about anything. "We did a doghouse once made to look like a little library," said Diane Dax, a vice-president at Calico Inc., which began making ersatz book backs in 1983. The company creates all types of books in leather and gold leaf, from presentation boxes to folio boxes for artists. "We make books with another use," Ms. Dax said.

The company also makes hideaway books, which look like books but can actually hold playing cards, pencils, notepaper, even clocks. The hideaway books have cloth spines and cardboard covers decorated with decorative paper. Hideaway books start at $5. Tooled leather books by the foot, or yard, cost $10 an inch. CALICO INC., Industrial Center, Lower Market Street, Wappingers Falls, NY 12590; (914) 297-2400. ✉

# BOOKBINDING, CUSTOM DESIGNS

A FEW YEARS BACK, Elspeth Coleman read the complete works of Martin Cruz Smith with mercenary intent. The author had ordered custom bookboxes for his manuscripts of *Gorky Park* and *Polar Star,* which Ms. Coleman, a partner in Weitz, Weitz & Coleman, the Manhattan bookbinders, adorned with the appropriate images—a fishnet, a soldier's epaulet and a red star, all in leather.

You can tell a lot about a book by its cover, as long as it is custom-crafted by a bookbinder. And Weitz, Weitz & Coleman, in business since 1909, makes all sorts of leather book coverings. Some are traditional, like a gilded elephant on a Kipling volume or pale rose leather, adorned with a camellia, for a copy of *Camille.* And a few are downright playful. For a Yankee fan, Herbert Weitz, a partner in the firm, devised a baseball-card box in navy and white pinstripe, then rubbed a little sand on it, "like a uniform after a game," he said.

A good bookbinder should be adaptable, with a feel for the craft's long history, according to Mr. Weitz. "Much of what we do is straight out of the 15th century," he said, standing by a cabinet holding 2,000 gold-embossing tools. Traditional touches include gilded pages, gold tooling and hand-sewn headbands, the fabric strips at the book's spine. Other aspects are pure 1990s, such as acid-free endpapers.

The company, which also sells rare books, will create new covers for old volumes, restore crumbling tomes and design wedding and photo albums. The specialty is leather covers enhanced with a drawing from the volume. For a rare edition of *Aesop's Fables,* illustrated by Arthur Rackham, Ms. Coleman adapted Rackham's rendering of the spider and the fly, fashioning a gilded web and black leather insects.

The price for a basic leather binding is computed by adding the book's length and width and multiplying by 17—$221 for a 5-by-8-inch book. Adornments are extra. Mr. Weitz also offers bookbinding classes, $250 for five sessions. WEITZ, WEITZ & COLEMAN, 1377 Lexington Avenue (near 91st Street), New York, NY 10128; (212) 831-2213. ✉

BARBARA MAURIELLO LEARNED BOOKBINDING 15 years ago, when she wanted to bind a collection of her small paintings. She liked the craft so much, she quit teaching art, apprenticed with a bookbinder and now operates her own bookbinding studio, in Hoboken. Her specialty is cloth-bound books in offbeat fabrics, like Hermes scarves (her scarf books graced a window display at Hermes in Manhattan) and vintage quilts (she inset a square from a quilt on the cover of a quilting book). She also fashions book covers from unusual paper and, occasionally, leather, though "it's not what I love," she says.

Much of Ms. Mauriello's work is restoring rare books, a painstaking process that can entail replacing missing paper near the spine with thin Japanese tissue. For extremely fragile books that can't survive rebinding, she fashions book boxes. Prices start at $45 an hour, materials additional. **BARBARA MAURIELLO;** (201) 420-6613.

WHEN DANIEL KELM DECIDED, 14 years ago, to quit teaching chemistry at the University of Minnesota and learn bookbinding, he moved, without hesitation, to Massachusetts. "There's a long tradition of book art here," he said. Mr. Kelm's studio, the Wide Awake Garage, which he owns, creates both traditional books (in leather) and artist's books (in paper, cloth or metal).

His leather books are elaborate, with some aspect of the text interpreted, often three-dimensionally, on the cover. (The detailed process entails using both wax and plaster molds to create the paper cast used on the cover.) "It's tradition with a twist," Mr. Kelm said. His artist's books also often have a three-dimensional aspect, opening into tetrahedrons, cubes and other shapes. Books range from $500 to $5,000. **WIDE AWAKE GARAGE,** P.O. Box 449, Easthampton, MA 01027; (413) 527-8044. ✉

FOR DO-IT-YOURSELF ENTHUSIASTS, the Center for Book Arts offers classes, including weekend workshops, on many aspects of bookbinding, from traditional to popups. The Center, which also teaches papermaking, holds regular bookbinding exhibitions and keeps slides of works by members who accept bookbinding commissions. Weekend workshops start at $150. **CENTER FOR BOOK ARTS,** 626 Broadway (between Bleecker and Houston streets), New York, NY 10012; (212) 460-9768.

# Books,
# DESIGN AND DECORATING

$P$EOPLE BUY BOOKS on decorating and design for lots of reasons—to drool over pictures of dream houses, to keep up with trends, to admire the work of a particular architect or designer. But for many, the reasons are more mercenary. "People come here looking for ideas," said Cynthia Conigliaro, a partner in Archivia (pronounced ar-KEE-vee-ah), a five-year-old bookstore devoted exclusively to volumes on the decorative arts, architecture, gardening and interior design.

For Ms. Conigliaro and her partner Joan Gers, a big chunk of the day is spent perusing their shelves and consulting catalogs to match customers with the right books. For somebody who needed a stencil for a chair rail, they found the required image in a book on porcelain. And for a buckle designer looking for new ideas, they unearthed some old ideas from vintage fashion books.

Both owners are veterans of the design book business. Ms. Gers ran two art book stores and her partner is a former buyer for Rizzoli International Bookstores.

These days, decorative arts books abound, yet it can be difficult to locate a specific volume. Most general-interest bookstores carry new design books exclusively. And large discount emporia, like the Strand Book Store (828 Broadway at 12th Street) and Academy Book Store (10 West 18th Street), stock a changing mix of used, sale and out-of-print design volumes.

But Archivia displays a carefully edited cross selection of new, out-of-print, foreign and rare books, from $9.95 to $12,000.

Books from overseas—from an illustrated book in French on Art Deco stylist Michel Dufet to a monograph on 19th-century German silver flatware—compose 25 percent of Archivia's stock. But the store's biggests sellers are two out-of-print American volumes from the 1970s—*Billy Baldwin Remembers* and *Billy Baldwin Decorates.* A mail order catalog is available. ARCHIVIA, 944 Madison Avenue (near East 75th Street), New York, NY 10021; (212) 439-9194. ✉

• • •

SOME OF THE MOST PRIZED decorative arts books have been out of print for only a few years, according to Forrest Proper, a partner in Joslin Hall Rare Books, a mail order company specializing in out-of-print decorative arts books.

A prime example: the exhibition catalog from a show of Federal period card tables at Yale University several years ago. Just 2,000 books were printed, but the card tables, which are small and not too expensive, are popular. "And that is the only book," Mr. Proper said.

Joslin Hall, which is six years old, publishes several catalogs a year, offering everything from a $20 volume, in English and Gaelic, on Irish silver to a $2,500 two-volume set in Spanish on embroidery, which features hand-done embroidery patterns in ink, with all letters of the alphabet decorated with flowers, birds and animals.

Books with engraved plates from the 18th century, while not about design per se, can serve as handsome decorative objects, Mr. Proper added. With sewn bindings and rag paper, they have survived better than many later books. Catalog available for $1. **JOSLIN HALL RARE BOOKS,** P.O. Box 516, Concord, MA 01742; (508) 371-3101. ✉

FOR MANY DESIGN ENTHUSIASTS, the thrill comes from owning a first or early edition of a notable volume. A recent reprint of Owen Jones's 1856 design encyclopedia, *Grammar of Ormanent,* from Studio Editions sells at the Strand for $34.95.

But Ursus Rare Books currently stocks the real thing, a $7,500 first edition with plates depicting Celtic, Greek and Egyptian design examples. "The plates in subsequent editions were not as vivid," explained William J. Wyer, who heads the rare book department.

Ursus generally devotes several bookcases to antique decorative arts volumes, from a 1917 edition of *The Decoration of Houses* by Edith Wharton and Ogden Godman, Jr., to the 1803 first edition of "Observations on the Theory and Practice of Landscape Gardening," by Humphrey Repton, inventor of the term "landscape gardening." Repton's book features 26 aquatints of gardens with removable flaps, which allowed him to show how gardens looked before and after his suggested improvements. **URSUS RARE BOOKS LTD.,** mezzanine of the Carlyle Hotel, 981 Madison Avenue (near East 76th Street), New York, NY 10021; (212) 772-8787. ✉

## CAMERAS, REPAIRED

WHAT IS THE WORST THING that can happen to a camera? Rick Rankin, president of Professional Camera Repair Service, opened a small red box and held up Exhibit A: a horribly melted Nikon that still contained a rancid roll of film, the victim of a fire that broke out in a photographer's studio.

"Fire and water damage," Mr. Rankin said, shaking his head.

Yes, he could fix it, but it would hardly be worth the effort. "We could keep a few inner parts," he said. "But it would need a new body."

Most cameras in need of repairs are in much better shape, of course. And they can usually be made to work again with far less time and cost. Battery corrosion is a common problem. So is dirt.

"Eighty percent of what we do here is clean cameras," Mr. Rankin said.

Cameras often need repairs after a trip to the tropics. Excessive moisture is harmful. So is sand. And salt water causes serious corrosion.

Professional, which has 16 technicians, can repair all types of cameras, though much of its work is on high-end equipment, including electronic cameras. The company, begun in 1946, is an authorized repair center for Leica, Nikon, Hasselblad, Pentax, Canon, Rolleiflex and several other manufacturers. The company also repairs vintage cameras, making new parts by hand if the originals are no longer available.

"Some older cameras are so well made, they're often easier to restore than the newer, high-tech cameras," Mr. Rankin said.

Professional also repairs unusual and obscure models, like the Russian Zenit.

But the company specialty is one-of-a-kind modifications. Just before Elizabeth Taylor's most recent wedding, a supermarket tabloid sent in several miniature spy cameras. One was to go in a pocketbook. Another was to fit into a packet of cigarettes. And the last was to hide in an hors d'oeuvres tray. "Mission accomplished," Mr. Rankin said with a grin.

Repairs start at around $60 an hour, parts additional. Estimates are free, except for electronic cameras. **PROFESSIONAL CAMERA REPAIR SERVICE,** 37 West 47th Street, New York, NY 10036; (212) 382-0550. ✉

A LOT OF NEW CAMERAS have been made in the last 20 years. And Harry Frei, owner of Photo Tech Repair Service, repairs most of them, from simple aim-and-shoot models to sophisticated electronic cameras.

In business for over 30 years, the company, which employs 14 technicians, is an authorized service center for ten manufacturers, including Canon, Kodak, Minolta, Nikon, Polaroid and Ricoh. Photo Tech also repairs flash equipment, VCRs, camcorders and Kodak slide projectors.

The top-line electronic cameras now require a computer for repairs. "These cameras are assembled by robotics," explained Isaac Hadid, technical service manager, holding a Nikon 8008. "You can't repair this type of camera without a computer."

With camera hooked to computer, Mr. Hadid called up the proper Nikon program. The computer promptly tests various parts of the camera and reports that 1,017 photographs have been taken.

Prices vary according to the problem and equipment needed. For electronic equipment, such as camcorders and VCRs, estimates are

$25, for cameras $5. Estimates are charged only if the work is not done. **PHOTO TECH REPAIR SERVICE,** 110 East 13th Street (near Fourth Avenue), New York, NY 10003; (212) 673-8400.  ⊠

TODAY'S VIDEO EQUIPMENT has made old 8-millimeter movie cameras and projectors obsolete. But Stephen Wong, who owns Projector Workshop, still gets requests to repair vintage equipment, including 8-millimeter, Super 8 and 16-millimeter. "There's still a lot of old film collectors out there," he says. "You can't get the same image with video as with film."

A number of customers have had old projectors repaired in recent years to see old home movies before transferring them onto video. Mr. Wong, who has repaired motion picture equipment for 15 years, also repairs slide projectors and motion picture cameras. Super 8 projector repairs cost $50 and under, 16-millimeter repairs are $200 and under. Free estimates.  **PROJECTOR WORKSHOP,** 34 West 46th Street, New York, NY 10036; (212) 354-1466.  ⊠

## CANE FURNITURE, REPAIRED

"CANE LOVES TO BE USED," declared David Feuer, president of Yorkville Caning. But caned seats, backs and tabletops are easily misused. Owners stand on them, animals claw them and kids love to poke things through them. Cane also disintegrates and dries with age, becoming brittle and breakable. But there are a variety of options—and price ranges—when recaning is needed.

Yorkville, in business just over a century, offers both hand caning, which is slow and costly, and machine caning, quicker and cheaper. The company also repairs wicker and rush.

Two types of hand caning are available. With traditional caning, holes are drilled all the way through the object's wood frame. Pieces of cane, made from the bark of the rattan plant, are then woven in the familiar openwork pattern by hand. With French caning, the holes do not penetrate the entire frame. The caner places the needed strands in each hole, glues them and secures them with a peg until weaving is complete. French caning is a must when chair backs are double-caned.

Prewoven cane, imported from Southeast Asia in large rolls, is the mainstay of machine caning. To install a machine cane seat, the frame is routed and cleaned, and a sheet of cane is set in, bordered with a single strand of bamboo.

The cane's size and weave are dictated by the furniture maker, said Mr. Feuer, who frequently recanes antique furniture. Machine-caned furniture can be converted to hand caned and the reverse, though Mr. Feuer discourages machine caning for valuable antiques. Properly cared for, hand caning should last 20 years, he said. Machine caning, which costs from $25 to $40 for an average, 15-by-15-inch chair seat, lasts about half as long. Free delivery available, $50 minimum. YORKVILLE CANING, 31-04 60th Street (near Northern Boulevard), Woodside, New York, NY 11377; (718) 274-6464.

OLEK LEJBZON, A WOODWORKING SHOP, offers all types of furniture repair and rehabilitation, from French polishing to upholstry. And the company, begun in 1950, has two craftspeople who do nothing but caning. Much of the company's work is on antiques, so hand caning is the specialty, both traditional and French ($2 for each frame hole). Machine caning is also available, from about $50.  OLEK LEJBZON, 210 11th Avenue, 11th floor (near West 25th Street), New York, NY 10001; (212) 243-3363.

CHAIR SEATS WEAR OUT FIRST, says Jack Hubsmith, owner of York End Caning. So Mr. Hubsmith, whose shop has repaired hand and machine caning for 18 years, often creates a new cane seat to match an old back. Weave must be identical, and new cane is stained to match old.

To prolong cane's life, Mr. Hubsmith suggests wetting or misting the cane with warm water periodically, especially in winter. A machine-caned seat for a Breuer chair costs $30. Hand caning costs from $2.00 to $2.75 a hole, or about $150 to $200 per seat. Free delivery.  YORK END CANING, 454 East 84th Street, New York, NY 10028; (212) 288-6843.

## CEDAR CLOSETS

A CEDAR-LINED CLOSET may not be considered one of life's necessities. "But it's a really nice finishing touch," said Marc White, a partner in D. W. Woods, a seven-year-old custom cabinetry company that has installed cedar closets throughout the metropolitan New York area.

Cedar has a warm, rustic appearance and a distinctive fragrance with a component that moths loathe. Cedar is also resistant to decay. And cedar closets are relatively easy to install and maintain. Both do-it-yourself enthusiasts and professional woodworkers can usually do the job. (Warning: Some people are allergic to cedar.)

Most cedar closets are lined with eastern red cedar, or Juniperus virginiana, which grows in a number of eastern states, including Kentucky, Virginia and the Carolinas. Two types of wood linings are available. Cedar planking, usually ⅜ inches thick and 4 inches wide, is solid aromatic cedar. A cheaper alternative is cedar strandboard, a composite, similar to plywood, made from mill leftovers and sapwood.

The costlier planking is prettier and, in the long run, more practical, according to Mr. White. With time, cedar pores seal and the fragrance disappears. But solid cedar can be revived with a light sanding. A gentle rubbing with cedar oil will also enhance the scent. The aroma will not return as readily to strandboard. Mr. White recommends strandboard panels for large areas, such as an attic or under a staircase.

The scent lasts longest when closets and chests are kept dark and shut. An airtight closet, however impractical, can go at least five years without a sanding, Mr. White said. But a closet sanded every few years can last half a century.

New York walls are almost never straight, added Mr. White, who with his partner Doug Robinson specializes in custom woodworking. So he usually covers the closet with a full plywood backing before installing the cedar planking. Installation, which usually takes one or two days, costs about $600 a day with two workers, plus materials. **D. W. WOODS,** 61 Greenpoint Avenue, Brooklyn, NY 11222; (212) 694-0250 or (718) 349-9861.

IF IT'S TOO COSTLY to cedarize an entire closet, cedar planking can be installed on a few large surfaces, according to Joseph Toledo, owner of Toledo Interiors, a six-year-old custom cabinetry firm in Brooklyn. "You can do a back wall, leave the sides alone and still notice the smell," Mr. Toledo says. But cedar closets can also be extremely elaborate, with shelves and moldings in cedar. Toledo specializes in custom woodwork, including one-of-a-kind pieces, but also does cedar closets upon request. The charge for installation is usually $50 an hour (half day minimum), plus materials.   **TOLEDO INTERIORS**; (718) 349-3610.

FOR DO-IT-YOURSELF CARPENTERS, most Pergament stores, including the large Valley Stream store, have a selection of aromatic cedar planking and strandboard panels. Most planking comes in highly varied lengths. But Ply-Gem's Cedarmate planking comes neatly precut in 16-, 32- and 48-inch lengths. Each board is ⁵⁄₁₆ inch thick and 3¾ inches wide. It costs $19.99 a box.   **PERGAMENT,** 36-21 13th Avenue, Borough Park, Brooklyn, NY 11218, (718) 633-7600; for locations of other Pergaments, call (516) 694-9300.

## CHILD-PROOFING A HOUSE

*E*LECTRICAL OUTLETS, open windows and cabinets filled with cleaning products are pretty innocuous—until there's a toddler in the house.

Parents and grandparents who want child-safe homes have several options these days. Baby stores and catalogs sell a variety of home safety products, from plastic outlet covers to guard rails for beds. There are also professional baby-proofers who make house calls, size up potential problems, then sell and install products. In addition, some architects offer custom baby-proofing items with a little esthetic appeal.

Mary Ann Simnowski, a baby-proofer who makes house calls, says she considers safety, practicality and esthetics when she recommends items for a baby's home.

Besides advice, Ms. Simnowski, co-owner of New York Baby Proofing Co. with her husband, Anthony, gives customers a checklist for each room, then sells and, if necessary, installs whatever items the family wants. "In an average three-bedroom home, there are probably 200 items you might need," she said.

Products fall into two categories. Some, like stair gates, outlet covers and window guards, halt life-threatening accidents. Others, such as Velcro for lamps and pictures and netting for plants, can prevent lesser injuries.

Since 1976, New York City, for example, has required landlords of buildings with three or more units to outfit windows with window guards and window stops in any apartments where children 11 years old and younger live.

Ms. Simnowski, who began her business during her pregnancy in 1990, suggests parents baby-proof a house when the child is five or six months old. That means the child will grow up accustomed to socket covers and drawer locks. "Stove knob covers can look like toys if they're new, and the child may want to play," she said.

Though Ms. Simnowski finds most parents get high marks for child-proofing the baby's room, they tend to be less aware of hazards in the rest of the house. "They put chairs next to banisters, leave out breakables or keep liquor bottles displayed on rolling carts," she said. First-time parents also underestimate a child's abilities, she added.

Ms. Simnowski charges $50 for a house call, which is deducted from labor charges if items are installed. If the company does not do an installation, Ms. Simnowski provides customers a comprehensive do-it-yourself guide.   **NEW YORK BABY PROOFING CORP.;** (212) 362-1262.

WHEN JOAN FABRY NEEDED window guards for her house in Washington, D.C., she remembered the glass window guards from her childhood. But glass guards didn't let in air. So Ms. Fabry, an architect, designed Plexiglas window guards with whimsical geometric cut-outs. The cut-outs, in circles, diamonds or squares, let air circulate but are small enough to prevent a child from falling out.

Ms. Fabry can design and fabricate custom Plexiglas guards for most windows. If the window has a frame, guards can screw on directly. For recessed windows, the guards come with a Plexiglas lip, outfitted with holes for screws. She can also provide colored Plexiglas guards.

Ms. Fabry charges $375 for a guard 2 feet 6 inches wide by 1 foot 6 inches long.

Note: New York City requires guards to be metal. **FABRY ASSOCIATES,** 1743 Connecticut Avenue NW, Washington, DC 20009; (202) 797-3601.

THE PERFECTLY SAFE CATALOG, published by Duncan Hill, Ltd., in North Canton, Ohio, offers 78 pages of child-proofing items, from the obvious (a packet of four stove knob covers for $5.95) to the less so (a pool alarm, for $39.95, beeps whenever anything that weighs 10 pounds or more disturbs the water).

The catalog includes a variety of socket and wire covers, guard rails in wood, plastic or polyester for banisters, rooms and stairs and protective pads for coffee-table edges. Besides outlet covers, big sellers include testers to determine lead in water, home ear examination kits and choke testers (sizers that determine if small objects can be swallowed), said Dan Angus, merchandise buyer for the catalog. **PERFECTLY SAFE,** 7245 Whipple Avenue NW, North Canton, OH 44720; (800) 837-5437. Catalogs cost two dollars. ✉

ALBEE'S, A 50-YEAR-OLD BABY STORE, devotes an entire wall to baby-proofing items, from lid locks for toilets to cushiony plastic bathtub spout covers. VCR slot covers, which cost $5.99, are a big seller, according to Cara Weintraub, store manager. **ALBEE'S,** 715 Amsterdam Avenue (near West 95th Street), New York, NY 10025; (212) 662-5740.

## CHIMNEY SWEEPS

A CRACKLING FIRE IS A PLEASURE on a crisp autumn day, provided the smoke goes up a chimney that's been properly cleaned and inspected. "There's a killer attached to your house if you don't take care of it," said Dennis Smith, owner of Chimney Doctors, an 11-year-old company.

A variety of problems can occur if a chimney isn't inspected and swept regularly. Animals can nest or even die in the flue, causing odors or blockages. A blocked or damaged gas furnace can send noxious carbon monoxide fumes into the room instead of up the chimney. And a buildup of creosote, a natural but flammable by-product of burning wood, can start a deadly chimney fire.

"Chimneys are designed to support temperatures of 1,000 degrees," said John E. Bittner, executive director of the National Chimney Sweep Guild, a 15-year-old trade association. "But a chimney with ¼ inch or more of creosote can easily ignite, taking the temperature up an additional 1,000 degrees in a heartbeat." The added heat can crack or shatter the chimney.

Creosote buildup occurs in three stages, each increasingly dangerous and difficult to remove. Loose, fluffy stage-one creosote, which can be swept away, develops in open fireplaces. Tarry, gummy stage-two creosote commonly occurs in fireplaces with glass doors or wood stoves. And stage three, a hardened glaze, is removable only by chemicals or powerful rotary tools.

With open fireplaces, Mr. Bittner advises a cleaning after burning a cord of wood, four feet high by four feet wide. Fireplaces with glass doors should be cleaned once a year, and wood-burning stoves every six months.

Mr. Bittner also suggests choosing a chimney sweep with liability insurance, a business that is several years old and has board certification. Certified sweeps, who wear identification badges, must pass a rigorous written exam. The Chimney Safety Institute of America in Olney, Maryland, provides names of certified sweeps by telephone or with a stamped self-addressed envelope: 16021 Industrial Drive, Suite 8, Gaithersburg, MD 20877; (301) 963-6900.

Mr. Smith, a certified sweep who works throughout the tristate area, regularly installs chimney liners, particularly in brownstones where fireplaces originally used coal. Coal dust produced sulfuric acid, which disintegrates chimneys. A new lining will make the chimney usable again. Cleanings range from $90 to $400, depending on location and difficulty.

Like many chimney sweeps, Mr. Smith wears the traditional top hat and black tailcoat, a custom that dates from 16th-century England. In those days, master sweeps were despised for using young boys to clean chimneys. The posh outfits were to burnish their lowly image. These days, professional sweeps like Mr. Smith clean chimneys with flexible fiberglass brushes and use closed-circuit televisions to detect chimney cracks.   **CHIMNEY DOCTORS;** (800) 877-9337 or (908) 475-2995.

WHEN HARRY RICHART CLEANS A CHIMNEY, he often shows the client how to build a proper fire. "A fireplace is not a garbage disposal," said Mr. Richart, a certified sweep whose 35-year-old company, Certified Chimney Contractors, services the tristate region. Christmas trees and vast quantities of paper and cardboard should not be burned in fireplaces. Prefabricated logs are safe but will dirty the chimney. And the shellac from newspaper magazine supplements can stick to walls when burned.

In addition to cleaning, building, lining and restoring fireplaces, Mr. Richart and his 28-man team often locate hidden fireplaces in houses and apartment buildings. "Usually we find them in the back of a closet," he said. Residential cleanings start at $74.50 in New Jersey, brownstone cleanings at $145 in New York City.   **CERTIFIED CHIMNEY CONTRACTORS,** 3122 Route 10, Denville, NJ 07834; (800) 432-1019 or (201) 361-1783.

WILLIAM PERRON, A CERTIFIED SWEEP who owns the Chim-Chimeny Chimney Sweeping Service, does a lot of work in Westchester, Putnam, Fairfield and Rockland counties. So while he regularly cleans and inspects chimneys, he often deals with dead or nesting animals.

"Animals are a big problem," said Mr. Perron, a chimney sweep for 15 years. Raccoons often have babies on the damper. "We have to remove these, put them in a cardboard box, then gently smoke the mother onto the roof," he says. To prevent a repeat entry, he usually caps the chimney top with a screen. Cleanings start at $89.   **CHIM-CHIMENY CHIMNEY SWEEPING SERVICE,** 190 Saratoga Avenue, Yonkers, NY 10705; (914) 965-4455.

# CHINA
# (LOCATING DISCONTINUED PATTERNS)

IT'S EASY TO BREAK A TEACUP. The challenge is to replace it, particularly if it comes from a china pattern that's been discontinued. But for the last decade or so, there's been a growth in the number of mail order businesses specializing in discontinued china patterns.

This is comforting news for tableware enthusiasts, since china patterns are being discontinued more quickly than ever before, according to Stacy Davidson, whose Pattern Finders Ltd. stocks over 100,000 pieces of discontinued china.

With computers, china companies can tell early on how well a pattern is selling. "Patterns used to have a shelf life of 20 to 30 years," said Ms. Davidson, who worked in Macy's china department before starting her mail order business in 1979. "Now people tell me the pattern they chose when they got married a year ago has been discontinued."

A china maker may discontinue a strong-selling pattern if it becomes too costly to produce. Fashion is also a factor. "Those sea green patterns from the late '50s aren't made anymore, though we do a good business in them," said Ms. Davidson, who scours auction houses, estate sales and china companies for discontinued merchandise. "There's a lot of sentimentality involved with dinnerware. People have wonderful memories of sitting around the dinner table."

Pattern Finders buys and sells china and crystal by over 100 international manufacturers, including Lenox, Royal Doulton, Royal Worcester, Haviland, Wedgwood, Spode and Rosenthal. Demand is particularly strong for Rosenthal's Moss Rose pattern, which was popular with American military families stationed in postwar Germany. A five-piece setting of Moss Rose costs $165, plus shipping. Single pieces are also available.   **PATTERN FINDERS,** 11 Traders Cove, Port Jefferson, NY 11777; (516) 928-5158.   ✉

"YEARS AGO, the hostess put the chipped plate at her place, but now she can usually find a replacement," says Jacquelynn Ives, whose 21-year-old company offers 18 lines of discontinued English and American china, including Adams, Coalport and Franciscan.

A common problem is finding replacements for discontinued china patterns that don't have names or numbers printed on the piece. Ms. Ives asks customers to photocopy the front and back of an unidentified piece and describe the colors; photocopies offer clearer details than pictures, she said.

Growing demand from brides who want traditional china patterns prompted Ms. Ives to start a bridal registry, available for mail order customers. All wedding china is gift-wrapped. A five-piece setting of Lenox costs about $135, plus shipping. Individual pieces are also available. JACQUELYNN'S CHINA MATCHING SERVICE, 219 N. Milwaukee Street, Milwaukee, WI 53202; (414) 272-8880. ✉

HOLIDAY CHINA IS A SPECIALTY of Hoffman's Patterns of the Past, a replacement service in Princeton, Illinois. Among the company's holiday patterns are Johnson Brothers' Merry Christmas, Mikasa's Festive Season and Royal Worcester's Holly Ribbons and Village Christmas. But Noritake's Christmas Memories, embellished with a hunter green border, holly leaves and a Christmas scene in the middle, is particularly popular. A dinner plate costs $26.

The company, which ships anywhere, stocks over 12,000 china patterns. HOFFMAN'S PATTERNS OF THE PAST, 513 South Main Street, Princeton, IL 61356; (815) 875-1944. ✉

WITH A GROWING NUMBER of placement services, prices for obsolete patterns vary, and it pays to shop. The International Association of Dinnerware Matchers catalog lists more than 60 replacement services across the nation. The catalog costs $2. INTERNATIONAL ASSOCIATION OF DINNERWARE MATCHERS, 112 North MacArthur Boulevard, Irving, TX 76061. ✉

# CHINA, RESTORED AND REPAIRED

CHINA BREAKS. But even when an object shatters, all is not lost. "This came to us in 20 pieces," said Lansing Moore, holding a Byzantine terra cotta bowl. The bowl was smooth, with little evidence that it had once been a heap of shards. "Restorations can be almost invisible," said Mr. Moore, president of Center Art Studio, which restores ceramic, porcelain, crystal, metal and enamel.

The company, founded in 1919, also does so-called museum repairs, stabilizing cracks and breaks so they won't worsen but making no attempt to hide them. "We assembled this but left it to look as it was," explained Iliana Engelke Moore, the company's vice-president, holding a Venetian Renaissance drug jar with cracks and chips.

About half the company's repairs are on ceramics and porcelains, from precious Ming vases to inexpensive teapots. The company can fill in cracks, repair chips and even replace large missing areas, like the lip of a jar. Reassembly is done with slow-setting adhesives.

Colors and patterns can be matched as well, by means of glazing, airbrushing and hand painting. Ceramics are never refired to set colors since they can explode.

It can often be cheaper to repair contemporary ceramics, such as dinner plates and lamps, than to replace them, according to Mr. Moore, who took over the company in 1981. "We guarantee restorations for a year of use if you do not put them in the dishwasher," he said. The company accepts mail orders, makes deliveries in Manhattan and charges a minimum of $100 a job.   CENTER ART STUDIO, 250 West 54th Street, New York, NY 10019; (212) 247-3550.   ✉

HESS RESTORATIONS, which restores china, silver, crystal, lacquer and ivory, has done museum restorations for years. But customers usually ask for invisible restorations, said Marina Pastor, a partner. "We fabricated the hands," Ms. Pastor explained, holding a flawless-looking Meissen statue of a nymph.

Ms. Pastor recently repaired a big porcelain washbowl that was missing a chunk of its base. The bowl, of sentimental value, had a transfer print of grapes around its base. "So I had to hand paint it to imitate the print," said Ms. Pastor, who studied art in Russia, where she grew up. She took over the company in 1988, with her mother, Nina Korabelnikov.

Do-it-yourself attempts at ceramics restoration can often prove costly, Ms. Pastor added. Botched repair work must be removed before the proper repairs can be done. Ceramic repairs start at $45. Mail orders accepted. HESS RESTORATIONS, 200 Park Avenue South (near 17th Street), New York, NY 10003; (212) 260-2255. ✉

WHILE CERAMIC AND PORCELAIN repairs can be nearly invisible, the object is weakened, said Jadwiga Baran, owner of Sano Studio for more than 20 years. Nonfiring glazes are water-repellant, but should be kept away from hot water and hot liquids, such as soups. And restored vases should be fitted with liners when filled with water.

Repairs from $50. SANO STUDIO, 767 Lexington Avenue (near 60th Street), New York, NY 10021; (212) 759-6131. ✉

## CLEANING SERVICES

CLEANING A HOUSE, according to David Eason, is an art. "Anybody can take a dustcloth and run it along a windowsill," said Mr. Eason, who owns Dirtbursters, a cleaning service that works in Manhattan and Brooklyn. "But we want to make it to look like you could have a party."

Even in the 1990s, spring cleaning is a big deal for services like Mr. Eason's. Customers with regular cleaning help often want a service to come in and do heavy cleaning each spring. Residents also call cleaning services for a grand once-over before moving into a new apartment or house.

Dirtbursters, in business since 1983, specializes in cleaning apartments, houses and small businesses. Clients can hire cleaners from the company on just about any basis, according to Mr. Eason. "We'll clean once a week, every other week, once a month or twice a year," he said. "We have one client who wants a cleaner every day."

A typical cleaning starts with a scrub-down for the kitchen and bathroom. All rooms are vacuumed or dust-mopped. And everything is dusted, Mr. Eason said. But each job is different. "We'll clean as thoroughly as the client wishes," he explained. Rough-hewn wood beams, for example, often can't be cleaned with a dustmop or feather duster. "If the client wants it clean, we'll pick the dust off by hand," he said.

Other notably difficult—and often nasty—tasks include old-fashioned ovens that do not self-clean, dishwasher interiors with mineral deposits from the water and range hoods. "People usually wait too long to clean those," Mr. Eason said of range hoods. He also advises clients to use liners in catboxes. "It means we spend less time washing out the catbox and more time on something else, like polishing the silver," he said.

The company does off-beat tasks, as well. "A woman asked to have someone stay with her dogs while she was away," Mr. Eason said. "We did it."

Residential cleaning is $18 an hour, and office cleaning is $18 an hour, with a three-hour minimum. DIRTBURSTERS; (212) 721-4357.

REVIVE, A THREE-YEAR-OLD cleaning service based in Queens, offers complete spring cleanings for both residences and offices in the greater New York area. But the company specialty is cleaning walls, panels and furniture in fabric or vinyl. "Once you get water damage on a fabric wall covering, you can either remove the wallpaper or remove the stains," says Steven J. Glick, the owner. "It's a lot cheaper to remove the stains."

All of Revive's work on fabric and vinyl is accomplished with a biodegradable, nontoxic soap made from coconut oil and kelp, according to Mr. Glick. Dirt is removed either with an extractor or with dry-foam, designed to minimize moisture on the fabric wall, panel or article of furniture.

Revive also cleans wall partitions and acoustical ceiling tiles.

Fabric walls costs 30 cents to 52 cents a square foot to clean. Chairs in leather or fabric are about $6 to $10. REVIVE, 6 Oxford Lane, Smithtown, NY 11787; (516) 979-2045.

SPRING MEANS LOTS OF CALLS for heavy cleaning, according to Les Goray, manager of Maids Unlimited, a large cleaning service begun in 1950. Tasks include scrubbing and scouring of ovens, stoves and cabinets, and washing walls and moving furniture to clean hard-to-reach spots. "It's real hands-and-knees work," said AnnMarie Sneed, who supervises cleaning personnel. The company can clean carpeting and draperies as well.

Maids Unlimited also offers light cleaning—dusting, vacuuming, wet mopping and laundry, provided laundry facilities are in the building.

Maid service costs $60.62 for four hours; heavy cleaning is $25 an hour without supplies, with a four-hour minimum.  MAIDS UNLIMITED, 230 East 93rd Street, New York, NY 10128; (212) 369-9100.

## CLOCKS, CLEANED AND REPAIRED

NORMAN STEINKRITZ'S TINY SHOP is noisy in an oddly comforting way. Chimes ring out on the hour. And in the background is the constant ticking of old-fashioned mechanical clocks, the kind Mr. Steinkritz has repaired for over 40 years.

In an era of quartz clocks and batteries, a few craftsmen, like Mr. Steinkritz, still prefer working with old-fangled timepieces, the kind that run with wheels, pivots and bearings. Properly cared for, a good mechanical clock can last for years. And when an old clock becomes erratic or simply stops, it can usually be repaired.

"The important thing is to wind a clock once a month and let it run," Mr. Steinkritz said. "If you just let it stay there on the mantle, the oil will start to congeal."

Congealed oil is, in fact, the main reason clocks stop. "Clocks dry up," Mr. Steinkritz explained. "Instead of being a lubricant, the oil becomes an abrasive and stops the wheels."

Clock parts wear out as well. Cables snap on grandfather clocks, pendulums break, and wheels lose their teeth. Mr. Steinkritz can also make a silent cuckoo clock tweet again by replacing the clock's tiny, but strategicially placed, wood-and-paper bellows.

Finding proper parts is a problem as mechanical clocks grow scarce. But Mr. Steinkritz has a huge inventory of keys, wheels and pivots, as well as vintage clocks ripe for a little cannibalization. "I throw nothing away," he said proudly. When necessary, he makes parts, using a large lathe.

Mr. Steinkritz also converts mechanical clocks into quartz clocks. "If a clock is completely worn down, it's a cheaper alternative," he says, holding a French, gold-plated bracket clock from the 1930's that is now battery run. Clock repairs range from about $40 to $900.   **HENNOR JEW-ELERS AND CLOCKMAKERS,** 966 Lexington Avenue (near 70th Street), New York, NY 10021; (212) 744-1058.

JOHN D. METCALFE, who has repaired and restored mechanical clocks for over 20 years, wants nothing to do with quartz clocks. "Antique clocks are more fun," he said, standing by a newly restored French Empire clock in rosewood and ormolu. "Some of the soul of the clockmaker went into each clock. You can live for 300 years and never see all the variations."

For over six years, Mr. Metcalfe was surrounded by historical clocks as curator of the National Association of Watch and Clock Collections in Lancaster, Pennsylvania. He went into business for himself in New York in 1992. Among his restorations is an English lantern clock from 1680 with a rather loud hammer chime. "I try to persuade the owners that they will soon get used to the striking," he said.

Mr. Metcalfe, who learned his trade from the British Horological Institute, enjoys doing cosmetic work on clock cases, polishing brass mounts, resilvering dials and cleaning ormolu. He also makes replacements for worn parts and seeks out old clocks for parts.

Restorations start at $185 for both spring-driven and weight-driven shelf and pendulum wall clocks. Mr. Metcalfe also restores antique music boxes.   **JOHN D. METCALFE,** at Frederick Victoria, 154 East 55th Street, New York, NY 10022; (212) 832-0941.   ✉

IF A CLOCK ACTS TESTY, it may just be in need of restoration, according to Gerald Grunsell, a clock restorer for over 40 years. "The clock will tell you when it's time for repairs," he said. "The timekeeping will become erratic or it will squeak when it strikes."

Mr. Grunsell, also an alum of the British Horological Institute, cleans clocks by taking them completely apart, polishing all pivots, burnishing worn bearings and replacing broken springs. The clock is then oiled and reassembled, with adjustments made along the way.

A clock mechanism can either be repaired so it works properly or be restored so it both looks and works as it did originally, Mr. Grunsell said. "It's a question of what the customer wants to pay."

Mr. Grunsell's specialty is repairing English clocks from the 17th through 19th centuries. But he will also repair modern mechanical clocks and pocket watches.

Minor adjustments start at about $10 to $15, but complete restorations can cost $1,000 and up. **THE HOROLOGIST OF LONDON,** 450 Main Street, Ridgefield, CT 06877; (203) 438-4332.

## CLOCKS (MAIL ORDER PARTS FOR DO-IT-YOURSELF REPAIRS)

WHAT HAS MORE THAN 300 faces and nearly 400 pairs of hands? The catalog from Klockit, a Wisconsin mail order company that sells clock parts, clockmaking kits and completed clocks, including German cuckoo clocks.

"People are often scared of touching clock movements, but it's not difficult to make or repair your own clocks," said Fred Koermer, who started the company over 20 years ago.

Klockit sells everything from second hands, which start at 35 cents each, to a kit for making a grandfather clock with brass weights and a carved oak case ($1,849.95). The company also offers a variety of quartz movements, including a battery-powered minimovement, less than three inches square.

Interest in do-it-yourself clockmaking and repairs grew dramatically with the introduction of quartz movements in the late 1970s, said Larry Heskett, Klockit's vice-president for marketing. Quartz movements also made it possible to create clocks out of unlikely items like automobile hubcaps and silkscreen prints.

Klockit, which also sells music-box movements, has technicians who will help customers over the telephone. **KLOCKIT,** P.O. Box 636, Lake Geneva, WI 53147; (800) 556-2548. ✉

PRECISION MOVEMENTS, which has sold clock and music-box parts and kits by catalog for over 10 years, specializes in quartz movements, including the latest types that chime or strike the hour. The chiming movement includes a speaker, and with the flick of a switch, gives the owner a choice of either Westminster or Whittington chimes.

The catalog's collection of do-it-yourself kits includes one for a miniature grandfather clock with either an arabic or walnut dial ($39.95) and for a scaled-down street clock in black bezel or brass ($29.95).

The company, which provides technical help by phone, also offers miniature clocks, pocket watches, clock faces, movements and cases. PRECISION MOVEMENTS, P.O. Box 689, Emmaus, PA 18049; (800) 533-2024.  ✉

# CLOSETS, ## ORGANIZED AND CUSTOMIZED

RUMMAGING THROUGH A CROWDED CLOSET can be traumatic, particularly when items crash down unexpectedly from the upper shelves. But the right combination of rods, shelves and drawers, smartly placed and securely installed, can add storage space and demystify even the most Byzantine closet.

Since the late 1970s, the closet organization business has grown, both with franchises, such as the California Closet Company, and with single businesses. Typically, a closet organizer comes to your residence, measures your closets, tallies up belongings (shoes, belts, hanging items) and presents a simple sketch. Installation usually takes a day.

"A closet three feet deep and six feet wide can easily be a walk-in closet," said Mort Olin, a closet organizer for over 20 years. Shelves can go against the back wall, with shoe racks on the door and twin poles for short hanging items in the side recess.

Mr. Olin works with the two common partitions—melamine-covered particle board and wire shelf systems. Plastic laminated melamine is sturdy, ideal for drawers and adjustable shelves. But wire is cheaper and offers more design options, Mr. Olin said. To prevent wire imprints on folded clothes, he sells Plexiglas shelf covers. He prefers wire coated in baked epoxy instead of vinyl. "It doesn't get sticky," he said.

Wire shelving costs $9 a linear foot, melamine costs $75 a linear foot. MORT OLIN, 13 Mansfield Court, Livingston, NJ 07039; (201) 992-0168.

GEORGE WILD, A CABINETMAKER for over 25 years, makes custom closet interiors from melamine. But he also works with fine woods, including ash, birch and mahogany, which can be stained in a variety of finishes. Frequently, clients ask for a closet interior that matches wood used in the room.

His closet partitions stand on the floor (most melamine partitions are suspended from the walls). Pull-out shelves are a specialty, as are secret compartments. "We can hide a safe," he says. Melamine costs $85 a linear foot, woods start at $160 a foot. GEORGE WILD CLOSETS, 1595 York Avenue at 84th Street, New York, NY 10028; (212) 737-4658.

MIKE BELFOR, WHO OWNS European Closet & Cabinet, offers custom closet interiors in exotic hues, including bright red, besides the standard colors (white, black, almond and wood tone). His company also custom cuts shelves, drawers and partitions for do-it-yourself installation. "You save 30 percent but lose the installation warranty," he said.

In addition to melamine, Mr. Belfor's company, begun in 1985, makes closets from furniture-grade birch, which can be stained or painted. "Some people want a more natural wood look," he said. Custom closets can also be outfitted with brass-plated hardware in a variety of styles. "We make it look like furniture," he said.

The worst closets to organize have more depth than width, Mr. Belfor added. If a deep closet has some width, it can be made into a walk-in. Otherwise, "It's a problem closet," he said. EUROPEAN CLOSET & CABINET, 42-81 Hunter Street, Long Island City, NY 11101; (718) 784-3232 or (516) 454-0011.

## COMPUTERS
## (PERSONAL TRAINERS)

$T$HOUGH PERSONAL COMPUTERS are now standard equipment in many homes, mastering an Apple Macintosh or IBM Think Pad is considerably more challenging than learning to use a vacuum cleaner.

Enter the personal trainer, the computer consultant who makes house calls and tailors hardware and software to an individual's requirements. While computer consultants have been hired by small businesses for years, many will also work with individuals, from raw beginners to seasoned cybernauts.

A good personal trainer works closely with a client, sizing up the person's reasons for using the computer. Most work with clients both in person and on the phone and will advise on the correct machine and software to buy, teach how to use the machine, solve problems when they occur, help the individual trade up to more sophisticated programs and modify old equipment as needed.

Indeed, though Julie Packer, co–head writer for *As the World Turns,* uses her Dell desktop computer mainly as a word processor, she hired computer consultant Bruce Stark, president of Computer Tutor, to set up a fax modem and help smooth out problems she had with software. "I'd rather spend time writing than reading the manual," she said.

Computer clubs, found in most cities, often have lists of computer consultants. Two in Manhattan are the New York Mac Users' Group, (212) 473-1600, and the New York Personal Computer Users' Group, (212) 686-6972.

Many consultants specialize in either Apple- or IBM-compatible equipment and software. The following work with individuals as well as small businesses throughout the New York metropolitan area.

David Pogue, author of *Macs for Dummies* (IDG Books Worldwide, $19.95), believes in teaching beginners the skills they need without burdening them early on with superfluous information. "If you're taught too much the first day, you tend to block it out," said Mr. Pogue, personal trainer to composer Stephen Sondheim, among others.

A composer himself, he often works with musicians, like Ray Pool, the harpist at the Waldorf-Astoria's Peacock Alley, who bought a Mac so he could self-publish harp arrangements. Since Mr. Pogue installed Finale, a music notation program, in his Mac, Mr. Pool has self-published 11 volumes for harp, including a harmony guide called *Blazing Pedals.*

Mr. Pogue, who charges $90 an hour, also "cleans up machines," as he puts it. Most Apples come with options the average user does not need, such as data for hooking up the computer to a mainframe or connecting it to a local area network. Once rid of them, the machine gains memory and speed. He also streamlines the Mac's behind-the-scenes filing system, which almost always results in a speed boost. **DAVID POGUE;** (203) 359-8200 (e-mail address: Pogue@aol.com).

CLIENTS OFTEN ASK Eric Rode, a consultant specializing in IBM, Compaq, Dell, Gateway, Packard-Bell, Zeos, AST and other PCs, to upgrade existing equipment, from adding storage space to installing a larger monitor. Additions are fairly easy, provided the computer was purchased in the last couple of years. The cheapest and easiest way to add storage is with a second hard drive, said Mr. Rode, a consultant for eight years.

Mr. Rode, who charges $50 an hour, often advises clients on the best computer for their needs. "If all you're doing is a letter a week, you might as well keep your old IBM AT," he said. "It's like an old car you drive to the market and back."

But he rarely advises purchasing used computers. "Unless you take it apart completely, you have no idea how much life is in it," he said. **ERIC RODE,** 109 Mountain Boulevard, Watchung, NJ 07060; (908) 757-0203.

WHEN BRUCE STARK OPENED his businesses, the Computer Tutor and the Computer MacTutor, in 1982, 99 percent of his clients wanted basic training. And while he still teaches beginners, most clients are computer literates who want to use more sophisticated skills and equipment.

Mr. Stark regularly installs fax-modems, CD-ROMs, soundboards and video capture boards. He also customizes existing software to meet a client's needs. For a retired man interested in the stock market, he created a stock-tracking program that mimicked the man's personal method for following stocks. He also customized a database enabling a recent political campaign to track donors.

Computer Tutor specializes in PCs and Computer MacTutor in Apples. Each charges $85 to $125 an hour. **COMPUTER TUTOR;** (212) 787-6636. **COMPUTER MACTUTOR;** (212) 362-6241.

MURRAY GORDON, PRESIDENT of Quetzal Information Systems, often deals with emergencies, such as retrieving lost or scrambled information. A writer recently called him after her hard disk crashed, taking all her story files with it. "A lot of information was still there but badly scrambled," said Mr. Gordon, a PC consultant since 1987. When the machine was up and running again, he explained how to create backup tapes to avoid a similar mishap.

Quetzal, which charges $75 to $85 an hour, also installs hardware. For a writer with a work computer, home computer and laptop, he hooked up Laplink, enabling the person to transfer files as needed between machines. **QUETZAL INFORMATION SYSTEMS;** (212) 988-0109 or (718) 375-1186 (e-mail address: QUETzal@panix.com).

BOOSTING CONFIDENCE is a big part of teaching someone to use a computer, according to Debbra Lupien, president of Lupien Ltd. and a Mac consultant for six years. "The first time I used a computer, I was convinced it would blow up in my face," she said. Most home users ask Ms. Lupien to set up computers for word processing, desktop publishing or managing their finances. When there's a kid in the house, she usually equips the computer with a CD-ROM player that offers educational functions, including teaching programs and encyclopedias.

Ms. Lupien, who charges $50 an hour, often works with professional photographers, providing programs so they can use the computer to keep track of images. **LUPIEN LTD.;** (718) 693-0584 (e-mail address: Debbra@aol.com).

PETER FREEMAN, a Mac consultant since 1986, often works with beginners. But these days, clients usually call him when they get a new piece of software or want new hardware, such as a fax modem, installed. "Some people don't want to be bothered with putting in a software program themselves," he said. Clients also call when a program crashes or two pieces of software won't work together effectively, added Mr. Freeman, who writes about computer equipment for *Electronic Musician* magazine and accepts clients only in Manhattan. He charges $60 to $125 an hour. PETER FREEMAN; (212) 642-8255 (e-mail address: e-glide@interport.net).

## COMPUTERS (WHAT TO DO WITH OLD MODELS)

To COMPUTER ENTHUSIASTS, the term closetware has nothing to do with shoes or suits. It means computer limbo.

Every year, thousands of outdated computers, including machines that are only three or four years old, get relegated to the closet, usually by frustrated owners who don't know what to do with them. There they sit, gathering dust and becoming more obsolete by the second. And the problem is growing. A 1991 study by Carnegie-Mellon University predicts that by 2005, the nation will discard approximately 150 million computers.

Not surprisingly, the quest for a computer made from recyclable materials that are easily dismantled has become a grail for manufacturers both here and abroad.

In Germany, computer makers are already required by law to take back old machines owners no longer want. And American manufacturers, including I.B.M. and Hewlett-Packard, are currently working on ways to efficiently reclaim and recycle used computers.

For now, computer owners eager to clean out their closets have three basic options. They can donate old computers to nonprofit organizations for a tax deduction (usually the machine's current market value). They can sell them for a fraction of the original purchase price. And a growing number of vendors, such as Micro Exchange in Nutley, New Jersey, and Crocodile Computers in Manhattan, accept old computers as trade-ins, like used cars.

In any case, the task may require a little initiative. Salvation Army–style pick-up trucks are rare in the used computer world. Donors and sellers with only one or two computers are usually responsible for packing and transportation costs. However, when the recipient is a charitable organization, documented transportation costs are tax deductible, according to Rubin Gorewitz, a certified public accountant in Manhattan.

Donors often successfully place old software and computers with churches, schools and other local nonprofit organizations. But too frequently, even the well-meaning give recipients equipment they can't use. One way to insure that old computers find the right home is to donate through a large placement service, such as the National Cristina Foundation.

Cristina, with a national network of recipients, from the National Easter Seal Society to countless schools and job-training programs, matches computers with donors. "When technology is no longer of use in its first place, it should be transferred to a second place of use," said Yvette Marrin, president.

The twelve-year-old foundation accepts working computers from the old I.B.M. XT model on and any Macs. As with all placement services mentioned here, donors receive documentation for tax deductions. **NATIONAL CRISTINA FOUNDATION,** 591 West Putnam Avenue, Greenwich, CT 06830; (800) 274-7846.  ✉

UNLIKE MOST PLACEMENT SERVICES, East West Education Development Foundation in Boston accepts computers in any condition. At its warehouse, technicians fix what's necessary, produce rehabs complete with mouse, modem, software and adapters and send them to the needy throughout the world. East West recipients include the *Oslobodjenje Journal,* Sarajevo's remaining newspaper; Hands Across Watts in Los Angeles; and the International Rice Institute in the Philippines.

Multicomputer donors can choose their nonprofit recipients. "Bankers Trust sent 25 old computers and asked that they go to Hungary, where they were opening a branch," said Alex Randall, the organization's founder.

Mr. Randall, who accepts any Macs and anything from the I.B.M. XT on—"our target machine is the 386," he said—believes even obsolete models offer years of service. "Only three percent of the people on the planet have ever touched a computer," he said. "In the right hands, they are mind-enhancing tools." EAST WEST EDUCATION DEVELOPMENT FOUNDATION, 55 Temple Place, Boston, MA 02111; (617) 542-1234. ✉

"PLACEMENT AGENCIES HAVE LOTS of requests and plenty of places for these old computers," said John L. German, director and founder of Non-Profit Computing, a national service. The trick is getting the right raw material.

Though his organization accepts almost any used computer, Mr. German prefers donations in good shape. But he recently found a home for broken machines with a school that trains women to repair computers. To avoid needless transport, he tries to place donations with organizations near the donor. NON-PROFIT COMPUTING, INC.; (212) 759-2368. ✉

SINCE 1991, THE Student Human Rights Exchange has sent used computers to human rights organizations in Nepal, Mongolia, Cambodia and Russia, among other places. The organization accepts Macs and I.B.M.s from the XT on. STUDENT HUMAN RIGHTS EXCHANGE; (202) 625-1214.

THE ROBIN HOOD FOUNDATION, a seven-year-old nonprofit organization, distributes used computers to 85 New York City poverty-fighting organizations, including housing programs, youth groups and job-training programs. They accept Macs and the I.B.M. 286 and up. ROBIN HOOD FOUNDATION, 111 Broadway (near 18th Street), New York, NY 10006; (212) 227-6601.

FOR SELLERS, PROFITS are highest if the owner can find a buyer directly, often through a classified ad, whether with a large online service, such as America On-Line and Compu-Serve, or in computer publications. David Pogue, author of *Macs for Dummies,* has sold several old computers through the *Mac Street Journal,* the monthly magazine of the Mac Users' Group in New York ([212] 473-1600). "You get market value, which is about one third of what you paid for it last year," he said.

PC owners can seek out buyers at the monthly meetings of the New

York Personal Computer Users' Group. For information, call (212) 533-6972.

SECONDHAND COMPUTER VENDORS also buy equipment. (Look for ads in such publications as *Computer Shopper*.) "You get a quick sale," said Bob Cook, president of Sun Remarketing, a mail order concern specializing in used Macs. "But you get a wholesale rate."

Sellers must ship computers at their own expense, which costs about $25 via U.P.S., Mr. Cook said. To pack, he suggests sellers protect each computer with a plastic garbage bag, then place it in a sturdy cardboard box, filled liberally with plastic peanuts. He buys Mac SEs, which originally sold for $2,495, for about $180, and sells them for $279.   SUN REMARKETING INC.; (800) 821-3221.   ⊠

TOM BUECHEL, OWNER OF Rockaway Recycling in Rockaway, New Jersey, gives sellers two choices. Customers can place marketable computers, like the 286, on consignment at A Second Byte, a warehouse store in nearby Dover. There, a typical used 386 with a working monitor and printer sells for $300 to $500, with a 15 percent commission to the company.

And unsellable dinosaurs, like original PCs, can be dropped off at Rockaway Recycling, which cannibalizes about half a million pounds of computers a month. But while old computers contain bits of precious metal, such as gold, owners with just one oldie rarely make money. "I have to pay to get rid of the monitor," Mr. Buechel said. "And that offsets the price of the printer and other pieces."   ROCKAWAY RE-CYCLING, 311 Main Street, Rockaway, NJ 07866; (800) 317-5865.   A SECOND BYTE, 18 North Salem, Dover, NJ 07871; (201) 989-7752.

CROCODILE COMPUTERS, which sells new and used computers, buys second-hand Macs from 1989 on, used 386s and up and all sorts of parts.   CROCODILE COMPUTERS, 240 West 73rd Street, New York, NY 10024; (212) 769-3400.

MICRO EXCHANGE, which sells new and refurbished computers, buys secondhand Macs and PCs from the 386.   MICRO EXCHANGE, 682 Passaic Avenue, Nutley, NJ 07110; (201) 284-1200.

## Costumes to rent

"WE MAKE PEOPLE LOOK like their fantasies," said Susan Handler, co-owner of Creative Costume Company, a 14-year-old costume rental company in Manhattan.

Halloween is, of course, high season for fantasies—and costume renters, like Ms. Handler. People want to look pretty or sexy—or both, according to Ms. Handler, who with her partner Linda Carcaci, has designed over 1,000 different rental costumes. On the glamorous side are a Cleopatra gown in pleated gold lamé and a billowy Ginger Rogers dress. (There's a complementary Fred Astaire top hat and tux.) On the sexy side are a Lady Godiva bodysuit and a sassy French Maid's dress, popular with men and women alike.

There's also a selection of Halloween standards: witches, devils, skeletons, bats and weird Freddy Kruger from the film *Freddy's Dead*. Movies are a big inspiration for the costume business, Ms. Handler said.

Halloween isn't the only time of year for dressing up, of course. Ms. Handler once designed an Elvis costume for a groom who wanted to sing "Love Me Tender" to his bride at their wedding reception. Seasonal costumes include Santa Claus, Uncle Sam, George Washington and a big satin Valentine built for two people. Costume rentals from $20 to $200. CREATIVE COSTUME COMPANY, 330 W. 38th Street, New York, NY 10018; (212) 564-5552.

FRANKIE STEIN OF FRANKIE STEINZ Costumes used to be a certified public accountant. But she quit years ago when she discovered designing and renting costumes, not to mention dressing up in them, was more fun. Ms. Stein's costumes range from a vintage satin flapper dress with cloche hat to her slinky Diana Ross dress, purchased from a stripper. "I like unusual stuff," she said, holding a Christmas tree suit for a child.

Ms. Stein's specialty is vintage costumes: clothes from the '20s through the '60s (Peter Max vests, beaded headbands). Theme costumes are another specialty: decks of cards, the *Wizard of Oz* characters.

Robin Hood and *Star Trek* are typically hot costumes at Halloween, Ms. Stein said. "They're really colorful and theatrical." And for the renter who wants to make a memorable entrance, Ms. Stein designed a ball gown with a train that looks like a gigantic pumpkin. Costume rentals from $65 to $100. FRANKIE STEINZ COSTUMES, 24 Harrison Street, New York, NY 10013; (212) 925-1373.

RUBIE'S COSTUME CO., which opened over 40 years ago, is enormous, with thousands of costumes. "I can't even count," said Terry Goldkranz, secretary to the president. The shop is jammed with togas, clown suits, flamenco dresses, Dracula capes, medieval gowns, sailor suits and reindeer outfits (yes, the noses light up and they're red).

Halloween stand-bys include vinyl *Terminator II* jackets and Morticia Addams gowns. In addition to new costumes, Rubie's also offers full-cut costumes for large people (choices include samurai warriors and Madame Butterfly). Rentals from $35. RUBIE'S COSTUME CO., 120-08 Jamaica Ave., Richmond Hill, NY 11418; (718) 846-1008.

THERE'S ONLY ONE TRUE SANTA CLAUS, of course, but would-be helpers, or imposters, can choose from five types of classic red-and-white suits at Allan Uniform Rental Service, in business for over 30 years. The fully lined deluxe model ($125) comes in red velvet, while budget-minded Santas can opt for velour or corduroy ($75). Wig, beard, belt and boot coverings are included, with optional stomach padding ($20). Men's sizes range from 42 to 60. ALLAN UNIFORM RENTAL SERVICE, 121 East 24th Street (near Lexington Avenue), New York, NY 10010; (212) 529-4655.

## CRYSTAL CHANDELIERS, CLEANED

WHAT HAPPENS TO A CRYSTAL CHANDELIER that isn't cleaned at least once a year? That depends on where the chandelier is hanging, said John Sander, who has cleaned chandeliers in private homes for over 25 years.

Sometimes the crystal becomes dirty and dusty. Sometimes it just loses its sparkle. And if there's a smoker in the house, it can actually change color. "I remember I once was called to clean a beautiful chandelier I thought was amber crystal," Mr. Sander recalled. "It turned out it was clear crystal, and the owner had been smoking his cigar under it every day."

It isn't difficult to clean crystal chandeliers, but common sense is required, said Mr. Sander, who learned his trade at Marvin Alexander Inc., a Manhattan chandelier shop. Chandeliers should never be turned or spun when cleaned as they can unscrew and crash to the floor. And the person cleaning the chandelier should never touch the pins or bronze accoutrements with an ammonia-soaked cloth.

Mr. Sander cleans crystal with ammonia, water "and these golden fingers," he said with a chuckle, holding up his hands. Ammonia cuts through grease and soot, doesn't need to be rinsed and washes right off, he added. Mr. Sander also brings extra pins and wires in case the prisms are starting to fall off.

John Sander charges $100 for the first two hours and supplies everything except the ladder.   JOHN SANDER; (212) 751-5974.

CRYSTAL CHANDELIERS always sparkle just after they are cleaned. But some shine more than others, said Larry Deblinger, president of Crystal Maintenance Co., a more-than-30-year-old family business. "With plain glass, you'll get a shine, but it won't be the same as with fine lead crystal," he said.

Besides ammonia and water, Mr. Deblinger and his team of six cleaners use a little soap powder to remove grit. Mr. Deblinger does not recommend drip-dry spray-on cleaners. "They can leave spots," he said. "We dry each crystal individually, then hang them back on individually."

It is also important that crystal prisms face the right way to enhance sparkle and reflection. The cut part of the glass should face inside, so the light hits it and bounces off, Mr. Deblinger said.

Crystal Maintenance, which cleans chandeliers in hotels, restaurants and private homes, charges about $150 to clean a large chandelier and supplies everything, including ladder and drop cloth.   CRYSTAL MAINTENANCE CO., 1650 Broadway (at 51st Street), New York, NY 10019; (212) 582-2207.

"SOMETIMES PEOPLE DON'T REALIZE things are missing from their chandeliers," said John McCahill, who has cleaned chandeliers in private homes for over 20 years. Pins and prisms can come loose with age. So if a chandelier needs missing parts or rewiring, Mr. McCahill will do the necessary repairs before cleaning. Mr. McCahill gives free estimates, brings his own ladder and drop cloth and charges a minimum of $50 a job.   JOHN McCAHILL; (718) 762-0623.

## CRYSTAL CHANDELIERS, CUSTOM-MADE AND REPAIRED

LEAD CRYSTAL HAS A NUMBER of attractive properties. It has clarity and weight and is easier to cut than ordinary window glass. "And it sounds nice when you hit it," said Maurine Locke, a partner in Versailles Lighting, which designs, manufactures and repairs chandeliers.

Crystal can also break or chip. Finding a match for a broken prism, globe or bobeche, as a candleholder on a chandelier is known, can be a challenge. But Versailles, which opened in 1982, has a vast collection of chandelier parts, old and new, including prisms and arms. "I've been collecting these for 25 years," said Max Guedj, a partner who began making chandeliers more than 35 years ago in France.

Prisms come in colored glass, modern glass and costly rock crystal as well. There are elaborately cut crystals stems, arms, globes and hurricane lamps.

Versailles's specialty is customized crystal chandeliers, from sleek modern examples to copies of vintage fixtures, all made on the premises. "You can have this chandelier for $600 or $5,000," said Ms. Locke, as she touched a sparkling crystal light fixture.

The price for Versailles's crystal chandeliers, custom-made on the premises, depends on the crystal's thickness and quality. Arms and prisms can be of heavy antique Baccarat crystal, or modern glass that merely looks old. Or the fixture can be a combination of the two.

The company repairs chandeliers as well, by replacing broken parts or refashioning old parts into a new model. It also repairs lamps, sconces and metal light fixtures. Custom chandeliers cost from $275 to

$10,000; prisms start at one dollar. VERSAILLES LIGHTING INC., 124 West 30th Street and 224 West 30th Street, New York, NY 10001; (212) 564-0240.

LOUIS MATTIA LIKES TO restore broken chandeliers. "We'll rewire them, replace whatever parts are missing, reassemble them and clean them," said Mr. Mattia, who has repaired lighting fixtures for over 30 years. And if a customer wants to add prisms to a candleholder or sconce, Mr. Mattia can drill the necessary holes and supply the prisms. Complete repairs, including cleaning, start at $300; prisms start at $2.50. LOUIS MATTIA, 980 Second Avenue (near 52nd Street), New York, NY 10022; (212) 753-2176.

## CURTAINS, COUTURE AND READY-MADE

*I*T'S NO MYSTERY why curtains are often compared with fashion.

A century ago, curtains were an interior decorator's version of a Worth gown—ruched, furbelowed and spangled, built of countless yards of costly damask with petticoats galore. So it comes as no surprise that, as in fashion, curtains are available in couture and ready-to-wear varieties, some costing thousands of dollars, others little more than a double CD.

Many custom curtain makers started their careers with hemlines and runways in mind. Some still think that way on occasion. "I once worked on a bias-cut curtain that hung like a 1930's dress," said Madeleine Boutte, a former dress designer who is now a partner in Alphapuck Designs, a custom workroom.

Like fashion, too, curtains ride waves of popularity. In New York City, two window treatments have held sway for decades. One is the elaborately constructed, deeply romantic curtain, ornamented with enough swags and jabots to outfit the Three Musketeers. The other is the reductivist SoHo special—big, bare, defiantly nude windows.

Lately, however, even those stubborn windows are getting dressed, but barely. Enter the curtain as undergarment, filmy panels that resemble an old-fashioned slip in silk taffeta, organdy, muslin, even parachute nylon. These can be found in catalogs (Ballard Designs, Pottery Barn, Spiegel) or can be custom-made.

Even cheaper varieties can be stylish. Urban Outfitters' tab-top curtains, in pale blue cotton chambray, are reminiscent of well-worn overalls.

"If we're not working with a decorator, we make suggestions depending on the the house," said Kandie von Waggoner, a partner at Alphapuck Designs. In a modern house, that may mean Roman shades. Or in a more traditional setting, curtains with swags and jabots.

Ms. Boutte and Ms. von Waggoner often accompany clients who need help when shopping for fabric. Or they provide swatches. "We enjoy working with different fabrics, particularly when they're weighty," Ms. Boutte said. The exception: double-knit polyester. "A client wanted it, but it puckered," she said. "Never again."

Lined roman and balloon shades cost $18 to $22 a square foot. Lined curtains cost $100 to $150 per fabric width. Prices include linings but not fabrics. ALPHAPUCK DESIGNS, 139 Fulton Street (near Broadway), New York, NY 10038; (212) 267-2561.

THOUGH VIVIAN WHITE, owner of White Workroom in SoHo, works mainly with decorators, she makes curtains for walk-in customers, provided they know the type of curtain they want.

One such client with a strong design sense wanted curtains with Ming-the-Merciless drama—navy blue panels with red trim wired to look like lightning bolts. A photograph of the curtain wound up in *HG* magazine.

Ms. White also makes unlined silk drapes that attach to a custom-made pole with narrow silk strips that knot. "They look like fine lingerie," she said. "Curtains don't have to be lined, but lining catches the dirt," she added.

A pair of side panels with interlining, lining and center-edge trim for a nine-foot window starts at $350. WHITE WORKROOM, 525 Broadway (at Spring Street), New York, NY 10012; (212) 941-5910.

"EVERYTHING HAS BEEN DONE in the past 300 years," said Jay Perlstein, a partner in Regency Drapery. Still, good custom curtains can look highly original. "We take an element from this style and that style and use different fabrics to get something very modern," he said.

Regency, which works frequently with decorators, is known for traditional curtains with lots of hand-sewn dressmaker details. (The company routinely makes muslin mockups for complex designs.) "Our curtains are usually fancy," Mr. Perlstein said.

Demand is still strong for curtains that "puddle" fabric on to the floor, but a bit less so for heavy fringes and rosettes. Elaborate shower curtains, in turn, can be eight feet long.

Folding accordion-style when drawn, Roman shades, four feet by six feet, range from around $400 (unlined) to $900 (elaborate trim, lining and inner lining), fabric not included. REGENCY DRAPERY LTD., 42-25 Vernon Boulevard, Long Island City, NY 11101; (718) 482-7383.

THOUGH CURTAIN DESIGNER Mardi Philips often makes sheers on overhead tracks, she favors Roman shades as an attractive alternative. "They're nice in pale fabrics, and I use natural fiber linings so they can be cleaned easily," she said. When working with private clients instead of decorators, Ms. Philips advises on the type of curtain and fabric to choose, doing the fabric shopping if necessary.

She also makes muslin mockups. "If the clients can see something they can approve, they become more confident," she said. "The average person has a hard time imagining proportion." Roman shades for a 54-by-72-inch window start at $300, without fabric. MARDI PHILIPS; (212) 924-2604.

BESIDES A CUSTOM CURTAIN-MAKING DEPARTMENT, ABC Carpet & Home stocks fashion-conscious ready-made curtains. Their intensely pleated silk tissue curtains in metallic gold, silver or beige are a hip version of sheers ($195), while panels of pleated silk Charmeuse are reminiscent of a classic Fortuny dress ($195). And light shimmers through a large gold panel curtain with an organza center that is heavily embroidered with leaves and curlicues and bordered with raw silk ($595). ABC CARPET & HOME, 888 Broadway (at 19th Street), New York, NY 10003; (212) 473-3000. ✉

FOR A HUGE SELECTION of ready-made curtains, Country Curtains, a mail order company since 1956, offers three different catalogs. Their oldest, Country Curtains, features 68 pages of curtains, mostly un-lined—everything from ruffled calicos (from $21.50 a pair) to simple ribbon-trimmed curtains with tab tops (from $17 a pair). The City Curtains catalog features more sophisticated styles in damasks, floral tapestries and lace fabrics, many with tab tops. And More Window Ways offers formal treatments—swagged or scalloped valances (from $45) and moiré-lined draperies (from $80). COUNTRY CURTAINS, the Red Lion Inn, Stockbridge, MA 01262; for a catalog call (800) 876-6123. ✉

EVER WONDER WHAT HAPPENS to curtains that hang in show houses, appear in photo shoots or are used for display by the big fabric houses? Some wind up at The Drapery Exchange, a consignment shop for quality curtains, bedding and pillows in Darien, Connecticut.

They range from simple curtains for a child's room (from $60) to highly elaborate silks and damasks (one dramatic window treatment in silk with braided tie-backs and inner lining recently sold for $6,000). The shop, which arranges alterations, lets clients take curtains home on approval. THE DRAPERY EXCHANGE, 1072 Post Road, Darien, CT 06820; (203) 655-3844.

# CURTAINS,
# FINIALS AND HARDWARE

IF CURTAINS ARE LIKE DRESSES for windows, then finials and their attendant hardware—brackets, rods and rings—are window jewelry, grace notes that lend fabric and glass a dash of style, ornament and fun.

While functional in origin—*something* has to hold up the window coverings, after all—hardware is the window's finishing touch, the wing of curved iron or burnished steel that sets off a billowy silk or heavy brocade.

The classic curtain of the 1980s, sumptuous, swagged and serious, demanded imposing hardware like mighty stained wood poles and swirling finials that look like soft ice cream in gilded wood or polished brass.

But curtains today have lightened up, and so has hardware, in both heft and mood. Instead of the perennial acorns and globes, the newest finials are whimsical. Some could be called Robin-Hood-meets-New-Age, with lots of arrows, starfish, moons, suns and spears. The latest metal poles are rough-hewn but skinny, and forged metal has replaced brass as the material of choice.

Almost anything goes, it seems, as long as it's witty. For a steak-house in Milwaukee, Mary Bright, a Manhattan curtain designer, used huge S-shaped meathooks to hang black rubber draperies from a rod.

In the '90s, the latest hardware need not be costly. Michael Aram's curtain hardware line in sand-cast iron and brass includes lighthearted finials and tie-backs shaped like twigs, leaves and fleurs-de-lis. A complete window-treatment set—finials, brackets and a 10-foot solid brass rod—costs about $130.

The collection is available at Simon's Hardware, 421 Third Avenue, near 29th Street ([212] 532-9220), and at Platypus, 126 Spring Street, near Greene Street, in SoHo ([212] 219-3919).

At Gracious Home, 1217 Third Avenue, near 70th Street ([212] 517-6300), curtain hardware covers an entire wall and includes resin starfish tie-backs in gold or black ($90 a pair). ABC Carpet & Home, 888 Broadway, at 19th Street ([212] 473-3000), stocks antique flower-shaped tie-backs in pressed milk glass ($55) and simple egg-shaped finials in unpainted wood (from $8).

And Martin Albert Interiors, at 9 East 19th Street ([212] 673-8000), stocks a range of more serious curtain hardware, including wooden rods ($30 a foot) with orb-shaped finials. All can be covered with fabric.

A number of craftspeople offer ready-made designs and custom styles. Since 1990, Mike Braun, a woodworker, and Nicholas Trujillo, a metalworker, have devised rough-hewn finials and rods in torch-cut metal.

Stock designs include an arrow, sunburst and spear, all heavily, rustically textured. They also do custom work. Stock finials cost $85 a pair.

**BRAUN & TRUJILLO,** 15223 Northwest 60th Avenue, Miami Lakes, FL 33014; (305) 558-0623.  ⊠

FOR YEARS, JOSEPH BIUNNO, who owns a custom carpentry shop, offered hand-carved wood finials that were elegant but expensive. But three years ago, he started a line of polyurethane finials taken from rubber molds, and they cost about $65 each.

These finials, which look a bit like old ivory, can be used as is or can be painted, gilded or faux-painted to resemble wood. Mr. Biunno also has finials in Art Deco, Biedermeyer and Russian styles, as well as animal heads.  **JOSEPH BIUNNO,** 129 West 29th Street, New York, NY 10011; (212) 629-5630.  ⊠

CLIENTS OF TOM PENN, whose metal designs have classic lines and graceful curves, often visit his workshop in Long Island City, Queens, for ideas before commissioning hardware.

"When a form appeals, it can be made into anything, a drawer pull, the end of a spoon, a tie-back," he said. And it can show up elsewhere, for example, in bronze pulleys for Venetian blinds. A pair of custom finials in bronze costs around $200.  **TOM PENN,** P.O. Box 7092, Long Island City, Queens, NY 11101; (718) 784-4537.  ⊠

IF CLIENTS DON'T SEE SAMPLES they like among the swirls, curlicues, arrows, flames and other classic shapes at Wainlands Mark II metalworking shop, Mark Wainland, a partner, suggests a custom design or a reworking of a classic.

Though Mr. Wainland's brass and wrought-iron hardware can be heavy, everything is hollowed out to lessen the load. A complete window treatment—finials, brackets, 20 rings and pole—costs about $500 in wrought iron.  **WAINLANDS MARK II LTD.,** 1108 First Avenue (at 61st Street), New York, NY 10021; (212) 223-2376.  ⊠

## DECORATORS (ONE-DAY)

ON A MUGGY SUMMER MORNING, Lauri Ward, owner of Use What You Have Interiors, strode briskly into a prewar apartment on Manhattan's Upper East Side and got down to the whirlwind business of being a one-day interior decorator.

She scrutinized the cluttered living room. Then, following a spirited discussion with the owner, who bravely announced, "Anything can go," she began moving things around, consigning some items to the basement, artfully rearranging others.

Just over two hours later, the room looked airy and less chaotic. After compiling a suggestion list for future improvements, Ms. Ward was ready to collect her check (she charges $195 to redecorate rooms under 19 by 19 feet, $300 for larger rooms) and leave. "I never know what to expect when I walk in the door," she said. "But with this job I'm used to thinking on my feet."

Ms. Ward, whose firm is 15 years old, qualifies as a trailblazer among one-day decorators, a small but diverse group in sync with the scaled-down style of the 1990s. For the most part, one-day decorators deal with decorating's prosaic, but confusing, aspects, advising on fabrics, paint, floor plans and other basics.

"A lot of people with great design ideas have problems with practical matters, like spatial issues," Ms. Ward said. "They see a color that looks great on a swatch but looks awful when it goes up on a wall."

A one-day job is precisely what it claims to be. Unlike conventional decorators, who handle a project's every facet—choosing cabinetmakers, overseeing the painters, buying fabrics—one-day decorators are essentially consultants. While the best come up with imaginative solutions to specific design problems, it is up to the client to get the job done.

The appeal of the one-day decorator is obvious. With flat fees or hourly rates, the bill is rarely an unpleasant surprise.

Most one-day decorators will happily work with what the client owns. And since the client can choose whether to implement the decorator's edicts, the à la carte decorator can seem less intimidating than a full-project person who many homeowners fear will take charge of their lives and leave his or her signature all over the place.

For no additional charge, one-day decorators like Ms. Ward also arrange for clients to visit design showrooms that normally deal exclusively with the trade. And some will shop with the client, usually for an hourly fee. USE WHAT YOU HAVE INTERIORS; (212) 288-8888. ✉

FROM A TOLL-FREE 800 NUMBER, Barbara Landsman, a Manhattan decorator, reaches a national audience with her Dial-a-Decorator telephone advisory service. For a $100 check, Ms. Landsman studies photographers, blueprints and even videotapes of rooms sent by clients, then calls them back, at the client's expense, with ideas.

Much of what she uncovers are technical problems. "If a room is too dark, the lampshades are often paper," she said. Her advice: replace paper with something more translucent. Like many one-day decorators, she maintains it is not necessary to set foot in a room to decorate it. She started her business in 1986, in fact, because she found she was giving free advice constantly on the phone. She does, however, make house calls in Manhattan. DIAL-A-DECORATOR; (212) 799-5586 or (800) 486-7336. ✉

HOUSE CALLS, priced at $125 an hour with a two-hour minimum, are the specialty of Joann Eckstut and Sheran James of Room Redux, a New York service that began in November 1992. Though the two women rearrange furniture, they spend much of their visits devising new color schemes, suggesting fabrics and tiles and coming up with a new concept for the room.

A few days after the visit, clients receive a customized workbook, detailing ideas for each room—"For your windows, we would recommend a simple curtain treatment because the windows are so nice," reads a bedroom entry—and listing sources.   ROOM REDUX; (212) 534-6319.

FOR CLIENTS WILLING TO PAY THE PRICE, many well-known designers are available for just a day. To free more time for her writing, New York decorator Alexandra Stoddard cut back project work in favor of one-day consultations. "If you have the experience, you can decorate a whole house in a day without question," said Ms. Stoddard, who charges $3,500 for a day that encompasses visits to source shops in Manhattan and lunch.

Sessions, which entail copious note taking by the client, cover floor plans, color schemes and lighting as well as quick tips. "Every room needs a touch of yellow for warmth," Ms. Stoddard said. "It can be as simple as a polished brass candlestick or a bouquet of tulips." ALEXANDRA STODDARD; (212) 289-5509.

## DOLL HOSPITALS

IRVING CHAIS SITS IN A BRIGHTLY lit room above Lexington Avenue, surrounded by dolls, dolls, dolls. Some are headless, some have broken arms, and a few look as if they've had too much love. But by the time they leave the New York Doll Hospital, nearly all will look new, or almost new.

"We can fix any kind of doll, windups, battery-operated, cloth, wax, papier-maché," said Mr. Chais, the hospital's owner and head surgeon. "We've been in business since 1900 and never lost a patient yet."

The hospital, which accepts patients from all over the world, was opened by Mr. Chais's grandfather, a toymaker from Germany. These days many patients come in for restringing, a process that keeps the doll's limbs in moving order. The hospital also does hair transplants (new wigs start at $20), limb replacements, eye surgery and general restitching and cleaning.

For some patients, the hospital is like a spa. Beth Laporte, a nurse at the hospital, makes new clothes for dolls in any style, from a velvet drop-waist frock for a 19th-century bisque doll to a red polka dot dress for a Shirley Temple doll.

The hospital treats stuffed toys, as well. Ailing teddy bears are taken completely apart, lined with muslin and restuffed. When possible, original eyes and noses are used, and all original labels are reattached.

The hospital also sells healthy dolls dating from before the mid-1960s, including vintage Madame Alexander dolls, Betsy McCalls, Shirley Temples, Patti Playmates, Kewpies and, of course, Barbies.

Repairs start at about $15; Mr. Chais always gives an estimate before admitting a patient. The hospital accepts mail orders and ships. NEW YORK DOLL HOSPITAL, 787 Lexington Avenue (near 61st Street), New York, NY 10021; (212) 838-7527.  ✉

SHE'S KNOWN AS THE DOLL LADY, and Iris Brown relishes the sobriquet. Since 1967, Mrs. Brown has sold and repaired antique dolls, specializing in her favorites, Victorian dolls from Germany and France. "Children in Victorian times were not allowed to play with most of these dolls, so you can still find a lot in very good shape," she said.

Her tiny East Side shops, painted romantic Victorian red, is pleasantly cluttered with antique dolls in all sizes, shapes and costumes. Palm-sized dollhouse dolls sit next to big baby dolls with wax faces. In a glass case are two 19th-century crèche dolls, dressed for a Christmas tableau. Old Santas from Germany and Sweden grace the window. And everywhere are vintage accessories—tiny gloves, parasols, shoes, handbags and hats.

Repairs, which start at $20, are done in the shop's balcony. Mrs. Brown, who works only on antique dolls, does restringing, cleaning, paint touchups and wig restorations. She also dresses old dolls in period clothes, choosing from her vast selection of antique frocks and acessories. In addition, Mrs. Brown has a selection of vintage Christmas ornaments. "Dolls and Christmas kind of go together," she said. IRIS BROWN'S VICTORIAN DOLL AND MINIATURE SHOP, 253 East 57th Street, New York, NY 10022; (212) 593-2882.

## DOORBELLS

P EOPLE INSTALL NEW DOORBELLS for all sorts of reasons. But most want a bell that is both functional and attractive. They want a louder bell, or a nicer sound. Or they upgrade the house and decide to get something different.

Though it's a household accessory that attracts minimal attention at most, a doorbell can be an appealing, and amusing, grace note. It can be weirdly evocative, like the household buzzers that sound like high-school bells. Or showy: The Westminster chime, redolent of the BBC, is a big seller, in both four-note and eight-note versions.

And for residents who can't decide how a bell should sound, there are musical doorbells that can be programmed to play anything from the opening notes of Beethoven's Fifth Symphony to Happy Birthday.

Two basic types of doorbells are available these days—electrical chimes and mechanical bells. Tudor Electrical Supply Company sells the former and stocks a variety of styles, with many on view in its showroom where visitors can try them out. The most popular chime is a simple, rectangular unit, in beige or white, that goes either ding or ding-dong.

Wireless chimes that run on a radio frequency and units that light up for the hearing-impaired are also available.

J. Ralph Corbett, an attorney-turned-radio-producer, gets credit for popularizing the electric door chime in 1936. With the help of an acoustics expert, he fashioned a chime from a talcum powder can. His manufacturing company, NuTone, is currently one of the largest electrical chime manufacturers in the United States.

Electrical chimes run on 16 volts and require a transformer, and often an electrician, to install. "But if you're handy, you can install one yourself," said Chuck Wetzel, national service manager for NuTone.

Tudor also sells industrial doorbells—round metal bells that ring with a striker. Industrial bells range from two to six inches and start at $10. "They make a real bell-like sound," said Mike Zarre, Tudor showroom manager.  **TUDOR ELECTRICAL SUPPLY COMPANY,** 222 East 46th Street, New York, NY 10017; (212) 867-7550.

A LARGE PART OF A MECHANICAL doorbell's appeal is its traditional appearance, according to Bob Crawford, owner of Crawford's Old House Store, a 12-year-old mail order company specializing in reproduction Victorian hardware and accessories. Crawford's sells a highly decorative twist-type mechanical bell for $31. The bell is all brass, including the key.

A mechanical doorbell isn't practical on a house with a storm door or screen door; the mechanism that rings the bell needs to go through the door, Mr. Crawford explains. But the bells can often be used on apartment doors. They can also be set in doorframes.  **CRAWFORD'S OLD HOUSE STORE,** 550 Elizabeth Street, Waukesha, WI 53186; (800) 556-7878.  ✉

# DOORS
# (HARDWARE)

*T*HEY'RE MEANT TO BE FUNCTIONAL, but doorknobs and levers can also be a handsome finishing touch for any type of room. They're the jewelry of the house, and like necklaces or bracelets, they come in an enormous range of styles, shapes and even materials.

"We have over 50,000 styles of hardware," said Andrew Ward, chief executive officer of P. E. Guerin, makers of decorative hardware for 135 years. "We make them all ourselves, in the foundry upstairs."

Mr. Ward and his associate, Martin Grubman, stood in the company's 100-year-old Greenwich Village showroom, an old-fashioned, high-ceilinged room of drawers and glass cases filled with brass doorknobs and levers. Drawer pulls, faucets and other types of ornamental hardware were also on view. The company, founded by a distant relative by marriage of Mr. Ward, makes period-style hardware from the

Gothic era to Art Moderne, with stops along the way at the Renaissance, the three Louises (XIV, XV, XVI), Empire, Art Nouveau and Arts & Crafts.

Demand is particularly strong for unusual pieces, including levers shaped like mermaids, dolphins and swans. The company will modify any of its existing designs or create entirely new ones.

With each case devoted to knobs or levers of a distinct era, a browse through the room is a concise history of ornamental hardware. French 18th-century knobs and levers are P. E. Guerin's specialty. Hardware designs from the Louis XVI era often display reliefs of laurel and ribbon, beading, acanthus leaves, daisies and sunflowers.

In contrast, hardware inspired by the Louis XV years was "soft, asymmetrical and abstract, almost feminine," Mr. Grubman explained. And Louis XIV hardware is distinguished by shells, symmetrical lines and deep carving.

Hardware is made by a centuries-old method called sand casting. A model of the doorknob or lever to be created is covered with sand. Next the model is removed and hot melted brass is poured into the cavity, where it hardens. Hardware straight out of the mold looks rough and rather crude, and requires extensive cleaning, chasing and polishing before its decorative images are clear and sharp. Then it is plated. A variety of finishes are available, though gold is the most popular.

Doorknobs and levers start at around $40 and go over $1,000 apiece. **P. E. GUERIN, INC.,** 21-25 Jane Street (near Eighth Avenue), New York, NY 10014; (212) 243-5270. ✉

THOUGH APPEARANCE AND STYLE are obvious factors when choosing new doorknobs, so is comfort. Egg-shaped knobs are the perfect shape for the hand, according to Walter Ress, who manages Simon's Hardware, a large retailer of decorative hardware. "The egg has some bulk to it, but also a grace the round knob doesn't have," he said.

Simon's, in business since 1909, represents 12 large hardware manufacturers and devotes nearly an entire room to doorknobs and levers. Most knobs are brass, though a variety of finishes are available, including contemporary-looking combination finishes in brass and chrome or chrome and black metal. The company also sells Lucite knobs shaped like balls or disks, popular in Art Deco–style homes, Mr. Ress said. A large selection of porcelain knobs are available as well, including white knobs decorated with painted flowers.

Doorknobs and levers start at around $50 for a two-knob set. A 608-page catalog is available for $25, which is used as a merchandise credit.   SIMON'S HARDWARE, 421 Third Avenue (near 30th Street), New York, NY 10016; (212) 532-9220.   ✉

FOR YEARS, CUSTOMERS brought old doorknobs, levers and faucets to Crown City Hardware, a conventional hardware store in Pasadena, California, when replacements were needed. There were so many requests, the store began commissioning reproductions of hard-to-get decorative hardware about 10 years ago. Crown City now offers close to 500 different types of door hardware, from the elaborate brass levers found in Victorian houses to the octagonal crystal knobs popular during the 1920s ($100 for a pair with brass base and shank). The clear crystal knob sells best, though a range of colors are available, including cobalt blue, Depression green, Depression pink and amethyst.

Many of the company's most unusual styles are pictured in a 225-page catalog ($6.50, payable by check).   CROWN CITY HARDWARE, 1047 North Allen Avenue, Pasadena, CA 91104; (818) 794-1188.   ✉

## DOWN BEDDING, CUSTOM-MADE AND REPAIRED

*O*UNCE FOR OUNCE, down is the warmest filling ever devised for a comforter, according to Abe Studin, who has renovated comforters and pillows since he got out of the army in 1946. And properly cared for, down can last for years. Mr. Studin, whose father opened the Madison Quilt Shops in 1924, recently renovated a 25-year-old comforter. The frayed cotton cover had to be replaced. But the goosedown filling was still fluffy and soft.

"A lot of people have comforters with heirloom fillings made from old feather beds their grandparents brought over from Europe," Mr. Studin said. Almost any good down or feather filling can be recycled.

Mr. Studin recently made a comforter using the down from two old sleeping bags.

Mr. Studin can revive down pillows while the customer waits. "That way you don't have to be without your pillow," he said. The old fabric cover is discarded. The contents, usually a mix of down and feathers, is sterilized and fluffed in a machine. Additional down or feathers are added if necessary. And everything is sewn in a new cotton covering that won't leak.

Mr. Studin, who also makes customized comforters and pillows, offers three types of fillings. White goose down, taken from the bird's belly, is the lightest and costliest. It can be mixed with feathers for a firmer feel. Lambswool is advised for customers allergic to down. And dacron polyester, the cheapest, is washable. Mr. Studin recommends it for children's comforters.

Prices for renovated pillows start at $12 for a standard size, $14 for queen size. Quilt renovations start at $160 for a queen size.  **MADISON QUILT SHOPS,** 2307 Grand Concourse (near 183rd Street), Bronx, NY 10468; (718) 733-2100.

DOWN COMFORTERS SHOULD never be stored in plastic bags, according to Miss Kay, a long-time employee at J. Schachter, which has made, sold and renovated quilts and pillows since 1919. Miss Kay, who was in the quilt-renovating business for many of her 78 years, also suggests rotating the pillow with each linen change. "That freshens it and gives it a chance to breathe," she said.

Schachter's renovates and re-covers pillows while the customer waits (from $16 for standard size). Quilt re-covering, including sterilization of fillings, starts at $140 for a king size.  **J. SCHACHTER,** 5 Cook Street, Brooklyn, NY 11206; (718) 384-2732 or (800) 468-6233.

# DRAPERY CLEANERS

THE EQUIPMENT AT HAIRO BAGHDASSARIAN'S dry-cleaning establishment in Queens looks as if it was designed for giants. The examining tables, where the staff inspects fabrics before cleaning, are the size of banquet tables. The pressing machines measure 110 inches long. And there's a huge contraption with wooden teeth for stretching draperies.

The outsize equipment is necessary for cleaning draperies and curtains, according to Mr. Baghdassarian, who opened Drapemasters of America more than 25 years ago. "You cannot press eight-foot drapes on a regular garment press," he explained, shaking his head.

A competent, and trusted, dry cleaner should be able to treat most household curtains and draperies, according to William Seiz, president of the Neighborhood Cleaners Association, a trade association in Manhattan. But it can be a good idea to take costly or complicated draperies to an establishment that specializes in cleaning window coverings.

In addition to large-scale machinery, a drapery cleaner uses different cleaning techniques than most garment cleaners. A professional drapery cleaner should also be equipped to take down and rehang drapes on site at the customer's request.

The biggest problem with draperies is shrinkage, Mr. Baghdassarian said. Shrinking happens even in dry cleaning, particularly from heat. Two percent shrinkage is typical for most drapery fabrics. "It doesn't sound like much," Mr. Baghdassarian explained. "But with a 96-inch drapery for an eight-foot ceiling, that's two inches."

Draperies are treated with the same solvents as garments, he added. But they should be dried at lower temperatures to prevent shrinkage. If shrinking still occurs, they can be stretched on a blocking machine.

Customers should be very careful when choosing drapery fabrics. Surface prints often bleed, screen prints can fade, and chintz usually loses its luster when dry cleaned. Even fabrics that claim to be dry cleanable often aren't, Mr. Baghdassarian said.

Manufacturers of vinyl blackout liners, often used in bedrooms, usually suggest dry cleaning with Stoddard solvent. "It's made with petroleum and it's now illegal," said Mr. Baghdassarian, holding a vinyl fabric swatch. "We can't clean this."

Mr. Baghdassarian suggests cleaning draperies every 18 to 24 months. "Fabric absorbs dust, soot, smoke, cooking smells," he said. "Vacuuming helps, but it won't do the entire job."

Drapemasters, which also makes drapes, services New York, New Jersey and Connecticut, and charges $2.50 a pleat for unlined, eight-foot drapes, $3 a pleat lined. This includes pickup and rehanging. The average window has about 30 pleats. **DRAPEMASTERS OF AMERICA,** 89-01 Astoria Boulevard, Jackson Heights, Queens, NY 11369; (718) 446-6666.

WHILE DRAPES SHOULD USUALLY be dry cleaned, curtains often can be washed. Majestic Drapery Cleaners in Brooklyn has the large-scale machinery to clean both household and commercial draperies. But the company, which started in 1928 as curtain cleaners, still wet cleans and starches most types of white lace curtains.

Washing is better than dry cleaning for some curtains, according to Arnold Rothstein, a partner in the firm. The finished product can look brighter.

"The biggest headache is when people leave their draperies up five or six years without cleaning them," he added. "Sunlight and heat deteriorate them." According to a drapery-cleaning leaflet published by the Better Business Bureau, window dressings may appear in good condition when taken to the dry cleaners. But they can, in fact, be so fragile that even the moderate agitation necessary to remove soil will rip them to shreds. A cleaner should inspect window coverings before cleaning to prevent mishaps.

Majestic, which services New York City, Nassau County and lower Westchester, charges $3 a pleat, which includes pickup and cleaning. Rehanging is additional. **MAJESTIC DRAPERY CLEANERS,** 740 Pine Street, Brooklyn, NY 11208; (718) 272-0010.

"LININGS ARE SACRIFICIAL," said Steve DeMarco, Sr., president of Triple S, a drapery- and rug-cleaning concern in Connecticut. "You let the sun eat up the lining instead of the drapery. It's easy to replace the lining." Triple S, which has cleaned commercial and residential draperies throughout Connecticut and Weschester County for 20 years, also alters and repairs window coverings.

After cleaning, all long drapes are finished in a special machine, called Adjust-a-Drape, that blocks the fabric, adjusts length if necessary and sets in pleats, Mr. DeMarco said. Triple S charges from $11.25 a fabric width (approximately five pleats) for lined drapes, from $10.50 unlined, with a 20 percent discount for drapes brought to the shop.

TRIPLE S, 337 Westport Avenue, Norwalk, CT 06851, (203) 853-2121; 400 West Main Street, Stamford, CT 06902, (203) 327-7471; 1800 Stratford Avenue, Stratford, CT 06497, (203) 333-0555.

## DRESSFORMS

"ALL PEOPLE ARE NOT PERFECT," said W. Burdette Hunton, strolling past a row of dressforms made by his firm, the Wolf Form Co., in Englewood, New Jersey. Most of the forms were, in fact, a perfect size 8, which clothing manufacturers favor for sample garments. But there was also a custom-made woman's size 16, with inches added to waist and bust, a child's form with a removable head and a generous man's size 50, ordered by an opera company.

Home sewers with polished skills and pattern-perfect measurements seldom have problems fitting garments. But for the majority of sewers, a clothing form can be a vital tool, particularly if it is customized. Fitting problems, a major worry for home sewers, are often eliminated by using a form. And for sophisticated methods of clothing construction, like French draping, a form is a necessity.

A custom form is helpful also when shaping clothes to disguise a sloping shoulder, a raised hip or other minor imperfections.

The recession and sky-high clothing prices have contributed to a boomlet in home sewing after years of decline. "Some people also find it satisfying to make their own clothes," said Bruno Ferri, president of Wolf Form.

Wolf, which dates from the early years of the century, creates garment forms primarily for designers, clothing manufacturers and fashion schools. But the firm sells directly to individuals, as well, and accepts custom orders. Clients can either stop by for a fitting or fill out a detailed measurement form, available by mail. Forms start at $460.

A Wolf form gets its shape from a sturdy papier-mâché core, made from molds. Cores are padded with cotton stock, covered with cream-colored Irish linen and placed on adjustable metal rods. The company has over 1,200 molds in stock but makes new ones when needed. Sizes and shapes change, after all. "When I started here in 1931, a women's size 10 was a 34½-inch bust, 24½-inch waist, 34½-inch hip," Mr. Hunton said. Today a size 8 measures 36-26-38.  **WOLF FORM CO.,** 17 Van Nostrand Avenue, Englewood, NJ 07631; (201) 567-6556 or (212) 255-4508.  ✉

"THE WORD 'DRESSFORM' makes you think of something Grandma had in the attic," said LaVina Scott, a fashion design instructor for 25 years. So when Mrs. Scott invented a do-it-yourself method for making dress-forms in 1968, she decided to call them fashion forms. In 1975, she published a book, *Sew Clothes to You,* detailing step-by-step instruc-tions ($24.95, available by mail). Based in Stockton, California, she now travels widely, teaching seminars on making fashion forms.

"The idea was to make a form that fit the body perfectly," Mrs. Scott said. "A form that duplicates you offers proficiency in fitting, draping and pattern alteration." She also wanted a lightweight form the sewer could plunge pins into with ease. Her solution was to make a papier-mâché model of the sewer's body, then fill it with liquid polyurethene. Then the form is padded and covered.

Forms take between 40 and 80 hours to make. "And you need someone to help you put the papier-mâché on yourself," she said. Mrs. Scott suggests sewers be a few pounds over average weight when mak-ing a fashion form since it easiest to fit fabric snugly onto a form.

Mrs. Scott also offers a three-hour video on French draping with a fashion form ($49.95).  **LAVINA SCOTT,** 875 West Sonoma Avenue, Stockton, CA 95204; (209) 463-3989.  ✉

"IT'S SO MUCH EASIER to sew with a dressform," said Alan Wootton, sales manager of National Thread & Supply Corp., a mail order com-pany since 1948 specializing in sewing supplies. National offers several dressforms, all currently under $150. Biggest seller is the Dritz My Dou-ble, a flexible plastic shell covered with a blue-gray nylon knitted mate-rial ($119.95). A small wheel at the neck, bust, waist and hips adjusts each measurement.  A free catalog is available.  **NATIONAL THREAD & SUPPLY CORP.,** 695 Red Oak Road, Stockbridge, GA 30281; (800) 331-7600.  ✉

# DYEING

WHEN ELISSA TATIGIKIS Iberti begins her work, she puts on a mask and gloves, and makes certain her little boy is no where nearby. Ms. Iberti is a professional fabric colorist, and dyeing can be dangerous business. "You have to know the different pigments and how they will affect fabrics," she said, standing by the much-used washing machine in her studio. "There's also a certain health hazard," she added. "Some dyes are toxic. Dyeing is chemistry."

With the recession in full swing, dyeing is one way to liven up a wardrobe without investing too much money. Dyeing can also be a way to salvage a favorite blouse or dress that has become spotted or stained. The problem is finding individuals or companies willing to accept a single garment for dyeing.

Most large dyeing concerns deal with bulk lots and won't dye a lone party dress. And specialized companies, like Manhattan's Fabric Effects, formerly 20/20 Colorists, and the Martin Izquierdo Studio, which does costume dyeing, do not usually deal with the general public.

Ms. Iberti, who has a masters degree in art, learned dyeing during her seven years as a costume coordinator at the Metropolitan Opera. Before she accepts a garment, she always explains dyeing's pitfalls. Natural fibers, like silk, cotton, linen and canvas, generally accept color best. Wool can shrink. And blends, such as polycotton, will only tint. (She will not work with pure synthetics. "No polyester bridesmaid dresses," she said.)

A possible problem is a natural fiber garment with lots of topstitching in polycotton thread. The garment most likely will accept the new color, but the topstitching may stay the original color or tint. "If you expect that, it's fine," Ms. Iberti said. "If not, you're horrified."

Once a garment is dyed, Ms. Iberti recommends dry cleaning. And she cannot guarantee an even result on old, well-worn garments, with perspiration stains.

For badly stained garments, Ms. Iberti usually suggests painting over offensive spots. Using fabric paint or a fiber-reactive dye, she can create florals, geometrics, ethnic prints—"whatever interests the person," she said.

Her minimum charge for dyeing is $55. Hand-painted fabric is $74 a yard. Ms. Iberti also teaches seminars on dyeing. Topics include color mixing, the science of dyeing and cotton dyes. The fee is $125.  ELISSA TATIGIKIS IBERTI; (516) 244-3092.

DRY CLEANERS OFTEN OFFER dyeing services, and Madame Paulette Dry Cleaners, in business since 1957, has provided dyeing for several years. Dyeing is done off the premises. But before a garment is accepted, customers receive a lengthy explanation of things that can go wrong. Trimmings, zippers and thread often won't take the dye, said owner/ manager John Mahdessian. "But if you still have a blue zipper after the dress is dyed black, we can change the zipper." The company will also remove buttons before dyeing and sew them back on afterward.

For dingy-looking white and off-white silks and cottons, Mr. Mahdessian suggests an overnight bleach. The cost is $25 per piece for silks and woolens. Dyeing starts at $140.  MADAME PAULETTE DRY CLEANERS, 1255 Second Avenue (65th Street), New York, NY 10021; (212) 838-6827.

## EMBROIDERY

*E*MBROIDERY COMES IN MANY GUISES, from bathrobe monograms and evening gown embellishments to the New York Knicks logos stitched on sweatshirts and caps. "It can be very personal," said Dan Weisner, publisher of *Stitches* magazine, a publication for the embroidery trade.

Oddly enough, custom embroidery is more widely available now than it was a decade ago. Hand embroiderers still stitch with needle, thread and an embroidery hoop. Machine embroiderers still create big, satiny monograms on special sewing machines.

But behind embroidery's increased availability is a new generation of computer-programmed sewing machines. With a range of disks and commands, the machines can stitch dozens of standardized monograms and images, from dinosaurs to teddy bears. The machines can also sew original images, which a programmer copies onto a disk using a mouse.

In the past, elaborate machine embroidery was accomplished by plotting each stitch, then translating the pattern onto punched tape, which was fed into sewing machines like old-style teletype. "It was slow," Mr. Weisner said. "The personal computer changed the embroidery industry."

Despite its speed and accuracy, computerized embroidery is not right for every job. Sandy Perlmutter, whose company, L. Allmeier, has done custom embroidery and alterations for over 50 years, offers hand embroidery, machine embroidery and computer embroidery.

"Nothing looks quite like a hand-embroidered monogram on a shirt," he said. "It's classier. And there's a little bit of character in the monogram." Mr. Perlmutter offers over 30 different styles, all hand stitched by women at his Brooklyn factory ($12.50 to $40).

Mr. Perlmutter has 12 styles of computer-embroidered shirt monograms as well ($6 to $8). Most shirt monograms go on the top pocket or the left collar; some clients even order monogrammed laundry markers in the collars.

Mr. Perlmutter also uses the computer to stitch baseball bats and ballet slippers on a line of personalized bibs ($9.95) and hooded towels ($29.95) he sells for kids. **L. ALLMEIER,** 109-111 West 24th Street, New York, NY 10011; (212) 243-7390. ✉

EDWARD THE MONOGRAMMER, aka Edward Sacher, learned his trade from his father, a machine embroiderer for over 30 years. And the old-style embroidery machine, which looks like a heavy-duty sewing machine, is ideal for the large, satiny monograms Mr. Sacher makes for towels, bathrobes, fur coats, sheets and shower curtains.

Seated at the machine, Mr. Sacher stitches initials freehand, making it look as easy as writing. "This is standard monogram script," he explained. "My handwriting doesn't look like this." Besides new monograms, Mr. Sacher can change or repair old monograms, usually on fur coats. "The woman gets divorced or gives the coat to her daughter," he explained.

Mr. Sacher offers over 50 monogram styles. Shirt monograms cost $6 to $8, freehand monograms $7.50 and $12, towel monograms $5 to $10. **EDWARD THE MONOGRAMMER,** Maxene Cleaners & Tailors, 750 Columbus Avenue (at 97th Street), New York, NY 10025; (212) 749-7300. ✉

TONY MCLAUGHLIN AND PETER BUCHANAN, who own Stitch Works, offer the standard range of monograms, crests and other images available on their computer. But the house specialty is custom design. Clients bring in a drawing they want converted to embroidery. Using the computer mouse, Mr. McLaughlin or Mr. Buchanan copies it onto a disk. When the design is complicated, it can take hours to make a disk. But it takes just minutes to sew the image once the machine is threaded with the right colors.

Stitch Works can produce a custom embroidery design for just one item, though their service is more cost effective for multiple orders. As party favors, a client asked them to embroider King Tutankhahamen's image onto V-neck sweaters. They offer personalized items, such as a chaise longue cover embroidered with a name or initial ($45) and embroidered baby blankets ($50). And recently, they initiated a line of decorative pillows with embroidered motifs. **STITCH WORKS,** 27 West 24th Street, New York, NY 10010; (212) 255-2573. ✉

MOST OF CHRIS BOBIN'S hand-stitched embroidery is for one-of-a-kind items, such as wedding and christening gowns. Unlike machines, hand embroiderers do an array of stitches, from herringbone to couching (a raised stitch). "There's literally a dictionary of stitches you can do by hand," she said. Machines do just two stitches—a flat stitch and satin stitch. Ms. Bobin charges $75 an hour. **CHRIS BOBIN;** (212) 475-7268.

# ERGONOMISTS (HOME OFFICE CONSULTANTS)

A HOME OFFICE CAN BE A HAVEN FROM THE NOISE and stress of conventional workplaces. But even a rudimentary office—a laptop computer on the dining-room table—should be set up with a knowledge of ergonomics, the science of designing and arranging tools to fit the user's physical and psychological requirements.

"The home is a neglected area of ergonomics," said Dr. Emil Pascarelli, professor of clinical medicine at Columbia Presbyterian Eastside and author, with Deborah Quilter, of *Repetitive Strain Injury: A Computer User's Guide* (Wiley; $14.95). "People rightfully insist on an ergonomically correct office, then go home and play Nintendo or work on the computer in an unsatisfactory setting."

An ergonomically incorrect work area can result in severe, often crippling injuries, from back ailments and eye strain to repetitive strain injury, or RSI, which harms muscles, tendons and nerves in the neck, forearm, hand and shoulders. RSI, which stems from repeated, forceful or awkward hand movements, makes it difficult to do the most mundane tasks, such as opening doors. For some, the damage is permanent.

In the 14 years since personal computers changed the way people do everything from writing letters to balancing checkbooks, the incidence of RSI has grown dramatically. In 1987, 10 repetitive motion ailments were reported for every 10,000 full-time workers, according to statistics from the U.S. Labor Department. In 1993, there were 38 cases for every 10,000 workers.

And an increasing number of these injuries occur in home offices. "I see a lot of professors who get injured when they take off six months to stay home and write a book," said Philip L. Witt, an associate professor of physical therapy at the University of North Carolina at Chapel Hill School of Medicine.

Ergonomists say the reason for such ailments is no mystery. A typist working on a manual machine used the entire upper body, from the shoulders down. But most computer jobs keep the upper body immobile while the forearms, hands and fingers work overtime. "It's like a baseball player throwing a 90-mph ball from the wrist," said Dr. Pascarelli.

Common sense is a key element of an ergonomically correct work area. But many people need additional guidance, whether from books and software on ergonomics or from a house call by an ergonomics consultant.

Most ergonomists agree the chair is the most important office component. The seat should go up and down so the feet are flat on the floor, the seat pan should adjust so the pelvis tilts forward slightly and the back rest should adjust to support the spine.

"If you're working at a kitchen table, which isn't the right height for using a computer, you can adjust the chair," said Paul Berglund, president of B.P. Associates, a midtown Manhattan showroom stocked with ergonomic office equipment. And if the feet, consequently, do not reach the floor, "you can use a footrest," he added.

B.P. carries a range of adjustable chairs by Hag, a Norwegian manufacturer (from $250 to $2,000). The five-year-old showroom also handles adjustable computer tables (from $500), foot rests (from $20) and glare screens (from $50). B.P., which does not sell directly, provides names of local retailers who carry their lines. **B.P. ASSOCIATES,** 155 East 56th Street, New York, NY 10022; (212) 759-1300.

"WE LIKE TO HAVE PEOPLE come in and sit in our chairs to see what's comfortable for them," said Tricia Martin, regional sales manager for Girsberger, a 107-year-old Swiss company that makes adjustable office chairs. A strong seller is the Consens chair, designed in conjunction with the College of Orthopedic Surgeons. It starts at around $400. **GIRSBERGER OFFICE SEATING,** 150 East 58th Street, New York, NY 10155; (212) 750-7760.

CLIENTS WHO CALL ELLEN KOLBER, an occupational therapist about to get a masters degree in ergonomics, usually have RSI or are concerned about getting it. Ms. Kolber, a staff member of the Miller Institute, which treats RSI, makes house calls to create or adjust home work stations to the client's needs. She often adjusts distances of the components, including the mouse, so there is no awkward stretching.

She also watches how the person uses the computer. "Some people need retraining, so they won't hit the keyboard too hard or hold their wrists wrong," she said. Ms. Kolber charges about $125 a visit. **ELLEN KOLBER;** (718) 789-4762.

JOHN KELLA, WHO OWNS COMPUTER HEALTH TRAINING, makes house calls to individuals and corporations to advise on ways to set up work stations and provides retraining on proper use of the keyboard and mouse—even explains how to hold the telephone to avoid injuries. "Some people need telephone headsets," he said. Some adjustments are inexpensive, such as outfitting pens with pads for clients who grip writing implements too tightly. Mr. Kella charges from $250 for his services. **COMPUTER HEALTH TRAINING;** (212) 246-0557.

MARLENE GREEN'S BACKGROUND is in computers rather than medicine. But she began studying ergonomics when she realized most computer specialists were knowledgeable mainly about hardware and software rather than ways to avoid injury at the work station. Though Ms. Green, who owns the Comfort Zone, often provides ergonomic consultations on the phone, she says visiting clients can expedite problem solving. "Some people have fully adjustable $400 chairs, but they don't bother adjusting them and wind up sitting on the edge of the chair," she said. She charges from $50 an hour.   THE COMFORT ZONE; (201) 659-4836.

CHARLES PAPPAS, RESEARCH EDITOR AT *Home Office Computing* magazine, makes house calls to evaluate how everything from lighting and air circulation to general stress level affect a work station. He also sells a set of pamphlets on work stations called "Is Your Computer Killing You?" Pamphlets cost $20, house calls are from $50 to $75.   ERGO COMMUNICATIONS; (212) 535-0344.

IF USING A COMPUTER becomes impossible, people with severe RSI often turn to voice-activated equipment. But many people need a training session with a speech pathologist to avoid strain to their vocal cords. One training session is often enough, said Lynda Marvin, a speech pathologist at the Miller Institute, who charges $150 an evaluation. LYNDA MARVIN, at Miller Institute; (212) 532-6202.

## EYEGLASSES, CHILDREN'S

LITTLE BOYS LIKE ROUND, preppie frames. And little girls like purple. That, at least, is the observation of Richard Hogg, president of Superspecs for Kids Only, a big store in Closter, New Jersey, that stocks nothing but eyeglass frames for kids, from the age of six months to 15 years.

Superspecs, which opened in 1992, carries over 1,000 frames, including kid-size ski, cycling and swimming goggles that can accommodate prescription lenses. Many frames have cable temples, which wrap around the ear, so kids can't yank them off. And durable materials, like bendable metals and super-tough plastics, abound. The shop is also outfitted with coloring books, television monitors showing cartoons and two corrugated pipes kids can crawl through if they get bored.

Though many children and young teens need eyeglasses to correct anything from weak eye muscles to myopia, finding frames for kids can be difficult. Adult optical stores often stock a limited range of young people's frames, or none at all.

Children are less likely to sit still during a fitting than adults, which some opticians find disruptive. Children also can be difficult to fit; glasses frequently leave red marks on young noses, which are cartilage instead of bone. And for years, eyeglass manufacturers produced a limited number of styles.

But about three years ago, companies that cater to the youth market, such as Disney, Crayola, Fisher-Price and even Nintendo, began making frames specifically for kids. Some are unisex, in colorful metallics and plastics. Some are snappy, with polka dots, plaids or stripes. And many are whimsical: One metal frame at Superspecs has the alphabet jumbled across the nose bridge.

There's even a growing frame selection for infants. Superspecs stocks 70 pastel itty bitties on headbands so babies can't pull them off.

Superspecs charges $65 to $200 for frames, $30 to $45 for discontinued models and $90 for most lenses. **SUPERSPECS FOR KIDS ONLY,** Closter Shopping Center, Closter, NJ 07624; (201) 768-1717.

JON GRUEN, WHOSE GRUEN Optika stores carry frames for children as well as adults, believes that kids usually should choose their own glasses. "If they don't like them, they have a tendency not to wear them," he said. A "miniaturized retro look," including metallics in geometric shapes, is popular for kids at the moment, he added. Frames and lenses for infants to 16-year-olds start at $168. **GRUEN OPTIKA,** 1225 Lexington Avenue (near 83rd Street), New York, NY 10028, (212) 628-2493; 2382 Broadway (near 87th Street), 10024, (212) 724-0850; 1076 Third Avenue (near 64th Street), 10021, (212) 751-6177; 740 Madison Avenue (near 64th Street), 10021, (212) 988-5832.

"FRAMES FOR KIDS ARE colorful, unusual and a lot more daring that they used to be," said Lloyd Chautin, whose Eyeman shop has a section devoted to children's glasses. Metallics are popular because they show off the kid's face. But most heavy plastics and old-style aviator glasses are no longer in vogue, he added. Frames and lenses cost $120, $145 or $165.　**THE EYEMAN,** 2266 Broadway (near 81st Street), New York, NY 10024; (212) 873-4114.

## FANS (DECORATIVE), REPAIRED

ANGELO L. MONTAPERTO RESTORES ANTIQUE furniture and specializes in marquetry, wood carving and French polishing. But when the weather gets warmer, clients often bring him decorative European fans to repair.

Repairing an antique fan, which usually has a mother-of-pearl frame or inlays, is quite similar to restoring inlays on furniture or jewelry boxes, Mr. Montaperto said. The hard part is finding shells to closely match the thickness, color, grain and translucency of the original mother-of-pearl.

To illustrate, Mr. Montaperto opened a metal box filled with mother-of-pearl in a variety of thicknesses and shades. "Mother-of-pearl is made from  shells that come from the Pacific," he said. "Because of differences in the grain and transparency, it is harder to work with than ivory, for example."

Mr. Montaperto, who learned his trade 20 years ago in Florence, Italy, can also restore fans with wood frames. Age, maintenance and climate changes are the main reasons antique fans need repair. Humid weather can prise an inlay from a frame. It can also damage the wood veneer. Mr. Montaperto's repairs start at about $100.   ANGELO L. MON-TAPERTO COMPANY, 131 Varick Street, New York, NY 10013; (212) 255-8626.

CHUN K. BECK CAN REPAIR all types of Asian fans, from huge paper Chinese fans to the pleated-silk lollipop-style fans of his native Korea. There's just one caveat. "After a paper fan is repaired, it can go on a wall," he said. "But it should never be used."

Mr. Beck, who also repairs jade, porcelain, coromandel and Asian screens, is adept at masking holes in both paper and silk. He dyes either paper or silk to match the proper color, then affixes it with a specially mixed glue that dries colorlessly.

He can also repair bamboo frames and will hand cut the tiny patterns seen in many Asian frames. Mr. Chun, who has worked in Manhattan for 10 years, also repairs mother-of-pearl fans. His prices start at $50.   ORIENT ANTIQUE RESTORER, 280 Madison Avenue (near 40th Street), New York, NY 10016; (212) 696-4762.

FANS IN VARIOUS FORMS account for a large part of Suetada Mitsuhashi's work. A custom framer and antiques restorer, Mr. Mitsuhashi repairs Japanese and Chinese paper fans, using glue to mend torn paper and hand-painting restored areas.

But Mr. Mitsuhashi's specialty is making frames for European and Asian fans. Fans, mounted on paper or silk, look best in a three-dimensional box-style frame, he said.

Frames that accommodate an average fan start at around $400. Red or black lacquer and other materials and colors are available.

Mr. Mitsuhashi also makes custom fan-shaped frames, which start at around $1,500. A cheaper alternative—about $500—is a ready-made fan-shaped frame from Italy, which Mr. Mitsuhashi can paint.   GAKU, 540 La Guardia Place (near West 3rd Street), New York, NY 10012; (212) 533-6610.

# FLAGS

$F$OR PRESIDENT'S DAY, the Fourth of July and other flag-waving events, it helps to have a flag. And the classic stars and bars come in a variety of sizes and fabrics, from modest tabletop models to elaborate versions worthy of a courthouse.

AAA American Flag Decorating Co., a flag shop, carries 11 sizes of American flags, from 2 feet by 3 feet to 20 by 30. The firm, owned by Ian Flamm, sells state and territorial flags as well as flags for more than 150 countries. Mr. Flamm also sells specialty flags as demand requires. During the Persian Gulf War, he stocked a 3-by-5-foot white flag printed with a big yellow ribbon and the legend "We Support Our Troops; Come Home Soon."

The life of a flag depends on where and how frequently it is flown, as well as the material, Mr. Flamm said. Flags flown at sea by the United States Navy are replaced every 96 hours, he noted.

A flag flown outdoors usually lasts about a year. Flapping breaks down a flag's fibers, and rain, which can be acidic, causes fabric to deteriorate.

Mr. Flamm's stars and stripes feature machine-sewn stripes and embroidered stars, and come in cotton, nylon or woven polyester.

For a standard 3-by-5-foot flag, Mr. Flamm recommends the $26 cotton version if the flag will be flown only on holidays. For more frequent use, he said nylon, at $32, is more cost effective. And the $39 woven polyester flag, used by the United States Navy, is believed to last the longest.

AAA American Flag also sells flagpoles.   **AAA AMERICAN FLAG DECORATING CO.,** 40 West 37th Street, New York, NY 10081; (212) 279-3524.   ⊠

ONE OF THE MORE POPULAR ITEMS at Ace Banner and Flag Company is an American flag for indoors that comes with stand, pole and eagle-shaped finial for $164.30. The 3-by-5-foot nylon flag, with embroidered stars and machine-sewn stripes, has a gold cord and tassel. "You see a lot of these in offices," said Carl Calo, who has owned Ace for more than 15 years.

Ace also offers a modest $14.50 flag set, which includes a 3-by-5-foot printed flag with pole and plastic eagle finial. Machine-sewn foreign flags, nautical flags, state flags and armed forces flags are also available. ACE BANNER AND FLAG, 107 West 27th Street, New York, NY 10001; (212) 620-9111. ✉

ABACROME INC., a flag and custom banner shop, stocks a large range of machine-sewn American and foreign flags, as well as miniature printed flags for each team in the National Football League (two dollars each). Abacrome's American flags, which have embroidered stars, are available in cotton, nylon or woven polyester. The shop has a glossy brochure. Minimum order $25. ABACROME, 151 West 26th Street, New York, NY 10001; (212) 989-1190. ✉

WHEN A NEW FLAG WEARS OUT, it is usually cheaper to discard it than repair it. Flags with historical or sentimental value are another matter.

"There is a huge market for Civil War flags right now," said Fonda Thomsen, whose nine-year-old company, the Textile Preservation Association, is a leader in flag conservation and restoration. Ms. Thomsen has worked on a variety of historical flags, including the 12-foot-by-24-foot flag flown during the battle of Fort Sumter.

Each flag presents a singular set of problems. Historical flags should never be washed or ironed, Ms. Thomsen said: "You'll destroy all evidence of battle—the smoke, combustion particles, soil samples, salt spray if it was by the sea." Flags should never be mounted on boards, and they should be kept away from light.

The Textile Preservation Association routinely analyzes each flag's materials to determine authenticity. "One so-called historical flag brought to me was sewn with mercerized thread," Ms. Thomsen said. "We knew it wasn't right."

The Textile Preservation Association provides treatment reports, charges $75 an hour and will ship finished products. TEXTILE PRESERVATION ASSOCIATION, P.O. Box 606, Sharpsburg, MD 21782; (301) 432-4160. ✉

## FLATWARE
## (LOCATING DISCONTINUED PATTERNS)

"IT OFFENDS NO ONE," Beverly Bremer explained. Mrs. Bremer, who owns the Beverly Bremer Silver Shop in Atlanta, Georgia, was discussing Chantilly, a well-known silver flatware pattern produced since 1898 by Gorham.

But even though Chantilly is still made, adding matching pieces to an existing set can be a problem. Knife blade styles changed over the years, for one thing. "There are lots of different Chantilly blades," Mrs. Bremer said, ticking off a long list. "If you inherited your mother's pattern and wanted to buy more knives, you'd need to know exactly which blade she had."

Adding pieces to a flatware collection can be even more challenging when the pattern has been discontinued. But a growing number of replacement services can usually locate discontinued or obscure pieces, such as duck shears or sardine forks. Some companies, including Mrs. Bremer's, deal exclusively in sterling silver. Others will match discontinued or hard-to-get silverplate and stainless steel.

Mrs. Bremer, in business since 1975, specializes in American silver, selling new and used sterling, in both active and discontinued patterns. Since sterling can be polished to look new, used silver can be a bargain. She charges $129 for a new four-piece setting of Chantilly and $99 for a used quartet.

Her biggest discontinued sellers are Etruscan (1913) by Gorham, Louis XIV (1924) by Towle and Marlborough (1906) by Reed & Barton, a copy of an English Victorian pattern. Mrs. Bremer, who accepts mail orders, suggests customers who can't identify their silver patterns send a photocopy. "It's also a good idea to look at the hallmark with a magnifying glass," she said. BEVERLY BREMER SILVER SHOP, 3164 Peachtree Road NE, Atlanta, GA 30305; (404) 261-4009. ✉

"NO OTHER COUNTRY IN THE WORLD has produced the variety of flatware patterns America has," said Bill Banker, a sales representative at Jean's Silversmiths, in business since 1911. And Jean's, set in a long, narrow midtown shop with a tin ceiling, has a huge supply of both new and discontinued sterling patterns. Much of the shop's discontinued stock is by Gorham. "But that's because they had more patterns than anyone else," said Mr. Banker, leafing through a book of American silver patterns.

Among silver cognoscenti, Jean's is perhaps best known as a source of used and discontinued Tiffany silver. "Tiffany retains its value more than most if you want to resell it," said Mr. Banker. Jean's sells used Tiffany for 20 percent less than list price. Strong sellers include Faneuil ($112 for a serving spoon), Flemish ($112 for a serving spoon) and the more elaborate English King ($123 for a serving spoon).

Much of the old silver at Jean's is monogrammed. And occasionally, a monogram enhances sales, even if it isn't the buyer's. A good seller at Jean's is the engraved Continental service from 1934 once owned by the American soprano Rosa Ponselle. "People have bought it because it had her monogram," Mr. Banker said. Some have even copied Ponselle's distinctive '30s deco RP monogram onto other patterns. JEAN'S SILVERSMITHS, 16 West 45th Street, New York, NY 10036; (212) 575-0723. ✉

ALICE KORMAN, who owns a discontinued china business in Merrick, New York, also deals in flatware. But silverplate and stainless steel are her specialties. Thanks to the popularity of stainless steel, silverplate doesn't have the enthusiastic following it had just after World War II. But Mrs. Korman, who runs a mail order business, often sells replacement pieces for inherited sets, notably Morning Star (1948) and White Orchid (1953), two popular postwar patterns by Community/Oneida.

Much of Mrs. Korman's silverplated flatware is actually new, purchased from department stores that went out of business. Priced according to condition, knives and forks start at nine dollars each. ALICE'S PAST AND PRESENT REPLACEMENTS, P.O. Box 465, Merrick, NY 11566; (516) 379-1352. ✉

# FLOORING
# (NATURAL FIBER)

A CENTURY AGO, spring was the time for ritual-minded Victorians to roll up the oriental rugs and bring out the sisal. Spring is still sisal season. Large carpet showrooms routinely hold spring sales of sisal, coir, seagrass and other floor coverings woven from natural vegetable fibers.

For nearly a decade, wall-to-wall sisal (pronounced SIGH-sul) and coir (pronounced KOY-er) have created neutral but textured floors, perfect backdrops for area rugs. But now, the growing natural-fiber family encompasses a wide range of colors, weaves, styles and blends, including sisals dyed coral and plum and such combinations as jute and wool, which is easier on bare feet than scratchy sisal.

Simple sisal rugs can be dressed up with borders in leather, tapestry fabric, colored jute or linen. And properly sealed, sisal and coir can even be used outdoors. Jeffrey Bilhuber, a New York decorator, was impressed by a sisal-covered porch he saw in Maine that was completely painted with white marine deck paint. "You just repaint every year," he said.

Designers are also trying out unusual fibers and blends, such as cogolin (pronounced KOH-goh-lin), a tightly woven carpet of raffia and cotton, and medieval matting, a densely woven rush that originally covered floors in drafty old castles.

Depending on quality, design and country of origin, fibers can be inexpensive or costly—a 9-by-12 coir rug can cost $99 or more than $1,000. Tanzanian sisal, smoother and finer than sisal grown in Mexico or Brazil, costs more.

"And a sisal woven in Belgium will be more expensive than something woven in India," said Hiram Samel, owner of Merida Meridian, a large vegetable fiber wholesaler in Syracuse, New York. Because of superior spinning qualities, sisal woven in Belgium, Switzerland and Germany tends to look particularly clean and smooth.

Painted sisal rugs are also democratically priced. Mary Emery, a sisal painter in New York, creates one-of-a-kind rugs, often painting area rugs on wall-to-wall sisal ($5 to $20 a square foot depending on number of colors used for art only).

But Ms. Emery, a rug painter for more than 10 years, also has a line of rugs in a set of patterns, from $800 for a 6-by-9-foot rug. Rugs are hand-painted and customers can choose colors. Designs range from traditional florals to crisp geometrics.

Sisal stains easily. Even water can discolor it, though damage can be prevented if the spot is blotted with paper towels, covered with potato flour overnight, then vacuumed. If stains are permanent, a custom paint job can often revive stained sisal. "I can design a pattern to mask the dirt," Ms. Emery said. Catalogs cost three dollars. MARY EMERY, Box 2103, New York, NY 10185; (212) 533-3387.  ⊠

SISAL RUGS CAN BE PAINTED to look like anything from Aubussons to faux marble, according to Jennifer Stewart Day, a rug painter for more than 15 years. Ms. Stewart once copied a Renaissance rug from London's Victoria & Albert Museum using 99 colors of dye. "Sisal is like silk," she said. "Each piece takes color a little differently."

Besides a line of machine-made printed rugs ($7 a square foot at Einstein Moomjy), Ms. Stewart accepts commissions. She recently designed a kitchen rug based on a client's china pattern ($32 to $65 a square foot, art only, at Einstein Moomjy). Her rugs can be ordered through retail outlets as well as the fabric company Schumacher and furniture manufacturers including Drexel, Hendredon and Century. JENNIFER STEWART DAY, 4850 Northway Drive NE, Atlanta, GA 30342; (404) 250-0077.  ⊠

LINDA PETTIBONE, A SISAL PAINTER in San Francisco for nearly ten years, always makes stencils for every image she designs for her rugs. "It's a no-mistake deal," she explained. "You can't erase on sisal." Her favorite designs are geometric, often with a southwestern flavor. Navajo rugs and Middle Eastern kilims are among her favorite influences.

And she often uses only a few colors, allowing the sisal to show through. "I want the design to stand out, not the color technique," she said. Ms. Pettibone charges $9 to $36 a square foot for her art; sisal is additional, $24 a square yard. LINDA PETTIBONE, 144 Parnassus, Suite 19, San Francisco, CA 94117; (415) 681-0283.  ⊠

MOST SISAL IS BACKED WITH LATEX to hold fibers in place. But Jack Lenor Larsen, a carpet and fabric design concern, also has a line of cotton-backed sisal. Besides being biodegradable, the cotton-back sisal can be cut easily into circular rugs and creates a more subtle seam than latex-backed sisal, according to Stephanie Kahane, marketing director.

Larsen's sisal and coir, made in Switzerland, is densely woven and comes in both solids and a mix of colors. Sisal and coir in simple designs cost $9.40 a square foot. Larsen sells to the interior design trade, only. JACK LENOR LARSEN, 232 East 59th Street, New York, NY 10022; (212) 674-3993.

UNUSUAL BORDERS IN TAPESTRY FABRIC, leather and broadloom carpet are a specialty at Patterson, Flynn, Martin & Manges, a floor-covering concern. Besides traditional mitred outer borders, Patterson offers rugs with fabric insets; resulting rugs appear to have an outer border of sisal.

Patterson also sells sisal and coir tiles, which can create the appearance of a parquet floor. Patterson, in the D & D building, sells only to the trade. PATTERSON, FLYNN, MARTIN & MANGES, The D & D Building, 979 Third Avenue (near 59th Street), New York, NY 10022; (212) 688-7700.

MOST LARGE CARPET STORES CARRY VEGETABLE fibers. But among the fibers at Einstein Moomjy are area rugs in raffia, made from reeds, and abaca, made from banana plants. The rugs are thick, with large open weaves. A raffia area rug 4 feet by 6 feet costs around $800. The store also sells a jute in herringbone patterns ($47.99 a square yard) and sea-grass that looks like English tweed ($26.50 a square yard), as well as wool and nylon sisals, softer and easier to clean than natural sisal (from $22.99 a square yard). EINSTEIN MOOMJY, 150 East 58th Street, New York, NY 10155; (212) 758-0900. ✉

BESIDES A RANGE OF AREA RUGS in vegetable fibers, ABC Carpet & Home sells broadlooms in basketweave, boucle and herringbone-patterned sisal, 13 feet 2 inches wide ($21.90 to $29.90 a square yard), and Karastan wool sisal, 12 feet wide, in herringbone, boucle and box patterns ($39.90 a square yard). ABC CARPET & HOME, 888 Broadway (near 19th Street), New York, NY 10003; (212) 473-3000. ✉

# FLOORS, WOOD

IT's EASY TO IGNORE FLOORS. People walk on them, scuff them and grind their heels into them. But like furniture, floors are a basic design element, with the size and scope to be a room's star attraction.

"I have always considered the floor to be the fifth wall of a room," said Juan P. Molyneux, a Manhattan interior designer. He adapted elements of an inlaid wood floor in Russia's Pavlosk Palace for an intricately painted floor at a recent Kipps Bay show house.

These days wood, whether strip, parquet or inlaid, is the floor of choice in a growing number of homes. With built-in graining and a range of natural colors, wood floors can be as subtle as a sisal carpet or as complex as an oriental rug. And with the move toward clean, architectural interiors, bare wood floors wearing only a satiny glow are no longer unusual.

Though wood floors are oddly timeless, they still follow the whims of fashion. Pickled and bleached floors, underfoot everywhere throughout the 1980s, have been supplanted by more natural-looking tones that range from honey to deep walnut.

"There is a tendency away from anything that might seem faddish," said Basil Walter, a partner in the Manhattan architectural firm of Sweeny Walter Associates, who has designed many wood floors.

High-gloss, basketball-court finishes have been dulled down to the softer gleam of an old-fashioned waxed floor. And while laser cutters have brought detailed inlays to a wider market, a plain plank floor with a handsome border is still an appealing option.

Homeowners in the market for new wood floors have more choices than ever, from prefinished planks to custom floors in classic herringbone patterns. Maintenance methods have improved, as well. Long-lasting water-base finishes are now available in addition to easy care polyurethane and traditional waxing.

The National Wood Flooring Association offers installational and maintenance advice on its hotline ([500] 443-9663). Calls cost 25 cents a minute.

Janos P. Spitzer bristles when he hears people say the workmanship found on beautiful old brownstone floors is no longer available. "We have better tools, better skills and better glues today," he said. Before he and his artisans cut custom wood floors in their workshop, they discuss the size and use of the room, then plot out a floor pattern. "You don't want to end up with a little sliver of pattern at one end," he said.

"The hottest designs are old," he added, pointing to an elaborate Fontainebleau-style sample treated to look antique. Though Mr. Spitzer creates designs to client specifications, his showroom is stocked with samples, from geometric fields to intricate borders. And though American white oak, found in many prewar New York apartments, remains popular, exotic woods from Africa and South America are easier than ever to find, he added. Custom floors range from $10 to $100 a square foot. Repairs and resanding also available. **JANOS P. SPITZER FLOORING COMPANY, INC.,** 133 West 24th Street, New York, NY 10011; (212) 627-1818.

PETER DOWNS, OWNER OF The New Wood Company, once created a new floor of walnut, oak and maple in the pattern of a Shaker quilt. But many of the floors he installs are of old wood. Some use the original floorboards removed from old houses, such as 200-year-old New Hampshire farmhouses. Others feature wide planks found on barn siding, a cheaper alternative. A third option is antique resawn beams harvested from old Reconstruction-era buildings from the South. "Older wood has more patina and a denser grain," said Mr. Downs, who also restores and resands wood floors. He recently replaced a worn-out portion of an elaborate wood border in an Upper West Side apartment, aging the new pieces to match the old. New oak floors start at eight dollars a square foot. **THE NEW WOOD COMPANY,** 301 West 96th Street, New York, NY 10025; (212) 222-9332.

DOZENS OF SAMPLES FROM MOST of the top wood floor manufacturers in the United States and Europe are on view in the appointment-only showroom of Hoboken Wood Floors, a large wood flooring distributor. Hoboken offers floors in a wide range of prices and styles, from prefinished maple or birch ($10 to $12 a square foot without installation) to wood with marble inlays.

"Maple, which has less intense graining than oak, is hot right now," said Denise Engedal, a Hoboken associate. At the elaborate end, Hoboken carries colorful inlaid designs by Dynamic Laser Applications, which has made inlaid floors to match patterned doors and stained-glass windows. Hoboken does not sell directly to the public, but will provide names of retailers. **HOBOKEN WOOD FLOORS,** 979 Third Avenue, New York, NY 10022; (212) 759-5917.

SINCE HER DAYS IN ART SCHOOL, Veva Crozer has been fascinated with color. So it's small surprise she specializes in wood floors stained every shade of the rainbow. Ms. Crozer's custom-color floors, using her patented water-base stain, can be embellished with fish, flowers and birds. She also sells prefinished nine-inch parquet squares in 3,500 colors ($20 to $22 a square foot without installation) and, for do-it-yourselfers, stain in quart cans for $11. **LUKKEN COLOR CORP.;** (203) 869-4679. ✉

EVERY YEAR, MOST OF the 4.6 billion feet of hardwood lumber used for shipping pallets becomes garbage after just one use. But Big City Forest, a division of South Bronx 2000, a recycling concern, recently devised a method for turning used red oak pallets into tongue-and-groove flooring strips, two to four feet long. The strips, which sell in packs, can be installed by contractors or do-it-yourselfers. **BIG CITY FOREST,** 1809 Carter Avenue, Bronx, NY 10457; (718) 731-3931. ✉

WILLIAM J. ERBE CO., a family business since 1908, is known for high-end custom wood floors at high-end prices. These days clients usually want subdued floors in traditional French patterns. Owner William Erbe also imports antique floors from Europe occasionally. "The pre-1830 floors were cut by hand, are delicate and constantly break," he said. "But they're an ego trip for some people." Antique floors can cost around $400 a square foot. **WILLIAM J. ERBE CO.,** 560 Barry Street, Bronx, NY 10474; (212) 249-6400 or (718) 991-7281.

IF AN ELABORATE NEW INLAID FLOOR IS TOO COSTLY, an alternative is a floor painted to appear inlaid. Juan P. Molyneux, who has designed several painted floors, often interprets Georgian and Neoclassical ceiling designs for the floors. A floor similar to his Kipps Bay floor costs about

$9,000.   **J. P. MOLYNEUX STUDIO LTD.**, 29 East 69th Street, New York, NY 10021; (212) 628-0097.

# FLY RODS,
# CUSTOM-MADE AND REPAIRED

As ED FODY SEES IT, owning a custom fly rod is like having a suit specially made by a tailor. "You can really adapt a bamboo rod to a person's needs," said Mr. Fody, who builds split bamboo fishing rods by hand in Stewart Manor, Long Island.

Bamboo fly rods, crafted from Tonkin cane that is split, planed, glued and varnished, originated in the 19th century, and were popular until the end of World War II, when fiberglass rods came on the market. These days most rods are made from graphite blanks, which are round, hollow, easy to care for and quicker to build than bamboo. But about a decade ago, bamboo rods made a comeback.

"It's a rod people want," said Mr. Fody. "The feel and action of a bamboo rod is unique." A bamboo rod can be tailored for cagey fish, from trout to salmon. It can be made either fast and flexible or slow, often by adding or subtracting as little as one thousandth of an inch from the tip.

Today's bamboo rods will also last longer than vintage versions, due to the strong epoxy glues that replaced the animal-hide glues of the past.

Mr. Fody, an enthusiastic salmon fisherman, began building bamboo fly rods over a decade ago, after reading *A Master's Guide to Building a Bamboo Fly Rod* by Edmund Everett Garrison and Hoagy B. Carmichael (Martha's Glenn Publishing, 1977). His six-sided bamboo rods, which take 80 to 100 hours to make, start at about $700.   **ED FODY**; (516) 352-7716.   ✉

EDWIN ROBERTS BEGAN REPAIRING vintage bamboo fly rods 18 years ago in an effort to learn how they were made. These days, he builds customized bamboo rods and sells rod-building kits. But his specialty is repairing collectibles. He recently restored a 15-foot rod by H. L.

Leonard, an old rod-making concern in Maine, that will go into the American Museum of Fly Fishing in Manchester, Vermont.

The goal is to make an old rod look new. Mr. Roberts often buys old rods for their period parts, such as guides, reels, even cases. A restored rod can often, though not always, be used. "Sometimes you have to hang it on the wall," he said.

Complete restorations start at $200. A brochure is available for two dollars. **E. F. ROBERTS CUSTOM RODMAKER,** 21C Seymour Road, East Granby, CT 06026; (203) 651-8402. ✉

A CUSTOM ROD can be tailored for specific uses, says graphite rod maker Tom Cooney, whose company, Rodcraft Components Inc., sells rod-making components. "The types of rods you can make are infinite," he said. Mr. Cooney's specialty is rods for catching Midwestern lake fish, including walleye, perch and blue gill. "A little more sensitivity is needed in a rod for catching walleye instead of bass," said Mr. Cooney, who has taught rod making for eight years.

Tom Cooney's customized rods range from about $175 to $980. A free brochure is available. **RODCRAFT COMPONENTS, INC.,** 3640 West 111th Street, Chicago, IL 60655; (312) 779-4312. ✉

## FRAMES (CONSERVATIONALLY CORRECT)

A PICTURE FRAME THAT MERELY LOOKS GOOD is a failure, says Jared Bark, who owns Bark Frameworks in SoHo. "A frame is a structure to protect the artwork," he explained. "It should never damage the work." The procedure should also be reversible, meaning the mat, pastes and other materials used can be removed without harming the art.

Bark, in business for more than 20 years, is one of the growing handful of framers that practice conservation framing. In the early 1970s, the art world became aware that certain framing materials and methods used for years were actually harming prints, photographs, pastels and other works on paper. For example, mat boards made from wood pulp can stain or yellow the work and make it brittle. Rag board mats, the 100 percent cotton alternative, are costlier but safer; Bark offers rag board mats in a variety of colors and thicknesses.

Framing methods are important, too. Art should never touch a wood frame, which is acidic. And space should be left between artwork and glazing, allowing the work to expand or contract with humidity changes. "If a work gets wavy and is too close to the glazing, the damage can be permanent," Mr. Bark said.

Glass is fine for protecting small artworks, he added. Lightweight, unbreakable acrylic glazings, like Plexiglas, are better for heavier art. And if the work is exposed to sun or fluorescent light, Mr. Bark suggests an acrylic glazing with an ultraviolet shield.

Bark also designs frames in hardwood (silver and gold leaf are available) and metal, including welded aluminum, brass, bronze and copper. A simple hardwood frame, 20 by 24 inches, with rag board mat and Japanese paper hinges, starts at $125. BARK FRAMEWORKS, 85 Grand Street (near Greene Street), New York, NY 10013, (212) 431-9080. ✉

"A LOT OF CONSERVATION PROBLEMS come from poor framing," said Philip Feld, a conservation framer for over 15 years. But even when works are framed to conservation standards, Mr. Feld suggests opening the frame every five to seven years to check for acid buildup.

Mr. Feld favors using strips of Japanese paper, which is thin but sturdy, for hinging or securing the artwork to its backing. This is the conservationally correct alternative to masking tape. Placement of hinges is important; if the artwork falls off the wall, the hinges should tear instead of the art.

Mr. Feld also does restoration work on both antique and damaged frames.

Custom rag mats start at $15, natural wood frames at $45. PHILIP FELD, 32 Union Square East, New York, NY 10003; (212) 254-7518. ✉

FOR DO-IT-YOURSELF FRAMERS, University Products has sold conservation materials by mail since 1975. "The demand for preservation materials has doubled in the last 10 years," said sales manager Scott Magoon, whose father David started the company. The company sells rag board mats, mounting weights and metal frames in 12 colors ($9.75 for a 20-by-8 inch frame; hardware kit for $1.10 needed to assemble frame). Free catalog available. **UNIVERSITY PRODUCTS,** P.O. Box 101, Holyoke, MA 01041; (800) 628-1912.  ✉

# FRAMES (THAT LOOK LIKE ANTIQUES)

CHOOSING A PICTURE FRAME requires sensitivity and care, according to Charles Schreiber, president of House of Heydenryk, a custom frame shop on the Upper East Side. "If you notice the frame first when you look at a picture, we've made a mistake," he said.

The company, begun in 1935 by Henry Heydenryk, scion of a Dutch frame-making family, sells, repairs and restores antique frames. But a large portion of the business is reproducing antique frames, anything from elaborately carved 18th-century French frames to popsicle-stick frames made by Depression-era hobo artists.

Demand for reproduction frames, which can look almost exactly like the originals, has grown in recent years, as antique frames have become more expensive. Certain artworks look best surrounded by the neat wood molding and  aged gilt of a vintage frame. And the right antique frame reproduction can turn a mirror into a minor work of art.

Heydenryk has over 3,000 antique and reproduction frames in stock, many dating from the '40s, when the shop devised frames for Edward Hopper's newest works. The shop's samples are complete frames, not corners, so customers get an idea of how the art and frame will actually look, Mr. Schrieber said. Each frame has a name. The Dali flower frame is a copy of a 16th-century Spanish frame artist Salvador Dali had reproduced. And the Buddha frame is a series of carved wood swirls, inspired by the curls on a Buddha's head.

House of Heydenryk, whose customers include museums and interior designers, has a staff of carvers, carpenters and gilt craftsmen working above the saleroom. Frame reproductions, which take about four weeks, start at $100, and average around $500 to $800. **HOUSE OF**

**HEYDENRYK,** 417 East 76th Street, New York, NY 10021; (212) 249-4903. ✉

LARRY SHAR, PRESIDENT of Jullius Lowy Frame and Restoring Company, stood next to several antique gilt frames from different styles and periods. Beside each frame was a reproduction corner molding identical to the original. The company, begun in 1907, has created antique frame reproductions for the Museum of Modern Art and the White House, among others. Lowy, which has two Manhattan showrooms, also sells antique frames, does frame restoration, reproduces antique furniture and does painting conservation.

The secret to making a new frame look old is to employ the same materials and methods as the original frame maker, said Mr. Shar, who took over the business in 1979 from his father, Hillard. Lowy has a large staff of carvers, carpenters and gilt craftsmen, who work above the East Side showroom.

Lowy will copy any of the 8,000 antique frames in stock or anything a customer brings in. For quick jobs, the company has a large inventory of gilded moldings that can be turned into antique frame reproductions in about a week. Other frames take about four weeks. Reproductions start at $200 and average around $1,000 for a 25-by-30-inch painting. **JULLIUS LOWY FRAME AND RESTORING COMPANY,** 223 East 80th Street, New York, NY 10021; (212) 861-8585. ✉

BRANDON COPANS'S SECOND-FLOOR WORKROOM in Westwood, New Jersey, smells pleasantly of wood, hardly surprising since an entire room is filled with raw lumber. Mr. Copans, a sculptor who has made antique frame reproductions since 1986, favors air-dried wood and finishing methods identical to those used by frame makers in years past. "You don't want a reproduction that looks brand new," he said.

Mr. Copans's specialties are Georgian-era English frames, with clean lines, and American folk art frames. To create an aged appearance in folk art frames, Mr. Copans will often drill tiny holes in the wood, to simulate insect bites and allow grime to collect in brand-new crevices. "I try to achieve the look a frame would have after being left in a barn for 200 years," he said.

Mr. Copans's frame reproductions usually take about two weeks.

Prices range from $11 a foot for simple frames to $60 a foot for more elaborate jobs.   **CREATIVE WORKS BY BRANDON COPANS,** 215 Westwood Avenue, Westwood, NJ 07675; (201) 664-2718.

## FRENCH POLISHERS FOR FURNITURE AND WOODWORK

*F*RENCH POLISH IS AMONG the most overused—and misused—terms in the lexicon of furniture finishes. To begin, it is not a material but a technique: Shellac is rubbed by hand onto a wood surface in a circular motion with a cloth pad to create a smooth, glassy finish.

"People mistakenly call anything rubbed on with a pad French polish," said James Boorstein, president of Traditional Line, an architectural restoration firm that has done French polishing for over a decade. Lacquers, synthetic varnishes and polyurethanes, for example, can make a furniture surface glisten, but they are not used in a proper French polish.

French polish is also extremely labor intensive and, consequently, can be costly. "You don't use French polish in a rumpus room for kids," said Anthony Lefeber, vice-president of operations at the company. "But it's applicable for fine antiques, particularly for something that was originally French polished."

The Traditional Line restoration crew once worked on a badly damaged 1880 Herter Brothers sideboard in Brazilian rosewood. They fabricated missing parts, restored existing woodwork, then applied a French polish and touched up the gilding.

The key element in French polish is shellac, a thin, amber varnish made by dissolving flakes of shellac in denatured alchohol. Shellac flakes are secretions harvested from the lac bug, a comma-size creature found in the jungles of India near Calcutta. Lac dye was also used in the 18th-century red coats British soldiers wore, according to Mr. Boorstein.

Shellacs come in a range of shades, from amber to colorless. (Mr. Boorstein has a piece of wood displaying eight different hues.) "The shellac you use depends on the piece," Mr. Boorstein said.

Depending on the size and condition of the piece, a complete restoration ranges from about $300 to $5,000, which includes French polishing. TRADITIONAL LINE, 143 West 21st Street, New York, NY 10011; (212) 627-3555.

THE HEYDAY OF THE FRENCH POLISH was the early 19th century, when neoclassical furniture was popular throughout France and much of Europe.

Often, the glow can be restored while preserving the original finish. Wax can build up over the years, attracting dirt. Once the dirt is cleaned off, the craftsman can apply a French polish. "But if the finish is deteriorated, we must start over," said Peter Triestman, president of Olek Lejbzon, a 50-year-old firm that specializes in high-end custom cabinetry. That means the piece must be stripped and the wood sanded, so the French polish will penetrate the wood's pores.

Almost any surface can take a French polish, though the process is less successful when used on sprayed synthetic finishes.

Items that are French polished thrive best in rooms with a relative humidity of 68 to 70 percent. If a room is too dry, the finish starts to crack. With excessive moisture, the finish becomes hazy and milky.

Olek Lejbzon charges about $700 to French polish a chest of drawers that also requires touch-ups and small veneer repairs. OLEK LEJBZON, 210 11th Avenue, 11th floor (near West 25th Street), New York, NY 10001; (212) 243-3363.

RICHARDS JARDEN CAN FRENCH POLISH furniture, but he prefers to do entire rooms. "It's slow and expensive," explained Mr. Jarden, who owns The Composition Group, a seven-year-old company that specializes in faux painting and unusual wall finishes. "But from a lasting standpoint, there's no better finish. It needs nothing but dusting the first 100 years."

Mr. Jarden, an artist who formerly headed the sculpture department at the Rhode Island School of Design, French polished a mahogany-paneled library for a television executive. The wood was chemically dyed for luster, brush sealed, then French polished with pads and shellac. (The polisher wears a mask and gloves.)

The process for French polishing a room is similar to that for working on furniture. The wood is lightly sanded to open the pores. Next shellac is applied to a thick wool pad, which is covered with a soft cloth. By continuous rubbing, the shellac is squeezed into the wood's pores. Subsequent layers of shellac bind to it and, eventually, create a shine.

Composition Group charges $75 an hour. Day rates and job rates are by estimate. **THE COMPOSITION GROUP,** 17 Fourth Avenue, Nyack, NY 10960; (914) 358-5546.

## GAMES
## (VINTAGE BOARD GAMES,
## JIGSAW PUZZLES AND CARDS)

Most years produce a fashionable new game, or two. But for some, the most memorable games are from the past, from kitschy board games based on defunct television shows to stylish card games from the 1920s.

"Every decade is the heyday for a distinctive type of game," said David Galt, whose 20-year-old company, Games & Names, sells and rents more than 5,000 games from 1882 to 1976.

"The 1980s were the heyday for trivia games," he said. The 1940s, predictably, featured war and patriotic games, like Flying Aces and Victory Rummy. And in the Depression-ridden 1930s, the hottest new games were about making money, notably Fortune, Easy Money, Big Business and, of course, Monopoly.

People buy vintage games for all sorts of reasons. Some are fascinated by weird or attractive boards. Others collect games by themes, such as transportation games, literary games or cartoon character games. Some simply want the games of their youth for their own kids. Though rules stay the same, the look and presentation of games can change over the years. "With Candyland, the path is not as long now as in the original," Mr. Galt said. And today's Careers for Girls looks somewhat different from the 1957 Careers.

Mr. Galt, whose old games range from $15 to $500, also invents and designs games, from name games for children's parties to elaborate card games for 100 people. Rentals start at $50.  GAMES AND NAMES; (212) 769-2514.  ✉

GAME SHOW, a five-and-a-half-year-old company with two Manhattan shops, offers a selection of out-of-print games and vintage games, including a patriotic version of Mah-Jongg credited to singer Kate Smith (the tiles form a flag with 48 stars). But the company's main strength is new games by small companies not normally stocked by major toy emporiums. Typical are Terrace ($31.98), an attack-and-capture strategy with a board, and Mind Trap ($28.98), a collection of over 500 conundrums. (Example: What food do you throw away the outside, cook the inside, eat the outside and throw away the inside? An ear of corn.)

The shops also carry reference books for people who want to invent their own games.  GAME SHOW, 474 Avenue of the Americas (between 11th and 12th Streets), New York, NY 10011, (212) 633-6328; 1240 Lexington Avenue (between 83rd and 84th streets), 10028; (212) 472-8011.  ✉

"THERE'S A GAME FOR EVERYTHING," said George Darrow, whose shop, Chick Darrow's Fun Antiques, has stocked antique toys and memorabilia, including games, for 30 years. Most of the shop's 200 games hail from the 1940s through the 1960s. "TV games are big," said Mr. Darrow, citing Concentration, Truth or Consequences, I Dream of Jeannie and, in particular, The Dating Game. Games range from $5 to $300. CHICK DARROW'S FUN ANTIQUES, 1101 First Avenue (near 61st Street), New York, NY 10021; (212) 838-0730.  ✉

# GARDENERS, CITY

CITY DWELLERS may not have lots of space, but that's no reason not to plant a garden, says garden designer Catherine Fitzsimons of Willowtown Gardens. "I encourage people to take advantage of every situation, be it a terrace or a window ledge," she said. "The city is a harsh place, and a garden creates comfort and a sense of beauty."

Ms. Fitzsimons, who studied at the Conway School of Landscape Design, designs and installs all types of gardens, both in cramped city spaces and in larger areas. She also tries to increase each client's ecological knowledge. She installed a trim cedar compost box, which turns leaves and twigs into fertilizer, in a tree-filled Brooklyn backyard garden she designed. And she tries to use native American plants, such as bayberry and witch hazel.

Gardens don't have to be expensive. "Putting morning glories around a door is very cheap but a real showstopper," said Ms. Fitzsimons, who installed a public garden near her home in Brooklyn Heights. And gardens can fit into tight spaces. "All you need is 12 inches of soil," she said.  Plants can also hide urban ugliness. Ms. Fitzsimons recently planted ivy to cover grafitti on the front of a Brooklyn brownstone. Ms. Fitzsimons's consultation fees start at $50 an hour. CATHERINE FITZSIMONS; (718) 243-1257.

A TERRACE GARDEN is really like another room, says garden designer Andrew Graves. "I try to design the garden in a way that will relate to the house," he said. "If it's outside a blue bedroom, I'll use blue and white flowers."

Mr. Graves, a garden designer for over 10 years, studied at Kew Gardens in London. He designs everything from window boxes to estate gardens, and will also select house plants.

In redesigning a garden that receives little light, Mr. Graves often works with existing plants that have become accustomed to living without much sun. "Don't kill a plant that's doing fine," he said. "Work with it."

He charges $40 an hour.   **ANDREW GRAVES;** (500) 288-6234, (212) 996-2652.

THERE'S AN ART TO PUTTING TOGETHER a garden in the city, says Richard Bianchi, owner of Newscapes Garden Design and a specialist in urban landscaping since 1988. Weight constraints are often an issue when choosing plants that will reside on a terrace. And city light tends to be extreme, veering from immense amounts of sun when a garden is on a high floor to forest darkness in backyard gardens.

"I'm not going to try to plant hibiscus in a shady backyard," Mr. Bianchi said. On the other hand, certain plants can thrive in smog, notably birch trees, spruces and black pines.

If a customer insists on a certain plant, Mr. Bianchi usually installs it, so long as the client knows it may only thrive for a year. His love of plants is deeply rooted. He grew up in the country, and though he studied business in college, he has worked in landscaping for much of his life. Mr. Bianchi charges about $40 an hour, though the price varies with the job.   **NEWSCAPES GARDEN DESIGN, INC.,** 246 Fifth Avenue, New York, NY 10001; (212) 689-4563.

# GIFTWRAPPING

*T*HIS YEAR JOANNA-FAITH Whitney had Christmas presents for her entire family all wrapped up by Thanksgiving. Ms. Whitney is one of those rare people who actually enjoy wrapping presents. And since 1986, she has wrapped gifts professionally for a variety of private and corporate clients.

A graduate of the School of Visual Arts, Ms. Whitney is vice-president of data processing for a large real estate company. She calls giftwrapping, done by appointment, her creative outlet. "I don't like to make any two packages the same," she explained, holding a bright red box garnished with green and white paper fans.

Some of her wraps are simple. Ms. Whitney wraps each box top and bottom separately, so the wrap can be reused (from $6). A specialty is a brightly colored reusable paper dome that slips over a wine bottle ($6). She also does elaborate wraps, covering boxes inside and out in brocades, satins and silks. She wrapped a wedding present in white velour. And a recent creation featured a brocade box secured by a handsome cummerbund. "Cloth boxes can be used later for sachets," Ms. Whitney said. And they can cost $100 and up.

The nature of the wrap depends on the present, the receiver and the bill. Before wrapping, Ms. Whitney likes to know a few details about the receiver, the occasion for the gift and the relation between giver and receiver. She "wrapped" a selection of embroidered handkerchiefs by turning them into an elaborate bouquet, fanning each into a flower and adding stems. And a party-giving client asked her to disguise the hors d'oeuvres trays to look like stacks of Christmas gifts and books. WRAPPINGS; (212) 996-5258.  ⊠

"I LIKE MAKING THINGS PRETTY," said Judy Moshan, who, with her partner, Risa Bergman, has done giftwrapping for over five years. Fairfield Baskets wraps individual packages.

But the specialty is gift baskets, with presents and trimmings that follow a theme. For a skier with broken bones, Ms. Moshan fashioned a large, round basket adorned with curling ribbons, tiny toy skis and mountains of tissue paper. It held chocolates, T-shirts—and ski magazines. Baskets from $25, giftwrapping from $10.  FAIRFIELD BASKETS, 55 Craven Street, Huntington Station, NY 11746; (516) 254-0810.  ⊠

# GILDING

*E*LI RIOS, an antiques restorer in Manhattan, recalls with pleasure a somber black and brown Portuguese screen with Japanese imagery. The client, believing the screen consisted of black paint on brown leather, asked Mr. Rios to clean the brown background. Instead, Mr. Rios concentrated on the black, which turned out to be silver gilt darkened with tarnish. The client wound up with a gleaming silver and brown antique screen.

Dictionaries define the ancient art of gilding as a process of applying a thin layer of real or imitation gold as a decorative element on a plainer surface. Still, all that's gilded isn't necessarily gold. Through the years, platinum, palladium, silver, aluminum, white gold and even tin have been used to impart a silvery image. (All but tin are still used.)

Even the gold applied in gilding varies widely. Pale 16-karat gold leaf is lightened with so much silver it has to be sealed with varnish so the silver won't tarnish. Twenty-two-karat gold is found on picture frames. Twenty-three-karat gold is used for exterior gilding. And 24-karat gold is considered too soft to work with. A cheaper alternative to gold leaf is metal plating, which merely looks like gold. Gold-colored gilding can even be silver. In the early 18th century, silver leaf colored with gamboge, a yellow varnish, appeared on frames and furniture.

Mr. Rios, who owns ECR Antique Conservation and Restoration, Inc., and charges from $45 an hour, has gilded a variety of surfaces, from silver-leaf sconces to gold-leaf ceilings. Since much of his work is conserving antiques, he needs to duplicate the type of gilt originally used. In conservation, the idea is to save as much of the original gilding as possible while halting deterioration. "The gilding is the object's history," said Mr. Rios, who teaches furniture conservation at the Fashion Institute of Technology. Restoration allows the gilder more pronounced changes that can make an object look new.

Mr. Rios also needs to analyze the method used to impart the gilt. Sometimes an object is simply painted gold. In oil gilding, gold leaf is set onto a sticky varnish. The more traditional water-gilding method, which dates from the ancient Egyptians, requires a primer of gesso, followed by bole or colored clay affixed with rabbit-skin glue. After the bole is smoothed with horsehair, gold leaf is applied, then burnished with agate for brightness.   **ECR ANTIQUE CONSERVATION AND RESTORATION,** 515 West 29th Street, New York, NY 10001; (212) 643-0388.

GOLD LEAF IS REMARKABLE, said Eve Kaplan, a partner in Fitzkaplan, a Manhattan furniture restorer since 1985. It lasts hundreds of years if it's not abraded in cleaning. It doesn't rust, like copper, or tarnish, like silver. "On most antiques, the material beneath the gold deteriorates first," she said.

In many instances, it's considered esthetically pleasing for hints of colored clay to peek out from under the gilding. For furniture conservation and restoration, Ms. Kaplan's specialty, she works with clay that matches the original, usually in a range of reds and browns. "Clay color can be used to authenticate a piece," she said. Clay colors differed in France, Germany and Italy, for example. Even gray clay was popular in England and the United States during the Victorian era.

Fitzkaplan charges between $40 and $50 an hour. FITZKAPLAN, 131 Varick Street, New York, NY 10013; (212) 989-8779.

THE LOBBY AT 381 PARK AVENUE SOUTH, a Manhattan office building, is garnished with bright gold leaf, hardly a surprise since Sepp Leaf, a leading supplier of gilding equipment, is situated upstairs. Most of Sepp Leaf's clients are professionals, who purchase brushes, agates, clays and books of gold leaf ($40 for 25 leaves, 3⅜ inches square).

But for beginners, the 24-year-old company offers an introductory gilder's kit based on the Kolner System, a simplified version of the water-gilding method. Developed by Paul Brauer, a German gilder, Kolner clays are designed to sidestep traditional gilding's complex mixing and heating processes. A video is also available ($39.95).

For first-time gilders, Ines Sepp, who manages the company, suggests flat, simple items, such as a small picture frame or the rim of a bowl. SEPP LEAF PRODUCTS, 381 Park Avenue South, New York, NY 10016; (212) 683-2840. ✉

## GLASS (CARVED)

VISITORS TO NEW YORK Carved Glass, John Claude Fevrier's downtown Manhattan workshop, inevitably ask the same thing: How is that stuff made? The "stuff" is carved glass, decorative windows, panels, mirrors and other glass surfaces patterned with frosty-looking images.

Though usually associated with Victorian and Art Deco times—think of frosted windows in London pubs or carved-glass naiads on old movie hall mirrors—carved glass can look thoroughly contemporary. For the dining room of a client with a prominent oriental rug, Mr. Fevrier carved the rug's pattern into a glass tabletop.

And for another client, Mr. Fevrier carved Manhattan's street grid onto thick glass shaped like the island.

Carved glass really isn't carved; patterns are actually sandblasted onto the glass. For a frosty but flat look, Mr. Fevrier blasts just the top layer of the glass. But he can carve deeply into the glass's surface, to give a three-dimensional appearance to a flower's petals, for example.

The most complex carvings are those cut into multiple layers of glass. Before electricity, acid was used to etch glass, a caustic and dangerous method seldom used today.

To blast a design, Mr. Fevrier puts on protective clothing, sets the object in his windowed blasting chamber, then stands outside it, inserting his arms into the chamber through a fringed plastic curtain. To blast specific images, he draws a pattern, tapes a stencil onto the glass, then blasts accordingly.

A glass carver for more than 30 years, Mr. Fevrier inherited the 65-year-old company from his father. Prices depend on designs. A simple Victorian design on a small transom costs $450 and up.  **NEW YORK CARVED ARTS,** 115 Grand Street (near Broadway), New York, NY 10013; (212) 966-5924.  ✉

FLAT PIECES ARE NOT the only type of glass that can be carved. Patricia Patenaude, an owner of Patenaude-Close, next to Mr. Fevrier's shop, blasts designs onto architectural glass blocks. She also carves out shapes in the blocks, then fills them in with color.

Though most of her glass blocks wind up as walls and partitions in corporate buildings, such as Hoffman-LaRoche's building in Florence, South Carolina, she often carves blocks for apartments that need light but look onto unappealing cityscapes.

Ms. Patenaude also creates frosted windows and doors with Victorian designs for brownstones. If part of a double-paned door is missing, she can copy the existing pane by making a rubbing. She also creates her own Victorian-influenced designs.

In addition, Ms. Patenaude frosts stained glass, which she and her partner, Frank Close, make. Their carved glass, including the blocks, costs $30 to $300 a square foot.  **PATENAUDE-CLOSE,** 115 Grand Street (near Broadway), New York, NY 10013; (212) 925-1140.  ✉

CARVED GLASS BY THE Shefts brothers, Charles, Sam and Isidore, can be seen in a number of Manahttan restaurants, including Tavern on the Green and Felidia. The brothers, in business for more than 40 years, are known for elaborate carvings in glass as well as stone.

A recent commission for a residence included a dining-room window, partition and tabletop in an Art Deco design that will be filled in with color. The company can also add gold and silver leaf to glass carvings.

The Shefts' company also carved some of the favorite poems and sayings of the Reverend Dr. Martin Luther King, Jr., in 12 languages, on two-and-a-quarter-inch-thick Pyrex for a new King memorial in San Francisco.

Carved Glass by Shefts also does simpler work, including frosted-glass windows for brownstones. Custom-carved glass costs $30 to $300 a square foot.   **CARVED GLASS BY SHEFTS,** 697 East 132nd Street, Bronx, NY 10454; (718) 665-6240.   ✉

## GLASS, MADE TO LOOK OLD

STEVEN JAYSON, a vice-president at S. A. Bendheim, a glass-importing firm, has strong ideas when the subject is windows. "Plate-glass windows in an old house stand out like a sore thumb," he said. An alternative is restoration glass, which is new glass that looks old. "Those little pits and bubbles are what people pay for," Mr. Jayson said, looking through a mildly blurry pane.

The distortions and imperfections result from glass-making methods in the days before machines. Like glass in the 18th and 19th centuries, today's restoration glass is made using a blowpipe. For over a decade, blown-glass windows have been increasingly popular with architects, historical societies and homeowners.

Bendheim, begun by Mr. Jayson's grandfather, Sem Bendheim, in 1927, sells two types of restoration glass windows from Europe. Full restoration is ⅛-inch thick with pock marks, bubbles and a fairly high level of distortion ($15.95 a square foot). Light restoration is thinner with less distortion ($13.95 a square foot). Customer choice depends on the origins of the house, grandfather's clock or other item in need of glass. A Bendheim customer recently bought light restoration glass to cover a Dürer print.

Light restoration glass is also available with an ultraviolet coating.

And for insulation, the blown glass can be paired with a pane of modern glass; the resulting window, while thick, still distorts.

In addition, Bendheim offers a large range of other types of antique glass, as blown glass is called, including colored glass and textured glass. **S. A. BENDHEIM COMPANY, INC.,** 122 Hudson Street, New York, NY 10013, (212) 226-6370; 61 Willet Street, Passaic, NJ 07055. ✉

THE BLENKO GLASS COMPANY began making blown-glass windows in clear and colored glass in 1893. And the family-owned company still makes antique glass, as well as decorative glassware and large commissions, such as the Art Deco glass slabs in New York's Rainbow Room.

Blenko makes two types of blown-glass windows. Wood mold windows have a minimal amount of bubbles and striations. Iron mold windows are more mottled and can even be used in bathrooms, said vice-president Richard Blenko. Wood mold windows cost $7.80 a square foot. Iron mold windows cost from $6.99 to $7.61 a square foot, depending on color (reds, oranges, yellows and blues are the more costly hues).

The company also makes hand-blown rondels, the large panes with the raised bull's-eye in the middle. **BLENKO GLASS COMPANY,** Box 67, Milton, WV 25541; (304) 743-9081. ✉

## GLASS, REPAIRED AND RESTORED

"YOUR OUTFIT WILL BE GRAY when you leave here," warns Augustine Jochec (pronounced JOE-check) when visitors settle in at Glass Restorations, his repair shop. Good glass is as clear as, well, crystal, but repairing it can be a messy business requiring grinding wheels, pumice and other dust-inducing materials.

Yet when the dust settles, glass that's been repaired often looks almost as good as new. Chips can be ground out, weblike cracks can be planed, and broken bits can be attached with colorless adhesives. "Sometimes the repair line is visible," said Mr. Jochec, holding a heavy Steuben dish with a subtle line where a glass curlicue was reattached.

But when breaks occur on a seam, sensitive repairs are almost impossible to see. Lifting a Steuben squirrel, Mr. Jochec showed where he had reattached an ear. To an unschooled eye, the repair was invisible.

Any repair, large or small, entails a four-step process. First, the chipped area is ground on a so-called rough wheel, until it looks etched. Next it is smoothed on a sandstone or aluminum oxide wheel. An initial polishing with pumice is accomplished on a felt wheel. Then the object is polished again on a muslin buffer with cerium oxide for sheen.

Mr. Jochec learned his trade nearly 40 years ago in Czechoslovakia with his twin brother, Antonin Jochec (a report on him follows), and restores all types of glass.

Lead crystal is the easiest to work. Besides being heavier and refracting light better, glass with a lead content of 15 to 50 percent is softer than lead-free glass.

But all glass repairs are challenging. Occasionally, glass with a simple chip will explode when it's ground for a repair. "Glass is volatile," Mr. Jochec explained.

Sudden temperature changes also can weaken glass. Mr. Jochec cautions against washing good glass in extremely hot water. "And never put it in the dishwasher," he added. Repairs start at $18 to remove chips from drinking glasses.  GLASS RESTORATIONS, 1597 York Avenue (near East 84th Street), New York, NY 10028; (212) 517-3287.  ⊠

NOT ALL DAMAGED GLASS is broken. Sometimes glass turns gray or cloudy, due to air pollution, acid from wine or a blend of harsh detergents and hot water in a dishwasher. But discolored glass can often be polished so it sparkles again, according to Antonin Jochec, Augustine Jochec's twin brother, whose company, Art Cut Glass Studio, is in his New Jersey home. Exteriors can be polished easily, but vases and decanters need at least a three-inch opening for a successful interior polish.

In addition to repairing all types of glass, from chipped wine glasses to scratched paperweights, Mr. Jochec fabricates decorative glass objects, including engraved blocks, cut-glass sculptures and commemorative glass plaques.

Repairs start at $10.   ART CUT GLASS STUDIO, R.D. 1, Box 10, Fawn Drive, Matawan, NJ 07747; (908) 583-7648.   ✉

SOMETIMES A GLASS OBJECT has been shattered and required major reconstruction. Indeed, most glass objects are in shards when owners bring them to Center Art Studio, where Lansing Moore, and his wife, Iliana Engelke Moore, have repaired glass and ceramic objects for 15 years. In particular, glass that is colored, molded or etched can often be restored almost invisibly. "Generally, if the object is not too small and is in less than 50 pieces, it can be reassembled," Mr. Moore said.

Repairs to glass are made with epoxy resins, which can be subtly tinted to match the original object. Missing areas also can often be rebuilt with resin.

When a glass object breaks, Mr. Moore suggests wrapping each piece separately to avoid scratches. And take the piece to a restorer quickly. "Dirty glass doesn't bind as well," he said. Repairs start at $100.   CENTER ART STUDIO, 250 West 54th Street, Room 901, New York, NY 10019; (212) 247-3550.   ✉

## GLASSWARE (LOCATING DISCONTINUED PATTERNS)

CRYSTAL STEMWARE is probably the most fragile item that goes on a well-dressed dinner table. In fact, some goblets and sorbet dishes break so easily owners don't even bother to look for replacements, particularly for discontinued or hard-to-find patterns.

But companies specializing in obsolete crystal stemware do exist. Replacements, Ltd., a mail order business begun just over 10 years ago by owner Bob Page, is the largest in the United States. The company, which also handles discontinued china and flatware (silver, silver plate and stainless), stocks hard-to-get patterns by more than 30 crystal makers. These include Baccarat, Cambridge, Galway,  Mikasa, Orrefors, Rosenthal, Seneca, Sasaki and Stuart.

Many of Replacements's patterns were made by American companies no longer in business—Imperial, Heisey, Tiffin and the hugely popular Fostoria, which stopped making crystal in 1982. "A number of American companies made crystal that was very labor intensive and required a lot of hand work," said Mr. Page, a former tax auditor who honed his interest in discontinued crystal at flea markets. The crystal was often simply too costly to make, he added.

Replacements's biggest seller is American by Fostoria, a heavy diamond-patterned crystal sold since the 1920s. "We have 1,772 customers on file for that pattern," Mr. Page said. A water goblet costs $24. For more obscure crystal patterns, customers can leave pattern names on file free of charge. The company will contact them when the requested pieces are located.

Replacements also identifies mystery patterns, using original catalogs and a five-person research team. Identification can be challenging, since few manufacturers signed their work or etched names onto items. Customers with mystery patterns can send a rubbing or a photograph. **REPLACEMENTS, LTD.,** 1089 Knox Road, P.O. Box 26029, Greensboro, NC 27420; (910) 697-3000 or (800) 562-4462. ✉

HELEN SLOAN went into the china replacement business more than 20 years ago when she discovered that Wedgwood's Napoleon Ivy, her favorite pattern, had been discontinued. These days her mail order business includes discontinued stemware by Lenox, Gorham, Cambridge, Royal Doulton, Waterford and Wedgwood, among others. Prices can vary widely, depending on the delicacy, rarity and original price of an item. A Fostoria American flat-based tumbler, for example, costs $20. Customers can register their hard-to-find patterns with the company, which will contact them, free of charge, when pieces are located. **LOCATERS, INC.,** 908 Rock Street, Little Rock, AR 72202; (800) 367-9690. ✉

FOSTORIA'S AMERICAN is so popular that Mildred Brumback, who started her china and crystal replacement service in 1981, specializes in the pattern's rarest pieces, such as shrimp bowls, condiment sets and ice buckets. Ms. Brumback, who stocks crystal by Lenox, Tiffin, Stuart, Cambridge and Gorham, among others, says she particularly enjoys locating hard-to-find patterns, such as Fostoria's elegant but simple Sheffield ($50 for a goblet). A Fostoria American water goblet costs

$25.   **MILDRED G. BRUMBACK CHINA MATCHING**, 420 Belle Grove Road, Middletown, VA 22645; (703) 869-1261.   ⊠

# GLOVES, CLEANED AND REPAIRED

*T*HOUGH THE HEAVY-DUTY glove season lasts only a few months, the glove rehabilitation season lasts all year.

Tired-looking gloves can usually be revived with a professional cleaning and pressing if stains are not left on the gloves for too long. Seams can be sewn closed. And loosened ornaments, such as bows, buttons and sequins, can often be reattached. Even white kid gloves of the Queen Mum variety can usually be revived, provided the leather is still in good condition.

Storing gloves properly is particularly crucial to their appearance, according to Jay Ruckel, a partner in La Crasia, a glove-designing concern in Manhattan. "Look at the difference," he said. In one hand he held a perfectly pressed brown suede glove. In the other was its messy mate, which had been crumpled into a ball. But after a quick press on a stainless-steel, hand-shaped machine, the second glove looked just like the first. A heavy wood weight was placed over the glove to make it even smoother.

With his partner La Crasia Duchein, Mr. Ruckel has designed and manufactured fashion gloves for women and men since 1973. And he is adamant that gloves must never be stored in plastic. Plastic can trap moisture, which can become acidic and eat away at the gloves. Different-colored leathers should also never be stored on top of each other as dyes can rub off. "In Victorian times, they kept gloves in cloth glove bags," he added.

La Crasia, which specializes in customized gloves, does not clean gloves, but Mr. Ruckel will press wrinkled gloves (one dollar) and repair tears on seams when possible. "We have to be able to match the stitching," he said. And if a glove is not too badly creased, Mr. Ruckel suggests a do-it-yourself pressing. "Place the glove on your knee and pull the fingers a bit," he said. "The heat from your leg will smooth out wrinkles."

The company has also opened a retail shop down the street from its Garment District factory. In addition to high-fashion gloves for all seasons, the shop sells gloves in a variety of Victorian designs, many inspired by the antique gloves on view in the La Crasia glove museum, also in the shop.  LA CRASIA, 6 East 32nd Street, New York, NY 10016; (212) 532-1956.  LA CRASIA GLOVE COMPARTMENT, 304 Fifth Avenue (near 32nd  Street), New York, NY 10016; (212) 594-2223.  ✉

GLOVERSVILLE, NEW YORK, about 45 miles north of Albany, was once a flourishing glove-making center. And Robison & Smith, a large Gloversville dry-cleaning concern, has cleaned gloves for over 30 years ($7.70 for wrist-length suede, $9 for wrist-length leather). Unlike most dry cleaners, Robison & Smith is equipped with hand-shaped glove stretchers that heat to 220 degrees; the concern will mail rehabilitated gloves all over the country.

Not every pair of leather gloves can be cleaned. "If leather gloves have been stored in a warm room, the oils in the skins can dry out," said Floyd King, manager of Robison & Smith.

Multicolor leather gloves are the hardest to clean since leathers bleed. Driving gloves are also challenging. "They're usually loaded with perspiration, which is salty and hardens the leather," Mr. King said.

Ink, lipstick and coffee are among the most common glove stains. If a stain can't be removed completely, the gloves can often be refinished with a light dye coat. Robison & Smith also wet cleans cloth gloves, though Mr. King says owners may want to do the job themselves. "Just be sure to rinse out all the detergent so the gloves don't get stiff and yellow," he said.  ROBISON & SMITH, 335 North Main Street, Gloversville, NY 12078; (518) 725-7181.  ✉

MOST OWNERS DON'T CLEAN black leather gloves as often as they should, said Norman Tarbous, an owner of R & S Cleaners, which has cleaned leathers for over 20 years. "They can't see the dirt and don't realize it's building up," he said. Too much dirt, and too little oil, will dry out gloves, causing them to eventually crack and peel.

Suede gloves are usually harder to clean than leather, which can be refinished. But suede has a nap, or fuzzy surface, and won't evenly absorb dyes. "Suede gloves will come out cleaner, but they may not look totally clean," Mr. Tarbous explained.

R & S can repair broken seams, if the stitches are similar to those they provide. But it's usually too expensive to create a replacement for a missing mate. "It's a lot cheaper to buy a new pair," Mr. Tarbous said. Glove cleaning costs $15. **R & S CLEANERS/THE LEATHER MASTERS,** 176 Second Avenue (near 11th Street), New York, NY 10003; (212) 674-6651.

## GOURDS

*E*ACH OCTOBER, more than a thousand gourd growers, craftspeople and collectors converge upon tiny Mount Gilead, Ohio, for the American Gourd Society's World's Largest Gourd Show. There they celebrate the wonders and uses of these ancient, inedible plants, which are hard, colorful and often, wonderfully weird.

Dozens of varieties exist, from the palm-sized dwarf hardshell gourd, with a two-inch base diameter, to giant gourds with 16-inch base diameters. And gourds have as many uses as varieties, says gourd society secretary John Stevens.

Smooth bottle gourds, with wide bases and narrow necks, have been used for centuries as percussion instruments by Africans, Hawaiians, Native Americans and other cultures. Gourds make sturdy birdfeeders, birdhouses and planters, as well as bowls, boxes, vases, dolls, baby rattles, jewelry, table arrangements and even Christmas decorations. "They don't break like glass balls," said Mr. Stevens.

"No two gourds are alike," said Linda Lindberg of the Gourd Factory, who with her husband, Peter, raises 30 acres of gourds in California's sunny San Joaquin Valley. The Lindbergs, who have grown gourds for more than 20 years, specialize in bottle gourds for percussion instruments but also raise kettle gourds, with wide bases and pointy tops, squat canteen gourds and teardrop gourds. All come in a variety of sizes. They also grow ornamental egg gourds, once used by farmers as sham eggs to encourage hens to be more productive.

The long, slow growing season is a key reason California gourds have smooth, hard shells, said Mrs. Lindberg, whose customers have included the New York Philharmonic. "It takes a whole year to grow a gourd." The seeds, often as large as arrowheads, must be planted by hand. Frequent weeding is needed to uproot bugs, which can scar the gourds. Bright green while growing, most gourds turn the color of straw when dried, with darker or mottled variations.

The Gourd Factory, which accepts mail and telephone orders and ships, charges $1 for an ornamental egg gourd and up to $25 for a giant hardshell gourd, with a base diameter over 12½ inches. A price sheet with illustrations of the gourds is available.   THE GOURD FACTORY, P.O. Box 55311, Stockton, CA 95295 (209) 887-3694.   ⊠

MOTORISTS OFTEN TURN OFF U.S. 1 IN WRENS, GEORGIA to the farm where Lena Braswell displays and sells the wide variety of gourds she grows on her 60-acre farm. Mrs. Braswell, who also takes mail and telephone orders and ships, has raised gourds for 16 years, ever since her aunt wanted gourds and couldn't find any. In addition to bottle gourds and ornamental egg gourds, she raises bushel gourds, huge creations shaped like tubs, and dipper gourds, round gourds with long "handles" growing from one end. "People used them as dippers for syrup in the olden days, but they can be used as dippers for water or punch," Mrs. Braswell said. Dipper gourds are also popular percussion instruments. Her specialty is kettle gourds, which are made into birdfeeders and birdhouses for the purple martin. (While in residence, purple martins conveniently eat insects, including mosquitoes.) At the customer's request, she will hollow the gourd and cut a hole for the bird.

Mrs. Braswell's gourds start at 50 cents. She asks mail order customers to send a sketch of the shape and size they want with a stamped, self-addressed envelope.   LENA BRASWELL, 1089 Hoyt Braswell Road, Wrens, GA; (706) 547-6784.   ⊠

FLORENCE HAIBER of La Grangeville, New York, has grown gourds since the mid-1960s on 3½ acres of land near Poughkeepsie. But she didn't open her business, Mona's Gourd and Garden Art, until she retired in 1988 after 25 years as a fifth-grade teacher.

Mrs. Haiber, whose nickname is Mona, grows a variety of gourds, including bottle gourds, dipper gourds and roundish gourds with bumpy surfaces. She will sell gourds in their natural state. But she also offers decorated gourds, which she embellishes herself. She paints dipper gourds to make dolls. She makes gourds into boxes, painting the surfaces to look like leather.

She also sells painted birdhouse gourds, complete with holes drilled. Mrs. Haiber's small hand-painted gourds cost about $6.50 and up. Her painted birdhouse gourds start at $40. **MONA'S GOURD ART**, Reilly Road, La Grangeville, NY 12540; (914) 223-3269.  ✉

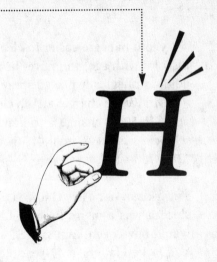

## Hats,
## CLEANED AND REPAIRED

"A WOMAN HAS TO WEAR a hat if she's really dressed," declared Horace Weeks, who cleans and renovates hats for both women and men at his shop, Peter & Irving. Mr. Weeks, a hat doctor for close to 30 years, can clean, block and decorate almost any type of hat, from fur-felt fedoras to multicolor pillboxes. But his specialty is women's hats, including straws.

"Straw is fragile," he said, patting a pale blue straw crown. But there is hope even if a straw hat is hideously bent out of shape. (Mr. Weeks does not renovate men's straws.) The damaged hat is dampened, steamed and shaped by hand on a wooden block so the crown has the proper form. The brim, also dampened and steamed, is pressed over a wooden flange. Then the hat goes into a metal box, heated to 250 degrees, to dry.

Mr. Weeks can rewire hats, dye hats, patch hats and install new linings, ribbons and trimmings. As Mr. Horace, he also decorates hats, old and new.

Cloth hats are easier to clean than straw. And white straws, which discolor with age, will never be snowy again, even after a cleaning. But a little strategically placed spray dye can turn them white again.

Mr. Weeks charges $25 to clean a women's hat, $25 for a reblocking and $16.50 to change a trimming. Men's hats are $27.50 to clean and reblock.  **PETER & IRVING,** 36 West 38th Street, New York, NY 10018; (212) 730-4369.

THE WORST HAT ABE GRUNFELD ever saw was run over by a car. But since it was a men's fur-felt fedora, he was able to reshape it. "Straw would have been impossible," admitted Mr. Grunfeld, who purchased Van Dyke Hatters, a 47-year-old hat renovating concern, several years ago.

Owners can get very attached to their hats, Mr. Grunfeld said. "We get hats here that are 30 years old." If a hat is well-worn, it can be cleaned but will still show its age. But an old hat that's hardly been worn will look like new once it is cleaned and reblocked.

Much of Mr. Grunfeld's work these days is on cowboy hats, which require a large-crown block and curvy flange for the brim. "People who wear western hats have a little style," he said.

Mr. Grunfeld cleans and blocks hats by hand. Linings are removed and cleaned separately. And hats get new bands for the outside and leather liners for the inside. Though men's hats are his specialty, he cleans and rehabilitates women's hats occasionally. Mr. Grunfeld also manufactures new hats, mostly men's fur-felt brimmed hats.

He charges $20 to clean and reblock a hat at his Brooklyn workshop. He also renovates hats for dry cleaners and shoe repair shops throughout New York City and can refer customers to the nearest shop. (Prices may vary elsewhere.)  **VAN DYKE HATTERS,** 463 East Ninth Street, Brooklyn, NY 11218; (718) 469-7420.

TO MIKE DELUCA, a hat renovator in Greenwich Village, Harrison Ford is a hero. For years, the hat-renovating business was slow. Then along came *Raiders of the Lost Ark.*

Bingo.

"We had a window full of old men's hats, some dating from when the shop opened, in 1927," said Zoya DeLuca, Mr. DeLuca's wife and partner in Champion Hat and Shoe Renovating Shop. The movie played at the nearby Greenwich theater. Within days, the old hats were sold. And the hat rehabilition business has been brisk ever since, particularly for fedoras, porkpies and cowboy hats.

The DeLucas, in business for over 15 years, clean and block cloth and straw hats. They can size and stretch hats. They also make cosmetic changes. "In the '40s, the bows were in the back of the hats," Mrs. DeLuca said. "Some people like that."

Top hats are particularly hard to rehabilitate, according to Mr. DeLuca. "The springs that make them collapsible can break," he said. In addition, many are *old*, 100 years and over. And the silk can be worn.

A hat will retain its shape if it is stored properly. Mr. DeLuca suggests keeping the hat in a box with the brim up. "When you wear it, snap the brim down," he says. When the hat is stored, gently roll up the brim. "And try not to pinch the hat in the center of the brim," he added. That can cause a weak spot.

Cleanings start at $15. **CHAMPION HAT AND SHOE RENOVATING SHOP,** 94 Greenwich Avenue (near West 12th Street), New York, NY 10011; (212) 929-5696.

## HOUSE PAINTERS, ARTISTS WHO MOONLIGHT AS

ONE OF THE QUICKEST, easiest and, relatively speaking, least expensive ways to liven a room is with decorative paint, whether it is a simple color wash over linen-white walls or a dining-room mural of a fanciful garden. And an obvious way to get the job done is to hire an artist.

While actors typically work as waiters to help pay the rent, artists often moonlight as house painters. The ranks of well-known artists who once wielded rollers and ladders is large and impressive, from Willem de Kooning to Frank Stella.

House painting is, in fact, a natural and practical way for artists to earn money. "You're painting all the time, so you're developing your skills," said Judith Eisler, a Manhattan artist who paints on canvases and walls.

For clients with blank walls, artists can be good value. Besides having a trained eye for color, many artists are skilled at a range of sophisticated painting techniques, from glazing and subtle stippling to metal leafing and faux woodwork. The right artist can paint a mural as handily as a molding. In addition, artists are often more willing than commercial house painters to experiment with new techniques and paints.

"It's very reassuring to have somebody who is a fine artist painting your house," said Donna Warner, the editor in chief of *Metropolitan Home* magazine. "You have a great deal of faith in both their ability and their taste level, assuming you like their art."

Ms. Warner recently hired Jeffrey Damberg, an artist with a studio in Greenwich, Connecticut, to paint her kitchen. "He was wonderful with helping me choose colors," she said.

As a student at the Lyme Academy of Fine Arts in Old Lyme, Connecticut, Mr. Damberg worked as a house painter to pay his tuition. These days, Mr. Damberg's happiest hours are spent painting portraits in his studio. But he still paints houses to earn money.

"You can't compare the enjoyment of painting a room with painting a face," he admitted. "But you always end up with a nice project you can see at the end of the day."

Helping a client choose colors is a big part of the job for Mr. Damberg, who mixes paints when commercial colors aren't quite right. "The color people want is usually much duller than the color on a sample chip," he explained. "I may change the color subtly on one wall if a lot of light shines on it," he added.

In Ms. Warner's kitchen, for example, Mr. Damberg created custom-color yellow walls that become subtly, but progressively, lighter moving from the entrance hall through the kitchen and eating area.

Mr. Damberg frequently paints murals in private homes, weaving in likenesses of family members and even pets when requested. For a dining-room mural, he included the owner's home in a rural Connecticut scene painted in the primitive style of Grandma Moses.

He also enjoys working with imitation metal leaf in silver or gold. Mr. Damberg charges $50 an hour for consultations, between $750 and $1,200 to do a small room in imitation metal leaf. For an average room, painting runs $500 to $1,000. JEFFREY DAMBERG, P.O. Box 433, Cos Cob, CT 06807; (203) 661-8234.

WHEN HE GETS THE TIME, Raymond Bugara does large-scale paintings juxtaposing realistic and abstract images. But most of his working hours are set aside for his other painting business, Faux Real Decorative Painting.

Mr. Bugara took up decorative painting 11 years ago, when he graduated from Cooper Union School of Art.

Besides a range of glazing techniques, he creates murals, notably monochromatic landscapes in sepia tones. He painted the doors of Ivana Trump's office in Trump Tower to look like marble. And at the offices of *Forbes* magazine, he painted the library's walls to look like mahogany.

Mr. Bugara especially likes trying out new paints and experimenting with colors. Instead of painting a simple latex wall, he is more inclined to add glazes or washes for a less flat finish.

A favorite technique is mixing a glaze from three pigments, such as blue, yellow and brown, then applying it with cheesecloth. When the pigments are crushed, a variety of colors come through, he explained. Mr. Bugara charges from $600 to $1,000 to apply a wash or pigmented glaze for a small room. **RAYMOND BUGARA, FAUX REAL DECORATIVE PAINTING;** (212) 228-3925.

KATIE MERZ SPENT YEARS PAINTING walls in homes, nightclubs and stores after graduating from Cooper Union School of Arts. "I love spackling and plastering," she said. But these days most of her house-painting efforts are decorative murals in the colorful, cartoony style of her paintings.

Ms. Merz recently created a large mural for an exercise room in a loft patterned with whimsical characters lifting barbells and sweating on exercycles. She got the job after the loft's owner bought one of her paintings during a show at the Jack Tilton Gallery in SoHo.

And for a bathroom in Westchester, she used chalk to create an absract mural to the owner's specifications and waterproofed it with latex polyurethane. Ms. Merz charges a day rate of $300 to $350, somewhat more for murals. **KATIE MERZ;** (212) 475-3940.

IN HER FIRST JOB AS A HOUSE PAINTER, Judith Eisler, who studied fine art and architecture at Cornell University, helped create the etched plaster walls for the Manhattan nightclub Nell's. And she discovered she enjoyed decorative painting, particularly elaborate plasters and glazes.

She painted the bathtub and light fixtures to match the walls in one recent room. And in a more elaborate effort, she copied a Monet landscape onto a safe in a Manhattan office.

Ms. Eisler charges $1.50 a square foot for the first coat and $1.00 a square foot each additional coat.   JUDITH EISLER; (212) 941-7875.

## IRONWORKERS

ASK JOEL SCHWARTZ what he makes for a living and he succinctly replies "house jewelry." Mr. Schwartz, owner of Schwartz's Forge and Metalworks in Deansboro, New York, is a contemporary blacksmith. And though he began his career fashioning real jewelry in silver and gold, these days he creates decorative balustrades, staircases and other large ornaments in forged steel and bronze.

A number of metal artisans make house jewelry, which comes in all sizes and guises, from hooks and handles to furniture that mates steel with wood, stone and glass. Some fabricate and repair exterior house jewelry, as well, notably wrought-iron window rails, tree guards, fences and gates.

Many artisans use thoroughly modern techniques, cutting metal into shapes and welding the pieces together with sophisticated equipment. Others adhere strictly to the classic principles of blacksmithing and forging, in which steel is heated, then hammered into shape. And a few, like Mr. Schwartz, handily mix techniques.

Iron's ability to achieve beauty was demonstrated in the late 19th century with the Eiffel Tower. Its current popularity, both inside and outside the home, comes from several factors. Iron is versatile and relatively inexpensive, and it can simply be made into interesting shapes.

New York architect Basil Walter of Sweeny Walter Associates, a New York architectural firm, likes iron because it can provide contemporary buildings with historical references. "Look at the Chelsea Hotel," he said, citing the late-19th-century structure's distinctive ornamental wrought iron. "You incorporate something like that in a new building and it refers to something historically significant."

Artisans and architects have also begun experimenting with unusual finishes for iron. Cold, chromey 1970s-style steel is no longer the only option. Chemical treatments with salts, acids and even ordinary water can create a range of warm finishes, from a rusty, woodlike patina to a greenish hue. Mr. Schwartz often uses a traditional wax-based finish on interior metalwork.

Mr. Schwartz first forged household accessories—"contemporary interpretations of traditional objects, like fireplace tools," he said. These days his commissions are usually large adornments, including bronze doors and wrought-iron fences for New York City brownstones.

Besides his own designs, he makes historic reproductions for listed buildings. He once fashioned a handrail for the handicap ramp at Gracie Mansion sympathetic to the building's historic style. Custom balustrades average about $700 to $1,000 a linear foot. **SCHWARTZ'S FORGE AND METALWORKS, INC**. P.O. Box 205, Route 315, Deansboro, NY 13328 (near Utica); (315) 841-4477.

JEAN WIART (PRONOUNCED WE-ARE), a French blacksmith, came to New York in 1984 to lead the French team that created the new torch and flame for the Statue of Liberty. He decided to stay, and in 1986 became a founding partner in L.M.S. Corps., the U.S. subsidiary of Les Métalliers Champénois, an architectural metalwork concern in Reims, France.

L.M.S. divides its jobs between historic restorations and new designs. The firm created the copper pineapple dome for Brooklyn's City Hall and frequently fashions wrought-iron railings in both contemporary and 18th-century French styles.

A specialty is repoussé work, in which copper, iron or aluminum is hammered or pressed on the reverse side to create decorative shapes, such as leaves or rosettes. "Using repoussé, we can adorn gate railings or stair railings with foliage," Mr. Wiart said. "Then it can be gilded." Custom stair railing starts at about $900 a linear foot.  **L.M.C. CORPS. (LES METALLIERS CHAMPENOIS),** 77 Second Avenue, Paterson, NJ 07514; (201) 279-3573.

JAMES GARVEY, a sculptor with Koenig Ironworks, likes creating both large and small objects from iron. On the large side are the stainless-steel armature bars he replicated to replace the original wrought-iron bars that surround the Statue of Liberty in 1986.

But he also has a line of pot racks, hooks and bookends in blackened steel. His $150 tripod stool with an elliptical top is light enough to hang from a hook. And a $300 stainless-steel valet with a ladder back, seat and low legs looks a like a quirky MacIntosh chair.

A blacksmith for over 20 years, Mr. Garvey particularly enjoys creating outdoor utility products, such as the forged-iron trash cans used in parts of Tribeca. And his tripod bicycle stand looks like a maypole, with chains and locks suspended like ribbons. **JAMES GARVEY AT KOENIG IRONWORKS,** 223 West 19th Street, New York, NY 10011; (212) 924-4333.  ✉

STEEL FURNITURE AND HARDWARE are designer Harris Rubin's specialties. But he is best known for making elegant steel objects that don't look like steel. From a distance, his slender oval endtable could be of darkly finished wood. He also works with smooth rusted steel. For a professor from Mexico, he created a glass-top coffee table with rusted legs shaped like Mayan pyramids.  "Steel furniture doesn't have to be your basic welded thing," he said. "It can have color, warmth and texture. And it is very strong."

Mr. Rubin, who accepts commissions, likes to match metal with wood and recently devised an Arts & Crafts–style coffee table from wood and glass with blackened steel ornaments. He also finishes his furniture with a range of patinas, including gun bluing, a bluish-black patina used on firearms. Endtables start at $600.  **HARRIS RUBIN,** 84 Front Street (under the Brooklyn Bridge), Brooklyn, NY 11201; (718) 858-6165.  ✉

FOR YEARS, Warner Wada, a SoHo photographer, rolled out an old Steinway piano top when he needed a table for dinner parties. So recently he teamed with architect Fritz Johnson and metal sculptor Jim Zivic to produce Burning Relic, a line of tables that feature piano tops set on hand-made steel bases.

The curved base for the baby grand table ($4,200) was inspired by the Paris Metro's ornamental ironwork. And the concert grand Prairie Table ($6,500) is balanced atop a forged iron base that looks like a bridge. BURNING RELIC, 37 Greene Street (near Grand Street), New York, NY 10013; (212) 226-5159. ✉

## JEWELRY
## (COSTUME) REPAIRED

GERARD ZIERLER, A JEWELER, works with lots of materials that sparkle and shine. But all that glitters isn't 14-carat gold. "I'm dealing essentially with junk," he admitted.

Mr. Zierler repairs costume jewelry—bracelets, necklaces, earrings and even rhinestone-encrusted tiaras. In business on Manhattan's Upper West Side since 1959, he also repairs fine jewelry and watches. But about 15 years ago, Mr. Zierler discovered the charms of cubic zircona, colored glass and painted plastic.

In recent years, many people have begun wearing costume jewelry during the day and keeping good jewelry in the vault, he says. At the same time, interest in vintage costume jewelry from the 1940s and '50s grew. And much new costume jewelry has become better and better, a far cry from the discount store adornments also available. "When a piece of costume jewelry costs $200 or $300, as many now do, people don't mind paying $50 for a repair," Mr. Zierler said.

Oddly enough, repairing costume jewelry can be more of a challenge than restoring the Real Thing. "When you have gold and fine stones, not much can go wrong," said Mr. Zierler. "With costume jewelry, you have to expect the unexpected." Figuring out what the original materials were can often be difficult. What looks like metal can be plastic. And since plastics can't be soldered, Mr. Zierler often has to use threads to hold a piece together.

Special cements must be used as well, since many costume jewelry materials will blacken with ordinary glues. Mr. Zierler also keeps a stock of false stones in all sizes and colors. On rare occasions when he can't find the right stone, he creates a new fake with filler and colors it with nail enamel. "Everything is salvageable," he said. "It just depends on the amount of work, and how much the customer is willing to pay."

Mr. Zierler's costume jewelry repairs start at $10. He also converts earrings from clip-ons to pierced (or the reverse) and replaces watchbands. **G. ZIERLER,** 202 West 96th Street, New York, NY 10025; (212) 749-1360. ✉

## JUKEBOXES, REPAIRED AND SOLD

Rᴵᴄᴋ Bᴏᴛᴛs, the editor of *Jukebox Collector* magazine, has a theory about why people collect vintage jukeboxes.

"They're always associated with pleasure," he said. "You'd go out to eat, a jukebox was there. You'd go to a tavern, a jukebox was there."

Mr. Botts's pleasure principle can apply to other coin-operated devices, such as pinball machines, gumball machines, soft-drink machines, slot machines and even old cash registers. Coin-operated amusement machines turn up regularly at flea markets or in attics. Electronic versions are also collectible, though they have been around only 15 years or so.

And even the most battered machines can usually be made to look and work like new. Indeed, to enthusiasts, old jukeboxes are like electric trains to some people.

Jukeboxes tend to be complicated, with amplifiers and push buttons. Even the decorative touches are complex, including things like revolving color pilasters and heat-operated bubble tubes.

Electronic pinball machines are also intricate, with dot-matrix displays and microcomputers that mastermind all moves.

But video machines are relatively simple, even showy ones like Street Fighter II, a hot box in the early 1990s. JUKEBOX COLLECTOR MAGAZINE; (515) 265-8324.  ⊠

IN 1983, STEVE HANSON decided to repair an old Seeburg jukebox just for fun. He enjoyed it so much that he repaired another, and another. These days, his business, New England Jukebox, near Hartford, sells and restores all types of coin-operated amusement machines.

Jukeboxes date from the early nickelodeons, which were first made in 1889, but some of the most desirable models are from the 1940s and '50s, Mr. Hanson said. The big-time makers were Wurlitzer, Seeburg, Rockola and AMI. Wurlitzer's heyday was the 1940s; Seeburg's the 1950s.

"They used a Seeburg in the TV show *Laverne and Shirley* and a Seeburg and a Rockola in *Happy Days*," he said.

Pinball machines were invented in the early 19th century. A stick that was much like a pool cue was originally used as the plunger. Flippers date from 1948, Mr. Hanson said. And electronic pinball began around 1977.

To rehabilitate a vintage pinball machine, Mr. Hanson cleans all contacts and flipper controls, refinishes the cabinet, paints the details and replaces the rubber rings that the balls bounce off.

Repairs from $45 an hour. NEW ENGLAND JUKEBOX, 77 Tolland Turnpike, Manchester, CT 06040; (203) 646-1533.

JUKEBOXES ARE REMARKABLY RESILIENT, said Wendy Johnson, a partner in John T. Johnson's Jukebox Classics, which sells and repairs vintage amusement machines. "Someone brought in a jukebox that had been sitting in a foot of water," she said. "We had sound coming out of it in 35 minutes."

A jukebox, slot machine or pinball machine left unused in a basement for years usually needs an overhaul, even if there is nothing wrong with the machine. Parts dry up, handles stick and everything needs to be cleaned.

Mrs. Johnson and her husband, John, the other partner, also refinish exteriors, replate chrome work and apply paint and enamel.

A lot of business comes from do-it-yourself enthusiasts who try to repair an old jukebox or pinball machine and make everything worse, Mrs. Johnson said.

Repairs by the Johnsons start at $75 for a small slot machine. House calls start at $100 in Brooklyn and $200 in Manhattan.   JOHN T. JOHNSON'S JUKEBOX CLASSICS, 6742 Fifth Avenue (near 68th Street), Brooklyn, NY 11220; (718) 833-8455.

## KNIFE SHARPENERS

Wʜᴇɴ ᴀ ᴋɪᴛᴄʜᴇɴ ᴋɴɪꜰᴇ or a pair of scissors needs to be sharpened, you will know, says Cam Weigmann, manager of Henry Westpfal & Co., Inc., an 85-year-old company that sharpens cutlery, scissors and leather-making tools. Hair starts to fold when barber scissors are dull. Fabric edges will gather if pinking shears lose their edge. "And if you can't cut a tomato, you know your knife needs sharpening," said Ms. Weigmann, who has been with Westpfal for 40 years.

Westpfal, which recently moved into a white-walled shop in the West 30s, sharpens nearly anything with a blade, including cuticle nippers, scalloping scissors, tailoring shears, hunting knives, straight-edge razors, chef's knives and dinner knives with sterling silver handles. These last must be sharpened entirely by hand as the vibrating from the grinding wheel, used in most sharpening, can loosen the handles, according to John Chapman, a grinder at Westpfal for almost 20 years.

To sharpen an ordinary knife, Mr. Chapman follows a four-step process. First, the knife is reshaped and repaired using a grinding wheel and water. Next, the edge is sharpened on the wheel. Polishing, which gets rid of rust, follows. Finally, the knife is honed by hand.

The process is similar for scissors, which are taken apart for sharpening. Mr. Chapman, who is left-handed, specializes in sharpening left-handed scissors.

Westpfal also sells a range of leather-making tools as well as Wiss scissors, Wusthof cutlery, Buck hunting knives and Swiss army knives, offering discounts off the list prices.

Scissors sharpening starts at $4, depending on condition and size. Knife sharpening starts at $2.50 for a paring knife. Pinking shear sharpening begins at $7.95. And it costs $9.95 to sharpen a straight-edge razor. Jobs are usually accomplished in two or three days. HENRY WESTPFAL, 105 West 30th Street, New York, NY 10001; (212) 563-5990. ✉

GRACIOUS HOME, A LARGE hardware and repair shop on Third Avenue, offers knife sharpening daily except Tuesdays and Saturdays. Sharpening is done by hand with a traditional grinding wheel. Knives and scissors can be sharpened while the customer waits. Gracious Home will sharpen all types of knives but does not do pinking shears. Knife sharpening usually costs one dollar an inch, but the price drops if customers bring in several knives. GRACIOUS HOME, 1220 Third Avenue, New York, NY 10027; (212) 517-6300. ✉

# KNITTING AND NEEDLEPOINT (PEOPLE WHO COMPLETE UNFINISHED PROJECTS)

ALMOST EVERYONE WHO HAS EVER KNITTED or done needlepoint has at some time wished for a helper to complete a half-finished sweater or canvas.

People put off finishing their projects for all sorts of reasons, said Judi Alweil, who owns Judy & Co. in Dix Hills, New York. The company completes unfinished needlepoint by hand.

"People get bored or find a particular design is too intricate to complete," she said. "Often they'll put off starting a new project because they feel guilty that the old piece has never been finished."

Judy & Co. will complete the stitchery on any kind of needlepoint canvas, including petit point, the tiniest canvas available.

Unfinished canvases, with yarn and instructions, are sent to the company's 20-year-old factory in Haiti, where a team of more than 15 workers matches colors and stitches. The company will also stitch entire canvases from scratch, using colors the client selects.

Most work is done in basketweave, a basic stitch. But unusual stitches, such as bargello and counted cross-stitch, are available at additional charge. Canvases are stitches on frames; finished works are blocked before their return. Prices start at 25 cents a square inch for a large-hole canvas.

Though Judy & Co. does not accept direct orders, Ms. Alweil will refer prospective clients to needlepoint shops offering her finishing service.   JUDY & CO.; (516) 499-8480.

KNITTING IS LIKE HANDWRITING, according to Sandy Eisenberg, owner of Sandy's Knit 'N' Needles in Queens. "No two people knit exactly the same way," she said. "When you pick up someone else's knitting, you have to match the tension of the stitches."

Sandy's is primarily a yarn shop, but Mrs. Eisenberg's knitters will complete knitting of nearly any kind, including sweaters, hats and scarves, even if the yarn has been bought elsewhere. The more-than-20-year-old shop will also knit garments from scratch.

Sandy's assembles knitted items as well, which entails fitting the garment, putting in seams and blocking. Knitting is completed from $12 to $15 an hour.   SANDY'S KNIT 'N' NEEDLES, 154-03B Union Turnpike, Flushing, NY 11367; (718) 380-0370.

## LACQUER FURNITURE, RESTORED AND REPAIRED

LACQUER, A LUSTROUS, DURABLE finish for wood, has been popular for over a thousand years in various guises. Slow-drying natural lacquer, made from the sap of sumac trees in Southeast Asia, was used for centuries on furniture crafted in India, China, Korea and Japan. And when lacquer furniture imported from Asia could no longer satisfy European demand, 17th-century craftsman, notably in France, England and Spain, devised a similar look, called japanning, using layers of paint and varnish.

These days lacquer furniture usually gets its lustre from synthetic spray finishes in acrylic or polyester. Oriental lacquer, japanning and synthetic lacquer can all be restored, though each process is distinctive.

Diane Fitzgerald and Eve Kaplan, co-owners of Fitzkaplan, specialize in the restoration of oriental lacquer, water gilding and antique painted finishes, including japanning. While japanned surfaces are seen in a variety of colors, natural Asian lacquer comes in just red, black or green, which is actually black lacquer coated with yellow shellac.

Lacquer furniture needing restoration often looks wrinkled or corrugated, resulting from contraction of the underlying wood. Ms. Fitzgerald, a restorer for 11 years, uses reversible materials, such as gesso and fillers made with gypsum or plaster to even out the surface. She matches the original colors using dry powder pigments and stains, adding shellac only if it was on the piece originally. (Oriental lacquer, which can be poisonous to skin when wet, is not readily available in the United States.)

Matching the original color is the key to a good restoration. "With lacquer, black isn't a flat black," she said. "There's a richness and depth of color that has to be matched."

Fitzkaplan can also clean and restore painting on both lacquer and japanned pieces. Fitzkaplan gives free estimates and charges between $40 and $50 an hour. FITZKAPLAN, 131 Varick Street (near Spring Street), 10th floor, New York, NY 10013; (212) 989-8779.

"GOOD LACQUER HAS DEPTH," said Oswaldo Novaes, whose company, Joia, has made and repaired synthetic lacquer furniture for over 20 years. Most of Mr. Novaes's furniture designs, which include Art Deco reproductions available only to the trade, are finished in acrylic lacquer. But Mr. Novaes's Long Island City workshop repairs a variety of synthetic lacquers, including polyester lacquer, a new, tough finish, for the general public.

Small nicks and even deep scratches in acrylic lacquer that do not penetrate the underlying wood can often be patched with about five coats of lacquer, each preceded by sanding. Complete stripping and resurfacing is usually needed for nicks that expose large areas of wood. "If a hole is big, you cannot fill it with lacquer and expect it to hold," Mr. Novaes said.

Polyester lacquer, which is like epoxy, is difficult to patch and usually requires a total stripping.

Joia (Portuguese for jewel) gives free estimates and charges about $750 to relacquer a small table. Repairs start at about $100. JOIA INTERIORS, INC., 149 East 60th Street, New York, NY 10022; (212) 759-1224.

# LAMPS,
## CUSTOM DESIGNS AND SPARE PARTS

OVER THE YEARS, Karl Muller has worked with a range of items: milk cans, vases, helmets, baskets, bottles, statues, even chamber pots. "You can make a lamp out of almost anything," said Mr. Muller, a staff member at Grand Brass Lamp Parts, in business in Manhattan for more than 90 years.

"Even if a customer comes in with a real piece of junk, we'll make it into a lamp," he added.

Grand Brass, which has converted household objects into lamps for decades, specializes in spare parts for lamps, including finials, switches, cords, glass shades and all sizes of stems and bases in brass, wood and marble. The shop also stocks an array of obsolete parts for old lamps as well as the latest energy-saving bulbs.

To convert an object into a lamp, it is usually necessary to drill holes, attach a base, add wiring, affix a harp, which holds the shade in place and finally attach a shade. Grand Brass sells plugs in a variety of colors. Silk cord in brown, gold and silver is also available, in addition to plastic.

Grand Brass, which charges from $25 to around $100 to convert an object into a lamp, also makes lamps from scratch, customizing them according to the client's wishes. **GRAND BRASS LAMP PARTS,** 221 Grand Street (near Elizabeth Street), New York, NY 10013; (212) 226-2567. ✉

MUSICAL INSTRUMENTS MAKE WONDERFUL LAMPS, says Matthew DeCillis, owner of Columbia Lighting & Silversmiths. "With trumpets, trombones and clarinets, there's already a hole in the middle. Just don't bring in a piano," he said. Columbia has converted a wide range of items into lamps over the years, including bubblegum machines, parking meters, even a stuffed zebra's foot.

In business since 1935, Columbia also sells lighting fixtures and lampshades. Simple shades are usually best when an object is converted into a lamp, said Linda DeCillis, a co-owner. "The lamp makes the statement itself," she said. Columbia charges from $65 to convert an object into a lamp. Musical instrument conversions start at $200. COLUMBIA LIGHTING & SILVERSMITHS, 493 Third Avenue (near 33rd Street), New York, NY 10016; (212) 725-5250.  ✉

# LAMPSHADES, CUSTOM DESIGNS

IF A LAMPSHADE IS THE FIRST THING you notice when you enter a room, the shade, most likely, is all wrong.

"You want shades that are pleasing to the eye, but not jarring," said Susanne Wellott, a custom lampshade designer in Bronxville, New York. "You want to think, 'What a lovely room,'" she explained. "Then you notice the details, the great pillows, the lovely lampshades."

Ready-made lampshades come in a dazzling variety of sizes and shapes these days, from rectangles and ovals to high-fashion coolies, with narrow tops and wide bottoms. But often, a custom-made, fabric-covered shade is the best choice. The lamp base may require a shade with an unusual shape or proportions. Or the owner may want shades that match the sofa or curtains.

A number of prominent custom shade makers, including Ruth Vitow and Abat-Jours in Manhattan, deal only through interior decorators. But Ms. Wellott's company, Shades from the Midnight Sun, works with both decorators and private individuals.

Ms. Wellott, in business for five years, studies the lamp base and the site it will occupy when she designs a shade. "A six-sided shade often looks good if you have a round base on a square table," she said.

She also relies more on her eye than on rigid rules of proportion when devising a size and shape. For years, the shade's circumference was supposed to be the height of the lamp's stem. But with tall candlestick bases, for example, the stem is often much longer.

Color can be a problem as well: The shade looks different when the bulb is lit. Recently, Ms. Wellott deliberately swathed a shade in three colors of chiffon so the shade changed color surprisingly when the light went on.

Custom frame making requires time and extensive hand sewing.

The metal frame is first covered with cotton tape, then a pattern is made for the lining and cover. Each is pinned together and hand sewn. Then comes braid, flounces, fringe—"whatever trim your little heart desires," Ms. Wellott said. She charges from $60 to $900 for a custom shade, depending on size, style and covering. SHADES FROM THE MIDNIGHT SUN; (914) 779-7237. ✉

KNIFE PLEATS, BOX PLEATS, shirt pleats and smocking are a few of the lampshade styles Charlotte Moss & Co. has offered since entering the custom lampshade business. The decorating boutique also carries whimsical finials ($9.50 to $27.50), including miniature brass urns and cobalt crystals.

The store provides an array of fabrics including silks, cottons and designer prints. Or the customer can supply the fabric. "Cream is still the most popular color," said Martha O'Hearn, who runs the shade department. "But prints can be wonderful," she added, touching a shade in blue and white check. Shades range from $85 to about $500. CHARLOTTE MOSS & CO., 1027 Lexington Avenue (near East 74th Street), New York, NY 10021; (212) 772-3320. ✉

FOR DO-IT-YOURSELF ENTHUSIASTS, lampshade making can be a rewarding craft. But frequently the requisite parts, particularly frames, are hard to find. Old frames in good condition can be recovered, of course. But the Smart Lamp and Shade Factory in Queens sells new metal frames (from about $5 to $30) as well as the tape, fabric and thread to cover them.

The company also makes custom shades, both fabric-covered soft shades and hard shades, according to owner Stanley Meyer. "Silk can be pleated or stretched," he said. Hard shades can be covered with the client's wallpaper. SMART LAMP AND SHADE FACTORY, 127-03 20th Avenue, College Point, Queens, NY 11356; (718) 358-8454.

THOUGH IT SOLD FABRIC to the millinery business when it opened in 1923, Friedman & Distillator has supplied classic lampshade fabrics, notably silk shantung, silk pongee and fine linen, to shade makers for years. The company offers braids, fringes, ribbons and other trims as well. "You can add an unusual trim to a mass-produced shade to make it distinctive," said owner Toni Peikes. Silk pongee starts at $12.50 a yard, silk shantung at $15.50 a yard. FRIEDMAN & DISTILLATOR, 53 Leonard Street (between Church and West Broadway), New York, NY 10013; (212) 226-6400.

# LEATHER FURNITURE AND ACCESSORIES, REPAIRED AND DESIGNED

LUSH IS THE WORD LEATHER artisan Michele Costello uses to describe parchment, a thin, translucent, cream-colored leather made from sheepskins that are dried instead of tanned.

"I like the fact that every piece is different," said Ms. Costello, who works with all types of leathers, from gold-tooled leather for desktops to exotic leathers such as parchment and shagreen, a shiny, grainy leather made from stingray, dogfish or shark.

A leather artisan for over 10 years, Ms. Costello makes customized home accessories, such as wastebaskets, lampshades, tabletops and screens in parchment, often hand-tooled with gold leaf. She can cover walls with parchment. She also accepts large commissions. She recently created huge, chocolate-brown leather doors for the New Jersey State Supreme Court House in Trenton, embossed with state seals and elaborate rope patterns (the new doors re-created the look of the building's original doors).

Parchment, used since biblical times, has veered in and out of style through the years. It was a fashion leather in the 1920s and '30s, favored by French interior designer Jean Michel Frank for walls and screens in Art Deco rooms. "It's very durable," Ms. Costello said. "In its natural state, you can erase pencil marks on it." When lacquered, it can even cover bathroom walls, she added.

Ms. Costello prefers the costly shagreen, which can be dyed, as an accent leather on such customized accessories as picture frames and jewelry boxes.

Ms. Costello's prices start at $60 a square foot for tooled leather, $160 a square foot for parchment commissions, and $300 a square foot for shagreen. Prices include leather and labor.   COSTELLO STUDIO, 315 East 91st Street, New York, NY 10128; (212) 410-2083.   ✉

"RESTORATION WORK CAN GO JUST SO FAR," said leather artisan Robert Falotico, who has worked with new and antique upholstery leathers for over 30 years. Still, a good leather chair or sofa can often be cleaned, restored and made usable once again.

Mr. Falotico, who learned the leather trade from his father, can remove oil stains left by skin and hair, clean scouring powder stains and dye discolored areas to the leather's original hue. And if a leather sofa or tabletop is beyond repair, Mr. Falotico can usually make a new one, distressing the leather to make it appear old.

Mr. Falotico also makes tooled-leather tabletops and fake bookbindings, the leather spines with gold-tooled titles seen increasingly on cabinets that hide video equipment.

To make a customized tabletop from cowhide, Mr. Falotico stretches the leather and adds a gold-tooled border, using a 500-year-old process that blends heat, gold leaf and a gilding wheel. A variety of border patterns are available, though Mr. Falotico often suggests something relating to the table's period.

Mr. Falotico charges $85 an hour plus materials. ROBERT FALOTICO STUDIOS, 315 East 91st Street, New York, NY 10128; (212) 369-1217.   ✉

# LEATHER GOODS, REPAIRED, RESTORED AND CUSTOM-MADE

W HEN DESCRIBING WHAT HE DOES FOR A LIVING, Donald Moore could use some before-and-after photographs. Mr. Moore, a partner in Artbag Creations, repairs handbags, belts, wallets and other leather goods. And the results can be striking.

"We'll restitch the handles and refinish the leather," said Mr. Moore, holding up a badly cracked, tooled-leather bag. And to revive a tired-looking black patent-leather attaché case, Mr. Moore installed a new lining and replated the hardware.

Handbags typically get a lot of wear, but the proper repairs can add years to the life of the bag. Artbag repairs or replaces zippers, sews loose stitches and fixes or duplicates leather handles. In business for more than 60 years, the company also does modifications, updating old-style clutch bags with shoulder straps and shortening or lengthening belts.

Much of Mr. Moore's business is custom work. For a policewoman, he devised a bag with a gun holster inside. And for a woman who needed to travel with a large amount of jewelry, he designed a bag with a hidden compartment.

Artbag charges from $60 to replace a zipper and from $125 to reline a handbag. **ARTBAG CREATIONS INC.,** 735 Madison Avenue (near East 64th Street), New York, NY 10021; (212) 744-2720. ✉

FOR CUSTOMERS UNHAPPY WITH THE APPEARANCE OF A HANDBAG, Tony Pecorella, president of Modern Leather Goods, offers a simple solution—alterations. "We can cut down a bag and shorten it, put a pocket on the bottom or put a loop on the bottom or side to hold an umbrella," he explained, demonstrating on a soft leather shoulder bag with a round base.

Most leather repairs are pretty standard, said Mr. Pecorella, whose business has been in his family for more than 60 years. Modern revives attaché cases with new locks and feet, replaces leather trim on key cases and wallets, and makes new linings in silk faille, leather, vinyl or suede.

Customers frequently ask to have worn-out handbags, belts or attaché cases copied if they are no longer sold in stores. Modern charges $35 and up to reline a bag and from $20 to $40 to replace a zipper. **MODERN LEATHER GOODS,** 2 West 32nd Street, fourth floor, New York, NY 10001; (212) 947-7770. ✉

ON A RECENT AFTERNOON, Jakov Dopter, who owns Kay Leather Goods Repair Service, installed new gold-plated hardware on a pink suede bag for a customer while she waited. "We have all this," said his wife, Valentina, pointing to a large cabinet filled with gold-plated snaps, hooks, loops and chain handles. "Some is cheap and some is expensive," she added. "The customer can choose."

Mr. Dopter, who trained as a shoe and bag designer in the Ukraine, repairs handbags, belts and attaché cases. And he improvises a bit when needed. He masked a large blemish on the front of a leather shoulder bag with a matching strip of leather that looked like a decorative stripe.

Mr. Dopter also makes custom belts from leather or fabric, often working with buckles supplied by his customers. Handbag linings start at $25. Custom belts start at $20. **KAY LEATHER GOODS REPAIR SERVICE,** 333 Fifth Avenue (near 33rd Street), New York, NY 10016; (212) 481-5579. ✉

FRED KINIGSBERG'S FACTORY, Custom Accessories of New York, is located in the heart of New York's Garment District, and most of his belts, bracelets and other accessories are made for well-known clothing designers. But Mr. Kinigsberg fashions one-of-a-kind belts for individuals as well. Customers usually bring in a buckle from a belt that wore out, then explain the type of belt that's needed. Besides leather and suede, which he can supply, Mr. Kinigsberg makes belts in a customer's fabric. "We can even braid the fabric," he said.

Customers also can design their own buckles, which are covered in leather, suede or fabric. "You're limited only by your imagination," Mr. Kinigsberg said. Not long ago, he made a belt using a heavy chrome logo from a motorcycle. And he recently acquired the machinery to embellish belts with nailheads and rhinestones. Belts start at $20, with the customer's buckle. **CUSTOM ACCESSORIES OF NEW YORK, LTD.,** 153 West 27th Street, New York, NY 10001; (212) 229-1860. By appointment.

# LEATHER (UNUSUAL KINDS)

IT TAKES A SPECIAL KIND OF LEATHER to upholster a sofa, says William Feigin, owner of Dualoy Inc., which sells upholstery and specialty leathers. Sheepskin can be too weak. Stronger goat and pigskin are often too small. But cowhides are big and durable and can cover large parts of a sofa without requiring unsightly seams.

Still, not all cowhides belong on fine furniture. Upholstery leather should be clean, with no blemishes or holes. That means the best hides come from pampered European cows, which, unlike American cattle, are neither branded nor exposed to bruisings from roaming the range, according to Mr. Feigin. "There is also a history of upholstery leather in Europe."

The average cowhide provides several types of leathers. The thick top side, exposed when the tanner removes the animal's hair, is the grain, backed by a heavy suede. The next layer is a lighter-weight suede.

Dualoy, which has sold leather since 1962, carries grained cowhides in a variety of colors, including the deep greens and cocoa browns used for Mission furniture. The company also stocks suedes and the fashionable antiqued cowhides seen in libraries and traditional clubs.

Another Dualoy specialty is exotic leather, such as cream-colored parchment, made from outer sheepskins dried instead of tanned, and shagreen, a pricey, grainy leather made from sting ray, shark or dogfish.

Upholstery leathers can be used on tabletops, as wall coverings and for accessories. Leather from Dualoy to upholster a chair costs about $600.  DUALOY INC., 45 West 34th Street, New York, NY 10001; (212) 736-3360.  ✉

LEATHER'S USES CONTINUE TO GROW, says Robert Katz, co-owner of Hermes Leather Corporation. Pigskins, now available in purples and fuschias, make handsome pillows or small chairs. And leather floor tiles can soundproof a room. "High heels are no problem," said Ralph Elias, Mr. Katz's partner. "Just don't drag the furniture across them."

Hermes, which has sold upholstry and fashion leather since 1927, stocks full European cowhides, averaging 60 to 65 feet, in 30 colors ($8.50 a square foot). But the company also offers custom coloring, using German hides, averaging about 75 feet, and an American tannery ($7.50 a square foot).  HERMES LEATHER CORPORATION, 45 West 34th Street, New York, NY 10001; (212) 947-1153.  ✉

· · ·

NOT ALL LEATHER IS SMOOTH. W. Pearce & Brothers, importers of English leathers for more than 45 years, offers an array of hairy leathers, stencil-dyed with leopard spots and tiger stripes. So-called hair-on leathers, tanned to retain the animal's hair, can be used as bedroom rugs, wall hangings and even chairs.

Top-grain cowhide can be bumpy. Pearce has a range of embossed leathers, including an alligator-embossed calfskin (from $3.80 a square foot).

Pearce also stocks vegetable-tanned leathers, or "naked leathers," which have no protective finish. "When you rub it, it gets a lustre," said director Lowell Chandler, Jr. Naked leathers can line walls but should not go on furniture.   **W. PEARCE & BROTHERS, INC.,** 363 Seventh Avenue (near 30th Street), New York, NY 10001; (212) 244-4595.   ✉

# LIGHTING DESIGNERS

MOST HOMEOWNERS HAVE LITTLE difficulty choosing lamps for the living room and bedroom. The problems tend to come with the more demanding settings or displays: the kitchen, the bathroom, art collections, even the backyard birch trees.

While an architect or an interior designer can often do the job, an alternative is a lighting designer, trained in the esthetics, technology and conservation of lighting.

Typically, a lighting designer studies the space, considers its function and comes up with a plan covering everything from fixtures and bulbs to the lighting's overall effect.

"When a room is used for a party, the light should tell the people where to mingle, where to find the buffet," said lighting designer Hervé Descottes.

Some designers are willing just to provide the grace notes—customized strip lighting for bookcases or strategic places in a room to emphasize, say, the shape of a staircase. But most will design and execute fixtures.

For a large dining room, lighting designer Ann Kale drew up plans for an Art Nouveau–style hanging fixture. The plans called for hiding in its elegant alabaster bowl a low-voltage spotlight (like ones used in slide projectors) "to make the crystal and flatware sparkle," she said.

Above the spotlight, but also hidden, would be two standard bulbs to provide general light so that guests wouldn't look ghoulish in the shadows created by the spotlight.

Until fairly recently, most lighting designers worked almost exclusively on commercial projects, such as hotels, museums and office buildings. But a growing number accept residential jobs as well, particularly when an intriguing challenge is involved.

For a new house in Old Westbury, Long Island, Thomas Thompson, the owner of Thomas Thompson Lighting Design in SoHo, devised what he calls table lamps for the ceiling. The client, who entertains a lot, didn't want lamps on the tables, Mr. Thompson said.

His solution was to encase bulbs in a series of customized aluminium-frame boxes partly recessed into the ceiling, with each box covered with white fibrous acrylic. "We wanted a softly glowing light to make people look good," he said.

Mr. Thompson, who teaches residential lighting at Parsons School of Design, tries to avoid using recessed spotlighting.

He charges $120 an hour. THOMAS THOMPSON LIGHTING DESIGN, 31 West 21st Street, New York, NY 10010; (212) 366-1760.

KITCHENS, WITH THEIR CULINARY and social uses, pose special lighting challenges, said Ms. Kale, who started Ann Kale Associates in SoHo in 1988. She avoids track lights in kitchens because they are impractical for the myriad tasks performed there. She often lays fluorescent lights on top of cabinets that are not flush with the ceiling. "It costs next to nothing, and you can use the space above as a display shelf," she said.

Ms. Kale said that low-wattage incandescent task lights attached to the undersides of cabinets make food look appealing. But as incandescent bulbs get hot, "You have to watch the wattage," she cautioned. "Incandescents can cook the canned tomatoes in the cupboard above."

Fluorescent lights pose a cooler alternative, if a less attractive one. But for a high-tech kitchen, she screened fluorescent lights with perforated metal.

Ms. Kale charges $125 an hour. ANN KALE ASSOCIATES INC., 75 Spring Street, New York, NY 10012; (212) 431-0954.

MR. DESCOTTES, WHO RUNS L'OBSERVATOIRE INTERNATIONAL, the New York branch of his Paris firm, thinks residential lighting should adapt to the owner's mood. "Some people like cool light, some like warm light and some like both," he said.

He avoids recessed spotlights in the home ("They make you feel like you have something to confess," he said) and enjoys lighting integrated into architecture.

Mr. Descottes often works with landscaping, as well as public and private art collections. He recently lighted the Mona Lisa in the Louvre, a challenge because of shadows created by a large new frame and a thick covering of bulletproof glass. "The glass changed the color of the painting," he said. He had to use filters to get the original color.

Mr. Descottes charges $130 an hour. L'OBSERVATOIRE INTERNA-TIONAL, 7 Weehawken Street, New York, NY 10014; (212) 255-4463.

PROPERLY USED, NEON CAN PROVIDE EFFECTIVE INDIRECT LIGHT, said Thomas P. Richmond, a lighting designer based in White Plains. For the solarium in a large house in New Jersey, he recently used two rows of neon in blue and orchid, hidden by a case at the top of a wall. "Neon is dimmable," he explained. "And you can bend the tubes to fit the architecture."

To light bookcases, he installs a long, one-inch-deep metal channel directly under the shelf to accommodate tiny lights. The metal can be painted or given a faux wood grain to blend with the shelf.

And unlike conventional bookcase lights, encased in plastic tubes, individual lights can be easily removed when they burn out.

Mr. Richmond charges $95 an hour. THOMAS P. RICHMOND, 79 Longview Avenue, White Plains, NY 10605; (914) 428-2511.

CHRISTINE SCIULLI (PRONOUNCED SHE-YU-LI), who has worked on exhibition lighting at the Solomon R. Guggenheim Museum, usually asks residential clients what effect they want and on what budget.

"Just as much can be accomplished with a hidden string of Christmas lights as with an expensive low-voltage xenon light strip," she said. Some rooms need little more than fine-tuning of existing lights. "There are several different colors of seemingly white fluorescent light," she said. "Some have better color-rendering properties than others."

She charges $50 an hour.  **CHRISTINE SCIULLI LIGHTING DESIGN;** (212) 420-0151.

RETAIL LIGHTING STORES OFTEN HAVE CONSULTANTS who visit residences and give advice. Cliff Starr, the lighting consultant at Lighting by Gregory, makes house calls with a suitcase full of bulbs, trying out different lighting combinations to determine what each room needs.

"Sometimes people are using the wrong bulbs, and all we need to do is increase the wattage," he said. At other times, he suggests new lights and fixtures. "But if the client is on a budget, we often work with existing lamps," he said.

A two-hour consultation costs about $250, depending on location. **LIGHTING BY GREGORY,** 158 Bowery (near Broome Street), New York, NY 10012; (212) 226-1276.

A GOOD WAY TO FIND A LIGHTING DESIGNER is through the International Association of Lighting Designers.  **INTERNATIONAL ASSOCIATION OF LIGHTING DESIGNERS,** 18 East 16th Street, New York, NY 10003; (212) 206-1281.

# LINENS (ANTIQUE)

*F*OR CENTURIES, WEALTHY EUROPEANS slept on white linen sheets, often embellished with embroidery and lace. And for the last decade or so, antique bed linens have gained a small but ardent following in the United States. "There are people who, once they have slept on linen sheets, will not sleep on anything else," said Muriel Clarke, who has sold antique linens for over 10 years.

Trouvaille Française, Mrs. Clarke's tiny shop, consists of two snug linen-filled rooms on the top floor of her East Side townhouse. Snowy Victorian pillow shams with lace ruffles cover a narrow bed. Embroidered French linen sheets are folded on a couch. And a wooden chest holds dozens of freshly laundered tea-table cloths.

Mrs. Clarke discovered antique linen's appeal during a vacation in

France, when she slept on old sheets. "Linen absorbs heat and moisture and is very cool for summer," Mrs. Clarke said. Her customers tend to use their antique sheets and tablecloths, instead of locking them away.

Bed and table linens over 100 years old can be used for years to come, provided they are in good condition and get good care. Linen sheets without lace inserts can be laundered carefully in the washing machine, Mrs. Clarke said. For professional laundering, she recommends the Park Avenue French Hand Laundry.

Antique linen's attractions include the embroidery and lace that can grace even modest pieces, and the cloth's soft, smooth feel. Repeated washings alter linen's texture, removing a micromolecular layer over each fiber.

Prices at Trouvaille Française range from $4 for a guest towel to $400 for a 19th-century woven cotton Marseilles-style bedspread. Late Victorian pillow shams start at $65 each, linen sheets at $135, and table runners range from $15 to $95. TROUVAILLE FRANCAISE; (212) 737-6015. ✉

"I LIKE FUSSINESS," declared Françoise Nunnallé, who has sold antique linens and decorative pillows for over 10 years. "People can buy new linens if they want something tailored."

The linen sheets, pillow shams, tablecloths and bedspreads Ms. Nunnallé carefully unfolds in her romantic lilac sitting room are all fussy, lavishly embellished with embroidery, cut work and hand-made lace.

An image from a famous painting by Brueghel is meticulously embroidered in the center of a soft round linen pillow sham. And a large round tablecloth, with a Belgian lace border, is decorated with embroidered roosters, sheep and chickens.

Even more modest pillow shams, which start at $250 a pair, are elaborate, with lace, ruffles and embroidery. "When people walk into a room, they want to see something fabulous, with lots of lace and cut work," she said.

Ms. Nunnallé, who receives customers in her midtown apartment, prides herself on linens in pristine condition. "Some people think because it's old it should have holes in it," she said. "But I wouldn't want holes in an old master painting." Buyers should crinkle antique linens in their hands to test fabric strength, she says. Ms. Nunnallé also carries hard-to-find linens, including large 19th-century lace tablecloths from Belgium and France, some 18 feet long, which can cost $3,500 and up. FRANCOISE NUNNALLE; (212) 246-4281.  ✉

"PEOPLE THINK OF ANTIQUE LINEN AS A SPECIAL OUTFIT FOR THE BED, like a holiday dress," said Jana Starr, co-owner of Jana Starr/Jean Hoffman Antiques, antique linen and clothing dealers in the East 80s for over 10 years.

Ms. Starr suggests customers combine antique pieces, such as pillow shams and bedspreads, with contemporary linens. "You add these for some oomph," she said, holding a $295 linen sheet embroidered with putti.

Antique linens can have a variety of unusual uses. Runners can serve as curtains. Lacy bedspreads make attractive canopies for beds. And linen sheets can become shower curtains when liners are added. Long linen sheets with embroidery at one end can also be made into duvet covers, Ms. Starr said.

Starr/Hoffman's tailored pillow shams start at $65 apiece; more ornate shams cost up to $175. Runners are priced from $75 to $150. And Marseilles bedspreads cost around $250.  JANA STARR/JEAN HOFFMAN ANTIQUES, 236 East 80th Street, New York, NY 10021; (212) 861-8256.  ✉

MOST FINE LINEN AFICIONADOS BALK at sending their favorite fabrics to the local dry cleaner for laundering. But specialty laundering services exist. The Laundery at Linens Limited is a mail order laundry in Milwaukee, Wisconsin, that washes, presses and repairs damask tablecloths, linen napkins, cutwork runners and other fine linens. All work is done by hand, from laundering (no dry-cleaning chemicals are used) to mending. Laundered linens, packed in acid-free tissue paper, are usually sent back in two weeks. It costs $62.50 to launder a three-yard damask tablecloth.  THE LAUNDERY AT LINENS LIMITED; (800) 637-6334 or (414) 223-1123.  ✉

# LINENS,
# CUSTOM DESIGNS AND MONOGRAMS

*F*INDING BED LINENS THAT FIT PERFECTLY can be a challenge.

Sometimes the problem is size: Standard commercial sheets are often too skimpy to cover the latest, extra-deep mattresses. But linens also should fit the look of the room, complementing the wallpaper, fabrics and furniture.

Léron Linens, a 78-year-old specialty linen shop, deals with both types of fitting problems. "I find what people like very much is white cotton with a hem stitch," said David Forster, whose family has run the business for years. Léron makes sheets for any size bed, from antique fourposters to yacht beds, and offers a variety of fabric colors and embellishments, including appliqué, embroidery and lace.

Working from a fabric or wallpaper swatch, the shop will adapt a corresponding design for top sheets, pillow shams, blanket covers, whatever. "We can also put the design on towels and bathrobes," said Carolina Donadio, a vice-president.

The best-selling sheets are 100 percent cotton. But Léron also embellishes no-iron poly-cotton sheets.

Cotton sheets with custom embroidery start at $250 for a queen-size top and bottom sheet and two standard pillowcases. A queen-size set of highly embellished Egyptian cotton sheets starts at around $600. LERON, 750 Madison Avenue (65th Street), New York, NY 10012; (212) 753-6700. ✉

BESIDES APPEARANCE, COMFORT AND PRACTICALITY are key considerations when choosing sheets. "Silk sheets launder beautifully," said Ric Barbatelli, president of E. Braun & Co., a 56-year-old specialty linen concern. "But if your three-year-old likes to throw herself on your bed with her orange juice, they're not the right thing."

E. Braun offers 100 percent cotton sheets with custom embellishments and sizing, in a variety of finishes including jacquard and sateen. Linen and silk sheets also are available. Cotton colors range from jet black to pale pink. "But 80 percent of our customers choose ecru or white," said Mr. Barbatelli.

Most Braun embellishments are adaptations of classic patterns—curlicues, stripes, scallops—updated in contemporary yarn colors. The company devises new designs, including monograms and crests, as well.

Embellished sheets and pillow shams for a queen-size bed start at $435 for poly-cotton and $705 for Egyptian cotton. E. BRAUN & CO., INC., 717 Madison Avenue (near 63rd Street), New York, NY 10021; (212) 838-0650. ✉

AFTER 74 YEARS ON MANHATTAN'S LOWER East Side, J. Schachter, a bed linen concern, moved to Brooklyn in 1993. But Schachter still offers custom and ready-made bed linens in poly-cotton, 100 pecent cotton, linen and even silk. "We've made sheets cut out at the corners for a mattress embedded in a fourposter bed," said Jay Rosenfeld, a co-owner for more than 15 years.

Though Schachter makes custom sheets for the new deep-mattress beds (about $50 for a 100 percent cotton queen flat sheet), Mr. Rosenfeld suggests customers first investigate Wamsutta's ready-made poly-cotton deep-fit sheets, which he sells for "under $30 a sheet," he said.

Schachter offers a range of embellishments in lace, appliqué and embroidery and can duplicate patterns customers bring in. Simple monograms start at around $25. J. SCHACHTER, 5 Cook Street (near Graham Avenue), Brooklyn, NY 11206; (718) 384-2732 or (800) 468-6233. ✉

## LINOLEUM, REDUX

IT'S HARD TO IMAGINE the first half of the 20th century without linoleum, the flooring of countless kitchens, bathrooms and recreation rooms. And it's almost equally hard to imagine linoleum as a hot floor covering for the '90s.

"It came in fifteen shades of brown," said Scott Hyman, an owner of Town & Country Flooring, recalling the classic linoleum of the Lucy and Ricky era.

But linoleum, *real* linoleum made with linseed oil, is back, turning up everywhere from restaurants to residences. The latest linoleums come in ultra-contemporary colors—raspberry reds, eggplant purples, mustard yellows—as well as the muted, marbleized grays, greens, aquas and browns of linoleums past.

Not surprisingly, a big part of linoleum's current charm is its retro quality, making it the flooring of choice when vintage houses and apartments are restored.

But interior designers are also treating linoleum with new respect. Hermes Mallea and Carey Maloney, partners in M (Group), a New York architectural firm, devised an elaborately patterned floor of hand-cut linoleum hexagons for an elegant dining room in the Kips Bay show house a couple of years back. Mallea and Maloney particularly like linoleum in entry ways, sitting rooms and other formal settings. "We use linoleum because it is great looking, practical, durable and unexpected," Mr. Maloney said. "The colors are great and can be very subtle, all shot with different colors."

Many homeowners also appreciate the natural ingredients that make up linoleum—wood flour, rosins, ground limestone, powdered cork, pigments, jute and linseed oil. The name, coined in 1863 by linoleum inventor Frederick Walton, comes from the Latin "linum" (flax) and "oleum" (oil) and refers to linseed oil, linoleum's vital component. Besides acting as a binder—and providing linoleum's distinctive scent—linseed oil oxydizes over time, creating a hard surface.

Linoleum's popularity faded fast in the 1960s, however, eclipsed by newfangled vinyls that were easier to install and maintain and were available in more colors. In 1974, Armstrong Floors shut down the last linoleum plant in the United States. (Flooring stores often incorrectly refer to sheet vinyl as linoleum.) Genuine linoleum is now imported from Europe, where it never fell from favor. And a handful of antique stores carry unused rolls of the real thing from the 1920s through the 1950s. Today's linoleums cost about the same as top-quality sheet vinyl.

Linoleum can be vacuumed, dusted with a dry mop and damp mopped with a neutral detergent. (Scrubbing and abrasive cleansers can pit linoleum.) New linoleum should also be sealed with at least four coats of an acrylic floor finish like Taski Ombra, which creates a matte finish. If a buildup occurs, it can be removed by a low pH stripping solution designed for linoleum.

For all its beauty, linoleum is still a challenge to install. Unlike vinyl tiles, which are often installed by do-it-yourselfers, linoleum usually requires a professional installation, particularly for custom-patterned floors. A reputable vendor can usually supply a skilled installer; companies that import linoleum, like Forbo (800) 842-7839 and Gerbert (717) 299-5035, can also provide names of installers and representatives in a customer's area.

Linoleum with inlaid patterns was popular in decades past, but today's linoleum is homogenous, with patterns extending all the way from surface to backing. B.I. Rosenhaus & Sons carries the latest lineoleums from both Forbo, which imports linoleum made by Krommenie in the Netherlands and Nairn in Scotland, and Gerbert, which imports linoleum made by DLW, or Deutsche Linoleum Werke, in Germany.

Each company offers a distinctive range of lineoleums in solid colors and patterns. Besides a line of pale, marbleized earth tones, Forbo's latest collection is patterned with intense, broad-brushed colors, inspired by the paintings of van Gogh, as a brochure puts it. DLW offers five lines, from pastels with subtle flecks of color to striated design known as jaspe patterns. The company also makes borders and inlay designs. Linoleum starts at $27 a square yard.   B.I. ROSENHAUS & SONS, 243 West 72nd Street, New York, NY 10023; (212) 873-1421.

ONE WAY TO GET THE LOOK of vintage linoleum is to buy the real thing. For over 20 years, Secondhand Rose, a SoHo antiques store, has stocked dozens of bolts of old linoleums, form Depression-era geometrics to cowboy patterns from the 1950s. Owner Suzanne Lipschutz's interest in vintage linoleum began when she needed to replace the linoleum in an old house she bought. She discovered a surprising amount of old, unused linoleum, still in rolls six- or nine-feet tall, much of it in old department and hardware store warehouses.

With over 300 rolls, Secondhand Rose's crowded basement offers a mini-history of linoleum—florals, marbles, wood grains, Jackson Pollock-like squiggles and children's pastels sprinkled with 1930s elephants and bunnies. There are linoleum rugs, too, which sport big border prints. "But you've got to want it," Ms. Lipschutz cautioned since linoleum that's rolled up for decades is hard to install. Old linoleum starts at $5 square foot.   SECONDHAND ROSE, 270 Lafayette Street at Prince Street, New York, NY 10012; (212) 431-7673.   ✉

BESIDES A FULL LINE OF LINOLEUMS from DLW, Town and Country Flooring, a large flooring distributor, offers custom-painted linoleum rugs. Designs can be hand painted or stenciled in whatever pattern the customer wants. The company can provide installations also, including inlays of elaborate designs cut with a laser. "We did clouds, rainbows and balloons for the floor of a children's hospital," said Mr. Hyman. TOWN AND COUNTRY FLOORING, 14 East 38th Street, New York, NY 10016; (212) 679-0312.   ✉

ARONSON'S HAS SOLD FORBO LINOLEUM for several years, but interest has grown particularly strong in the last year, says John E. Parry, a staff member. "Customers want bright colors," he added. But customers are also buying new lines of vinyls that offer the look of linoleum. Armstrong recently revived several old linoleum patterns for its stenciled vinyls, including Colonial Classic, a tiny brick pattern. Linoleum starts at $39.50 a square yard.   ARONSON'S, 135 West 17th Street, New York, NY 10011; (212) 243-4993.

ON THE WEST COAST, Linoleum City in Hollywood stocks Forbo linoleum as well as vinyl in late 19th-century Victorian patterns ($6.95 a square yard).   LINOLEUM CITY, 5657 Santa Monica Boulevard near Wilton Place, Hollywood, CA 90038; (213) 469-0063.   ✉

## LUGGAGE, REPAIRED

WITH STACKS OF SUITCASES BY VUITTON, Gucci and Mark Cross, Lou Jacob's upstairs workshop could be a luxury luggage store, if only the bags weren't so battered. Handles are missing, zippers are broken and leather corners are shredded. But by the time the bags leave the Fordham Repair Center, they should look almost like new, says Mr. Jacob, who started this luggage and handbag repair business in 1953. "There is no such thing as a lost cause," Mr. Jacob said, holding a tattered Gucci bag. "If you have the money, we have the talent."

Every job handled by Fordham is different, and Mr. Jacob needs to see the damaged object before estimating repair costs. Simple jobs, such as fixing a lock, start at about $10. But badly damaged bags, which can require a complete overhaul, may cost as much as $400.

"The buckles were strong and we kept the original vinyl," Mr. Jacob said, picking up large Vuitton suitcase. But nearly everything else on the bag is new, including the lining, the leather siding, the handle, the straps and the zipper. The idea is to closely match replacement parts and details with those originally on the bag.

Fordham Repair Center, located near the Empire State Building, repairs soft luggage, hard-frame luggage, handbags, attaché cases and even vintage alligator bags. When necessary, Fordham special orders parts, as with a piece of hardware that had to be custom-made for a Fendi suitcase. Fordham also cleans luggage, charging between $35 and $65.

To extend the life of a suitcase, Mr. Jacob suggests filling the bag to capacity with no empty spaces. "Accidents happen, but if treated properly, luggage can last for hundreds of thousands of miles." **FORDHAM REPAIR CENTER,** 10 East 33rd Street, New York, NY 10016; (212) 889-4553. ✉

"MANY TIMES CUSTOMERS THINK THEY NEED a new suitcase when in fact the old one can be repaired," said Thea Rosen, who, with her husband, Marvin, owns Superior Leather Restorers. Superior will install new zippers, tabs, buckles, feet and handles, replace worn leather corners and put in all-new leather sides. Mr. Rosen, who has repaired leather bags for over 30 years, will also add wheels and a pull strap for $50 to $75.

Superior, which sells new luggage and handbags, repairs handbags, attaché cases, leather garments, leather chair seats and leather sporting equipment, including baseball gloves. The shop also makes customized luggage covers in heavy duck for $200 and up.

"If somebody has been traveling with a bag for 15 years, I can't make it new," said Mrs. Rosen. "But I can make it better." Mrs. Rosen advises travelers to remove all shoulder straps and garment hooks from luggage checked onto a plane. "It's easy for them to get snapped off." **SUPERIOR LEATHER RESTORERS,** 133 Lexington Avenue (near 29th

Street), New York, NY 10016, (212) 889-7221; 138 West 72nd Street, New York, NY 10023, (212) 769-2099.  ✉

WHEN THE LATE JOHN R. GERARDO opened his luggage repair shop at the turn of the century, much of his business was repairing steamer trunks. Today his sons and grandsons run the family business out of the same shop in Manhattan's Garment District.

Most of their repair work is on suitcases, attaché cases and garment bags, but they still get the occasional trunk. "People buy Vuitton trunks at auction and want them refinished for coffee tables," said John Gerardo, Jr., who has worked at the shop for 25 years. "We clean out the inside, clean the brass hardware, repair the wood and shellac and varnish everything for a high-gloss finish."

Gerardo, which also sells new luggage and briefcases, will work on zippers, handles, locks, wheels and leather bindings. Cleanings start at $25. "We can get rid of some grease, but we can't do miracles," said Mr. Gerardo. The company also repairs molded suitcases, when possible. Cracks can usually be repaired with fiberglass filler as long as the two sides can still be joined.   JOHN R. GERARDO, INC., 30 West 31st Street, New York, NY 10001; (212) 695-6955.  ✉

## MAGIC SHOPS

W<small>ITH A GRACEFUL</small> <small>SWOOP</small> of his hands, Tony Spina makes balls float and eggs disappear and plucks playing cards out of thin air. None of this is surprising, since Mr. Spina, who owns Tannen's Magic Company, is a professional magician.

But with a little hocus pocus, and the proper equipment, most customers who visit his atmospheric upstairs shop achieve the same feats. "You'd be surprised how many magic enthusiasts are out there," Mr. Spina said.

For magic buffs, October 31 is like Christmas and New Year's rolled into one. Harry Houdini, the maestro of magicians, died that day in 1926 (admirers gather annually at his burial spot in Mechpalah Cemetery in Queens at 1:26 P.M.). And most magic shops celebrate Halloween with an array of new items. For the novice, a top-selling Tannen toy is Snake in the Basket ($45), a gimmick in which the snake selects a card.

Pros can try out One Night with You, a Polaroid camera effect for $25 that has the spectator pick a card and replace it in a deck. The "magician" next snaps a picture, and the instant photo shows the spectator standing next to an image of Elvis Presley, who holds the selected card.

Magic is as old as mankind, Mr. Spina said. "When they went into the pyramids, they found cups and balls, one of the tricks used today." Some in the trade even suspect Moses used a little abracadabra to turn his rod into a snake. "We sell canes like that," Mr. Spina said.

It isn't cricket to give away a magician's secrets. Still, Mr. Spina, Magician of the Year in 1974, admits there are 19 principles of magic and two distinct branches, divination and sleight of hand. He recommends the eight-volume *Tarbell Course in Magic* as a reference ($175). Volume 1 is a popular primer detailing 19 basic tricks ($17.50).

Tannen's, founded nearly 60 years ago by magician Louis Tannen, has a 350-page mail order catalog for $15, featuring 7,500 items, including ventriloquist dummies and card tricks. TANNEN'S MAGIC COMPANY, 24 West 25th Street, New York, NY 10010; (212) 929-4500 or (800) 564-6547. ✉

WITH A PAINTED CRATE Houdini once used and a collection of vintage crystal balls, the Flosso Hornmann Magic Co. looks like a museum of magic. The memorabilia collection reflects a parade of owners, starting from the Martinka Brothers in 1856 to Houdini himself. Its current owner, Jack Flosso, the son of a magician, has been a student of magic since childhood.

"Magic is a great hobby," Mr. Flosso said. "It helps a young child learn how to talk to other people. When he goes into business later and is called on to make a speech, he's lost his fear."

Mr. Flosso, who supplies beginners and professionals, has a range of items for kids. The Rope to Silk trick, $15, features a rope that bends, goes rigid and, with a sweep of the hand, turns to silk. And the pages of the *Magic Coloring Book*, $10, are blank, but figures appear when Mr. Flosso flips the pages. "When kids come up, the old ham in me makes me want to entertain them," he said. He also sells a $10 silk scarf that changes from red and blue to green and yellow. FLOSSO HORNMANN MAGIC COMPANY, 45 West 34th Street, New York, NY 10001; (212) 279-6079.

INTEREST IN MAGIC was low until Doug Henning brought his magic show to Broadway in the late 1970s, says magician Bob Riordan of Hank Lee's Magic Factory in Boston.

But it's been growing for the past decade, helped by David Copperfield's televised magic shows and an array of new gadgets and books. "Secrets are still not easy to come by, but this is 1990," Mr. Riordan said. "A lot more information is available."

Hank Lee's Magic Factory, which opened in 1975, specializes in magic books and the latest illusions. A wood-handled knife with a six-inch blade appears to penetrate the magician's arm and even draw blood, in the $95 Knife in the Arm effect. "It's kind of a neat geek trick," said Mr. Riordan. "In the end you emerge unharmed." The shop publishes a 500-page catalog ($8). **HANK LEE'S MAGIC FACTORY,** 127 South Street, Boston, MA 02111; (617) 482-8749. ✉

# MAPS, NEW AND ANTIQUE

IF MAP AFICIONADOS had an official holiday, it might be Columbus Day. Maps date back to the Babylonians. But without the explorations of Columbus and his followers in the 15th through 17th centuries, the so-called golden age of mapmaking, ushered in by such cartographers as Abraham Ortelius (1527–98) and Willem Blaeu (1571–1638), might never have dawned.

"The exploration of America coincided with the time that produced the most esthetically pleasing maps," said Robert T. Augustyn, a partner in Martayan Lan, antique map dealers.

Always a popular collectible, antique maps have grown increasingly popular since the Columbus quincentenary, which was commemorated in a slew of map shows in Manhattan.

Historic maps, which make handsome and interesting wall adornments, can be surprisingly plentiful and inexpensive. Nineteenth-century European maps start at around $20. Martayan Lan, in business since 1986, specializes in rarer, costlier maps, including decorative world maps from the 16th and 17th centuries, ranging from $500 to

$9,500. The shop also handles engraved hand-colored 17th-century maps for $300.

Demand is strongest for golden era world maps with decorative borders, in part because of their fine engraving. But dozens of types exist, including decorative star charts, town maps and navigational sea charts, called bluebacks because they are mounted on heavy blue paper. "Besides wear and tear at sea, sailors usually threw them away when they were superseded by something new," Mr. Augustyn said. "So not too many survived."

Columbus, of course, studied very different-looking maps before setting sail in 1492. Mr. Augustyn has a small geography book from 1482, similar to one Columbus consulted, with a trapezoidal map of a very small world. Africa extends to the bottom of the earth. And Sri Lanka is enormous. MARTAYAN LAN, 48 East 57th Street (near Park Avenue), New York, NY 10022; (212) 308-0018. ✉

RUTH SHEVIN, head of the Argosy Gallery map collection since 1952, isn't certain how many maps are in stock. But she knows there are thousands, from a colorful $4,000 world map by Gerhard Mercator (1512–94) to countless early maps of New York City, from about $50. (An 1857 map of lower Manhattan showing the original lots allocated by the Dutch East India Company costs about $55.)

Argosy's map room has shelves and shelves of maps, organized in folders. "If you ask for a map of Mississippi from 1830, I can hand it to you in as long as it takes me to get it," Miss Shevin said.

People collect antique maps for all sorts of reasons, she added. Maps can show where ancestors were born or places the collector has visited or lived. And some maps are simply pretty. "There's a lot of romance in maps," she said. Some people collect maps by certain cartographers for investment. And an 1835 map of Louisiana a lawyer purchased for $35 a few years back settled a multimillion-dollar boundary dispute. ARGOSY GALLERY, 116 East 59th Street, New York, NY 10022; (212) 753-4455. ✉

TODAY'S MAPS are more geographically accurate than anything Ortelius designed. Indeed, the *Hammond Atlas of the World* ($69.95) was put together entirely by computer using a digital database, explains

Leighton Warner, manager of Hagstrom Map and Travel Center, which stocks contemporary maps and atlases.

The rest of Hagstrom's new atlases are produced by hand, albeit using modern cartographic methods. They include *The New York Times Atlas* ($75), the *Great World Atlas* ($59.95) and the *Family World Atlas* ($34.95). The store also carries limited edition reproduction prints of vintage world, state and city maps, $20. HAGSTROM MAP AND TRAVEL CENTER, 57 West 43rd Street, New York, NY 10036; (212) 398-1222. ✉

# MARBLE, CLEANED AND REPAIRED

*T*HE 1980s were a decade of marble—marble floors, marble tabletops, marble everything. And the 1990s have become the decade of marble maintenance, restoration and repair.

Part of marble's appeal is that it is relatively easy to care for and repair. Owners can usually bleach out ink, grape juice and other stains using a stain removal kit. But scratches and ring marks, often left from alcoholic beverages, need to be sanded and repolished professionally.

"Marble can last a lifetime," said Sal Migliore, a partner in Empire State Marble Manufacturing, which has manufactured and repaired marble since 1932. It is usually cheaper to repair broken marble than to replace it with something new, he added.

When marble breaks, all chips should be saved. "We can put them back," Mr. Migliore said. The company, begun by Mr. Migliore's grandfather, can also repair chipped corners and, when necessary, make replacement corners, creating a template for a perfect match.

Marble reinforcements are another common repair. A client recently brought in a large marble tabletop that was bending due to a weak plywood reinforcement. So Empire State replaced the plywood with slate. "It weighs about 700 pounds now," Mr. Migliore said. Repairs start at around $60. EMPIRE STATE MARBLE MANUFACTURING CORP., 207 E. 110th Street, New York, NY 10029; (212) 534-7794.

JOHN GOULD, who owns J & C Marble Maintenance, makes house calls. For nearly 10 years he has polished marble floors, walls and, occasionally, smaller items, such as vanity tables. "People call me when things get spilled or when the floor doesn't shine," Mr. Gould said. "Even dull marble can be brought back to life, 100 percent." He uses a two-step process, drawing out dirt, then buffing and polishing the stone with large machines. The shine can remain a year or two, depending on foot traffic.

Mr. Gould charges about $2 a square foot, $350 minimum. J & C MARBLE MAINTENANCE, INC.; (201) 358-1431.

## MICROWAVE OVENS, REPAIRED

As RECENTLY AS THE MID-1970s, microwave ovens were a novelty. "Restaurants and rich people had them," said Andrew Heller, a partner in Micro-Ovens of New York, which has repaired microwave ovens since 1976.

These days, few homes are without a microwave oven. Some people even have two. "We recently repaired an upstairs kitchen microwave for a woman who used it just to heat food for her dog," Mr. Heller said.

The styles and varieties of microwave ovens have never been greater. Tabletop microwaves can weigh less than 40 pounds And they could become still lighter. "In the next two years, you'll probably see a portable microwave that runs on batteries," said Michael Liegner, a partner in Micro-Ovens.

A microwave oven can stop working for a variety of reasons. Fuses blow out. Switches get worn. "And people don't read the instruction books," said Mr. Heller. Owners should never use spritzers to clean the computerized switch panels. And users should always follow heating instructions, particularly for such items as microwave popcorn. "Sometimes people will leave popcorn in too long so all the kernels will pop," Mr. Heller said. "But when there's nothing left to cook, the oven gets destroyed."

Ovens that are not working properly can display a variety of symptoms. "People will call and say the oven is dead," Mr. Heller said. "But then there's all kinds of dead." The food may not heat, the light may not come on or the oven may not accept commands.

The first microwave ovens were made during World War II as an offshoot of radar. (Early microwave ovens manufactured by Raytheon were, in fact, called Radar Ranges.) Radar is a system for locating an object by means of ultra-high-frequency radio waves reflected from the object. The ovens work with magnetron tubes, which generate electromagnetic waves. The magnetron is constructed from powerful, rounded magnets and has an antenna to transmit microwaves.

By rapidly varying the magnetic field, the magnetron sends out microwaves that heat food by agitating water molecules. Plastic, wood and china, all invisible to microwaves, will normally not get hot from electromagnetic radiation. But metallic objects, which reflect energy, can set off sparks in the oven. "And if there's no water to absorb the energy," Mr. Liegner explained, "the energy reflects back into the machine and may damage the components."

Micro-Ovens, which also repairs air conditioners, is an authorized service center for 10 oven makers, including Amana, Panasonic, Sharp, Toshiba and Sunbeam. The company makes house calls in all boroughs of New York except Staten Island, northern New Jersey, southern Connecticut and Westchester and Rockland counties. The hourly rate is $46, plus $35 transportation for house calls. (To avoid the transportation cost, customers can bring ovens to the company's shop; repairs are done while the customer waits.) Minor jobs usually take about 30 minutes; major jobs run an hour to two hours. Parts are extra. MICRO-OVENS OF NEW YORK, 970 Woodmansten Place, Bronx, NY 10462; (718) 823-7101.

"A MICROWAVE OVEN is one of the safest appliances in the kitchen," said Albert Kain, president of Hearth Microwave Oven Service Corporation. A big concern of many oven owners is radiation leakage. But unless the oven door has been damaged or disturbed, leakage is seldom a problem, said Mr. Kain, who has repaired microwave ovens for over 25 years.

If an owner is concerned about leakage, most supermarkets sell inexpensive checking devices. But these are heat sensitive, and occasionally give inaccurate readings, Mr. Kain said.

Hearth Microwave is authorized to repair ovens by more than 10 manufacturers, including Litton, Goldstar, Sanyo, Emerson and Quasar. The company makes house calls in Brooklyn, Staten Island and New Jersey. House calls are $24.95 and up, depending on location, plus parts and labor. **HEARTH MICROWAVE OVEN SERVICE CORPORATION,** 108 Sheraden Avenue, Willowbrook, Staten Island, NY 10314; (718) 494-4444.

ONE REASON microwave ovens are so popular today is that they're affordable. In the 1960s, home microwaves cost around $3,000, according to Dan Lettiere, owner of A & D Microwave Ovens Service Corporation. A & D is an authorized service center for more than 10 different microwave makers, including Amana, Emerson, Panasonic, Samsung and Welbilt. (Authorized centers will honor warranties.) The company makes house calls in Queens, Nassau and Suffolk counties. House calls are $35, plus labor and parts. **A & D MICROWAVE OVENS SERVICE CORPORATION,** 90 Jericho Turnpike, Mineola, NY 11501; (516) 741-6521.

## MILK PAINT

*T*HE ANCIENT CAVE PAINTERS used a form of it. Samples of it were found in King Tut's tomb. And until World War II, many Americans still painted houses and furniture with it.

These days, however, milk paint, a durable, long-lasting paint made from milk protein, clay, earth pigments and lime, is almost a rarity. You won't find it at most hardware stores. And although it qualifies as a healthy paint, with no toxic ingredients or fumes, milk paint is still used mainly by decorators, furniture restorers and history buffs.

"Sherwin Williams isn't worried about me," said Charles E. Thibeau, owner and founder of the Old-Fashioned Milk Paint Company, in business for more than 20 years in Groton, Massachusetts.

Yet, while milk paint will never replace latex, some paint experts expect its appeal to grow in the 1990s, for environmental as well as esthetic reasons. "It's a really healthy, user-friendly material," said Matthew J. Mosca, a paint analyst in Baltimore, Maryland. Customers are ordering milk paint for kitchen cabinets and children's furniture, Mr. Thibeau added.

Milk paint's distinctive finish, which is flat and coarse, lends an authentic look to antique furniture, historic houses and stenciled floors. Mr. Thibeau's 16 muted colors—among them barn red, bayberry, mustard and pumpkin—are based on historical hues, made from earth pigments, such as ochre, umber and iron oxide. For pastels, he suggests adding white.

Properly adapted, milk paint works effectively with contemporary furniture and interiors, according to Mr. Mosca. "You can create a beautiful, translucent finish by waxing milk paint," he said. Linseed oil also adds a translucent quality. And straining will get rid of the particles that make milk paint feel rough.

Mr. Thibeau, a hobbyist furniture maker, began experimenting with old formulas in the early 1970s when he couldn't find milk paint in stores. "Certain types of furniture, like Windsor chairs and pencil post beds, were originally painted with milk paint," he explained.

It took him six months to devise a successful recipe based on powdered milk protein, known as casein. The milk protein makes pigments stick to a porous surface, such as wood. Lime is added so the concoction will mix with water. And since lime bleaches most pigments, stable earth colors are used.

Mr. Thibeau's paint is sold as a powder, sealed in foil-lined plastic pouches. You add water and stir. "It's like making chocolate milk," he said.

Once water is added, the paint must be used the same day since it starts to gel after a few hours. "It's a nuisance," Mr. Thibeau admitted. "But if it's not powdered, it's not milk paint."

Milk paint powder, available by mail order, costs $8.50 a pint, $14.95 a quart and $42.95 a gallon. It is also sold by distributors. The company will provide callers the name of the nearest distributor. **OLD-FASHIONED MILK PAINT COMPANY,** P.O. Box 222, Groton, MA 01450; (508) 448-6336.  ✉

FINE PAINTS of Europe doesn't sell milk paint, but the paint this seven-year-old company offers is unusual. Made in the Netherlands by Schreuder, a 300-year-old firm, the paint contains no extenders and features higher-quality resin, higher-quality solvents and a higher level of pigmentation than standard domestic paints, according to John Lahey, president of Fine Paints of Europe. The result is a long-lasting paint with an intense depth of color.

"Europeans do not move as often as Americans, so they make paints to last a long time," Mr. Lahey said. His paints are costly; a 2.5-liter container, which is less than three quarts, costs $68. "But that yields the same coverage as four to five quarts of most American paint," he said.

The line is available in 120 factory-mixed colors. The company also offers custom tinting. The paint is available by mail order and at some retailers.   FINE PAINTS OF EUROPE, P.O. Box 419, Woodstock, VT 05091; (800) 332-1556 or (802) 457-2468.   ✉

## MIRRORS
## (MADE TO LOOK OLD OR NEW)

MIRRORS, as Stanley Greenspan knows, can fool you. A new mirror can be made to look old, with silvery spots, dark webbing and a foggy reflection. And an old mirror can be cleaned up to look brand new.

Mr. Greenspan's company, Sundial Schwartz, is a hall of mirrors—etched mirrors, tinted mirrors, frosted mirrors and, occasionally, cracked mirrors. On a typical day, Mr. Greenspan's crew will work on all types of decorative reflectors, from old mirrors in need of rehabilitation to new mirrors to cover a ceiling or wall. Some mirrors will be re-silvered, a process in which a new reflective backing is applied. Others will have their edges beveled, a popular decorative touch.

While it's easy to take a mirror for granted, a mirror should complement its surroundings, be it a room or a frame. Spotting, which occurs when the mirror's reflective silver oxidizes, can look horrid on a modern mirror. But a too-perfect mirror in an antique frame can be equally jarring.

A new mirror can be made to look old in about half the time it takes for an old mirror to look new. All mirrors start out looking like a clear pane of glass, Mr. Greenspan explained. The glass is washed with soap, water and polishing powder, then rinsed in deionized water, which prevents discoloration. A tin solution is applied and rinsed off one side of the glass. This leaves a film so the silver solution, a blend of silver and chemicals that creates a reflection, will stick.

To make the mirror look like something Miss Havisham would have owned, a mild acidic solution is brushed on the mirror's back, creating the spots and blemishes of age. A sealing coat of lacquer is applied, followed by mirror-backing paint to prevent oxidation. "We can make it very heavily distressed or just mildly," Mr. Greenspan said.

Old mirrors can be made new by completely stripping the glass of all silver, paint and, in the case of very old mirrors, mercury. When the glass is once again clear, the silvering, and if necessary, antiquing can begin.

The only time a rehabilitated mirror won't look new is if the glass is scratched, clouded or damaged. Resilvering is most cost effective if a mirror is patterned, beveled or etched.

Besides mirrors, other decorative objects, such as chandeliers, bowls and lanterns, can be resilvered. Frosted glass can be resilvered as well, creating a stainless steel effect. "It's popular for shower doors," Mr. Greenspan said.

Resilvering starts at $11 a square foot, minimum five square feet. Antiquing, with glass supplied by Sundial Schwartz, costs $16 a square foot. Pickup and delivery is available in New York City. **SUNDIAL SCHWARTZ,** 159 East 118th Street, New York, NY 10035; (212) 289-4969 or (800) 876-4776. ✉

CUSTOMIZED MIRROR GLASS can get rather elaborate, according to Marcy Karpel, who, with her husband Jeffry, has owned Crosstown Custom Shade and Glass for nearly 10 years. Gold-veined mirrors were very popular a few years back, particularly in coffee shops. The company also makes customized mirrors with carved-out backs filled in gold.

In addition to resilvering old mirrors, Crosstown can distress new mirrors. Their process uses mercury harvested from old mirrors, then shaken onto the back of the new glass, "like from a flour sifter," Mr.

Karpel said. (Mercury is no longer used in new mirrors.) The mercury, mixed with new silver, causes spots, which spread as the mirror ages. And the mirror-backed paint seals in the mercury. Resilvering costs $20 a square foot; antiquing is $25 a square foot. **CROSSTOWN CUSTOM SHADE AND GLASS,** 200 West 86th Street, New York, NY 10024; (212) 787-8040. ✉

DAN TILSTONE, who owns the Antique Restoration Company in New-town, Pennsylvania, does all types of furniture restoration, from brass polishing and caning to mirror resilvering, antiquing and beveling. To-day's beveled mirrors usually look perfect. And unlike distressed mir-rors, which can look genuinely old, there's not a lot a mirror maker can do to make beveling look old.

"In the old days, beveling was done with a cast-iron wheel that re-volved slowly and horizontally," Mr. Tilstone said. "You'd see tiny chops in the bevel where the grinder varied the pressure."

But today's beveling machines are very precise, designed to neither wobble nor deviate.

Mr. Tilstone charges $22 a square foot for flat or beveled glass, $31 a square foot for etched glass. Minimum order $42. **THE ANTIQUE RESTORATION COMPANY,** 440 East Centre Avenue, Newtown, PA 18940; (215) 968-2343. ✉

ALFRED COHN, a spry octogenarian, sold his 70-plus-year-old mirror re-silvering company, New England Glass and Mirror in Norwich, Con-necticut, back in 1987. But he still reports for work six days a week as a consultant, making new mirrors by hand, restoring older mirrors and doing the elaborate etching or engraving that has earned him a special place in the world of custom mirrors.

Though Mr. Cohn works on simple items like small beveled mir-rors, he also tackles such elaborate jobs as antique mirrors with en-graved and beveled frames. These mirrors can have as many as a dozen parts. He often creates new parts to look like those too damaged to re-store.

From his Connecticut headquarters, Mr. Cohn accepts mail orders from all over the world. "I'll do it as long as I feel well enough," he said.

His resilvering method—"It's a lost art," he observed—is described in detail on a how-to video he sells for $20 to do-it-yourself enthusiasts. Taking a piece of ordinary glass, Mr. Cohn wipes it down with pumice powder and water, rinses it with tap water, sprays it with distilled water, then wipes it again with a combination of water and sensitizer. Next, he resprays it with distilled water, then sprays on a combination of silver and reducer. After drying, he brushes copper on the back to protect it from air damage. Resilvering costs $20 a square foot.   NEW ENGLAND GLASS AND MIRROR, 385 Central Avenue, Norwich, CT 06360; (203) 887-1649.   ⊠

# MURPHY BEDS

"IT'S NOT THE USUAL PULL-OUT COUCH," said Clark Murphy, president of the Murphy Bed Company. Mr. Murphy was, of course, discussing the Murphy bed, the steel-frame, pull-down wall bed invented in 1900 by his grandfather, William L. Murphy, and still manufactured, in an updated version, by the family company.

For years, Murphy beds were the basis of countless jokes in films by Charlie Chaplin and Buster Keaton. But the modern Murphy bed is a sedate piece of furniture that can be installed in an existing closet or a specially built cabinet with folding doors.

It has also come back into fashion, more or less, thanks to its space-saving qualities. Current customers include people with studio apartments, fire stations, ocean liners and retirement communities. "It turns a den into a guest room," said sales director Gene Kolakowski.

The company sells simple wood laminate cabinets for its beds, but specializes in folding steel frames. Murphy's latest steel frame, devised in 1964, has a spring-operated mechanism that bolts to the floor. The mattress foundation, used in lieu of a box spring, is of steel ribbon strips or a foam-covered wood frame. Beds are available for every current mattress size.

The company installs beds in the tristate area and can provide names of distributors elsewhere. Steel frames and foundations cost $600 to $745 for the Styleline, an every night bed, and $545 to $670 for the Econo-Recess, a guest bed. Mattresses and cabinets are additional.

MURPHY BED COMPANY, INC., 42 Central Avenue, Farmingdale, NY 11735; (800) 845-2337 or (516) 420-4330.

NOAH BLOCK, an owner of The Building Block cabinetmakers, calls the Sico wall bed the Mercedes of wall beds. "And it's at Mercedes prices," he added. The Sico, made in Minneapolis, is a panel bed that pulls down directly from the wall. When it is up, the underside, available in a variety of colors and woods, is flush with the wall. No doors are needed to cover it.

The Sico, anchored to the floor, pulls down with a compressed spring device. It uses both a conventional box spring and a mattress, sold separately. The bed frame and simple surrounding cabinets start at $3,000, including delivery, installation and tax. THE BUILDING BLOCK, 314 Eleventh Avenue (near 30th Street), New York, NY 10001; (212) 714-9333.

MOST PEOPLE WHO WANT A WALL BED are in a tight spot, both for space and for money, says Robert Meyers, owner of the Murphy Bed Center of New York. So Mr. Meyers, whose showroom opened in 1989, specializes in package deals.

Steel mechanisms, made by American Wall Bed in Lancaster, Ohio, can be purchased alone—from $495 for a twin, $550 for a full and $595 for a queen-size bed. But Mr. Meyers also sells accompanying cabinets. A folding-door cabinet, a frame and a mattress for a double bed start at $1,300. THE MURPHY BED CENTER OF NEW YORK, INC., 110 West 17th Street (near Sixth Avenue), New York, NY 10011; (212) 645-7079.

## MUSIC STANDS

ANTIQUE MUSIC STANDS can be difficult to find. But Gene Bruck and Marianne Wurlitzer, who deal in rare musical instruments, always have several models in their showroom.

Customers should be certain that what they get is a music stand, says Ms. Wurlitzer. Unlike a dictionary stand, a music stand is adjustable and should have a large lip to hold sheet music.

Many of Wurlitzer-Bruck's 18th- and 19th-century music stands hail from Europe, including several two-sided stands popular with quartets. The dealers also carry American stands. Currently in stock is an elaborate brass turn-of-the-century model with a light, balanced on three legs formed from naturally curving bulls' horns.

Wurlitzer-Bruck also has a range of tabletop music racks and folding stands, including a brass 19th-century model with candleholders. Music stands start at $750, music racks at $100. WURLITZER-BRUCK; (212) 787-6431.

THE MUSIC STANDS sold at Ideal Music are simpler, newer—and cheaper. In stock are black metal Hamilton stands and collapsible metal stands, which fold to fit into a briefcase.

The shop also sells Kliplites, bright lights encased in black metal that can clip onto a music stand. IDEAL MUSIC, 53 West 23rd Street, New York, NY 10011; (212) 675-5050.

## NECKTIES,
## CLEANED, ALTERED AND REPAIRED

WHEN NECKTIES GET WIDER, Andy Tarshis couldn't be happier. Mr. Tarshis's company, Tiecrafters, more than 40 years old, cleans and alters neckwear.

Not every tie has sufficient fabric to be widened. For those that do, Tiecrafters steams, reshapes and resews ties by hand. And when ties get narrow, the company slims down wide neckwear. "New ties are so expensive, it's cheaper to clean or alter your old favorites," said Mr. Tarshis, Tiecrafters' president for more than 10 years.

Frayed edges, usually at the knot or bottom triangle, can also be treated, either by folding under the fabric or by shortening the tie.

Most stains, including stubborn oils and inks, can be removed as well. The secret is to have the tie cleaned shortly after the spill occurs. Lots of customers are bringing in retro ties from the 1940s and '50s these days, Mr. Tarshis said. "But if the tie got dirty in 1945, it's going to be very hard to clean."

A few tie care tips: Always take the knot out of ties. Never pull loose threads. And keep cologne away from ties; it can damage color.

In addition, Tiecrafters makes customized neckties and bowties. Cleaning costs $5.75 a tie. Alterations are $8.50 a tie. And cleaning and alterations cost $11.50 a tie. Minimum four ties for all services. Customized ties start at $30 using client's fabric, $40 with Tiecrafter fabric. TIECRAFTERS, 252 West 29th Street, New York, NY 10001; (212) 629-5800.  ✉

THE TIE ORCHARD BEGAN altering ties in the 1960s, when narrow ties came in style. And the 40-year-old family-run business, which makes and sells ties, shirts and suspenders, has done neckwear alterations ever since.

The Tie Orchard does not accept mail orders. "The customer should come in so we can look and see if the work can be done," said Malie Berg, an owner. Alterations from $7.50.

The Tie Orchard also makes customized neckties and bowties. Necktie and handkerchief sets start at $20 with customer fabric. THE TIE ORCHARD, 41 Orchard Street (near Grand Street), New York, NY 10002; (212) 925-6285.

THE WORST THING A MAN CAN DO to a favorite necktie is tie a tight knot, says Ben Catanese, who owns Peerless Cleaners and has cleaned neckties for over 40 years. Tie fabric is cut on an angle, and once threads are pulled, ties are difficult to straighten.

Mr. Catanese also warns against ironing neckties. Instead, he places ties on a form, then shapes them using steam. Peerless charges $3.75 to clean and shape a tie. PEERLESS CLEANERS, 1660 First Avenue (near 86th Street), New York, NY 10028; (212) 722-3894.

# NEEDLEPOINT

IN RECENT YEARS, interest in needlepoint has grown. And with it, demand has increased for people who will put the finishing touches on completed canvases, making them into pillows, eyeglass cases, footstools, wall hangings, rugs, even backgammon boards.

Joan's Needlecraft Studio, near Gramercy Park, has finished needlework canvases since it opened more than 15 years ago. The shop makes needlepoint into a wide range of items, including handbags and tennis racket covers. But pillows are the most popular item, said owner Joan Linder. "People see them in all the decorator magazines."

Finishing a pillow entails several steps, including cleaning, if necessary, and blocking, which shapes the canvas. Blocking is important as the canvas's shape can become distorted as the stitcher works on it.

Joan's Needlecraft offers several styles of pillows. To make a knife-edge pillow, the needlepoint front and cloth back are sewn together, with a border of piping. A box-edge pillow has an extra piece of fabric, at least an inch wide, inserted between the front and back, making the pillow look like a box. A border of ruffles or gathers can also be added to knife-edge pillows.

Mrs. Linder's shop makes pillows in a variety of colors and three types of cloth. Velvet is usually preferred for pillows with floral patterns, corduroy for pillows with geometric and bargello patterns and moiré for dressier pillows, Mrs. Linder said. Pillows are usually stuffed with a polyester filling, though down is available at additional cost.

Joan's Needlecraft charges $44 for a knife-edge pillow, $49 for a box-edge pillow, and $54 for round pillows with a box edge, including materials. Prices are higher for pillows 18 inches and larger. JOAN'S NEEDLECRAFT STUDIO, 240 East 29th Street, New York, NY 10016; (212) 532-7129.

NEEDLEPOINT PILLOWS are getting larger and larger, according to Wallis Mayers, whose Upper East Side needlework shop has finished pillows for over 16 years. "The biggest-selling pillows are now 17 or 18 inches square," she said. Pillows in pastel colors for baby rooms are popular as well. And labor-intensive needlepoint rugs, usually three feet by five feet, are also newly popular with stitchers. Rugs are finished with a linen backing.

Ever since it opened Mrs. Mayers's shop has finished and cleaned needlepoint. Many of the shop's needlepoint pillows are elaborate, with tassels, trimming and different colors of piping. Pillows, stuffed with a dacron filler or, at additional cost, down, are usually made in velvet. Moiré is available at extra cost. The shop charges $60.50 to finish a knife-edge pillow and $70.25 for a box-edge pillow, both up to ten inches. Larger pillows are more costly. The shop also sells hand-painted needlepoint canvas and will customize canvas designs. WAL-LIS MAYERS NEEDLEWORK INC., 30 East 68th Street, New York, NY 10021; (212) 861-5318.

THE BEST REPAIRS to needlepoint and embroidery are almost invisible. Unfortunately, poor repairs can inflict nearly as much damage as water stains or time. Sarah Lowengard, a textile conservator for 15 years, will do restoration and conservation work on all types of needlework, old and new.

But much of her time is spent undoing the damage unwittingly inflicted on old needlepoint by well-meaning amateurs. This can mean remounting a textile for display using acid-free backing materials to prevent further deterioration or removing earlier repairs done improperly or in the wrong colors.

Ms. Lowengard, who has done work for the Museum of Natural History, will restore needlepoint or embroidery using the same stitches and colors, replace sections of broken canvas and repair stitches that have come loose. If a piece has faded, she can overdye a lighter color to achieve a close color match.

Though Ms. Lowengard will repair almost any type of needlework, she "draws the line at large things on plastic canvas with acrylics," she said. Her prices start at $50 an hour. SARAH LOWENGARD; (212) 860-2386.

MOST NEEDLEPOINT CANVASES are either printed or drawn with indelible magic marker these days. But Holly Clark makes canvases with hand-painted designs. Her custom canvases are in whatever design or color the customer wants. But she specializes in monograms. "They're a symbol of an age gone by," she said. Many of her monograms are classics, taken from old silver engravings. Ms. Clark's custom canvases start at $250. HOLLY CLARK; (212) 988-9550.

## NEON,
## CUSTOM-MADE AND REPAIRED

JEFF FRIEDMAN, a partner in Let There Be Neon/Neon City, stood beside a wall covered with clocks from the 1930s and '40s. Each was illuminated by bold neon bands. "A lot of people don't realize how easily neon can be repaired," Mr. Friedman said. "You don't have to throw the whole thing out just because there's a crack."

Let There Be Neon has designed, manufactured and repaired all types of neon objects since 1972, including signs, artworks, lamps, architectural embellishments, sculptures and, of course, clocks. Neon City, owned by Mr. Friedman's partner, Rudi Stern, has done similar work since 1981. The two companies merged recently and currently occupy a big, brick-walled workshop lit by dozens of old and new neon signs.

Neon is fashioned from glass vacuum tubes, which are shaped when heated and fitted with an electrode at each end. When filled with neon or argon gas, the tubes glow with color. "Neon is like drawing with light," Mr. Friedman said.

The process, invented in 1911 as a light source by Georges Claude, a Frenchman, was largely ignored until the late 1920s, when Americans began using it for commercial signs. Its popularity grew with the repeal of Prohibition in 1932, which created a sudden demand for jazzy signs advertising beer. Almost obsolete by the 1960s, neon lighting revived with renewed interest in 1930s design and with new uses devised for it by artists, craft workers and architects.

Repairs at Let There Be Neon start at $85, commmissions at $275. The company's custom neon clocks, priced from $550, are a specialty and can be seen at most branches of the Hard Rock Café. The concern also rents vintage neon signs. **LET THERE BE NEON/NEON CITY,** 38 White Street (near Church Street), New York, NY 10013; (212) 226-4883. ⊠

RITA RAMSOOK, who owns Neptune Neon, thinks neon's chief use will eventually be in architecture instead of on beer signs. In 1991, Ms. Ramsook became the new owner of Say It in Neon, a long-time neon business, when the former owner, Pacifico Palumbo, stepped down. Her renamed store offers a blend of architectural and decorative neon.

On the architectural side are her Neon Modular Systems, gas-filled acrylic tubes, which do not break as readily as glass. The modular neon-filled tubes, which can be used as sculpture or mounted on a wall for color accents or light, come in 26 colors, including solid colors and laser colors. The latter project a narrow band of color in the tube's center, like a laser, for a futuristic effect.

The tubes were used by video artist Nam June Paik in a new sculpture for the Dade County Airport in Miami. A set of four acrylic neon-filled tubes with transformer starts at $350. The tabletop sculptures fit interchangably into a black base and start at $225.

For something more whimsical, Ms. Ramsook also sells conventional neon signs and sculptures. "A little bit of neon is often all you want in a room," she said. Among her tabletop neon sculptures are renderings of palm trees, flamingos, parrots and big red hearts, which start at $225. Commissions start at around $200, repairs at $75.   NEPTUNE NEON, 288 Third Avenue, Brooklyn, NY 11215; (718) 625-1481.   ✉

## ORGANIZERS

$F$OR THOSE WHO ATTEMPT NEW YEAR'S RESOLUTIONS, organize the house, rearrange the home office and clean out the garage are right up there with lose ten pounds.

Whether such resolutions are observed, of course, is another matter. "They're usually too big or too vague," declared Stephanie Winston, a professional organizer and author of *Stephanie Winston's Best Organizing Tips* (Fireside/Simon & Schuster). Ms. Winston's commonsense advice is to keep resolutions precise, definitive and realistic: plan to clean up, say, the hall closet instead of the entire house.

"Once you get over the fear of it, organizing is energizing, liberating and really fun," she said. "If I feel restless or out of sorts, I organize the cabinets or drawers."

But not everyone does, which is why the ranks of professional organizers—people who do everything from bringing order to offices and filing systems to unpacking moving boxes—is growing.

When Ms. Winston, a former book editor, launched her career as an organizer in the mid-1970s, she was a pioneer. These days, the National Association of Professional Organizers, begun in 1985, lists over 700 members in 44 states. It also supplies anyone looking for an organizer with names and specialties of nearby members. The group can be reached at 15 North Mill Street, Nyack, NY 10962-3015; (914) 353-9270.

Ms. Winston, whose company is the Organizing Principle, credits the advent of the personal computer with the boomlet in her profession. Besides making communications quicker and more direct, computers increased the amount of information people receive. "People feel overwhelmed in a way they didn't before," she said.

Much of the information organizers supply is simply common sense. When cleaning a closet, for example, Ms. Winston suggests asking three questions before tossing out an item. Was it used in the last year? Does it have special meaning? Might it come in handy some day?

But a good organizer can also teach basic skills for managing time, space and paperwork. "What an organizer does is help analyze and break down that diffused feeling into steps and problems," said Ms. Winston, who has organized everything from kitchens and home paperwork to corporate offices. She charges from $100 an hour.   THE ORGANIZING PRINCIPLE; (212) 533-8860.

CLIENTS USUALLY CALL an organizer when they feel overwhelmed by some aspect of their life. "Organizing isn't rocket science, but often people don't know where to start," said Celia Wakefield of Wakefield & Company, an organizer since 1990. Ms. Wakefield typically spends time creating a physical setup—planners, files, whatever. "But a lot of my work is listening, talking and coming up with a consensus of what will suit the client," she said. "Some people want an empty desk, while others don't."

Ms. Wakefield, who specializes in time and money management, considers three organizational tools vital—a large planner, which can also hold credit cards and business cards; a good, up-to-date rolodex; and what she calls a tickler file, an open-sided accordion file for date-related material, from bills to theater tickets. She charges from $65 an hour.   WAKEFIELD & COMPANY; (914) 238-9257.

ORGANIZING HOME OFFICES is the specialty of Marcia Sloman of Under Control. In business three years, Ms. Sloman likes to deal with all aspects of an office, starting with physical layout, which she plots on a computer. Besides setting up personalized filing systems, she also outfits offices with what she calls a grab and go area—an easy-to-find place for storing business cards, marketing materials and other data her clients use frequently in meetings. Ms. Sloman charges from $50 an hour.  **UNDER CONTROL;** (914) 923-1057.

AN ORGANIZER SINCE 1988, Audrey Lavine of Life Support Systems says she has organized just about everything, from home offices for small businesses to a wedding in New York for an out-of-town client. "I found everything from someone to make the dress to the electrical equipment for the sound and lights," she said.

Much of her work entails dealing with clutter of the severest sort. Indeed, after rooting through one client's room for two days, she unearthed an antique spinet piano under mountains of books. "People hold on to things for sentimental reasons, often excessively," she said. Ms. Lavine charges from $60 an hour, four-hour minimum.  **LIFE SUPPORT SYSTEMS;** (212) 362-2399.

RONNI EISENBERG, an organizer for over 15 years, is adamant about teaching good organizational skills to children, something she has done with her own. Instead of saying, "Clean your room," she suggests specifying the task: "Please put your laundry in the hamper and make your bed." She also advises pointing out why a task should be accomplished. "Say, 'If we put your action figures away, you'll know where to find them tomorrow,'" she said.

The author of four books on organizing, including the new *Organize Your Office!* (Hyperion; $7.95), Ms. Eisenberg is a generalist, willing to organize anything from kitchens and closets to corporate offices. She charges $1,500 a day, from eight to ten hours.  **RONNI EISENBERG & ASSOCIATES;** (203) 227-1222.

A FORMER ACTRESS, Carol Crespo self-published an organizing workbook for actors, called *Taking Care of Business,* a few years back. These days she still does theater work occasionally (she devised rehearsal schedules and sifted through paperwork for a small New York City theater company recently). But most of her organizing concerns paperwork and time management for individuals and small businesses.

For clearing up clutter, she advocates assigning papers to piles initialed CRAFT—chuck, read, assign, file and take action. But when necessary, she uses a broom. "One client had a home office literally threaded with cobwebs," she said. Ms. Crespo charges $35 an hour. CAROL CRESPO; (212) 533-3707.

LINDA SAMUELS OF OH, SO ORGANIZED, in business for two years, splits her organizational time between offices and residences. Though she will organize entire houses, she often does just one room. A pregnant mother recently hired her to organize one room for her two-year-old. "The mother wanted all the toys and drawers organized for the older child before the new baby arrived," she said. Ms. Samuels charges from $50 an hour.   OH, SO ORGANIZED; (914) 271-5673.

AFTER 18 YEARS IN BANKING, Claudette Paäge of Paäge et Cie became an organizer last year. And instead of closets and schedules, she organizes financial matters, dealing with clients who need someone to pay bills, balance checkbooks and find information on matters like Individual Retirement Accounts and health insurance. "Some people just forget to pay their bills, while others find it tedious or time consuming," said Ms. Paäge, who charges $50 an hour.   PAAGE ET CIE; (914) 725-0343.

## OUTDOOR EQUIPMENT AND CLOTHING, CLEANED AND REPAIRED

COMMUNING WITH NATURE ON A TRAIL or in the woods may be great for the soul, but it's hard on clothing and equipment. Tents rip, zippers break, and after a few nights by a roaring campfire, a sleeping bag needs a good cleaning.

Most equipment manufacturers will repair their own tents, packs and sleeping bags, a process that can take weeks. A quicker alternative is to deal directly with a company that restores outdoor gear.

Leon Greenman, owner of Down East Service Center in SoHo, repaired outdoor equipment when he owned a camping goods store in Manhattan in the 1960s. He closed his doors in 1973 but stuck with the fix-it business.

These days his compact shop, with its extensive library of trail guides, fixes everything from hiking boot soles and mosquito netting to torn floors in tents. He alters nylon jackets, patches sleeping bags, replaces worn Velcro and repairs tears in climbing pants. He also restores fireman's coats, frequently attaching psychedelic yellow "reflexite" stripes. (Laminated reflecting tape, sewn on backpacks and jackets, is popular with cyclists and runners, as well.)

In addition, the company produces custom backpacks, overnight bags and instrument cases in heavy Cordura nylon, the staple fabric of soft luggage.

Mr. Greenman's most frequent repair is prosaic. "Zippers," he explained, "are not made of very hard metal. If they're caught in fabric, they can distort and open."

Rather than discard the entire zipper, he often replaces the metal slider, the part that goes up and down ($7.50 to $11.50). In contrast, it costs between $48.50 and $56.50 to replace a complete sleeping bag zipper.

Mr. Greenman stocks bins of buckles, loops, slips and clasps for backpacks, tents and overnight bags. His inventory consists mostly of heavy-duty plastic, though he prefers metal hardware. "It rusts, and the ends can separate unless they're welded together," he said. "But the plastic can break." **DOWN EAST SERVICE CENTER,** 50 Spring Street (near Lafayette Street), New York, NY 10012; (212) 925-2632. ✉

AS THE MOTHER OF A BOY SCOUT AND A GIRL SCOUT, Bea Maurer learned to repair camping equipment. "I was in charge of equipment for 37 troops," she explained. "It was cheaper to do the repairs myself."

These days the Boy Scout, all grown up, is part of Ms. Maurer's 40-person company, Bea Maurer, Inc., which repairs all types of outdoor equipment, from tents, trampolines and parachutes to golf bags and horse blankets. "The horses pull off the straps," Ms. Maurer explained.

The 15-year-old company, based in Chantilly, Virginia, near Washington, D.C., also manufactures products in canvas and Cordura, including computer covers, overnight bags and custom covers for Cessna airplanes.

Though most people are intimidated by the notion of repairing a sleeping bag or tent, many fixes can be stitched at home. "There's no reason you can't repair a nylon backpacking tent yourself on a sewing machine," Ms. Maurer said. Canvas tents require heavier machinery.

Besides sewing zippers on sleeping bags and tents, Ms. Maurer sells zippers to do-it-yourselfers. "It's hard to find this type of zipper at a fabric store," she said.

Bea Maurer, Inc., charges $30 an hour. A new zipper installed in a five-foot backpack tent costs around $30. **BEA MAURER, INC.,** 113 Executive Drive, Sterling, VA 20166; (703) 709-8088.  ✉

WHILE IT'S POSSIBLE TO LAUNDER down-filled items yourself in a large washer and dryer, it can be easier to take them to a commercial dry cleaner, preferably one accustomed to dealing with down. "Dry cleaners have bigger machines," said Charles Reiner, who owns Perry Process Cleaners. "Home drying doesn't always work as well, particularly for large items like sleeping bags," he added. For home drying, Mr. Reiner suggested adding a clean sneaker or tennis ball to help fluff the item.

Dry cleaning is usually preferable to washing, he added. "Water lowers the loft of down, but dry-cleaning solvents have no water." But since solvents disintegrate certain shell fabrics, like Gore-Tex, washing is often required, which Mr. Reiner's shop will do.

Mr. Reiner charges around $35 to clean a down-filled sleeping bag. **PERRY PROCESS CLEANERS,** 1315 Third Avenue (near East 75th Street), New York, NY 10021; (212) 628-8300.

## PAINT JOBS
## FOR APPLIANCES

APPLIANCES ARE OFTEN THE FIRST THING you notice in a kitchen, particularly if they're faded, scratched or painted a color that was in style 20 years ago. But like walls and furniture, appliances can be painted and rehabilitated to look new.

"A lot of people aren't aware that this process can be done," said James White, whose year-old company, Custom Spraying and Reglazing Co., refinishes kitchen appliances as well as countertops, metal cabinets and bathroom porcelain. "It's paint on metal, so it's the same process as refinishing a car. If it's done right," he added, "it can look beautiful."

People have kitchen appliances repainted for a variety of reasons. It's cheaper to paint a discolored refrigerator or dishwasher than replace it if it still works. "Refrigerators built years ago are better built and keep food cold longer than a lot of the new ones," Mr. White said. Appliances often need refinishing after being cleaned with a harsh product. Appliances that have been in fires can also benefit from a paint job.

Like Mr. White, most people who paint kitchen appliances also refinish bathtubs, tiles and sinks. But not all porcelain refinishers are willing to work on kitchen appliances. It can take nearly as long to prepare a refrigerator for spraying as a bathtub. But since appliances are smaller and cheaper to replace than bathtubs, the refinishing charge is less.

Preparation, of both appliance and room, is the most important part of the job, according to Mr. White, who is now 30 and has refinished porcelain and appliances since he was a teenager. Before spraying, the appliance must be sanded, tacked to remove surface lint and primed. Once this dries, the entire process is repeated. Nearby countertops, floors and surrounding entrances must be sealed off as well. And Mr. White puts fans in the windows to draw out paint fumes.

The actual spraying consists of seven to eight coats of acrylic enamel. Mr. White, who wears a mask when working, uses a hot-air turbine spray unit to cut down fumes and mess. He then applies a hardener, which keeps the finish from chipping and gives the appliance a high-gloss shine.

Appliances can be refinished in a variety of colors. Unusual hues can be specially mixed, as well. "I did a refrigerator in a raspberry puree color for a woman who had a raspberry puree–colored kitchen," Mr. White said.

Mr. White, a former competitive body builder who was Mr. New York City in 1988, charges from $145 to refinish a refrigerator in Staten Island and Brooklyn, from $170 in New Jersey, Queens and Long Island and from $195 in Manhattan.   **CUSTOM SPRAYING AND REGLAZING COMPANY,** 52 Rector Street, Staten Island, NY 10310; (718) 494-3751. ✉

MOST PEOPLE WANT KITCHEN APPLIANCES sprayed either white or almond, according to Diana Prieto, a partner in Authentic Porcelain Refinishing, a 15-year-old bathtub and appliance refinishing business in Queens. "But in recent months, we've been getting calls for black," she added. "Black appliances look sharp and modern."

An appliance can be sprayed any color, regardless of what its original color was. Both flat and textured surfaces can be sprayed, as well. The most commonly painted appliances are refrigerators, dishwashers, washing machines, cabinets and compacters. But just about anything with a metal surface is a good candidate for refinishing.

The best time to refinish a refrigerator is when the entire kitchen is being rehabilitated. Richard Prieto, the company's other partner, suggests spraying the refrigerator before the rest of the rehabilitation work begins, particularly in small kitchens. A basement is an ideal place to do the job as it's possible to spray freely.

Mr. Prieto charges $175 to $200 to spray a refrigerator, depending on travel time. He work in all New York City boroughs except Staten Island.   AUTHENTIC PORCELAIN REFINISHING, 55-23 31st Avenue, Woodside, Queens, NY 11377; (718) 726-1481.

IN ADDITION TO APPLIANCES and bathroom porcelain, Tom Peck refinishes wood cabinets using acrylic spray enamel. The spray gives cabinets a high-gloss, high-tech finish, according to Mr. Peck, a glazer for 10 years who began his own business, Dura-Gloss, nearly 10 years ago.

Mr. Peck, who works in New York City, Long Island, Westchester and southern Connecticut, charges $245 to spray a refrigerator. DURA-GLOSS; (516) 225-7213 or (800) 339-5037.


## PAPER CONSERVATORS

W HEN THE NORTHEAST DOCUMENT CONSERVATION CENTER opened more than 20 years ago, most of the jobs came from libraries with books in need of restoration and repair. But these days, the center, which specializes in paper conservation, restoration and repair, often works on family documents, from 19th-century immigration papers to old marriage licenses.

"Since the bicentennial, people have been more aware of roots and researching family history," said Mary Todd Glaser, director of paper conservation.

The center, which also does photo conservation, recently worked on a scrapbook from the debut of a 1920s Texas debutante. The paper had to be stabilized to prevent further deterioration. Crumbling corsages and ribbons were preserved as well.

The center also did work on the Emancipation Proclamation, which for some reason had been laminated. The plastic lamination film had to be removed and tears repaired.

"The enemy of paper is acid," Ms. Glaser said. Acids are often found in the backings and frames that hold documents as well as in paper made from wood pulp. Daylight is also extremely harmful. Paper items should be framed with acid-free materials and kept out of direct light. But it's best to keep them in the dark, in acid-free folders, Ms. Glaser said.

The center's 17 conservators can also work on maps, architectural drawings, parchment documents, drawings, prints, books and photographs, including large items. The charge is $85 an hour for private individuals and corporations, $200 minimum. **NORTHEAST DOCUMENT CONSERVATION CENTER,** 100 Brickstone Square, Andover, MA 01810; (508) 470-1010. ✉

MARTINA YAMIN, a paper conservator for 30 years, looked down at a costume sketch for a modern dance production from the 1940s. The pencil drawing on tracing paper was crumpled, torn and stained by yellowing scotch tape. But it wasn't hopeless, Ms. Yamin said. Tape stains can be removed. And even brittle paper can be treated.

Wrinkles are also often removable. One method is to place the paper on a suction table under a plastic bubble, and introduce a gentle mist. Ms. Yamin was able to eliminate deep creases, as well as stains, from a floor plan for a historic house in Staten Island. Mold is also often removable.

Ms. Yamin can treat a variety of paper items, including art and archival material. Prices start at $150. **MARTINA YAMIN;** (212) 532-6957. ✉

THE GRAPHIC CONSERVATION COMPANY has stabilized, repaired and restored a wide range of paper items, from architectural drawings and birth certificates to an eight-volume set of Audubon drawings. But the 15-year-old Chicago company is known for treating large works, such as movie and circus posters.

The company once worked on an enormous poster of a Civil War battle scene, 14 feet long, 8 feet wide. The company also recently restored a large antiquarian map of England. "Not many people have the large tables and big fiberglass sinks to work on these large things," said William Crusius, a partner in the firm.

The company charges $90 an hour.  GRAPHIC CONSERVATION COMPANY, 329 W. 18th Street, Chicago, IL 60616; (312) 738-2657.  ✉

NANCY WU, a paper conservator for 15 years, says it's important to know the historical importance of a work on paper before deciding how to treat conservation problems. "While it may be appropriate to treat foxing on an Andy Warhol or Jasper Johns, it may be totally inappropriate to treat the same condition on a Dürer," she said.

Ms. Wu does conservation work on flat items, like maps, books, prints, letters, as well as three-dimensional paper objects, including hat boxes and papier mâché by artists. Older paper items, made on 100 percent rag paper, are often easier to conserve than new ones. From the 1890s to the mid-20th century, paper was often filled with bleaching agents, which eventually promotes disintegration.

Ms. Wu visits New York once a week for consultations.  NANCY WU, FINE ART CONSERVATION SERVICES, The Pines, Tivoli, NY 12583; (914) 757-3812.  ✉

## PENS,
## SOLD, CLEANED AND REPAIRED

*B*OXES OF NIBS, barrels, springs, caps and levers line the wall above Richard Weinstein's desk at Authorized Repair Services, which has repaired fountain pens and mechanical pencils for nearly 30 years. The parts are for the vintage Parkers, Schaeffers and others, from the 1880s to the 1950s, that pen enthusiasts have collected in recent years. "These boxes are filled with memories," said Mr. Weinstein, who took over his father's repair business in 1989.

Mr. Weinstein's large stock of pen and pencil parts enables him to repair a variety of old and new writing implements, usually within 10 days to two weeks. Authorized Repair Services also fixes ballpoint pens, though often, Mr. Weinstein said, it is cheaper for a customer to simply discard a broken biro. (Ballpoint pens, invented by Lazlo Biro, are still commonly called biros in Britain, where they were first used in World War II by pilots of the Royal Air Force.)

The first dependable fountain pen was invented in 1883 by Lewis Edson Waterman, a life insurance salesman who lost a sale when an old-fashioned pen leaked ink on a client's application. Waterman's invention had a feed that both conducted ink to the pen point and allowed air intake to control ink flow. Since Waterman, literally hundreds of fountain pen models have appeared. Most have unique components, particularly nibs and feeding mechanisms, which must be matched or, failing that, specially made, Mr. Weinstein said.

The feeder systems in old fountain pens must also be refitted for today's inks, which are thinner than earlier inks. And Mr. Weinstein warns fountain pen aficionados to use only writing ink, never drawing ink, which can be thicker and may clog the pen's interior.

Repairs to vintage pens start at $35 for a cleaning and new ink bladder. New mechanisms for vintage mechanical pencils cost $35. Authorized Repair Services also sells new and vintage pens and pencils and purchases old models. AUTHORIZED REPAIR SERVICES, 30 West 57th Street, New York, NY 10019; (212) 586-0947.  ✉

"THIS IS VERY IMPORTANT," declared Steve Wiederlight, holding a tiny gold ring in his hand. Without that minuscule part, the pen it's designed for cannot be used. At the Fountain Pen Hospital, owned by Mr. Wiederlight and his brother, Terry, an entire room in the basement is lined with green metal drawers holding thousands of vintage pen parts.

The pen hospital's enormous collection of gold nibs, Bakelite caps and other writing essentials was almost discarded during the 1970s, when interest in fountain pens had waned. "We did maybe five or six repairs a week ten years ago," Terry Wiederlight said. These days the 50-year-old shop, located near City Hall, repairs close to 100 pens a week. "When computers came in, everybody wanted to start writing with fountain pens again," Steve Wiederlight said.

Pens admitted to the hospital are always cleaned inside and out. Points are straightened. Old rubber bladders are replaced. Failing mechanisms are repaired or replaced. And caps and barrels are buffed. Vintage pen repairs start at $19. Mechanical pencil repairs start at $10.

The hospital also buys and sells vintage pens and has over 1,000 old models in stock, including Parker Duofolds, Waterman Ripples and Waterman Safety pens. Prices range from $30 for a 1950s Esterbrook with a steel nib to $30,000 for Waterman's hand-carved sterling silver snake pen. **FOUNTAIN PEN HOSPITAL,** 10 Warren Street (near Broadway), New York, NY 10007; (212) 964-0580. ⊠

CARING FOR A FOUNTAIN PEN is quite simple, according to Marilyn Brown of Arthur Brown & Brother. "Rinse it out once a month with cold water," she said. And when riding in an airplane, it is a good idea to make certain a fountain pen is completely full or completely empty; air pressure changes may cause it to leak.

Arthur Brown, in business since 1924, carries a large selection of new and old fountain pens, ball point pens and pencils. New pens and pencils are discounted 20 percent off list price. The midtown shop also has an extensive selection of fountain pen inks and cartridges, including such colors as purple and mustard, ball point pen refills and pencil leads. Fountain pen repairs, including complete cleanings and bladder replacements, start at $40. **ARTHUR BROWN AND BROTHER,** 2 West 46th Street, New York, NY 10036; (212) 575-5555. ⊠

# PERFUME BOTTLES (ANTIQUE AND CUSTOM-MADE)

GEOFF ISLES, a Manhattan glass artist, held a graceful perfume flask with a big round stopper, designed just in time for Valentine's Day. The bottle was over 12 inches tall, embellished with bubbles that appear to float in the clear glass and provide a shallow hollow for the scent. "It doesn't hold much," Mr. Isles admitted. But very few of his scent bottles are ever filled with perfume. "They're mainly visual," Mr. Isles said.

Glass has been used since prehistoric times, and perfume bottles are among the earliest examples, dating from the ancient Egyptians around 2000 B.C. Glassmaking processes have changed relatively little over the years. Basically, the materials are fused at high temperatures, boiled down, skimmed and cooled. Molten glass is then poured into molds and pressed or blown. Glass can also be cut and beveled, crushed and molded or spread onto a mold.

To create the appearance of bubbles in his glass, which he calls Tuxedo Water Glass, Mr. Isles, a glassmaker for more than 15 years, adds baking soda to the molten mixture. The scent bottles, which cost $350, are then blown, ground and polished.

Mr. Isles, who also makes elaborate glass sculptures, accepts commissions and crafts his glass at UrbanGlass–New York Contemporary Glass Center, an enormous glassmakers' facility in Brooklyn outfitted with furnaces, studios and a sales and exhibition gallery of artists' works, including vases, art objects and, of course, perfume bottles. The workshop is open to the public. Classes in glassmaking are offered.

Mr. Isles's perfume bottles start at $60. GEOFF ISLES, Urban-Glass–New York Contemporary Glass Center, 647 Fulton Street, Brooklyn, NY 11217; (718) 625-3685.

NEARLY ALL THE BIG CRYSTAL PERFUME bottles on view in the window of Jean Laporte, L' Artisan Parfumeur, on Madison Avenue are old and hail from Europe. The shop specializes in scent but always keeps a small selection of antique bottles on hand. Examples range from cut glass and crystal to bottles embellished with silver.

The stoppers in these earlier bottles were not always airtight, and collectors often put colored water in them, said owner Regine Sicart. "The perfume companies were not thinking internationally back then." The scent bottles begin at around $200. L'ARTISAN PARFUMEUR, 870 Madison Avenue (near East 71st Street), New York, NY 10021; (212) 517-8665.  ✉

GALLERY #47 IN MANHATTAN claims to be the only shop in the world specilizing in vintage commercial perfume bottles. And, as a glance around the well-stocked shop indicates, commercial perfume bottles from the 1900s through the 1950s were often extraordinary.

Baccarat made some 500 different commercial flasks, often in experimental colors, such as jewel red and green. And besides designing bottles for their own stock, Lalique created flasks for 52 commercial perfumers from 1910 to 1940. "We have about 100 in stock," said Ken Leach, the shop's owner.

The shop, which carries over 2,000 bottles, also stocks Czech crystal bottles made between 1932 and 1939. "The bottles are lovely, but the stoppers are where the beauty lies," Mr. Leach said. Stoppers were often sculptural, with renderings of sinewy women. The Czechs used lots of color; their flasks were usually clear glass with frosted details.

Commercial bottles start at around $25—"But the really impressive pieces are around $450 to $500," said Mr. Leach, whose scent bottles appeared in the film *Bullets over Broadway*. And his stock goes up to $20,000, still shy of the $80,000 paid at auction at Bonham's London in 1989 for a Lalique bottle with a blue tiara top.  GALLERY #47, 1050 Second Avenue (near East 55th Street), New York, NY 10022; (212) 888-0165.  ✉

# PHOTOGRAPHS, RESTORATION AND CONSERVATION

A PICTURE CAN BE WORTH much more than the proverbial thousand words, be it a vintage work by a noted photographer or the sole surviving likeness of a family ancestor. But it isn't worth much to anyone if it is faded, stained or crumbling beyond recognition.

"Typically, it's the family photographs that are not well-maintained," said Mary Schobert, senior photography conservator at the Conservation Center for Art and Historic Artifacts, a nonprofit conservation laboratory that opened in 1981 in Philadelphia.

Often it is obvious when a photograph needs the attention of a conservator or restorer. Mildew, discoloration, creases and tears are common problems. But early signs of deterioration can be as subtle as a yellowed back on a snapshot taken as recently as the early 1960s.

"If the photograph is of historical importance, you need to take it to a conservator," said Robin Siegel, an officer in the photography division of the American Institute for Conservation of Historic and Artistic Works in Washington, D.C. "But if archival quality is not an issue, you can go to a good restorer," which usually costs less.

Conservators, by definition, can stabilize a photograph to prevent additional deterioration and improve the photograph's condition and appearance while doing as little as possible to alter the actual artifact. They use materials that can be removed, if necessary. The conservator also prepares a condition report.

Restorers, in contrast, can take drastic, but usually irreversible, steps to repair the image, including mounting and extensive retouching.

Most of the Conservation Center's jobs come from institutions. (Ms. Schobert spent months working on immigrant photos currently on display at Ellis Island.) But the center also accepts work from individuals, such as the woman who recently brought in old photographs documenting her father's boxing career. The center charges $75 for a condition report and $85 an hour for treatments. **CONSERVATION CENTER FOR ART AND HISTORIC ARTIFACTS,** 264 South 23rd Street, Philadelphia, PA 19103; (215) 545-0613. ✉

BRITTLE MOUNTING BOARDS that crease or tear are a major source of trouble with old photographs, particularly from the 19th century. "Often the photograph is in two pieces," said Peter Mustardo, a conservator for 11 years and a partner in the Better Image in Pittstown, New Jersey. In such cases, Mr. Mustardo and his partner, Nora Kennedy, offer two options. They can repair the actual photograph by removing the image from the board, mending the tear and inpainting lost areas. If the client cares more about the image than the artifact, they can make a negative, retouch it and make a print for display, a less costly process.

The best way to preserve family photographs is to keep the negatives, said Mr. Mustardo. "A lot of treatment work is circumvented when we have the negative." Condition reports cost $50, conservation work is $100 an hour. **THE BETTER IMAGE,** P.O. Box 164, Pittstown, NJ 08867; (908) 730-9105. ✉

BEFORE-AND-AFTER PHOTOGRAPHS decorate the showroom of Galowitz Photographics, Inc., a 15-year-old restoration concern in Greenwich Village. One before shot showed a badly faded 1920s image of two little boys. The after shot, clear and dark, was a photograph of the original, taken on high-contrast film with a blue filter.

"Ninety percent of the pictures that are 30 years old or older show signs of age," said owner Alan Galowitz. Much of the company's work is making copy negatives of originals, often after retouching, to preserve deteriorating images (from $22.35). The concern also cleans photographs, makes images from glass negatives and does retouching. Enlargements are also common. A poster-size image of baseball great Lou Gehrig leaning against a wall started life as a much smaller photograph.

Cleaning mold, mildew and bugs from photographs can be a challenge, Mr. Galowitz said. But often a kneaded eraser, used with extreme care, is all that's necessary to remove a child's doodles, he added. **GALOWITZ PHOTOGRAPHICS, INC.,** 50 East 13th Street, New York, NY 10003; (212) 505-7190. ✉

## PHOTOGRAPHS, RETOUCHING

THE CAMERA may not lie, but pictures handled by photo restorer Iris Devereux sometimes fib a little. Faces can have sleek new noses. Wrinkles can magically disappear. Eyelashes are added. Tattoos get subtracted. People can even be added or taken out of the picture.

"How many times have you seen a photograph and wished you could change your hair?" said Ms. Devereux, a former fashion photographer. "We can do just about anything to a picture."

Photographic retouching, popularized in the early days of Hollywood, is routinely applied to advertisements, fashion photography and glossy headshots of actors. But in recent years, customers have asked to have family snapshots and even heirloom portraits retouched, Ms. Devereux said.

Ms. Devereux once removed a neighbor child from a turn-of-the-century family portrait taken at a farmhouse. Another client asked to have her ex-husband erased from a picture taken on a cruise; the ship's captain was inserted in his place.

Devereux-Demetriad does retouching by hand, drawing in the needed backgrounds, shadows, skin tones or noses. "You have to know anatomy," said Ms. Devereux.

Restorations at Devereux-Demetriad take five steps. A copy negative is made from the original photograph. From this comes a copy print, which is retouched by airbrushing, drawing, bleaching and dyeing. A copy negative of the retouched image follows. The final photograph is then printed. Hand-tinting is also available.

Restoration usually starts at around $90. Devereux-Demetriad gives free estimates. **DEVEREUX-DEMETRIAD,** 119 West 57th Street, New York, NY 10019; (212) 245-1720.   ✉

RETOUCHING IS A LOT LIKE ILLUSTRATION, says Debora Musikar, who has retouched and hand-tinted photographs for 10 years. "If you remove things, you have to replace them with what would have been there."

Ms. Musikar, who accepts both commercial and individual jobs, does retouching on copy prints and will refer clients to a photo lab if copy negatives and final prints are needed. She gives free estimates. Small retouches start at $25, major alterations start at around $100. **DEBORA MUSIKAR PHOTO RETOUCHING,** (212) 627-9400; 2121 Cloverfield Boulevard, Suite 202, Santa Monica, CA 90404, (310) 449-4580.   ✉

# PHOTOGRAPHS, STOCK

*H*E'S NOT AN OBVIOUS PIN-UP. But a black-and-white image of Albert Einstein is a hot seller at FPG International, a photography archive in Manhattan.

The picture, by an unknown photographer, has plenty of competition. FPG owns the rights to more than five million images, from shots of Boy Scouts and bowlers circa 1955 to portraits of contemporary and historical figures.

But since 1988, when the company began promoting its collection of vintage photographs, rights to reproduce the image of Einstein have sold more than 100 times.

Most stock photograph companies, which own reproduction rights to old and new pictures, deal mainly with the advertising industry, magazine art departments and other professinals. But a smattering, such as FPG, also sell images for personal use.

This is good news for anyone who has ever wanted a print of a favorite magazine picture or has longed to adorn an office or dorm room with campy pictures of cheerleaders and malt shops.

In most cases, individuals contact a stock agency when they see its name next to a photograph they like in a magazine. But reproduction rights to stock photos can be hard to acquire and very expensive when a picture is for personal use, said Bob Roberts, a past president of the Picture Agency Council of America, a trade organization representing 86 stock companies.

Ordering historical and period photographs from FPG is easier. The company offers two glossy catalogs, $20 each, of celebrity and generic images. One is historical—Queen Victoria, Sigmund Freud, Mickey Mantle. The other is strictly nostalgia—gas station attendants, Laundromats, bathing beauties, dance marathons, dogs that play the piano. Prices begin at $125 for an 8-by-10-inch print.

FPG International, originally known as Freelance Photographers Guild, was started in 1936 by Arthur Brackman, a New York newspaper editor, to help photographers get work with the era's new picture magazines, such as *Life*. Eventually it became a general stock photo company.

Though most of FPG's photos are from contemporary photographers, Jessica Brackman, who inherited the business from her father and is its chairman, has promoted nostalgia images.

FPG images have decorated windows at Barneys New York from time to time. And FPG's antique fishing photos appeared on Sweden's Lotto posters a few years back. "Old pictures have become icons," said Barbara B. Roberts, president of FPG.  FPG INTERNATIONAL, 32 Union Square East (near East 16th Street), New York, NY 10001; (212) 777-4210.  ✉

MANY IMAGES FROM *LIFE* MAGAZINE fall into the icon category. And old *Life* images are easy to order from the Life Gallery of Photographs in Manhattan.

Not all the pictures that have appeared in the magazine were commissioned by *Life*, in which case the magazine does not hold the rights.

But the magazine will sell rights and a print for any image it owns, dating back to 1936, when the magazine began.

*Life* images for personal use start at $350 for an 11-by-14-inch print and go up to $10,000 for a 16-by-20-inch print of Albert Eisenstaedt's "Sailor Kissing a Nurse," in a signed limited edition of 250. Prints are made from original negatives when available.

In addition, the Life Gallery also represents the contents of the Associated Press's vast photography archive. "If they have the original negative, we can sell prints," said Maryann Kornely, manager of the Life Gallery. Among the collection's plums is Joe Rosenthal's famous World War II image of American soldiers raising the flag on Iwo Jima island. A signed print sells for $3,500.

"We suggest prints be matted on acid-free board and kept out of direct sunlight," Ms. Kornely said. Customers will get quicker service if they know the issue and date an image appeared, she added. LIFE GALLERY OF PHOTOGRAPHS, 1271 Avenue of the Americas (near West 50th Street), Room 2858, New York, NY 10020; (212) 522-4800. ✉

NOT SURPRISINGLY, *The New York Times* has a vast archive of photographs published in the paper from the mid-19th century to the present. The New York Times Picture Service will print photos the paper owns for personal use, with a glossy or matte finish, for $25 to $55, plus postage and handling (and a research fee, if any image is particularly hard to find).

Anyone interested in prints should provide as much information as possible, said Peggy Walsh, executive editor of The New York Times News Service. In addition to the photographer's name, publication date and section where the picture ran, a photocopy of the image is helpful. THE NEW YORK TIMES PICTURE SERVICE, 229 West 43rd Street, New York, NY 10036-3959; (212) 556-1617. ✉

# PIANOS,
# REBUILT AND RESTORED

RESTORING AN OLD PIANO can be a complicated business. There's the furniture part and the instrument part. And specialized skills are needed to return each to optimum condition.

"The wood may need refinishing or French polishing," says Kalman Detrich, a piano restorer in Manhattan for more than 35 years. "Veneer may be missing. Or a part may be gone, like the music desk."

Many things can go wrong with the instrument, as well. The tone will be amiss if the wood soundboard, which reinforces tones by vibration, is cracked. And cosmetic touches may be needed, including replacements for chipped or broken keys.

Mr. Detrich, who owns Detrich Pianos, takes a conservative approach to restoring and rebuilding pianos. "I like to keep as much of the original as possible," he said, standing by a rebuilt Steinway grand. Old Steinways are good pianos, he said. "They had quality wood, great metals and excellent craftsmanship." Soundboards were fashioned from solid spruce that grew on the north side of the mountain. "It got less sun, grew more steadily and had an even grain," he explained.

Mr. Detrich, who rebuilds American and European pianos, is adamant about saving old soundboards, even those with cracks. Cracks are a common problem, caused by drying or climate changes. Often an old board can be restored by wedging narrow wood planks into the cracks, then varnishing over the top, he said.

A good piano technician also makes adjustments. A slow, sluggish keyboard can be made faster. The sound can be regulated to be mellow or brilliant. And the touch can be heavy or light. "Nightclub performers usually want a piano with a light touch," Mr. Detrich said.

He also designs and builds pianos, often working with decorators. Offbeat designs include a stainless steel body with a lucite lid and a piano covered with mirrors. "The cases change the sound, but in such instances it's more important how the piano looks," Mr. Detrich said.

He charges from around $4,000 to rebuild a piano interior, $60 for a tuning. **DETRICH PIANOS,** 211 West 58th Street, New York, NY 10019; (212) 245-1234. ✉

LEOPOLD HOLDER SAT DOWN at a seven-foot Steinway Model B grand, circa 1943, and played a jazzy riff. "The bass is fine, but the treble is too sharp," he told an associate. The piano, he added, would be in fine voice by the time it was shipped to France, in a day or two, for an exhibition. New York Piano Center, which Mr. Holder opened in 1985, completely rebuilt it and refinished its polished black exterior.

Mr. Holder, a piano technician for 16 years, rebuilds and restores American and European pianos, inside and out. His company also tunes pianos ($75), does regulation and voicing ($800) and sells rebuilt pianos, mainly Steinway grands, though uprights are occasionally in stock.

Age is the main cause of problems in old pianos, Mr. Holder said. "Old pianos are susceptible to changes in humidity because they have so much wood." Abuse, lack of maintenance and natural disasters are the other big causes. "We had a piano in here with names carved on every inch of it," he said. "It left looking like this," he added, patting the 1943 Steinway. Another, older Steinway in Mr. Holder's shop was damaged in a flood. It received a new soundboard of silka spruce, new pinboards, which hold the tuning pins, and new strings, among other things. Eventually, its exterior will be refinished. Interior restorations from around $5,000. NEW YORK PIANO CENTER, 121 West 19th Street, New York, NY 10011; (212) 229-2600. ✉

SINCE 1968, THE NORTH BENNET STREET SCHOOL, a vocational school begun more than a century ago in Boston, has offered a piano technician's course (Mr. Holder is an alum). And the school has a reference service. People can call or write in and ask for the names of graduates in their area who rebuild, restore and tune pianos.

Students take classes in piano tuning, temperament, pitch, maintenance, action regulation, rebuilding and history, among other things. The course, which runs from September to May, costs $8,550 a year. NORTH BENNET STREET INDUSTRIAL SCHOOL, 39 North Bennet Street, Boston, MA 02113; (617) 227-0155.

# PILLOWS,
# UNUSUAL AND CUSTOM-MADE

IN *THE EYES OF LAURA MARS,* a suspense movie from the 1970s, actress Faye Dunaway sinks deep into a couch covered with pillows, nearly all made from kilim rugs. The pillows were designed by Marjorie Lawrence, whose company, the Pillowry, has created both ready-made and custom-made pillows from vintage fabrics for more than 20 years.

An oriental rug enthusiast, Ms. Lawrence began making pillows from colorful fabric fragments, salvaged from rugs that were too worn or damaged to use on the floor. "A flat piece of fabric may not look like anything," she said. "But put the proper backing and trim on it, and it takes on a new life."

The Pillowry stocks dozens of pillows, large and small, made from a variety of international fabrics, including Moroccan embroideries, French damasks, Aubusson textiles, Chinese silks, Japanese ikats and kilims. Pillows are backed in complementary colors in upholstery fabrics such as linen, velvet and cotton.

Much of the Pillowry's work is customized. Clients can use their own fabric or choose from Ms. Lawrence's stash of vintage textiles. A selection of braids, trims and cording is also available.

Pillows, closed with stitches instead of zippers, are priced from $25 to $2,500.  **THE PILLOWRY,** 132 East 61st Street, New York, NY 10021; (212) 308-1630.  ✉

A BEAUTIFUL PILLOW IS AN HEIRLOOM, says Lucy Sprunger, whose 12-year-old company, Thimbelina, designs pillows and pillow-making kits, many with needlepoint. Ms. Sprunger also creates shaped pillows, including down-filled moiré triangles garnished with fringe and bows.

Many Thimbelina pillows feature custom-designed needlepoint inserts, lavishly trimmed in braid and finished with hand-made tassels. Almost anything can dress up a pillow, Ms. Sprunger says. Among her favorite trims are the twisted crepe, seed pearls and beads used on bridal gowns. She has also decorated pillows with flounces and even sleeves from elegant old dresses.

Thimbelina pillows, all stitched closed, start at about $220. Kits, in-

cluding a needlepoint line designed by decorator Mario Buatta, start at
$120.   THIMBELINA, 69 North Main Street, Easthampton, NY 11937;
(516) 324-0729.   ✉

## PLANT SPECIALISTS
## WHO MAKE HOUSE CALLS

Sydney Rice has a stethoscope and a leafy plant printed on her little
green business cards. "I'm a plant doctor," said Ms. Rice, a horticulturist for 18 years. And the doctor makes house calls.

Though she can care for all types of plants, Ms. Rice prefers indoor
plants. Clients usually call when a plant isn't doing well. A variety of
problems can exist: insufficient light, too much or too little water and
bugs. Pruning may be needed. The plant may also be in the wrong pot.
"People often have plants in ceramic pots with no drainage, so the
plant is sitting in water," she said.

Ms. Rice frequently advises on the types of plants that do well in a
particular environment. Some plants, including the dracaena family,
adjust well to artificial light. The ficus tree likes sun. And African vio-
lets thrive in fluorescent light if room temperature is steady.

Ms. Rice cautions against throwing a plant away because it isn't doing well. Ficus from Florida, for example, need to acclimate to New
York. "A plant can go three months dropping leaves and still come out
of it," she said. A weakened plant is also attractive to insects, which
Ms. Rice usually kills with a mixture of alcohol and Ivory soap.

House calls are $50 an hour.   SYDNEY RICE; (718) 721-4846.

Jane Gill, a horticulturist who makes house calls, has an enormous,
15-year-old lime tree growing in her living room on the Upper West
Side. "You can have a citrus tree in the house if you get a lot of sun,"
she said. The trees require lots of water. "But they're fragrant," she
added.

Ms. Gill can sometimes diagnose what ails a plant over the telephone. Many factors can affect plant health, from the placement of the
nearest radiator to whether water appears in the plant's saucer. During

a house call, Ms. Gill can determine if a plant is infected with a pest, such as scale, white fly or spider mite. Her favorite prescription for mealy bug is alcohol.

Ms. Gill's specialty is big indoor trees, which she trims, prunes and transplants. She also advises on plant selection. Some plants, for example dieffenbachia, are poisonous, and should be kept from children and pets. House calls cost $60 to $70.   JANE GILL; (212) 316-6789.

## PLASTERERS WHO SPECIALIZE IN DECORATIVE WORK

MOST DAYS Bob Kaye walks to work. An ornamental plasterer, Mr. Kaye lives in a turn-of-the-century brownstone in Brooklyn's Park Slope district. Many of his jobs are in nearby houses with elaborate plaster ceiling medallions, moldings and wall ornaments in need of restoration and repair.

"Plaster can last for years and years," Mr. Kaye said. "But if a house settles or is on a busy street, it can crack."

Plaster embellishments for walls and ceilings were extremely popular in American buildings built before World War II. Public buildings flaunted vast amounts of elaborate plasterwork. Brownstones and townhouses in fashionable neighborhoods were also generously endowed, usually with ceiling rosettes and moldings in classic designs, such as Large Dentil, which looks like giant teeth, or Egg and Dart, a pattern of ovals flanked by arrows.

Mr. Kaye, in business since 1978, can restore old plasterwork as well as install new moldings, medallions and wall ornaments. In years past, brownstone dwellers often suspended new, modern-looking ceilings from old plaster ceilings, which remain more or less intact once the second ceiling is removed, he said.

Mr. Kaye, who also does plain plastering, works mainly on brownstones and townhouses. He provides free estimates and prefers jobs in Brooklyn, though he will take work in other parts of New York City. Prices vary from job to job, but wall moldings generally start at $20 to $30 a foot to make.   KAYE RESTORATIONS; (718) 788-1837.

"A LOT OF PEOPLE DON'T REALIZE the things done in plaster years ago can still be done today," said John Martorella, co-owner of Boro Plastering Corporation. "All you need is the money." Boro Plastering, begun in 1937 by Mr. Martorella's father, has done installation and restoration work on a number of New York buildings, including the Public Theatre and the New York Stock Exchange. But much of the company's work is done in conjunction with such interior designers as Peter Marino and David Easton for private residences in Manhattan and Westchester County.

Designs in ornamental plaster have changed little through the years. The plaster is much the same as well, though today's mix includes reinforced fiberglass, which makes the plaster lighter and stronger. Boro Plastering can duplicate an existing plaster design, making a mold from the original. For new designs, the company calls in a Brooklyn company, Saldonni and Pucci, which does sculpting and fabrication. Classic ornaments, such as rosettes and plaques, are also available ready-made and can be ordered through Boro, which will install them.

Boro Plastering accepts jobs in the tristate area and provides free estimates. Prices vary according to the job, but a day's work usually costs about $500. **BORO PLASTERING CORPORATION,** 1182 Broadway (near 28th Street), New York, NY 10001; (212) 684-3242.

## PORTRAIT PAINTERS FOR HOUSES

MICHAEL BRISTOL IS A HOUSE PAINTER, the kind who uses watercolors and small brushes instead of rollers and latex paint. For nearly 10 years, Mr. Bristol has painted portraits of houses, both exteriors and interiors, usually working from photographs.

"Painting old homes is a way to go back in time and still live in the real world," he said.

Most of Mr. Bristol's watercolors are commissioned by homeowners who like the idea of having the family residence immortalized in a painting. House paintings are also often commissioned as gifts.

Mr. Bristol's houses are meticulously detailed and set in their proper surroundings of trees, bushes, lawns or city sidewalks.

Though he favors old houses, he will paint structures from any period. But he keeps animals and people out of the picture. "I think buildings can stand alone," he said.

He charges from $300 to $2,500 for a portrait. He asks clients to send a photograph of the house and specify a size, then discusses details on the telephone. Mr. Bristol's portraits range from 14 by 18 inches to 20 by 24 inches.   MICHAEL BRISTOL, 3200 A Street, Lincoln, NE 68510; (402) 477-7636.   ✉

SUSAN STILLMAN BECAME A HOUSE PAINTER in a roundabout way. An illustrator and landscape artist since 1978—her work has appeared in *McCalls, Mademoiselle* and *The New York Times*—she noticed that her landscapes often included houses, which she enjoyed painting. So she decided to accept commissions for house portraits using oils or acrylics.

Ms. Stillman's work starts with photographs. She takes the pictures herself if the house is within a couple of hours of her studio in Westchester Country, New York, and uses photographs supplied by the client for houses farther afield. "I like to have the house photographed on a crisp day with strong shadows," she said.

She also interviews the homeowner, asking questions about the house, the grounds, the gardens and its history. "Some people want portraits of houses they no longer own," she said.

Ms. Stillman produces two types of portraits—small and medium-sized images on gessoed paper, which requires framing, and large portraits on canvas. For the paper portraits, she usually produces a pencil sketch for the client's approval. She creates color sketches for the large works. "When people see a sketch, they often suggest things," she said. "One man had me move around some sculptures and use different foliage."

Small portraits, usually about 14 by 20 inches, cost $500. Medium portraits, which average 18 by 24 inches, cost $750. And large canvases, about 38 by 48 inches, cost $1,800. There is an additional charge for framing.   SUSAN STILLMAN; (914) 682-3771.   ✉

A LONG-TIME ILLUSTRATOR, Richard Bennett has spent much of his career doing freelance work for such publications as *The Wall Street*

*Journal* and *The New York Times.* But in his spare time, he often did watercolor portraits of houses that appealed to him in Westchester County, where he lives. About 10 years ago, he turned house portraits into a business.

Mr. Bennett works from photographs, which he takes himself if the house is fairly near his own abode in Tuckahoe. Otherwise clients must supply photos. "I tell people the best way to photograph their house," he said.

Portraits, which include landscaping, are usually about 10 by 15 inches and require matting. Watercolor portraits start at $350 unframed. **RICHARD BENNETT;** (914) 779-8559. ✉

GAIL RODNEY, AN ILLUSTRATOR, was inspired to become a house painter by the picturesque surroundings in Manhattan's Carnegie Hill area, where she lives. "I like to sketch street life, the people, the shops, the houses," she said. Ms. Rodney, who makes commissioned pen-and-ink drawings and watercolors of buildings and views from apartments, likes to work on site in Manhattan. But she works from photographs for house portraits outside New York City.

Her drawings usually measure 8 by 10 inches. But they can be larger, depending on the subject. Among her larger efforts was a rendering of the Central Park reservoir as seen from an apartment window that overlooked it.

Ms. Rodney's line drawings start at $150 unframed; watercolor house portraits start at $200, unframed. **GAIL RODNEY GRAPHIC DESIGN AND ILLUSTRATION,** 130 East 94th Street, New York, NY 10128; (212) 348-8887. ✉

"I LOVE BUILDINGS AND HOUSES," said Claire Khalil, a New York artist. For more than 20 years, Mrs. Khalil has created fanciful oil or watercolor portraits of buildings that combine whimsical composition with scrupulous detail.

She has painted such well-known buildings as the Cloisters and the Frick Collection, complete with tiny renderings of artworks. Among her commissions have been a New York farmhouse, a 19th-century New England residence and an art collector's contemporary home in Idaho.

Instead of approaching a building literally, Mrs. Khalil usually shows interiors, with rooms pieced together like a puzzle. This maze of interiors is often set amid the building's landscape and is illustrated with figures, including family members. Mrs. Khalil visits the house, takes photographs, reviews floor plans and interviews the client for each painting.

Mrs. Khalil, whose commissioned house paintings start at $15,000, is represented by the Nancy Hoffman Gallery in SoHo.   NANCY HOFF- MAN GALLERY, 429 Broadway (near Prince Street), New York, NY 10013; (212) 966-6676.

THOUGH RICHARD TREASTER DOES NOT PAINT HOMES, his large commissioned watercolors are highly personal. "I paint representations of people's favorite things," he said. The results are large collages, 30 inches by 40 inches, that group whatever images a client chooses.

Mr. Treaster, who has done collages for individuals and corporations, likes to meet clients or have a long telephone conversation before determining each painting's elements. The watercolor renderings often feature such objects as an envelope with the stamp from a country where the client has lived or plane tickets for a favorite city.

"It would probably drive some artists crazy," Mr. Treaster said of the assignments. "But I enjoy working with people."

Watercolors 30 by 40 inches start at $4,500 and usually take one or two months. Mr. Treaster, who lives in Cleveland, is represented by Judith Selkowitz of Art Advisory Services in New York.   ART ADVISORY SERVICES—JUDITH SELKOWITZ; (212) 935-1272.   ⊠

## PRINTS OF FAMOUS ARTWORKS

BERNICE GALEF IS ALWAYS PLEASED when a splashy art exhibition opens or a painting sells at auction for a record-breaking price. In fact, just about anything that focuses attention on works of art gives Mrs. Galef reason to cheer.

Ms. Galef is a mail order print sleuth whose 16-year-old company, Print Finders, locates hard-to-find art reproductions, from print replicas to museum posters. And paintings that make news or attract fresh attention are in the greatest demand.

"There were lots of requests for George Seurat's *Sunday Afternoon on the Isle of Grand Jatte* after people saw the musical *Sunday in the Park with George,*" she said. But customers call and ask for prints of images they remember from childhood or enjoyed seeing in restaurants, art books, even hospitals.

Prints of well-known artworks are not exactly a rarity these days. Yet they can be difficult to locate. While most museums sell replicas of well-known works from their collections, customers do not always know where the particular Monet, Manet or Mapplethorpe they crave hangs. Reproductions of paintings from overseas museums can be especially hard to track down.

But with stacks of catalogs from the world's print publishers and a knowledge of art, Ms. Galef tracks down most requests. While she likes to have the name of the work and artist, she plays detective when necessary. For a man who wanted an image with a seltzer bottle, she located a Cubist-style poster advertising a French restaurant.

Though Ms. Galef does not deal in out-of-print images, she frequently locates prints no longer sold at museums or frame shops. She also keeps up with the replica market. Prints of celebrated paintings by Cezanne, Seurat and Matisse from the Barnes Foundation recently became available, for example.

Still, prints of certain works simply do not exist. "Just because an image is on a greeting card or calendar does not mean there's a large-size print," she said. Print Finders charges the print's retail price plus $7 shipping. Prints usually cost $20 to $40.   PRINT FINDERS; (914) 725-2332.  ✉

THE MASTERS' COLLECTION, a $6 mail order catalog, offers framed replicas on canvas of close to 300 familiar paintings, from English sporting pictures to American westerns. But the biggest sellers are Impressionists, notably works by Monet, Renoir and Mary Cassatt, according to Gregory Panjian, president of the H.A. DeNunzio Company, which produces the collection.

While clearly labeled as replicas, the company's canvases are nonetheless designed to ape the originals, complete with brushstrokes.

Using existing lithographs, a process is employed that lifts the ink off the paper and bonds it to a canvas. Next, a clear gel is applied to replicate brushstrokes. "They wouldn't fool an expert," Mr. Panjian said. "But it's a way to appreciate an artwork."

In addition to its catalog offerings, DeNunzio does custom work. "People can mail us a print they bought at a museum, and we'll transfer it to canvas," Mr. Panjian said. Owners of valuable paintings often lock up the original and hang a framed reproduction on the wall, he added.

Images cost $135 to $525 framed or 40 percent less without frames. THE MASTERS' COLLECTION, 40 Scitico Road, P.O. Box D, Somersville, CT 06072; (860) 749-2281 or (800) 222-6827.

PEOPLE WANT CONVINCING REPRODUCTIONS of famous artworks for lots of reasons, according to Diana DeWald, who owns an Ethan Allen furniture store. "They can't believe they can have something in their house from a museum," she said. "And there's no reason to insure."

Ms. DeWald's Lexington Avenue store stocks the Ethan Allen art collection—20 framed reproductions on canvas of works by Monet, Renoir, Cezanne and other warhorse Impressionists. The images are transferred from lithographs using a laser filtering technique. Colors are separated, then printed in layers, Ms. DeWald explained. A mold is taken from the surface of the original so brushstrokes appear where they should, she added.

A reproduction of Monet's large *Thunderstorm* costs $799; Matisse's much smaller *Dishes of Fruit* is $149. Prices include frames. ETHAN ALLEN, 192 Lexington Avenue (near East 32nd Street), New York, NY 10016; (212) 213-0600. ⊠

## QUILTS, CLEANED AND RESTORED

As RECENTLY AS THE EARLY 1970s, antique quilts were often regarded as little more than household items, to be tossed into the washing machine and casually repaired.

"Even museums didn't treat them the same as fine art objects," said Patsy Orlofsky, executive director of the Textile Conservation Workshop in South Salem, New York, and coauthor of *Quilts in America* (McGraw-Hill, 1974).

That attitude has changed. Several universities in the United States now offer textile conservation programs. And quilts are acknowledged as prime examples of American folk art.

There are two types of repairs for damaged quilts: conservation and restoration. The conservator tries to halt deterioration without actually replacing the quilt's fabric. The restorer will replace threadbare portions of the quilt, usually with fabric of the original vintage.

A large part of a conservator's job is knowing when to leave a quilt alone, said Mrs. Orlofsky, who started the Textile Conservation Workshop in 1978. To retain as much of the original quilt as possible, conservators hand-sew a layer of matching nylon netting over deteriorating patches.

"The netting protects the fabric of the quilt," Mrs. Orlofsky said. "And the owner can still use it."

The Textile Conservation Workshop, which employs 12 conservators, also washes quilts with deionized water, dry cleans fabric when wet cleaning is not possible, repairs stitching, fixes backing and attaches sleeves for hanging the quilt.

For each quilt an extensive condition report is prepared. It includes historical research, dye and fabric analyses, and treatment recommendations. All work is returned in acid-free wrappings for storage.

The workshop is in the old General Store in South Salem. It charges $75 for a condition report, $250 for wet cleaning and $50 an hour for repairs. The workshop also restores tapestries, samplers, lace and kimonos. **THE TEXTILE CONSERVATION WORKSHOP,** 3 Main Street, South Salem, NY 10590; (914) 763-5805. ✉

PIE (AS IN "EASY AS") GALINAT, who has restored quilts for over 20 years, regularly scours antiques shops and flea markets for old fabrics dating from 1840 to 1950.

"Early browns and reds are the most likely to rot," she said. "They are also the hardest to find." Silk, which is susceptible to dry rot, is particularly difficult and costly to restore. "My advice for silk is to frame it under glass or put it back into the cedar chest after it's restored," she said.

Ms. Galinat, who works out of her home in Greenwich Village, will replace top fabric, stitches and bindings, but does not do backings. She charges from $4 to $7 per fabric piece for cotton repairs and from $10 to $20 per piece for silk.

She also sells quilt stretchers, which her husband, Robert Self, makes from clear sugar pine. A set of stretchers, hinged to fold into quarters, costs $400 for a quilt under 90 inches square. **PIE GALINAT;** (212) 741-3259. ✉

BIG BAGS OF VINTAGE FABRIC fill Tracy Jamar's light-drenched West Side apartment, where she has restored damaged quilts for more than 15 years. "I get real pleasure out of matching the right period of fabric," she said.

Miss Jamar, who started sewing as a child in Minnesota, also does conservation when she feels it is necessary.

"Anything from the 18th century I leave as is, stabilizing with netting," she said. "But I have no trouble replacing or helping along quilts from the last half of the 19th century."

Sometimes a badly damaged quilt can be cut down. Sometimes an intact but fragile quilt can be hung on the wall. "And sometimes the best thing is just to fold it so the best part shows," she said.

Miss Jamar charges $40 an hour.

She also sells Walker Systems, a line of textile-hanging devices she invented with her father, Walker Jamar.

The hangers consist of aluminum bars that expand or contract to support the quilt or textiles. The bars are hung from fiberglass rods. The bars can also be hung directly on the wall with special brackets that come with the kit. Components to hang a quilt 72 inches square cost $34 to $65. JAMAR TEXTILE RESTORATIONS; (212) 866-6426 or (516) 329-0404. ✉

## RADIATOR COVERS

THE FIRST CAST-IRON RADIATORS, throbbing with steam heat, were invented during the Industrial Revolution. And almost immediately, radiator owners devised ways of covering them.

Radiators are not known for their beauty. Hot radiators can cause burns. And a tasteful radiator enclosure can enhance a room, doubling as a bookcase or windowseat. Properly designed, an enclosure should also help heat the room efficiently.

"If you look at the earliest buildings with architectural built-ins, you find attempts to incorporate the radiator into the architectural statement," said Stephen Pino, a furniture designer for The Building Block, a Manhattan woodworking concern.

Air-Lite, a home improvement shop in Queens, offers a large selection of radiator enclosures, including customized covers in metal, wood and Formica and ready-made, standard-size metal covers. Prices vary according to style and material. Painted steel enclosures with front grills in stock sizes, which slip over a free-standing radiator, start at $45 for a 21-inch width.

The simplest customized metal covers with grill fronts cost about $75 for a 24-inch width. And enclosures with louvers instead of a grill start at about $169 for 24 inches. Air-Lite's customized metal grills are supplied by Kero, a New Jersey firm which has manufactured steel grills for years.

Air-Lite, which has built, sold and installed radiator enclosures for 15 years, also offers KD or knockdown metal covers, which come unassembled in pieces complete with instructions.

Air-Lite will also build made-to-measure radiator covers in Formica (an array of colors and wood grains are available), mirrors with a Lucite grill, and hardwoods, such as oak, cherry and mahogany (unfinished from $215 for 24 inches, varnished from $299). Air-Lite's wooden enclosures have decorative aluminum grills in gold or silver. But modifications and enhancements, such as moldings, can be made, according to Joseph Rubino, owner of Air-Lite. Models are on view at Air-Lite's Queens showroom.

Mr. Rubino also suggests heat reflector panels (from $9.99) for the inside of wooden radiators to enhance the enclosure's life. And metal covers should be kept dry and buffed regularly with car wax to prevent rust. AIR-LITE, 212-57 Jamaica Avenue, Queens Village, NY 11428; (718) 464-0298.

ALL RADIATOR COVERS FROM BUILDING BLOCK are made of wood, and all are expensive, according to Noah Block, a co-owner. Most are ordered by customers who want a room of complementary built-in furniture, including bookcases and cabinets. But single radiator enclosures can be created as well, often to double as window seats.

Mr. Pino, who designs the enclosures, usually visits a client's home, sees where the enclosure will go, suggests woods and styles, then draws a plan. (Visits cost $100 for the first hour in Manhattan.)

Most Building Block enclosures are designed to hide their purpose: Enclosures can be fronted with shallow bookcases, for example. For a four-foot customized enclosure, prices start at around $1,500. BUILDING BLOCK, 314 11th Avenue (near West 30th Street), New York, NY 10001; (212) 714-9333.

·  ·  ·

THOUGH CUSTOMERS CAN TAKE THE MEASUREMENTS for the made-to-measure metal radiator covers sold by Crosstown Custom Shade and Glass, owner Marcy Karpel suggests a professional fitting.

"Once an enclosure is ordered, we can't alter the model or have it remade," she said. "We measure 99 percent of the covers we sell."

Crosstown, on the Upper West Side, sells metal enclosures by Kero, which has more than 20 models.

Empire, the simplest, costs $94 to cover a 24-inch radiator and has a front grate, but does not have an insulated top, which means the owner should not put plants or books on it.

Eton, much more elaborate, is painted to look like wood, has a louvered front, is flanked by bookcases and costs $292 to cover a 24-inch radiator. CROSSTOWN CUSTOM SHADE AND GLASS, 200 West 86th Street, New York, NY 10024; (212) 787-8040.

# RADIOS (VINTAGE), SOLD AND REPAIRED

ON A TRIP TO VERMONT IN THE LATE 1970s, Bruce and Charlotte Mager bought an old Zenith radio from the 1930s. "We started thinking about radios and the history of electricity in the home, and we were hooked," said Mrs. Mager. And that is how the couple decided to open Waves, a more-than-15-year-old shop that sells, buys, rents and repairs early radios and phonographs.

Interest in old radios, which include crystal sets, battery radios from the 1920s and tube radios made through the 1950s, has grown dramatically in recent years, fanned by a growing number of museums, collector clubs and nostalgia films, such as *Radio Days.*

Prices for early radios have risen as well. They currently range from $50 to more than $5,000, depending on size, rarity, model and original cost.

It can be a challenge to find people who repair early radios. The wiring in old radios, which used tubes and three different voltages, is totally different from today's solid-state. And vintage parts can be hard to find. "Radios are not difficult to repair, but it takes knowledge and the proper tools," said Mrs. Mager.

Waves, which sells tubes, knobs and grill cloth, does repairs off the premises. Estimates cost $10, included in the repair price. Repairs are to interiors only and start at around $50. The shop also sells $5 wiring diagrams by mail for do-it-yourself repairs. Manufacturer and model number are needed. WAVES, 32 East 13th Street (near University Place), New York, NY 10003; (212) 989-9284.  ✉

BOB ESLINGER, who owns Antique Radio Restoration & Repair, started fiddling with old radios as a teenager 30 years ago. But for the last two years, he has repaired early radios full-time. "From the tube technology to the beautiful woodwork, they are a no-compromise work of art," he said.

With the proper overhaul, many early radios can go 20 years without service, said Mr. Eslinger, who collects vintage radios. "Tube technology was good technology," he said. "There's a richness of sound you don't get with solid-state." Early radios, which receive short-wave and AM stations, can be adapted to receive FM broadcasts. "But most people don't want to modify the early technology," Mr. Eslinger said.

A complete rebuild, usually between $125 and $300, includes new tubes, new wire cord, new capacitors and a cleaning. Mr. Eslinger also checks resistors and refinished cabinets, cleans chassis, lubricates volume controls and cleans tubes. "It's a rat's nest in there sometimes," Mr. Eslinger said. Restoration of exteriors is also offered. Mail orders are accepted; radios should be double boxed for shipping. ANTIQUE RADIO RESTORATION & REPAIR, 20 Gary School Road, Pomfret Center, CT 06259; (860) 928-2628, between 10:00 A.M. and 7:00 P.M., Tuesday through Saturday.  ✉

ADVICE ON THE CARE AND REPAIR OF OLD RADIOS is provided in *Antique Radio Classified*, a monthly magazine for collectors. The magazine, begun more than a decade ago, also offers information about radio clubs and fairs, where vintage parts and equipment can be purchased or swapped. Subscriptions cost $34.95 a year. ANTIQUE RADIO CLASSI-FIED, P.O. Box 2, Carlisle, MA 01741; (508) 371-0512.  ✉

# REPLATING METAL

$I$T'S TEMPTING TO CALL Ruben Mirensky an alchemist, though he doesn't really turn base metals into gold. It just looks that way. Mr. Mirensky, who owns All Plating Corporation, is in the metal-plating business. And by stripping, polishing and plating, he makes objects in steel, zinc or other base metals look like brass, copper or even gold.

After years of use, household hardware, such as doorknobs, hinges, lamp bases and faucets, often needs a good polishing and plating. Polishing can restore luster and smooth the surface when an object in brass, copper or some other desirable metal is dull, pitted or dented. Plating is necessary if the veneer has worn off a base metal, such as steel or lead.

Plating is also required if you want to change an object's finish to fit a new color scheme. Brass, for example, can be plated in copper, chrome or a variety of antique finishes.

Such companies as All Plating, which Mr. Mirensky has owned for three years, polish metal using a variety of grinders and wheels. Electroplating is accomplished in huge vats of solvent that contain dissolved metals. Metal anodes hang on a positively charged bar in the tank, and the work to be plated hangs on a negatively charged bar. The current releases the plating metal, which is bonded onto the work.

"If you want this color of copper with a bit more red, we can add current or raise the heat of the tank," Mr. Mirensky explained.

Bright finishes in chrome, brass, copper and gold were high style for household hardware in the 1980s, but today many architects and decorators are requesting softer finishes. "Pewter, satin brass, satin copper and black nickel are popular at the moment," Mr. Mirensky said. "So are unusual finishes like green patina and brown patina." The latter two, usually seen on outdoor hardware, often turn up on seaside properties, where conventional copper finishes oxidize quickly.

Prime candidates for plating are metal objects in good condition. Painted objects, including doorknobs and hinges, pose few problems as paint can be stripped. "But sometimes it's cheaper to replace the object than to replate it," Mr. Mirensky said. Polishing and plating for a doorknob usually ranges from $7.50 to $15, depending on condition. All

Plating has a $75 minimum. **ALL PLATING CORPORATION,** 154-158 North 7th Street, Brooklyn, NY 11211; (718) 388-9360.  ✉

ED BYERS AND HIS CREW plate a vast number of doorknobs, drawer pulls and decorative metal grates each week. But Hygrade Polishing and Plating, which Mr. Byers has owned since 1981, accepts unusual objects, as well. In a box awaiting plating were a collection of dull-looking Emmy awards, the television industry's statuettes. Assorted chrome accessories from antique automobiles sat on a table nearby. And artists and architects often bring in abstract metal sculptures for plating.

Hygrade, which has rows of steaming electroplating baths in a cavernous workroom, also accepts outsize jobs. A client asked to have an enormous, one-of-a-kind circular staircase of solid steel plated to look like mirror-polished brass. And the company had to build a special plating tank to accommodate a gigantic chandelier commissioned for a palace. (It was plated in gleaming black nickel.)

"People tend to overclean metal fixtures," Mr. Byers noted. "You can clean chrome all you want. But with brass, too much cleaning will remove the protective lacquer. Once that goes, the piece will tarnish." He recommends cleaning polished brass with a nonscratch duster and no abrasives.

Hygrade offers a variety of finishes and will plate most metals, including such problem metals as aluminum and stainless steel. (These two metals must be specially coated to enable the plating solution to stick.) Hygrade charges from $5 to polish and plate a doorknob and from $10 for hinges.  **HYGRADE POLISHING AND PLATING COMPANY,** 22-07 41st Avenue, Long Island City, Queens, NY 11101; (718) 392-4082.  ✉

BESIDES HOUSEHOLD HARDWARE, Spectronics Electroplating Corporation, which opened in Brooklyn in 1989, polishes and plates jewelry, flatware, brass beds and ecclesiastical pieces, such as chalices and tabernacles. "I use a heavy gold and create an old dull look on the chalices," said owner Sam Williams, who has done plating for more than 15 years. Replating a chalice starts at around $30.

Mr. Williams also offers a range of antique finishes for the turn-of-the-century jewelry customers often bring for plating. Doorknobs start at around $4 for polishing and plating.  **SPECTRONICS ELECTROPLATING CORPORATION,** 66 South 2nd Street, Brooklyn, NY 11211; (718) 599-1447.  ✉

# RESIZING WOOD FURNITURE

IT'S EASY TO FIND THE PERFECT CARVED-WOOD ARMOIRE at an antique shop or flea market these days. And it's a pleasure to know there's an ideal place for it in the dining room or the den. But getting it past the front door can be another matter.

"The average doorway in New York is seven feet high," said Mario DiRe, a custom cabinetmaker for over 30 years. Furniture wider than 48 inches and deeper than 24 inches should be built to come apart in sections, he added.

That isn't always the case, of course. But a number of custom cabinetmakers, such as Mr. DiRe, can resize wood furniture, both old and new, strategically subtracting or adding where alterations are needed and refinishing the piece so the changes are invisible.

Mr. DiRe, who owns Telesca-Heyman, a nearly 50-year-old Manhattan cabinet shop, recently disassembled, trimmed and refitted a large cabinet with glass-fronted doors for a family moving from Queens to New Jersey. "They couldn't get it out of their apartment," explained Remo DiRe, Mr. DiRe's son. Telesca-Heyman's workers also altered the cabinet's interior so it became a bar, with glass shelves and a mirrored back. Then everything was reassembled on site in New Jersey.

The company can expand wood items as well, including sideboards, armoires and beds. Customers often want antique beds widened to queen- or king-size dimensions. "It's important to keep the same proportions when you resize furniture," said the senior Mr. DiRe, who learned his craft in Italy and Switzerland. Chairs, for example, are often best left as they are, though they sometimes can be cut down to fit a low table.

The company can also dismantle and reassemble architectural woodwork, including antique ceilings and wainscotting. Resizing starts at around $1,000, but with custom work, prices vary according to the job. **TELESCA-HEYMAN,** 304 East 94th Street, New York, NY 10028; (212) 534-3442.

FOR *BACK PAGE STORY,* a play performed at Lincoln Center a few years ago, an actor had to hide in an old-style roll-top desk on stage. "It was a real antique, very confining," said Leslie Neilson, who owns Barewood Architectural Woodworking, a custom cabinet shop in Brooklyn. So Barewood modified the back of the desk so the actor could slip in and out unseen.

Usually the company, which opened in 1975, resizes more conventional items, such as armoires, bookcases and beds. Mr. Neilson recently elongated a set of casement windows, adding two new panes at the bottom where the originals were removed to accommodate an air conditioner.

But expanding antique beds is a company specialty. Often wood must be specially selected, carved and stained to seamlessly match the original. For a recent job, Mr. Neilson salvaged the old posts at the bed's foot and created duplicates to replace decayed posts, using a restorer to copy the original decorative painting.

"When deciding to resize something, you have to consider appearance, structure and whether it's cost effective," Mr. Neilson said. "In a lot of cases, it's cheaper and faster to build something new than to resize it." Barewood charges $55 an hour. **BAREWOOD ARCHITECTURAL WOODWORKING,** 106 Ferris Street, Brooklyn, NY 11231; (718) 875-9037.

FURNITURE THAT NEEDS TO BE TAKEN APART to fit into a room will probably need to be taken apart again when it's time to move. So the craftsmen at Olek Lejbzon, a 50-year-old custom woodworking, upholstery and restoration company, will take apart armoires, bookcases and other items and redowel them so they can be easily dismantled and assembled. Customers receive instructions so they or their moving company can do the job.

Olek Lejbzon, which specializes in high-end custom cabinetry, has resized a number of items over the years. The company once lengthened the four posts of an antique canopy bed from 1830, adding hand-turned carved mahogany finials, with a gold-leafed acorn at each top.

"The idea was to do something in the spirit of the original," said Wayne Heyser, the manager. Routing was fitted at the edge before the finials were added. The company offers both stock finials and custom-turned finials.

Resizing starts at around $800. The price depends on the object's size as well as the work, touch-ups and refinishing required.   OLEK LEJBZON, 210 11th Avenue, 11th floor (near West 25th Street), New York, NY 10001; (212) 243-3363.

## RETINNING COPPER POTS

GOOD COPPER COOKWARE WILL LAST FOREVER, says Jamie Gibbons, brandishing a heavy copper saucepan. "If you bang it out of shape, we can put it back." And when the pan's tin lining wears out, Retinning and Copper Repair, Mr. Gibbons's 77-year-old workshop, can create a new, hand-wiped tin interior.

Professional chefs like copper cookware because it heats evenly and cools down quickly when removed from the flame. But since certain foods cooked directly on copper can become mildly toxic, copper pots, pans and kettles need linings. Inert metals, such as silver and gold, work just as well as tin, Mr. Gibbons said. "Tin's just a lot cheaper."

The art of retinning has changed little over the years. The pot is cleaned in a solution of caustic soda, scrubbed with sand, then rinsed. The copper is prepped so the tin will bind. Then, a stick of tin is rubbed onto the heated pot, like butter. Baths in cold water, hot water and sawdust follow. Finally, the pot is polished on an electric wheel.

Mr. Gibbons also does repairs and replaces rivets on handles. He has even retinned gas tanks from vintage Chevrolets and Cadillacs.

A word of caution: Tin melts at 450 degrees. "If you leave a teapot on the stove too long, and the water boils down, you can melt out the tin," Mr. Gibbons warned.

Retinning costs two dollars an inch. To measure, run a tape measure from lip to base, across the bottom and up the other side.

**RETINNING AND COPPER REPAIR, INC.,** 525 West 26th Street, New York, NY 10001; (212) 244-4896.  ✉

WHEN DOES A COPPER POT NEED TO BE RETINNED? When the hole in the worn tin lining is the size of a quarter, says Steven Bridge, whose father, Fred, opened Bridge Kitchenware in 1946. "But any time you see copper coming through, it's a good idea to get a pan relined," Mr. Bridge added.

Though tin linings eventually wear out, proper cooking utensils can a stretch a lining's life. Metal scrapers should never be used. Mr. Bridge recommends wood or heatproof plastic, such as the new Exoglass spatulas from France. And copper cookware should never go into the dishwasher. A nonabrasive pad or sponge is best for cleaning.

Retinning costs $2.10 an inch, $2.50 an inch for mail orders (shipping and insurance included).  **BRIDGE KITCHENWARE,** 214 East 52nd Street, New York, NY 10022; (212) 688-4220.  ✉

FOR COPPER COOKWARE AFICIONADOS who want to try retinning pots themselves, Aux Cuisines, a New Jersey concern, offers the Tin Lizzie Copper Retinning Kit. The kit, which consists of instructions, a nine-by-nine-inch square of tin and a bottle of flux, a chemical that allows tin to melt onto copper, costs $15.95 and is available at such stores as Zabar's, 2245 Broadway at West 81st Street in Manhattan, (212) 787-2000, and by mail from Aux Cuisines.

The kit works best for pots that are mildly worn in patches, according to Sue Lyon, president of Aux Cuisines. "Most pots wear out in a particular area, and it's cheaper to simply retin the worn spots," she said.  **AUX CUISINES, INC.,** 43 Saddle Ranch Lane, Hillsdale, NJ 07642; (201) 664-8775.  ✉

# REWEAVING

SEYMOUR SCHNALL HAS SPENT CLOSE TO A LIFETIME dealing with the consequences of mothholes, snags and burns. Mr. Schnall, who owns Superior Weaving and Mending Company, is a reweaver. And every week, he and his staff make holes and tears disappear on all types of garments.

"You reweave thread by thread to repair the damage," said Mr. Schnall, who joined Superior as a messenger before buying the company in 1931.

A good reweaver can fill in holes on a variety of fabrics so meticulously that it is impossible to find the original damage. Mr. Schnall held up a tan Donegal tweed jacket that had been pocked with over a dozen mothholes when it was brought in. To an unschooled eye, the rewoven holes were impossible to find.

A rewoven garment can also be strong. "Of course it can be dry cleaned," said Mort Schnall, a partner with his father.

One reason good reweaving seems invisible is that the work is done with the garment's actual yarn. The reweaver steals threads from inside seams and, occasionally, hems—"wherever we can get it," the younger Mr. Schnall said. This is then woven into the existing fabric in the identical configuration of the original weave. The only problem is when the garment's outer threads have faded.

Any kind of fabric with threads that can be pulled is usually a good candidate for reweaving. But larger weaves are better than fine weaves. Flannels reweave beautifully as do tweeds and even some polyesters. Satin is much more difficult. So is corduroy, because of its nap.

Colors can occasionally create problems as well. Dark and medium colors are excellent candidates for reweaving. But the process can occasionally show on light-colored fabrics. "It all takes time," the elder Mr. Schnall added. "And it's very hard on the eyes."

Reweaving starts at $20 for a simple sweater. The price goes up, depending on the size of the hole, type of fabric and labor. **SUPERIOR WEAVING AND MENDING COMPANY,** 41 Union Square West, Suite 423 (near 17th Street and Broadway), New York, NY 10003; (212) 929-7208.  ⊠

"IT'S LIKE WEAVING A BASKET," said Nat Singer, who opened the French-American Reweaving Company back in 1930. "It's a matter of replacing the missing threads one by one, exactly as the pattern exists."

The method can work equally well for solid and patterned fabrics. Mr. Singer recently rewove a hole on a colorful checked men's jacket in lightweight wool. A red tab taped on the sleeve was the only indication of where the reweaving had occurred.

"It looks like a wild design, but it is actually very regular," Mr. Singer explained. "But gabardine, which looks very regular, has a little ribbing in it and is very hard to simulate."

Mr. Singer and his staff reweave sheets, tablecloths and even antique fabrics as well as garments. The company also repairs lace, usually on tablecloths and bridal gowns. Mr. Singer once repaired nearly all the lace on a wedding gown that a cat had clawed.

Besides thread-by-thread reweaving, Mr. Singer does section weaving for large holes. A piece of matching fabric is placed in the hole and rewoven into the existing fabric.

Some garments, such as raincoats and leather jackets, simply can't be rewoven. Burberry raincoats, for example, are so tightly woven the reweaving can show. "So we improvise," Mr. Singer said. Unwanted slits can become plackets. False seams can hide rips. Darts can disguise tears on a bodice. And when the elbows of a sweater are too weak or costly to reweave, Mr. Singer will install patches in leather or ultrasuede. Reweaving starts at $25 a hole. THE FRENCH-AMERICAN REWEAVING COMPANY, 119 West 57th Street (near Avenue of the Americas), Room 1406, New York, NY 10019; (212) 765-4670.

ALICE ZOTTA LEARNED REWEAVING as a teenager in a large clothing factory in Valdagno, a tiny town in Vincenza Province in the Italian Alps. And for more than 30 years, she has had her own business, reweaving all sorts of items, from sweaters and jackets to tablecloths and even upholstery. "Reweaving requires a lot of patience," she said. "You have to like it."

Though the techniques have remained the same, fabrics have changed over the years. "The new fabrics have very intriguing designs, which can take time to reweave," she said.

Gabardine remains among the toughest to reweave, she added. "It is woven very tight. You can reweave two holes in another fabric in the time it takes to do one in gabardine."

Reweaving starts at $10 a hole for simple jobs. ALICE ZOTTA, 2 West 45th Street (near Fifth Avenue), Room 1701, New York, NY 10036; (212) 840-7657.

# RUG CLEANERS

STANDING IN A. BESHAR & COMPANY'S RUG-FILLED GALLERY, Jackie Mackay, the company's manager, offered a quick list of rug-care tips: Rotate rugs every year to slow fading and distribute wear. Add moth crystals when storing rugs. Keep potted plants off rugs (they can cause dry rot). And when rugs become dirty and dingy, take them to a professional rug cleaner.

That last comment hardly seems surprising, since Beshar, founded by the grandfather of owner Robert Beshar, has been cleaning rugs and carpets for 95 years. But rug cleaning requires special equipment, techniques and knowledge.

"You want to use someone who knows how to care for different types of rugs," said Claudia Ramirez, executive vice-president of the Association of Specialists in Cleaning & Restoration, which provides educational and technical services for members.

Some rugs look best after a wet cleaning with cold water and a neutral detergent. Rugs that aren't colorfast usually require dry cleaning. And delicate rugs need different care from broadlooms. "You need someone who knows when to use a machine rinser and when to work on the floor with a brush and foam," Ms. Ramirez said. The association, based in Annapolis Junction, Maryland, supplies names of members throughout the country who specialize in cleaning and restoration; telephone (301) 604-4411.

The decision to clean a rug should be made with care. If a dirty rug is left untouched, it can be damaged, particularly if it gets a lot of use. Dirt and grit will wear away the pile when the rug is trod upon frequently. But cleaning, which causes wear, should not take place too often, either.

To determine if your rug needs cleaning, dampen a white washcloth, wring it out and wipe your rug. "If it comes up gray, the rug needs cleaning," Ms. Mackay said. Rugs in the city should be cleaned every three years, she added. Clean rugs in the country every five years.

A rug will last longer if it rests on a pad. Rubber pads, 1/4 inch thick, are best for oriental rugs, according to Ms. Mackay, who also sells oriental rugs. A. Beshar charges $1.50 a square foot to clean oriental and broadloom rugs and from $3 a square foot for kilims, Aubussons and needlepoint rugs. **A. BESHAR & CO.,** 1513 First Avenue (near East 79th Street), New York, NY 10021; (212) 288-1998. For cleaning and restoration, call the company's plant; (718) 292-3301.

SEVERE STORMS THAT CAUSE HOMES TO FLOOD usually mean new business for Restoration by Costikyan, which cleans and repairs carpets and rugs. Though difficult, it often is possible to chemically strip colors that run, said Philip Costikyan, a partner in the Long Island City concern his great-grandfather began in 1886. The firm also removes stains, including troublesome pet stains.

Mr. Costikyan usually recommends wet cleaning wool rugs. "When wool absorbs water, it expands and forces out soil particles," he said. Dry cleaning may be better for certain painted rugs and Navaho rugs that aren't colorfast. And hand-made hooked rugs, which can deteriorate in water, are sponged. Prices vary according to rug type and labor. It costs from $250 to $500 to clean a 9-by-12-foot rug. **RESTORATION BY COSTIKYAN, LTD.,** 38-10 29th Street, Long Island City, NY 11101; (718) 786-9684.

FOR RUGS OF HISTORICAL IMPORTANCE, as well as newer high-quality rugs, textile conservators can provide a safe and careful cleaning. "We do a very thorough cleaning," said Marlene Eidelhart, head conservator at the Cathedral of St. John the Divine Textile Conservation Laboratory.

For over a decade, the nonprofit lab, which originally worked almost exclusively on the cathedral's vast collection of rugs and tapestries, has performed cleanings and conservation work on textiles for individuals, museums and other institutions as well.

With multiple soakings and rinsings as well as detergent applied by hand, it can take an entire day to clean a single rug. "Colors get brighter when dirt is removed," Ms. Eidelhart said. Besides cleaning, the lab repairs rugs and stabilizes deterioration. Prices for cleaning range from $12 to $15 a square foot. All other services, which include restoration, conservation, analysis and condition reports, cost $65 an hour. **THE CATHEDRAL OF ST. JOHN THE DIVINE TEXTILE CONSERVATION LABORATORY,** 1047 Amsterdam Avenue, New York, NY 10025; (212) 316-7523.

# RUG RESTORERS
# AND CONSERVATORS

S OME OF RONNEE BARNETT'S WORK graces the walls of apartments, houses, art galleries and even the New York University Law School. But much of it winds up on the floor, where people walk all over it.

A rug and textile restorer since 1978, Ms. Barnett always asks clients how they plan to use the rugs she is about to repair. "It is important to know what kind of stress will be on the rug," she explained, standing before a rainbow of yarns in her studio.

To prevent further disintegration of hanging rugs, it is sometimes possible simply to dye a piece of cloth, place it behind the spot that has worn bare and sew down the loosened threads. But holes, rips and tears in rugs that will receive foot traffic must be rewoven, duplicating the original weave and mix of colors.

Often Ms. Barnett dyes yarn for restorations. She also respins commercial yarns to duplicate the look of older yarns. A good restoration is almost invisible, Ms. Barnett said. "The eye should never go to the damage."

The restored rug must also be sufficiently strong to accept foot traffic. "A bad restoration creates so much stress on the original that tears occur," said Ms. Barnett.

Ms. Barnett restores several types of rugs, including flat-weave rugs such as kilims, Aubussons, Navaho and Hopi rugs, as well as pile rugs, rag rugs, hooked rugs and braided rugs. Flat-weave rugs get their design from the weft's horizontal threads. These cross the warp's vertical threads, which form the rug's foundation. A pile rug's foundation is made from the warp and weft; the design comes from rows of yarn looped through the weft.

Ms. Barnett also does tapestry restoration and reweaves disintegrating painting canvases. She charges $60 an hour in her studio. RONNEE BARNETT, 580 Broadway (near Prince Street), New York, NY 10012; (212) 966-3520. ✉

A RUG MAY NEED CONSERVATION OR RESTORATION for a variety of reasons, said Tina Kane, who has restored and wet cleaned rugs since 1973. Oxidation can cause woolen fibers to disintegrate, particularly in shades of dark brown, which contain high amounts of tannin.

Damage can also come from animal accidents, heavy furniture dragged across the rug and potted plants watered regularly and left on the rug for long stretches. "Owners should turn the rug from time to time so it wears evenly," said Mrs. Kane, who has a studio in Orange County, New York.

When the dyes in a rug are in good condition, Mrs. Kane likes to wet clean the rug before restoration. This allows her to see the colors accurately. Mrs. Kane can wet clean rugs up to 40 by 20 feet.

Weaving techniques used in textile restoration have changed little over the years, said Mrs. Kane, who has done tapestry restoration for the Metropolitan Museum of Art.

But dyeing techniques have improved dramatically in the last 20 years, resulting in long-lasting colors that match the original, even if it has faded.

Mrs. Kane restores flat-weave rugs, pile rugs, rag rugs, hooked rugs, braided rugs and tapestries, charging $45 to $50 an hour in her studio. Wet cleaning costs between $10 and $15 a square foot.  TINA KANE; (914) 986-8522.  ✉

## RUGS (BRAIDED)

BRAIDED RUGS HAVE BEEN AROUND for a long time, which is one reason these sturdy, all-American floor coverings have a fusty, grandmotherly image. But aficionados of the braided rug are trying hard to change that.

Such interior decorators as William Diamond have recently covered a number of stylish wood floors with braided wool. And Cathy Comins, whose company, Art Underfoot, offers custom handcrafted rugs, uses such adjectives as sophisticated and chic to describe the braided rug.

"A new braided rug can look like Granny's," said Ms. Comins, who represents 175 textile artists. "But it doesn't have to."

American braided rugs date from the early 1800s, according to *The Complete Book of Rug Braiding* by Helen Howard Feeley (Coward-McCann, Inc., 1957). Designed to warm cold floors and add color, early rugs used old scraps of wool, cotton and anything else in the house. Today's rugs are usually 100 percent wool.

To make a braided rug, a length of fabric is folded into four layers, then braided with two other lengths. Finished braids are then laced together so the stiches are invisible and the rug is reversible.

Traditional braided rugs often display a vast, seemingly random variety of colors, often called hit-and-miss. Bands of color in concentric circles are also a popular design.

"One way to update a braided rug is to use solid color. There's a chevron pattern in these rugs that's usually obscured by a mix of colors," Ms. Comins says. And though most braided rugs are round or oval, they can be square and even fringed.

Ms. Comins handles custom-braided rugs by Jan Jurta, who makes rugs in just about any size, shape and combination of colors. Mrs. Jurta's rugs are created on a small, patented braiding machine, then hand-laced with cotton thread. The wooden machine produces rugs that are more uniform than hand-braided models, according to Ms. Comins.

Ms. Comins, who also represents makers of rag and hooked rugs, charges $45 a square foot for a custom machine-braided rug. Sample rugs by artists represented by Ms. Comins can be seen at Patterson, Flynn and Martin, 979 Third Avenue, New York, NY ([212] 688-7700). ART UNDERFOOT; (201) 744-4171. ✉

VERNA COX'S HAND-BRAIDED RUGS have been displayed at the Smithsonian Institution in Washington, D.C., and on the pages of such magazines as *McCall's Needlework* and *Women's Day*. Mrs. Cox, a rug-braiding instructor for more than 12 years, has produced a trio of instructional videos, including step-by-step guides to making oval, round and rectangular hand-braided rugs ($39.95 each). She has also authored the *Illustrated Braiding Guide* ($9.95).

"I like rugs that are well designed and well made," said Mrs. Cox, a rug braider for over 30 years. She suggests novice braiders start with something small, like a two-by-three-foot rug, and learn to braid consistently. "If one braid is tight and one is loose, you have a problem," she warned. Braided wool strands can also be made into chair cushions, stair runners, wall hangings and place mats.

Mrs. Cox, who lives in Bucksport, Maine, also accepts commissions and charges $40 a square foot for a hand-braided rug.   COX ENTERPRISES, R.R. 2, Box 245, Bucksport, ME 04416; (207) 469-6402. ✉

NANCY YOUNG STARTED HAND-BRAIDING RUGS in Maine in the early 1950s while her husband was in the Korean War. And she's still making them, though she filled her house in Quakertown, Pennsylvania, years ago.

"I like the recycling aspect of braided rugs," said Mrs. Young, who has taught rug braiding for years.

Mrs. Young, who has sold her rugs at the Museum of American Folk Art shop, is pleased that braided rugs seem to be coming back in style. "People are extending the craft into different rug shapes," she said. "You see heart-shaped rugs, cloverleaf rugs." Her latest specialty is braided denim rugs, made, when possible, from old blue jeans supplied by the client.

Mrs. Young, who also repairs braided rugs, accepts commissions and charges $20 a square foot for most braided fabric rugs, $25 a square foot for braided denim.   NANCY YOUNG; (215) 536-1346.   ✉

TO DAWN RAPCHINSKI, braided rugs symbolize family life and its best traditions. She originally learned hand braiding in the early 1980s when she wanted a rug for her dining room in Ephrata, Pennsylvania.

Mrs. Rapchinski, who charges from $17 to $22 a square foot, creates hand-braided rugs in old-fashioned or contemporary designs. A recent hit-and-miss-style rug featured 18 hues. And big splashes of color covered a more modern-looking rug.   DAWN RAPCHINSKI; (717) 733-9026.   ✉

# RUGS (HOOKED), CUSTOM-MADE, CLEANED AND REPAIRED

No ONE REALLY KNOWS who gets credit for devising the hooked rug. Some view the rugs, made from fabric strips pulled through a woven base with a wood-handled crochet hook, as a true, born-in-America folk art. Others, notably W. W. Kent in his 1930 book, *The Hooked Rug,* trace the craft's origins to the sixth-century Copts and Bronze Age Vikings.

Whatever. During the last decade or so, hooked rugs, once relegated to the attic, have become popular, prompted, in part, by decorators who featured them prominently in country-style interiors. "A lot of young collectors who couldn't afford orientals also started buying hooked rugs," said Jessie Turbayne, author of *Hooked Rugs, History and the Continuing Tradition* (Schiffer Publishing; $39.95) and *The Hooker's Art* (Schiffer Publishing; $49.95).

Though she designs and makes custom hooked rugs, Ms. Turbayne's specialty is restoring wounded rugs, from flea market finds to heirloom oldies unearthed in basements. "If three quarters of the rug is missing, I can still fix it," she said.

Ms. Turbayne matches fabric and hooking technique to the original, dyeing cloth when necessary. Most rugs from 1930 to the present feature wool strips, with older models composed of silk, cotton, flannel, old shawls—any scrap fabric the maker had on hand. Backings range from burlap and jute for older models to linen for more recent rugs.

When buying a rug at a flea market, Ms. Turbayne advises pinching the rug's end. "If it cracks or turns to sawdust, don't buy it," she said. She also suggests avoiding rugs with latex-treated backings, which are all but impossible to repair.

In addition, hooked rugs should never be vacuumed. "Beater bar brushes suck up ends and unravel rugs," she said. "Sixty percent of my repair work is due to vacuum cleaners." She suggests using a carpet sweeper or broom.

Ms. Turbayne makes new rugs for $75 to $125 a square foot. Repairs start at $25.  **JESSIE TURBAYNE,** P.O. Box 2540, Westwood, MA 02090; (617) 769-4798.  ✉

UNLIKE BRAIDED OR RAG RUGS, hooked rugs can depict distinct images, representational and abstract alike. Ron Mosseller, a second-generation custom rug and tapestry hooker, often approaches his commissioned work like a portrait painter, working from photographs and visiting sites he's asked to re-create. "One man wanted all the animals on his ranch shown on one rug," he said. Another client asked to have his 1933 Buick immortalized on a rug.

Mr. Mosseller, who uses a hooking technique popular in the 1850s, also copies antique rugs. Commissioned rugs cost $65 to $150 a square foot.  **RON MOSSELLER,** 1205 Lynn Road, Tryon, NC 28782; (704) 859-5336.  ✉

BESIDES RUGS, HOOKING ENTHUSIASTS can make chair cushions, wall hangings, pillows, table runners and even handbags, according to Joan Moshimer, a rug designer who deals in hooking supplies for do-it-your-selfers.

Author of *The Complete Book of Rug Hooking* (Dover; $9.95), Mrs. Moshimer offers patterns for several thousand different rug designs, ranging from sophisticated geometrics to early American–style portraits of roosters, dogs and other animals (a catalog of designs costs $6).

"Colonial-style primitives are popular right now," Mrs. Moshimer said. "They also use wide strips, which make up more quickly because fewer are needed." Patterns, priced from $6, include backing, in burlap or linen, printed with a design.

Mrs. Moshimer, a rug hooker for over 25 years, also sells beginner's kits with precut strips. And she encourages all rug hookers, including beginners, to sign their work. "Your descendants will bless you," she said.  **JOAN MOSHIMER'S RUG HOOKER STUDIO,** 21 North Street, P.O. Box 351, Kennebunkport, ME 04046; (207) 967-3711 or (800) 626-7847.  ✉

# RUGS (RAG), CUSTOM-MADE, CLEANED AND REPAIRED

DURING HER DAYS AS AN ART STUDENT, Margareta Grandin Nettles learned to make traditional Scandinavian rag rugs in her native Sweden. But she thinks that her years on Nantucket, where she now lives and has a shop, are responsible for the distinctive look, texture and colors of her hand-made cotton rugs.

"The light, the water, the way peple use their homes all influence me," Mrs. Nettles said.

Rag rugs, as the name implies, originated in Scandinavia as a way to use up old clothing. A traditional rag rug is made from two long cotton strips woven into a cotton warp, which is a series of threads extended lengthwise in a loom. Rag rugs have even been woven from plastic for bathrooms and kitchens, but Mrs. Nettles uses only cotton for her rugs.

Mrs. Nettles, who taught weaving when she first came to the United States, uses a natural linen warp to give the rugs strength. "If we use fine cotton and push all that fabric, it might rip," she said. "And these rugs are very hard to repair."

For added strength and color, she weaves in three or four cotton strips, and prefers a braided edge because, she said, "Fringes will just disintegrate."

Her rugs, which are reversible, come in three styles: tabby, a mixed color flat weave that costs $40 a square foot; twill, a heavier, mixed-color diagonal, $48 a square foot; and checkerboard, $50 a square foot.

For each order, she creates a sample for $75, which is applied to the bill. Customers can go to her house, which doubles as her shop, or order rugs by telephone or mail. Orders take four to six weeks. **MARGARETA GRANDIN NETTLES,** 64 Union Street, Nantucket, MA 02554; (508) 228-9533. ✉

DOZENS OF READY-MADE RAG RUGS in a rainbow of colors are displayed in neat bamboo bins at the Gazebo, a boutique specializing in country home furnishings. Customers can also order rugs to their specification at no additional charge.

The rugs, $17.50 a square foot for stripes, $25 a square foot for checks, are made at the Gazebo's factory in Haiti on looms imported from Scandinavia. Each rug has a scoured linen warp, a cotton weft made from two pieces of cloth and fringed edges. The rugs use only American cotton, which is usually colorfast, according to Carolyn Barnard, the shop's owner. The reversible rugs can be washed or dry cleaned.

The rugs come in several styles. Mélange is a variety of colors running together. Stripes and checks can also be delineated. Rugs can be up to 11 feet wide without a seam.   THE GAZEBO, 114 East 57th Street (near Lexington Avenue), New York, NY 10022; (212) 832-7077.   ✉

# RUGS (WARP-FACE)

SEVERAL YEARS AGO, a curator at the Brooklyn Museum asked Elizabeth Eakins, a New York rugmaker, to reproduce an old American woven rug for a historic home. The rug was what weavers call a warp-face rug, which means its pattern comes mainly from threads running lengthwise. Ms. Eakins's specialty had been hand-raided rugs, but she promptly abandoned them to make warp-face rugs woven in wool.

These days, Ms. Eakins, who recently moved to an airy East Side shop, creates customized woven rugs in the crisp, geometric patterns that typify warp-face rugs. (She designed Gracie Stripe, formed from thick and thin lines, for a rug commissioned for Gracie Mansion.)

Her patterns, usually very simple, are mainly a device for showcasing colors. "Even in solid blocks, you see lots of different shades," she said, holding a sample rug in pale hues. "There are 40 different whites and creams in this."

Like Scandinavia's traditional cotton rag rugs, woven American rugs originated as a way to create floor coverings using old cloth. The earliest often blended wools and cottons, creating a durable, slightly coarse surface.

Ms. Eakins decided early on to work exclusively in wool. "The weaving process is as labor intensive as with a cotton rag rug," she said. "But wool gives you a structurally stronger carpet." It is also more formal. "It can go in a beach house or a Park Avenue apartment," she said.

To customize her rugs, Ms. Eakins consults closely with clients and decorators, who provide fabric samples, paint swatches and photographs. She also hand-dyes her mothproofed wools when stock colors aren't quite right.

The rugs, which have natural-colored Belgian linen hems, cost $88 a square foot for hand-dyed wool. For each order, Ms. Eakins makes a sample, which costs $200, is nonrefundable and becomes her property. **ELIZABETH EAKINS INC.,** 21 East 65th Street, New York, NY 10021; (212) 628-1950. ✉

HARRIET GILES, A KENTUCKY WEAVER, was inspired to create handcrafted floor coverings by her grandmother, who makes hooked rugs. "But weaving goes a lot faster," she said. "I like to see something get finished."

Mrs. Giles, who has woven warp-face rugs for over 15 years, specializes in traditional American designs, including plaids, stripes and mixed colors. Her rugs are called balance weave, since she uses a cotton or linen warp with a wool weft. (Weft threads cross the warp and appear as horizontal bars on Mrs. Giles's rugs.)

Many of Mrs. Giles's patterns are her own creations, with several adapted from the Colonial woven rugs she has either copied or restored for historic homes in Kentucky. For restorations, Mrs. Giles often creates a new warp while retaining parts of the original weft. "Sometimes I'll dye the new fabric with walnut hulls or coffee grounds to make it look old," she said.

Mrs. Giles, who works with the colors her clients request, also makes cotton warp-face rugs. But she prefers wool, which is softer and has more texture. "It holds the warp threads in shape better than cotton," she said.

Besides classic warp-face rugs, Mrs. Giles also makes rag rugs. Her rugs can be ordered through Art Underfoot in Upper Montclair, New Jersey. **ART UNDERFOOT;** (201) 744-4171. ✉

THOMAS PATTON, who weaves both warp-face and weft-face rugs, in Bath, Maine, has been a jazz drummer for years. So it's hardly surprising that he uses musical terms to describe the look and color of his sturdy wool rugs.

A weaver for more than 15 years, Mr. Patton prefers heathers, or Debussy colors, as he calls them. Many of his rugs feature 10-inch stripes of various hues, sewn together to make the rug the size the client wants. "The idea is to get syncopated counter rhythms with color," he said.

He has also created a variety of modern designs, including a vertical stripe called "D Minor 7" and a border-patterned rug, "Santa Fe."

Mr. Patton only uses wool for his fringed-edge rugs. "Wool has so much character, and the possibilities for color are great," he said. "Wool also has that indestructible feel." Mr. Patton charges $25 a square foot for his woven wool rugs.   THOMAS PATTON, Box 238, HCR 31, Bath, ME 04350; (207) 442-9798.   ✉

## SAFES

"OUR OBJECTIVE," says Richard Krasilovsky, "is to take the competitive edge away from the thief." That's an old line, he added. But since Mr. Krasilovsky is president of Empire Safe Company, which sells and distributes safes, it's apt.

Once used mainly by businesses and banks, safes are turning up in a growing number of houses and apartments. In part, this is due to the easy availability of inexpensive, fire-resistant safes sold by locksmiths, hardware stores and discount outlets. But a dizzying array of safes, large and small, heavy and (relatively) light, are on the market, for both residential and commercial use. And the widest variety is offered by companies, such as Empire, that specialize in safes and vaults.

The latest residential safes are highly specialized, so the customer can select a safe built to accomplish distinct tasks. Fire-resistant safes, designed mainly to protect papers, tend to be fairly light, with maximum insulation and minimal heat-conducting steel. "But they're easy for a burglar to open with common hand tools," Mr. Krasilovsky said.

Safes built to protect valuables have an array of options, such as multiple bolts, solid steel walls and automatic locking and relocking mechanisms, designed to slow the thief's progress. Many of these offer fire protection as well, from one to three hours.

Capacity, convenience and operating ease are additional qualities to look for when choosing a burglar-resistant safe, Mr. Krasilovsky said. Battery-operated digital locks, which the owner can reprogram, are easier to use than conventional combination locks. But they cost an additional $150 to $250.

Customers often request safes like those in hotel rooms, Mr. Krasilovsky added. But while these may successfully hide jewelry, passports and money from light-fingered housekeepers, they are not designed to withstand attacks from a crowbar.

Empire, in business since 1904, offers a number of residential burglar- and fire-resistant safes, including the compact, solid-steel-walled 220-pound Ave 1000, 14 inches tall, 14 inches wide, 17 inches deep, designed for apartments ($1,075 with digital lock, $925 with combination lock) and the 265-pound Pro 1212, 16 inches tall, 16 inches wide, 19 inches deep, equipped with added fire resistance for houses ($1,330 with digital lock, $1,080 with combination lock). Both models, which can be customized, come with flocked interiors to prevent scratches.

To deter petty thefts in apartments, Empire has also added a line of less costly digital safes from $400 to $900.

In addition, Empire has a selection of decorative one-of-a-kind safes designed by artists, including Richard Haas and Red Grooms. EMPIRE SAFE COMPANY, 433 Canal Street (at Varick Street), New York, NY 10013; (212) 226-2255.

PEOPLE ARE BEGINNING TO INSTALL safes in their homes instead of using safe deposit boxes at banks, according to David Garbar, vice-president of Acme Safe Company, dealers and distributors of safes since 1904. Residential safes are also increasingly popular with collectors of silver, coins and stamps as well as people in cash businesses, such as grocery store owners, who can't always make a bank deposit at the day's end.

Mr. Garbar recommends that safes weighing less than 700 pounds be anchored to the floor with heavy-duty bolts, a service his company performs at installation. "It's better to force a burglar to open it in your house when he's under pressure instead of letting him open it at his leisure in his garage," he said.

Acme also offers a floor safe, which can be installed in the concrete of a basement or garage. With a simple metal plate that fits over the door and lock, the safe is easily concealed by a rug or furniture.

Acme's most popular models include a steel, 70-pound apartment safe ($360 with combination lock, $520 with digital lock) and a 400-pound burglar- and fire-resistant safe with steel and concrete-filled walls ($870 with a digital lock, $720 with a combination lock).  ACME SAFE COMPANY, 419 Park Avenue South (at 29th Street), New York, NY 10016; (212) 226-2500.

THE CLASSIC WALL SAFE, seen in dozens of old movies, is still available. The problem is that most existing buildings aren't equipped to accommodate the safe's necessary depth. Still, these safes fit between wall studs in a sheetrock or plaster wall, said Charles Maffey, an owner of Maffey's Lock and Safe, in business for more than 80 years in Elizabeth, New Jersey. Safes typically weigh 60 to 100 pounds and start at $285.

Maffey's also offers gun safes, typically 60 inches tall, 22 inches wide and 14 inches deep. Often gun collectors can't get insurance unless guns are properly secured, a task accomplished by the safe, Mr. Maffey explained. Gun safes start at $800.  MAFFEY'S LOCK AND SAFE, 1172 East Grand Street, Elizabeth, NJ 07201; (908) 351-1172.

## SCREENS

*F*EW FURNISHINGS COMBINE GLAMOUR AND PRACTICALITY as flawlessly as decorative screens, the exuberant zig-zags that can shield the Stairmaster, create pockets of privacy and effortlessly evoke mystery, history and more than a whiff of romance (imagine the dressing room of a silent screen diva or Diaghalev dancer *without* a screen, swathed with a fringed silk scarf, of course).

Though never long out of style, screens are suddenly everywhere, from cheap chic versions in mail order catalogs to custom creations that look like gigantic pieces of jewelry. Designers can't seem to get enough of them.

"People are tired of all the fabric they used in the '80s and want a cleaner, more architectural look," said T. Keller Donovan, a New York interior designer who created a black-and-white desk screen for last summer's Southampton show house.

For space-starved New Yorkers, screens are a natural decorating tool, a clever ploy that adds definition to a boxy room, lends a welcome jolt of color and provides a hint of privacy. Screens can blend quietly or command attention, depending on the room's requirements.

And they can be fashioned from almost anything, as long as the final product is witty. Consider Los Angeles artisan Clare Graham, who devised a colorful, gracefully curved screen, 36 inches tall, from 630 yardsticks.

Indeed, in tune with the frugal '90s, screens can be individualized without being costly. Several mail order houses offer three-panel screens with fabric insets that can be dyed, stenciled or replaced with fabric to match the sofa or curtains. At Pottery Barn, a wrought-iron frame with whimsical scrolls at the top supports the screen's three cotton insets ($199) ([800] 922-5507).

Similar but simpler, the top of each lacquered steel panel of Crate & Barrel's folding screen is gently arched ($129) ([800] 323-5461). And the Domestications screen, in cherry-finished hardwood, features a large central panel flanked by two smaller side panels, each with removable fabric insets ($99) ([800] 746-2555).

Amusing screens are increasingly on view at department and specialty stores. Clodagh, the designer who created the romantic interiors at Felissimo, at 10 West 56th Street ([212] 956-4438), also devised the store's distinctive black wood zig-zag screen that holds 500 pencils, a blazing rainbow of color. Just 25 inches tall, it can sit on a tabletop or hide a nonworking fireplace ($680 for the screen, $500 for the pencils).

And Takashimaya, 693 Fifth Avenue, near 54th Street, ([212] 350-0100), frequently displays antique Japanese silk screens as well as quirkier offerings, like a pair of weathered wood doors with once-elegant moldings that seem straight out of Blanche DuBois's New Orleans ($1,195 a panel).

Besides their versions of such classics as Eileen Gray's wood-lacquered screen from 1922 ($2,868), Palazzetti, at 515 Madison Avenue, near 53rd Street ([212] 832-1459), carries three whimsical folding screens that look like enormous jigsaw puzzle pieces by Milan designer Silvio Russo ($1,800 to $2,500). Ideal for a kid's room, provided no one gets too rambunctious, the laminate-covered particle-board screens come in bold primary colors.

A number of artisans also offer both ready-made and custom screens. Furniture designer Chris Lehrecke, a long-time admirer of 1920s French bistro screens, devised a sleek wood screen from long oval strands of Finnish birch plywood.

Though somewhat similar to Charles Eames's classic undulating wood screen, the top of Mr. Lehrecke's is slightly shorter at the sides, creating a graceful slope, and rolls up like a carpet. Available in natural wood ($1,900) or oil-base stains ($2,100).   **CHRIS LEHRECKE FURNITURE,** 50 Douglas Street, Brooklyn, NY 11231; (718) 783-9150.   ⊠

AMANDA WEIL'S UNUSUAL SCREENS are a showcase for her work as a photographer. Each panel is made from a large photographic transparency that she either leaves black and white or colors with copper and blue toners. The transparencies are then sandwiched between glass and framed in sleek black wood or metal.

A recent screen shows images of Japanese bamboo while another is a seaside view with a dock reflected in water. Because the transparencies are, well, transparent, Ms. Weil will add gold leaf to the back of the screen if the client prefers something more opaque. She also will fashion screens around images a client chooses but she always takes the pictures herself. Ms. Weil's screens start at $3,000.   **WEIL STUDIO,** 34 Renwick Street, New York, NY 10013; (212) 229-0655.   ⊠

FOR A CLIENT WHOSE BEACHFRONT VIEW was marred by an unattractive new building, architect Dana Lee Sottile and jewelry designer Philip N. D.'Drennan devised a solution—and launched a new custom screen business.

Their screen is a thicket of polished steel rods in an ultramodern openwork pattern with slices of colorful stained glass artfully positioned here and there. The effect: a jewel-encrusted screen. Decorative finials in metal and stained glass, made to evoke fanciful sea creatures, such as jelly fish, parade across the top. Similar screens cost $8,000 to $10,000, less complex versions cost less. **DANA LEE SOTTILE AND PHILIP N. D.'DRENNAN;** (212) 877-5974. ✉

PAINTED WOOD SCREENS designed to fit a specific site, or purpose, are a specialty of Shawn Ranck, a woodworker for about five years. For a woman who wanted to hide a piece of exercise equipment in her bedroom, Mr. Ranck made a large three-paneled plywood screen, painted in bold Moroccan-inspired colors and images.

Typically, Mr. Ranck visits the client to see where the screen is needed, does a few sketches, then makes the screen the client chooses. Simple screens start at $550, with more complex versions from $1,200. **SHAWN RANCK;** (212) 777-2385. ✉

THE FOLDING SCREENS IN FURNITURE designer Kenneth Winslow's SoHo shop are classics with a slightly futuristic spin. Most impressive is an imposing lacquered mahogany screen with a rectangular center panel flanked by two sharply angled side panels. Three frosted-glass windows are set into each panel, and cylindrical nickel-plated hinges hold everything together ($2,500). **KENNETH WINSLOW,** 464 Broome Street, New York, NY 10013; (212) 219-9244. ✉

THE BOLD, SINGLE-PANEL DREAM SCREEN from the furniture design firm of Dialogica looks vaguely African, with a hand-carved solid maple frame and woven rush panel. Two panels can be connected to form a free-standing screen, or a single panel can work as a headboard ($2,030 a panel). **DIALOGICA,** 484 Broome Street, New York, NY 10013, (212) 966-1934; 1070 Madison Avenue (near 80th Street), New York, NY 10028, (212) 737-7811. ✉

THOUGH TRADITIONAL SHOJI SCREENS, formed from classic horizontal rectangles, are a staple of Miya Shoji, the custom Japanese screen company also makes decorative free-standing shoji screens in contemporary designs, such as geometrics and Art Deco patterns.

Among the newest is an open-grill screen with elaborate latticework. For a classic shoji look, the company also offers a beige cotton backing as an alternative to the popular plastic-coated silk. Most screens are made from bass wood, but specialty woods, such as red cedar, can change the effect. Shojis start at $240 a panel, open-grill screens from $400 a panel.  MIYA SHOJI, 109 West 17th Street, New York, NY 10011; (212) 243-6774.  ✉

NGUYEN VAN LAN, who owns the Japanese Screen Corporation, learned to make traditional shoji screens in Korea after escaping from his native Vietnam in a tiny boat. These days he designs and builds custom screens at his home in Queens, where he has a showroom.

Mr. Lan makes three types of screens: sliding screens, free-standing screens that fold in two directions and free-standing room dividers. He also blends Eastern and Western designs, as in a pair of wide-slat shoji doors designed for New York Telephone's corporate headquarters in White Plains. The door design can be specially ordered.

The screens have traditional hinge fittings instead of the staples used in cheaper, ready-made screens. Mr. Lan favors California redwood, which is light and durable, but will use more costly material on request.

His screens start at $221 for a pair of window screens three feet by four feet. Mr. Lan offers a brochure.  JAPANESE SCREEN CORPORATION, 23-37 91st Street, East Elmhurst, Queens, NY 11369; (718) 803-2267. ✉

A SURE-FIRE WAY TO SAVE MONEY and create something unusual is to make a screen yourself, which is precisely what T. Keller Donovan did for his Upper West Side apartment. To mask two uneven columns that flanked his windows, he devised two four-panel, fabric-covered screens using discarded folding doors—"the kind that never work well on closets," he said.

First, he padded the wood doors with a layer of one-inch-thick Dacron batting cut to fit each panel and applied with spray glue. Next, he stapled his cover fabric, a nubby white linen, to the four edges of each door.

For color and definition, and to cover the staples, he outlined each panel's edges with bright red grosgrain ribbon, applied with a glue gun. And he used 1¼-inch brass hardware hinges, installed with an electric drill, to put each screen together. "I did it all in a weekend," he said. Total cost: $245.

If bifolding doors aren't available, Mr. Donovan suggests chipboard panels. A good choice might be 7-foot-tall panels that are 18 inches wide and ¾-inch thick.   T. KELLER DONOVAN; (212) 759-4450.

# SEWING MACHINES, REPAIRED AND REVIVED

CROWN MACHINE SERVICE, George Grossman's cluttered repair shop on the Upper West Side, offers a concise history of the sewing machine. On a shelf in the back sits a tiny black-and-gold antique Singer, circa 1900. Nearby is a new computerized sewing machine. And on adjoining shelves are rows of portables from almost every decade in between.

"Most older machines can be put back in working order," said Mr. Grossman, who opened the store over 30 years ago. Motors can be replaced or rebuilt. And parts that are no longer made can often be cannibalized from the shop's collection of aging sewing machines. Most repairs cost under $100, Mr. Grossman added. New machines, in contrast, range from around $150 for a basic model to $3,000 for the latest computerized machine. "It makes sense to repair most machines," he said.

A sewing machine needs professional help if it breaks thread, sews irregular stitches or skips stitches, among other things. Thread can catch in the gears; with plastic gears, thread can bind and actually break gear teeth. And machines often go out of sync, losing the timing and tension needed for proper sewing.

Crown, an authorized dealer for Pfaff, Elna, Viking and Singer, repairs most makes of old and new machines and gives free estimates. Cleaning and oiling starts at $29, weekly rentals at $25.   CROWN MACHINE SERVICE, 2792 Broadway (near West 108th Street), New York, NY 10025; (212) 663-8968.

STANLEY ARCHIBALD, A REPAIR TECHNICIAN at Park East Sewing Center, believes in preventive maintenance. Those who sew infrequently should run their machines for a few minutes every two to three months, just to keep the parts moving. "You don't even need thread," he said.

And after every garment is completed, lint should be removed and the lint collection area cleaned with a vacuum cleaner or canned Air-flo, a spray.

Besides repairing sewing machines of all vintages, Park East fixes sergers or overlock machines, which finish edges, make decorative stitches and sew easily on silks and knit fabrics. "They're to sewing machines what microwaves are to conventional ovens," said Joseph Capece, Park East's owner for over 21 years. Once a garment industry tool, sergers, which are smaller than sewing machines and use four spools of thread, have been snapped up by home sewers for the past five years.

Park East, an authorized dealer for Bernina, White and New Home, offers sewing and serger classes. Cleaning and oiling starts at $45. Free estimates. PARK EAST SEWING CENTER, 1358 Third Avenue (near East 77th Street), New York, NY 10021; (212) 737-1220.

"A LOT OF THE OLDER SINGER MACHINES are still very good," said Jack Kaplan, owner of Kaplan's Sewing Machines in Fairlawn, New Jersey, for 45 years. With their metal interiors, older machines can usually outlast the newer models outfitted mostly with plastic parts. All that metal needs oil, however, and older machines should be oiled once a year. Mr. Kaplan advises using a thin, clear, white oil. "Nothing too gummy," he cautioned. "And never oil the motor. That can cause a fire."

Cleaning and oiling starts at around $35. Estimates are free. KAPLAN'S SEWING MACHINES INC., Amber Cycle Building, 11-02 River Road, Fairlawn, NJ 07410; (201) 796-0022.

## SHOES, REPAIRED AND REFITTED

NEARLY EVERYONE HAS A FAVORITE NEIGHBORHOOD shoe repair shop for simple tasks, such as getting lifts replaced or shoes resoled. But occasionally, more elaborate work is needed, such as dyeing pumps to match the bridesmaids' dresses or altering loafers to make the wearer taller.

Much of Carlos Mesquita's work at Top Service, the nearly 15-year-old Manhattan branch of a Paris shoe repair company, consists of adjustments to make old shoes stylish again. He adds decorative platforms to flat-soled shoes and sneakers, dyes fabrics and suedes, re-covers heels, trims fat straps and changes buckles.

"With little changes on a nice pair of shoes you're tired of, you'll want to wear them again," he said.

The quality and color array of shoe dyes have improved in recent years, though matching footwear and fabric can still be a challenge. "We have more than 64 shades of pink, but sometimes we still need to mix a color specially for the right shade," said Mr. Mesquita, who manages the shop. Before having shoes dyed, customers always should specify whether the shoes will be worn mainly indoors or outdoors, he added. "The lighting is different and will determine how we match the color," he said.

To weatherproof shoes, Mr. Mesquita suggests using sprays on suede or fabric and cream polish instead of liquid polish on leather shoes. "Spray protectors will disappear on leather the next time the shoe is polished," he explained.

Top Service charges $20 for dyeing and from $25 to $35 to add a platform. TOP SERVICE, 845 Seventh Avenue (near 54th Street), New York, NY 10019; (212) 765-3190. ✉

"YOUR FEET HAVE A TENDENCY TO TIGHTEN UP a bit when you try shoes on," said Thomas Bifulco, owner of T.O. Dey custom shoemakers, explaining why shoes often feel tighter at home than in the store. He also suggests buying shoes at day's end, when feet are a bit swollen. But if the shoe doesn't fit, Mr. Bifulco can add or subtract a size on most shoes for men, women and children.

Mr. Bifulco's company, begun in 1926, can also transform closed-toe shoes into open-toe models, make pumps into sling-backs and change the height of heels. "With cowboy boots, some people can't wear an extreme underslung heel," he said. "So we make the heels less extreme."

Many T.O. Dey customers need shoes adjusted for foot problems, such as club feet, weak feet, fallen arches or bunions. But the company does decorative work as well. One New York socialite has her shoes covered to match her clothes, whether in fabric, ultrasuede or suede.

T.O. Dey charges $29.95 to $49.95 to readjust a shoe size; custom shoes cost $650 for the first pair, $500 for each additional pair. **T.O. DEY,** 9 East 38th Street, New York, NY 10016; (212) 683-6300.

OFTEN A RELATIVELY SMALL FOOT PROBLEM can cause major misery. "On some people, the little toe tends to jump up a bit," said Alex Konstantinovski, an owner of Gelman Custom Made Shoes. The solution can be as simple as a piece of sponge, specially cut and precisely inserted into the shoe.

Mr. Konstantinovski, who learned his trade in Russia more than 30 years ago, can adjust shoes to alleviate a limp and alter shoes to add height to those who want it. He fashions custom-made shoes in the style and material the customer selects. An elevation of ½-inch costs about $25. He also makes custom shoes. **GELMAN CUSTOM MADE SHOES,** 404 East 73rd Street, New York, NY 10021; (212) 249-3659.

# SILVER, CLEANED AND REPAIRED

*T*HE BEST WAY TO CARE FOR SILVER is to use it, says Robert Routh, president of Thome Silversmiths, Inc. Silver used frequently has a soft, lustrous patina. And the more it's washed, the less it needs to be polished.

But even abused silver can be repaired, restored and polished to look new. "You won't recognize this when it's finished," Mr. Routh said, holding a tarnished silver cup melted and twisted in a fire. The base will be resculpted, dents will be removed, and polishing will eliminate scratches.

Mr. Routh has restored, repaired and replated silver and other precious metals for more than 35 years. He can add—or subtract—monograms, fill in holes, repair broken handles, fix broken hinges, repair necks ripped off candlesticks and, when necessary, make identical copies of existing pieces.

"We're involved in all aspects of silver," said Mr. Routh, holding a Georgian silver teapot with a broken ivory handle he plans to repair.

Mr. Routh also studies silver for its country and year of origin, as silver contents often differ. "Using the wrong solder can change the color," he said.

It is easy to care for silver, according to Jean Routh, whose father, Frank Thome, started the family business in 1931. Spots, which can eat into the silver, should be cleaned immediately with paste polish. Natural sponges clean better than nylon sponges. And steel wool should never be used.

Thome Silversmiths accepts pieces for repair by mail. Prices vary according to the difficulty of the work, but it costs $54 to put a handle back onto a knife blade. **THOME SILVERSMITHS, INC.,** 49 West 37th Street, Suite 605, New York, NY 10018; (212) 764-5426.  ⊠

WHEN SILVER IS SCRATCHED SO BADLY it's lost its luster, it's time for a professional polishing, says Morty Fogel, manager of Restore-All Silversmiths, a 50-year-old concern that repairs, restores, replates and polishes precious metals.

A good polishing also shows off the silver's origins. While sterling has a silver content of 92.5 percent, some continental silver is 80 percent silver; the rest is copper and other alloys. When highly polished, continental silver will often have a slightly reddish tone.

Replating starts at about four dollars for a small teaspoon. **RESTORE-ALL SILVERSMITHS,** 37 West 47th Street, Room 306, New York, NY 10036; (212) 719-1330.  ⊠

IT IS ALMOST IMPOSSIBLE TO REPLACE GLASS LINERS in silver saltcellars these days, says Richard Wyler, president of S. Wyler Inc., which has sold and restored antique silver for over a century. So Mr. Wyler suggests gold plating, known as vermeil, for saltcellar interiors. "Salt pits silver but not gold," he said.

Vermeil, popular in the 1960s, is coming back into style, Mr. Wyler added, holding an antique vermeil serving spoon. Soap and water is the best way to clean vermeil, as abrasives will remove the gold.

Repairs at S. Wyler start at about $50. **S. WYLER INC.,** 941 Lexington Avenue (near 69th Street), New York, NY 10021; (212) 879-9848.  ⊠

REVIVING STERLING FLATWARE chewed up by garbage disposals is a specialty at Precision Metal Finishing in Mobile, Alabama. "Sometimes those spoons have sentimental meaning," said Bill Carrigan, the owner, who charges about $20 to straighten out a mangled teaspoon.

The firm, in business since 1979, also electroplates silver, gold, copper, tin, nickel and brass, including brass beds and doorknobs.   PRECISION METAL FINISHING, INC., 1806 Sixth Street, Mobile, AL 36615; (334) 432-0155.   ✉

## SLIPCOVERS

SLIPCOVERS, ONCE UPON A TIME, were all about practicality, a good, quick way to make ugly furniture pretty and usable once again. But in the 1980s, they grew fashionable, with whimsical fabrics and flounces. And these days, in tune with the lean '90s, they blend fashion *and* practicality.

"After the '80s, everything got simple," said Mischelle Arcus, a Manhattan slipcover designer. "Lots of white linen with pleated corners and no shirring."

There are varying degrees of simplicity, of course. New Orleans designer Ann Dupuy, half of the team of Holden and Dupuy, recently fashioned a frill-free white linen slipcover for a Louis XV chair. "We kept it simple to contrast with the gold arms and legs," she said. She also uses lots of sheer fabrics these days. "The idea is not just to cover up a chair but to layer it."

The best slipcovers are like clothing for furniture, a new dress in a different color, fabric or style, be it a seasonal switch or something special for a party. Ms. Arcus, owner of Marcus Feilding, has two different sets of slipcovers for her living-room chairs. "In a small city apartment, the same look can get tedious," she said. "And when you send one set to the cleaners, you've still got something to put on the chair."

And though custom slipcovers, a must for most upholstered furniture, can cost several hundred dollars, ready-to-wears for generic chairs can cost much less. Gracious Home in Manhattan (1217 Third Avenue;

988-8990), for example, has a few navy piped, cotton duck slipcovers for metal folding chairs at $47.50.

Ms. Arcus, who learned sewing in her native New Zealand, has slipcovered hard-to-fit items, such as knoll sofas and sofa beds. Clients have had her slipcover bargain-priced showroom samples for a unified look and mismatched dining room chairs. (She recently fashioned a set in a heavy brocade.)

"You get these frumpy chairs and turn them into completely different people," she said. For simple jobs, she cuts muslin patterns on site. More complex furniture must be brought to her Tribeca workshop. She charges from $325, plus $95 a cushion, to slipcover an upholstered chair, fabric not included.   MARCUS FEILDING LTD.; (212) 349-1696.

"IF ANYTHING, SLIPCOVERS NOW HAVE A SENSE OF HUMOR," said Vikki Vandamm, owner of Vandamm Interiors in Greenwich, Connecticut, and a custom slipcover designer.

For a party, Ms. Vandamm fashioned shirt-tailored slipcovers for metal folding chairs with front and seat in pinstripe, with a white yoke at the top; the pinstriped back featured a white collar and a row of tiny shirt buttons. And for a room with a western theme, she slipcovered an armless chair in denim, added a petticoat of heavy lace and tied a bandana around the back.

She also devised a bikini slipcover for a wood-framed dining-room chair, with a skirt for the seat and a top for the back that exposed several inches of the curved wood in the middle. She charges from $240, fabric not included, to slipcover a chair, from $110, without fabric, for an ottoman.   VANDAMM INTERIORS, 375 Greenwich Avenue, Greenwich, CT 06830; (203) 622-9070.

MONTE COLEMAN IS KNOWN for fashioning witty, pleasingly quirky custom slipcovers to the specifications of designers, such as Vincent Wolf. For Mr. Wolf, who doesn't like slipcovers that "look upholstered," Mr. Coleman's creations often have a relaxed, loose look.

But Mr. Coleman also designs slipcovers. Several recent designs featured two skirts, one a bit shorter than the other, in different colors. Custom slipcovers for sofas start at $600, without fabric.   MONTE COLEMAN, 49 East 10th Street, New York, NY, 10003; (212) 995-2649.

F INE TAILORING AND DRESSMAKER DETAILS, often with a touch of whimsy, distinguish slipcovers by Pembrooke & Ives. The eight-year-old business specializes in custom, one-of-a-kind slipcovers, usually from sketches submitted by designers.

Owner Andrew Sheinman favors slipcovers with distinctive details—skirts with box or pencil pleats, shirred skirts, buttons "that actually button up the back." He prefers a tailored look with careful fit, "a cross between upholstery and a slipcover." Custom slipcovers for upholstered chairs start at $500 without fabric, from $900 for sofas. PEMBROOKE & IVES, 149 Wooster (near Houston Street), New York, NY 10012; (212) 995-0555.

COREY MANSUETO, a partner in Decor Couture, thinks even simple slipcovers should have details, such as kick pleats that show a peek of contrasting fabric. Mr. Mansueto, a prop designer for Broadway musicals, also favors slipcovers that look unstructured "but are fitted so they don't move around."

To give a slipcover the look of "something found in an aging Italian villa," he recently dyed fabric, then hand-stenciled it. And he just finished sofa slipcovers of unbleached painters' canvas. He charges from $250 for a dining-room chair, fabric not included; from $500 for a sofa. DECOR COUTURE; (212) 727-0123.

SLIPCOVER DESIGNER SAMI ROSENZWEIG, owner of Slips in San Francisco, makes custom ready-to-wear slipcovers for generic chairs, including directors' chairs, bentwood café chairs and folding metal chairs.

Customers can choose fabric, colors and details. He can add a magazine pocket to his basic directors' chair slipcover, for example. For mail order jobs, he usually requests a room picture, then sends swatches. Directors' chair slipcovers in cotton duck start at $65, fabric included. SLIPS, 1543 Grant Avenue, San Francisco, CA 94133; (415) 362-5652. ✉

HEADBOARDS, A POOL TABLE AND AN UPRIGHT PIANO are a few of the items Victoria Allen, owner of Custom Slipcovers and Interiors in Westerly, Rhode Island, has slipcovered. "The piano needed to face the room," she explained. "So I gave it a long box-pleated skirt in linen." She charges from $175 to slipcover a simple chair.   CUSTOM SLIPCOVERS AND INTERIORS, 157 Main Street, Westerly, RI 02891; (401) 596-5099. By appointment.

# SONGS,
# FOR SPECIAL OCCASIONS

"HAPPY BIRTHDAY TO YOU" is one of the most popular songs in the world, but it's hardly scintillating. That's why some people want something different for special occasions. A familiar tune, perhaps, with custom-tailored lyrics. Or a fresh melody with lyrics that gently, or not-so-gently, toast or roast the honoree.

A new song can be a present itself, particularly if it comes with sheet music suitable for framing or a cassette recording.

But finding someone to write, sing and record a custom song can be a challenge. Songwriters' organizations, such as ASCAP, do not routinely provide sources for such work. Still, a number of professional composers write original songs or parodies for both individuals and corporations. "It can be a pleasure," said Dennis Scott, a Nashville-based composer who won a 1981 Grammy Award for his children's album, *Sesame Country.*

Mr. Scott can write a completely new song. But his specialty is parodies. "I listened to a lot of Alan Sherman as a kid," he said.

A native of New York City, Mr. Scott's first album was *Songs that Tickle Your Funny Bone,* a collection of song parodies for kids. Ditties included "Please Put Your Toys Away" to the tune of "Anchors Away."

Since then, he has produced albums, written TV and video soundtracks and composed dozens of songs. In 1987, Ray Charles sang "Always a Friend," which Mr. Scott cowrote, on an episode of the TV show *Who's the Boss.*

For individual commissions, Mr. Scott gets lots of information about the subject. "Inside jokes, interesting traits, quirks, big events in the person's life—that type of thing," he said.

Though he usually writes new songs for corporate events, he thinks parodies of well-known songs work best at family gatherings. "That way people can concentrate on the lyrics and not strain to listen," he said.

Mr. Scott can also record his songs in his 16-track recording studio, offering piano or orchestral accompaniments. Songs start at $300, studio work is additional.   **DENNIS SCOTT PRODUCTIONS,** P.O. Box 150874, Nashville, TN 37215; (615) 292-9459.   ✉

SARAGAIL KATZMAN BENJAMIN, a composer for 20 years, saw a production of *The Music Man* when she was four years old and has been hooked on show tunes ever since. "I like the old stuff," she said. "Rodgers and Hammerstein, George Gershwin. If I wrote that kind of stuff today it would sound dated. But I like to stay with the basic ideas and structure and jet propel it into this era."

Ms. Benjamin, whose children's musical *The Alexandria Municipal Reading Library* was performed at Manhattan's Quaigh Theater in 1985, writes for weddings, birthdays and other events. She prefers to write all-new material, though she also does parodies. "It's easier to create a specific mood," she said.

Clients receive sheet music and a tape. Ms. Benjamin, who has been a cabaret singer, can also perform the work. Songs start at $300, performances are $300.   **SARAGAIL KATZMAN BENJAMIN;** (914) 576-3854. ✉

## SOUND RESTORERS

*S*OME CALL IT CRACKLE. Others say it sounds like bacon cooking. Whatever it's called, the background static heard on old phonograph records, from 78s and LPs to World War I–vintage diamond disks, is annoying. But it need not always be permanent.

For years, professional sound restorers have decrackled and enhanced historic sounds for the recording industry. Without restoration, few reissues of old recordings, from Caruso to Cole Porter, would be marketable as CDs and tapes. (Never mind that the hippest contemporary rock artists now consciously leave in background gibberish.)

The cleanup process is costly, however, and until recently, consumers with rare old recordings haven't been so fortunate. Some places that transfer old recordings to CDs do not have noise removal equipment. But a few professional sound restorers quietly take occasional jobs from private individuals when time permits. And in 1995, Quintessential Sound, a three-year-old sound restoration firm, extended its service to consumers, transferring rare records and tapes onto master compact discs.

Since then, the company has restored and transferred to tape or CD everything from vintage recordings of Gregorian chants to an opera singer's audition recordings from the 1930s. A lawyer who worked as a DJ in college had a CD made of his radio broadcasts—with the music he introduced edited out. And a woman gave her husband a CD of his high-school marching band as a birthday gift.

"A number of our clients are collectors with rare records they want to listen to without damaging the original," said Gabe Wiener, the company director. Other common CD transfers include 45s that were never issued on compact discs and old recordings that are unplayable because their owners no longer have the right turntables or tape machines.

"We're like audio archeologists," Mr. Wiener said. Indeed, the company also makes CDs from acetate discs, a precursor of tape recordings. "There was a place in Times Square during World War II where servicemen could record messages for their families," Mr. Wiener said. "We've transferred a number of those."

Audio archeology is a distinctly digital-age craft. The transfer starts on a turntable outfitted with a stylus that fits the record's grooves. Until the 1950s, groove sizes varied; using the right stylus enhances sound.

To electronically remove crackles, sound is fed into a computer system that looks like a tower of CD players. Pushing buttons and turning dials, the sound engineer programs the computer to eliminate as much unwanted noise as possible.

"The process is based on the fact that sound comes in the form of a wave," Mr. Wiener explained. Crackles are like breaks in the wave. The computer analyzes the wave mathematically and reconstructs the sounds that are not there.

Next, the engineer transfers the sound to a master compact disc, made from gold instead of aluminum. In factories, mass-produced CDs are stamped with a lathe. But to make just one, it is necessary to burn the program code onto a chemically treated disc. Since this requires a highly reflective surface, gold is used. Disks hold 74 minutes of sound.

Copyright laws prevent such companies as Quintessential from transferring certain materials for the public, notably recordings issued after 1971, recordings currently on the market or recordings that will be rereleased.

The setup fee for each compact disc is $100; restored material costs $2 a minute. It costs $200 to transfer a 50-minute LP to CD or $244 for a set of 12 78s that run three minutes a side. **QUINTESSENTIAL SOUND, INC.,** 1600 Broadway (near 48th Street), New York, NY 10019; (212) 586-4200.

FOR INDUSTRIAL CLIENTS, Electro-Nova Productions, a 19-year-old audio studio, edits out noise digitally, a costly process. To keep costs down for consumers, the company uses a simple filter, then transfers the recording to a gold master disc. "You may still have some pops, but we can usually clean it up a little," said Mark Sydorak, president. Electro-Nova charges $125 to transfer one hour of material from LPs, 33s, 45s or cassettes onto a disc. **ELECTRO-NOVA PRODUCTIONS,** 342 Madison Avenue (at 43rd Street), New York, NY 10173; (212) 687-5838.

MUCH OF THE BUSINESS at Master Cutting Room comes from recording companies that want extraneous noise, such as microphone buzzes, tape hisses and crackles, removed from soundtracks to be reissued on CD. But the 25-year-old sound restoration company occasionally removes unwanted sounds and transfers recordings onto CDs for individuals. The company also does forensic sound enhancements, amplifying background voices that may be important in legal cases. Typically, the setup fee is $350 plus $65 a minute, but prices vary depending on the recording. **MASTER CUTTING ROOM, INC.,** 250 West 49th Street, New York, NY 10019; (212) 765-8496.

DOUG POMEROY, OWNER OF POMEROY AUDIO, opened his audio studio in 1976, after working as a staff engineer for Columbia Records. Though he works mostly with professionals, he also removes extraneous sounds from recordings and tapes for private individuals. One secret of making a clean-sounding CD from a static-ridden recording is simply to play the record properly with the correct stylus. "That way you get less noise to begin with," explained Mr. Pomeroy, who has a large collection of custom styluses.

He also uses a sophisticated English computer-based system to remove unwanted sounds. Mr. Pomeroy charges $10 a minute for the computer processing, plus $75 an hour for manual editing by an engineer and $75 for each hour of programmed material. **POMEROY AUDIO,** 193 Baltic Street, Brooklyn, NY 11201; (718) 855-2650.

## SOUND SPECIALISTS

RECENTLY, Steve Plotnicki, president of Profile Entertainment, a record company, had a home theater installed in his Southampton house. It was designed to showcase a big picture and big sound, with a 32-inch TV, a 100-disc CD player, cassette tape deck, laser disc player, four powerful built-in wall speakers and a large subwoofer, which makes sounds pulsate.

"You get one of these and immediately go out and rent *The Terminator*," he said.

An electronics wizard familiar with the latest speakers, components and wiring could probably hook up a home theater with relative ease. But most people require the services of a professional systems designer.

With increasingly sophisticated electronics systems, such as projector screens and centralized audio, security and lighting systems, demand has grown for systems designers, who install and, in some cases, select and even create components to meet the customer's requirements.

A systems designer can also help those who quake at the prospect of hooking up a simple TV, speakers and CD player in the living room.

Customers often call a systems designer before an equipment purchase. "In a 20-by-16 foot room with a huge screen, you want a big sound to emphasize the image," said Paul Austi, president of Audio

Video Crafts, a custom systems designer in Long Island City. "But with a 35-inch screen in a smaller room, you don't need six speakers."

On large jobs, systems designers frequently work with architects or interior designers, as Mr. Austi did with designer Norman Michaeloff, who devised the 15-by-22-foot library in the 1994 designer show house in Southampton.

Following Mr. Michaeloff's instructions—"I didn't want it to look high tech, with everything blinking," the designer said—Mr. Austi put together a sound system consisting of a 53-inch TV, a surround sound receiver, six speakers, a 100-chamber CD library, tape deck, FM tuner, VCR and laser disc player, all hooked to a single remote control. The entire job including equipment came to about $12,000.

Mr. Austi's nine-year-old company also installs multiroom sound systems that store all electronic equipment—CDs, VCRs, tape decks—in a single closet and allow residents to listen to a different CD or tape in various rooms. AUDIO VIDEO CRAFTS, 37-31 30th Street, Long Island City, NY 11101; (718) 706-8300.

WHILE IT IS EASIEST TO INSTALL large electronics systems when a residence is being built or remodeled, a system that includes wall speakers usually can be fitted with minimal damage in postwar buildings with sheetrocked walls or homes with basements, where wires can be housed. Installations are usually more cumbersome in prewar buildings with thick plaster walls.

But sometimes wires can be run under wall-to-wall carpets. And for small rooms or rentals, Aaron Sacks, manager of Charos Custom Sound in Southampton, suggests thin white wire tape that can run along walls and be painted so it won't show as much.

Though Charos also sells sound equipment, the company will do designs and installations using some equipment other than their own. Labor costs from $45 to $100 an hour, per worker, depending on job complexity. CHAROS CUSTOM SOUND, 28 Cameron Street, Southampton, NY 11968; (516) 283-4428.

AUDIO DESIGN ASSOCIATES OF WHITE PLAINS, which manufactures and installs high-end multiroom audiovisual equipment and home theaters, frequently integrates household electronic systems, connecting push-button-control drapes, telephones and lights, with room-to-room audiovisual systems; commands are delivered on a touch screen, much like an ATM machine.

In one system, each room is equipped with an $800 keypad resembling a light switch that offers options from adjusting FM volume, station and bass to dimming the lights.

The 21-year-old company also designs security systems, including a new finger-touch scanner that memorizes fingerprints and unlocks doors accordingly. "There's no fumbling with keys," said Wayne Boyle, an ADA vice-president. The system costs $3,620 for one door, $1,500 each additional door.

Though ADA, which charges $125 an hour, or $425 a day for labor, specializes in large jobs, they can refer customers to affiliated installers for smaller jobs.   **AUDIO DESIGN ASSOCIATES,** 602-610 Mamaroneck Avenue, White Plains, NY 10605; (914) 946-9595.

THE COMPLEX SYSTEMS installed by Audio Command that include security, lighting and audiovisual for an entire house are usually controlled with a touch screen. But with the proper software, the entire home system can be monitored on a computer outfitted with a touch screen, according to Robert Kaufman, president of the 21-year-old company.

"With a computer, you can sit in your office in another city and close the drapes and turn on the lights in any room of your house," Mr. Kaufman said. His company charges from $50 to $65 an hour, $5,000 job minimum.   **AUDIO COMMAND SYSTEMS, INC.,** 46 Merrick Road, Rockville Center, NY 11570; (516) 766-5055.

THOUGH BORIS FERCOVICH, president of Audio Hi-Fi Consultants, has installed complex home theaters, he also does small jobs, such as hooking up a pair of speakers, a TV, CD player and receiver. "You need to find the best way to hide the cable," he said.

An important part of the job is teaching the customer how to use the equipment. "Otherwise, the person can find himself with a remote control and nowhere to go," he said. Mr. Fercovich, in business since 1981, charges $60 an hour plus a $30 travel fee.   **AUDIO HI-FI CONSULTANTS, INC.,** 37 Comet Lane, Levittown, NY 11756; (212) 741-6997 or (516) 731-7863.

ULTIMATE SOUND & INSTALLATIONS IN RICHMOND HILL, Queens, specializes in designing high-end audiovisual systems and home theaters. But the nine-year-old company also does smaller jobs, such as installing single-room systems. Simple multiroom systems also can be modified inexpensively.

"If a kid doesn't want to listen to what's playing throughout the house, we can install a jack where he can plug in his boom box and hear his own music through the room's built-in speakers," said Jack Borenstein, president of Ultimate Sound. Ultimate charges $75 an hour per worker. ULTIMATE SOUND & INSTALLATIONS, INC., 91-01 108th Street, Richmond Hill, NY 11418; (718) 441-6161.

# SPRAY PAINT FOR FURNITURE

"SOMETIMES IT'S KIND OF FUN to go out and find people who don't normally do what you need to have done," says Barbara Hill, an artist and movie set designer in Houston, Texas. And that is precisely what Ms. Hill did when she wanted a slick, lacquered look for a collection of wood and metal furniture from the 1940s and '50s for her house.

With a box of automobile paints in fuchsias, purples and blues, she took her furniture to a nearby auto-body shop and asked to have it sprayed. "They had never had a request like that," she said. But they did it, right down to the old, curved wood sofa legs. "I wanted something one-of-a-kind," Ms. Hill said. "And I didn't want to spend a lot of money."

Paint applied with a spray gun is sleeker and glossier than paint applied with a brush or roller. And when the spray gun is loaded with high-tech industrial paint, like that used on automobiles, the look is shinier still.

A recent sampling of auto-body shops in New York City indicates that not many are eager to take on jobs like Ms. Hill's. More often, a shop will paint an unconventional object for a long-time customer.

Ever since sculptor Leon Hariton asked him to paint several large metal artworks, Matthew Meng, owner of the Little Garage in Woodside, Queens—69-20 48th Avenue ([718] 446-3670)—has been willing to occasionally spray objects other than cars. "But it can get expensive," he said. "It's easier to estimate the price to paint a BMW than a filing cabinet."

A good alternative to auto-body shops is companies that restore porcelain bathtubs, spray paint large appliances or paint metal office furniture. While most make house calls for large items, small items must usually be brought to the company's shop.

Robert Leib's specialty is painting dental equipment (the most unusual item he ever painted was a CAT-scan). But he also spray paints kitchen cabinets, appliances and metal office furniture as well as wood furniture.

Though Mr. Leib, whose late father started A & B Spraying Co. more than 40 years ago, normally mixes colors, he recently sprayed a bedroom set for a client with glossy Benjamin Moore paint. But metal objects require a tougher finish, he said.

He charges $150 to refinish a refrigerator. A & B SPRAYING CO., 14 Sweetfield Circle, Yonkers, NY 10704; (718) 652-0132 or (914) 969-5999.

STONE SERVICES INC., NEAR YANKEE STADIUM, is a large, 57-year-old concern that specializes in spray painting office furniture. But they also do smaller, residential jobs. Stone Services can offer a variety of finishes, from simple enamels used on household woodwork to costly, high-tech paints such as Imron, which is "very strong, durable and flexible," according to owner Peter Maron.

Since spray paint magnifies imperfections, objects must be in good condition. If an object is rusted or dented, Stone will reshape and sand it. The company has spray painted artworks, wicker, wood furniture and, recently, a set of auditorium chairs.

Stone charges from $45 to paint a three-, four- or five-drawer file cabinet in enamel or epoxy. STONE SERVICES INC., 445 Gerard Avenue (near 144th Street), Bronx, NY 10451; (718) 292-6000.

AMONG THE METAL OBJECTS James White, owner of Custom Spraying and Reglazing, can spray paint are outdoor furniture, spiral staircases, file cabinets and desks. He recently started using the electrostatic refinishing process, which attracts paint to a metal surface magnetically and is considered more environmentally sound than some spray methods. He charges from $65 a chair to paint yard furniture, $150 minimum. CUSTOM SPRAYING AND REGLAZING, 389 Nome Avenue, Staten Island, NY 10314; (718) 494-3751.

CUSTOMERS USUALLY CHOOSE WHITE OR OFF-WHITE when they ask to have their kitchen cabinets spray painted, according to Diana Prieto, a partner in Authentic Porcelain. "But we can match colors and have color charts to choose from," she said.

Authentic Porcelain, which specializes in bathtub refinishing, can spray wood cabinets, including filing cabinets, and metal furniture. The company charges about $225 to paint a wrought-iron outdoor table and four chairs. The company only makes house calls, $225 minimum. AUTHENTIC PORCELAIN REFINISHING; (718) 726-1481.

## STAINED GLASS, REPAIRED AND CUSTOM-MADE

THREE STAINED-GLASS WINDOWS dominate the Gil Studio, Thomas Garcia's airy SoHo workroom. One is a new window Mr. Garcia designed for a South Carolina church. The second is a heavily leaded window, colorful but buckled, that fell from a Fifth Avenue church. And the third is an important turn-of-the-century window, pocked with bullet holes, from a Manhattan building.

The windows, which neatly sum up Mr. Garcia's range, also illustrate the tasks a small but growing number of glass studios can accomplish. A stained-glass artisan since 1973, Mr. Garcia designs and fabricates new windows in contemporary styles. He also does repairs and restorations, which the church window needs. It will require new leading and some new glass, which must be matched with the old.

Stained-glass conservation, Mr. Garcia's other specialty, is relatively new in the United States, though Europeans have practiced it for years. (The New York Landmarks Conservancy has a list of glass conservationists.) For windows with historical value, Mr. Garcia saves as much original glass as possible and documents every step, taking photographs, making rubbings and keeping meticulous notes.

His favorite job, to date, was repairing a floral skylight by D. Maitland Armstrong, a Tiffany contemporary, that was destroyed in a fire. "It was like detective work trying to figure out how the original was done and find the right glass," he said.

Prices depend on the job. Simple repairs start at about $50 for a lamp or stained-glass panel. Mr. Garcia gives estimates and accepts commissions from throughout the country. GIL STUDIO, INC., 145 Hudson Street, New York, NY 10013; (212) 219-8620. ✉

DECORATIVE STAINED GLASS was extremely popular in the United States around the turn of the century. And much of it is now in need of repair, according to Tom Venturella, a stained-glass artisan since 1969. "Glass made in this country holds up well, but the life of lead is about 80 to 90 years," he said. "You see a lot of buckled windows."

Mr. Venturella, who has a light-filled studio over Union Square, fabricates new windows and repairs old, including Frank Lloyd Wright windows set with zinc or brass instead of lead. He also specializes in conservation. Two years ago, Mr. Venturella spent a year working on seven turn-of-the-century windows for Pennsylvania's state capitol building in Harrisburg. His task included cleaning the windows and removing lead strips, used in previous repairs, which masked the windows's original images.

Despite modern refinements, the concept of leaded stained glass has changed little since the ninth century, Mr. Venturella said. His own interest in stained glass dates from his Catholic school days in the Midwest, when he would gaze at the windows of the choir loft and wonder "how they did that stuff." Mr. Venturella gives estimates and accepts jobs from throughout the country. Simple repairs start at around $50. VENTURELLA STUDIOS, 32 Union Square East, New York, NY 10003; (212) 228-4252. ✉

"A LOT OF PEOPLE COME TO US WITH LIGHTING PROBLEMS," said Bill Cummings, who owns Cummings Stained Glass Studios in North Adams, Massachusetts. "Our job is to affect the light in the room." The studio, which has been in Mr. Cummings's family since 1928, has done stained-glass fabrication, restoration and conservation for a variety of well-known buildings, including San Francisco's Neiman Marcus department store and the Old Executive Office Building in Washington, D.C. The latter, which recently received a G.S.A. design award, was a replication; the original turn-of-the-century stained-glass dome was removed and destroyed in 1947. The studio achieved a design, working with old black-and-white drawings and paint samples.

Cummings Studio, billeted in a vintage barn, will also take on smaller projects, particularly if complex lighting problems are involved. Stained glass can cut glare from nearby buildings or provide color and light for windows shaded by trees. The studio also fashions large stained-glass sculptures, which can create dramatic lighting effects when suspended between clear windows. Repairs range from about $300 to $1,000 a square foot.   CUMMINGS STAINED GLASS STUDIOS, 182 East Main Street, North Adam, MA 01247; (413) 664-6578.   ⊠

# STATIONERY, CUSTOM-MADE

"WE HAVE A LOOK," said Maria Thomas, whose 15-year-old company, Pendragon, Ink, specializes in personalized stationery, from wedding invitations and birth announcements to placecards and menus. The look is ornate and vaguely Victorian. Colorful hand-painted flowers garnish a message lettered in elaborate calligraphy and embellished with lots of curlicues.

Ms. Thomas, whose studio is a Victorian house in Whitinsville, Massachusetts, is one of a growing number of artists who design and create cards, announcements, invitations, envelopes and other personalized documents. Some started their businesses because they were bored with mass-market cards and invitations sold in stores. Others liked the idea of offering snippets of functional—and affordable—artwork, no matter how ephemeral.

Ms. Thomas, who began her six-person company for both of these reasons, also needed a job that kept her at home while she cared for her three children. "And I'm fascinated with letter forms," she said.

Prospective customers can order a packet of sample cards for $10. Ms. Thomas next creates the calligraphy, which is printed by offset on cream-colored stock. Using the Japanese brushstroke technique, she then hand paints flowers onto the printed cards. Though the rose is the most popular bloom, Pendragon, Ink, also offers lady's slipper, violets and holly. Ms. Thomas can add metallic tones to the buds, as well. "Gold looks very nice with peach," she says. Wedding invitations start at $420 for 50.   **PENDRAGON, INK,** 27 Prospect Street, Whitinsville, MA 01588; (508) 234-6843.   ✉

ON HER BIRTHDAY THREE YEARS AGO, Helene Dolney received a pad of watercolor paper measuring just four by six inches. She discovered she enjoyed making scaled-down watercolors of flowers and landscapes, which she affixed to cards and gave to friends. Before long, she was in business, taking commissions for hand painted thank-you notes, blank cards and invitations, which she can embellish, when necessary, with calligraphy.

Ms. Dolney, based in Manhattan, also sells hand-made cards decorated with origami animals (the good-luck crane is her favorite), dried flowers and details from original color photographs. "I love color," she said. "That's one reason I paint flowers."

Much of Ms. Dolney's work is customized and all of it is signed. For a company specializing in plant-based hair products, for example, she designed cards with a bright yellow arnica painted on the front. Cards cost from $5 to $25 each.   **HELENE DOLNEY;** (212) 598-0441.   ✉

"WE'RE TRYING TO COMBINE ESTHETICS WITH TRADITIONS," said Judith Brous, holding an elaborate, hand-painted ketuba, a Jewish marriage certificate. Judaic Creations, started in 1991 by Ms. Brous and her partner, Pamela Ostroff, offers a range of personalized Jewish documents, including birth, bar mitzvah and bat mitzvah certificates, designed by artists in Israel and the United States. Documents are lettered in Hebrew calligraphy, and most are decorated with classic Jewish symbols, such as wheat, grapes and the Star of David.

With the ketuba, which is traditionally framed and hung in the bedroom, customers usually order a one-of-a-kind document, designed to include images and text of their choice ($900 and up). "A couple married in the Central Park Zoo asked for a ketuba with stylized animals," said Ms. Ostroff. Another wrote an English text that concluded, "We will never go to sleep fighting."

The company also offers printed artist-designed documents, with suitable Old Testament quotations ($250 and up). Cards are available; newlyweds can order thank-you cards illustrated with their ketuba. Catalog availabe.   JUDAIC CREATIONS; (212) 724-2401.   ✉

WENDY R. MILLER'S CARDS can be very personal. Ms. Miller, in business since 1991, likes to work from photographs furnished by clients when she designs cards in pen and ink. For a 50th anniversary party, she worked with old wedding photos of the honored couple. And for a stockbroker, she created a greeting card incorporating a line drawing of the man with *The Wall Street Journal*'s Money and Investing logo.

Ms. Miller, whose company, A La Card, also designs personalized business cards and stationery, prints her drawings onto cards by offset. Then, using paint, she delicately hand-colors the black-and-white images. Standard four-by-six-inch cards cost three dollars to five dollars each, minimum order 25.   A LA CARD; (212) 753-5295.   ✉

## STATIONERY (OBSOLETE SUPPLIES)

WHATEVER HAPPENED to reel-to-reel typewriter ribbons, mimeograph stencils, old blue ledger books with cream-colored paper and other office supplies from the precomputer age?

They're still made, and while most superstores won't touch the stuff, traditional office and school supplies can be found at a shrinking number of old-fashioned stationery stores.

One such shop is William Klass's Upper East Side stationery and art-supply store, which looks much as it did when it opened in 1953. Much of the merchandise is also reminiscent of that vintage. Besides Speedball pen points and silk reel-to-reel typewriter ribbons, the store stocks adding-machine ribbons, carbon paper with pages attached and all types of erasers.

Besides the new stuff, such as post-its and hi-liters, Mr. Klass's well-stocked shop carries a small stash of discontinued art supplies, such as Bellini oil paint in tubes ($8 to $20 each) and picture postcards of famous artworks (30 cents each). **KLASS STATIONERS AND ART SUPPLIES,** 970 Lexington Avenue (near 70th Street), New York, NY 10021; (212) 737-4500.

THE LAST IBM SELECTRIC TYPEWRITERS rolled out of the factory in 1987. Many have been junked. But with 12.5 million made, plenty are still in use—enough, in fact, that Lexmark International, which makes and markets IBM typewriter products, still makes six styles of ribbon cassettes for Selectrics.

Ribbons are also available for the Model B Executive, an IBM electric typewriter introduced in 1956, and IBM's dot matrix printers. "Some of that hardware will last forever," said Ken Bissell, a communications manager at Lexmark.

Lexmark carries six styles of ribbon cassettes for Selectric typewriters (from $5.50) and has a stash of old golfball fonts in a variety of type styles, including Courier and Italic ($40 each). **LEXMARK INTERNATIONAL;** (800) 438-2468.  ✉

NORMAN KAUFMAN ADMITTED THAT CUSTOMERS were not clamoring for silk reel-to-reel typewriter ribbons at his 50-year-old Brooklyn stationery shop, Kaufman's Office Supply. "But I sell enough to keep ordering more," he said. And though self-inking stamps have made wood-handled rubber stamps almost obsolete, he still sells an occasional stainless-steel carousel to hold 8, 10 or 12 old-fashioned rubber stamps ($24.95, $26.95 or $29.95). **KAUFMAN'S OFFICE SUPPLY,** 167 Mineola Boulevard, Mineola, NY, 11501; (718) 693-4130 or (516) 873-7994.

## STENCILS

NINETEENTH-CENTURY NEW ENGLANDERS used them to liven up their furniture, fabric and walls. The Victorians embellished ceilings with them. And Pennsylvania farmers applied them to barns.

But it took the late-20th-century computer to make stencils an elaborate and sophisticated decorating tool. "You couldn't cut an intricate design like this by hand," said Mary Lou Smith of Stencil World, a mail order house specializing in stencils. "But a laser computer can read a design exactly as an artist draws it. The computer can also produce stencils in quantity."

Stencils, which come in many sizes, shapes and designs, are a quick, inexpensive and individualistic way to decorate just about anything, be it a room, a canvas bag or a worn-out piece of furniture. They are ideal for rental apartments, where wallpapering a room can prove too costly. And the choice of designs has never been greater.

"For years, stencils meant duckies and chickies, but no more," said Susan Saye, executive secretary for the Stencil Artisans League, an international organization based in Norcross, Georgia, that promotes stencil design and instruction.

In recent years, several mail order companies offering nothing but stencils have begun throughout the United States.

Ms. Smith learned to stencil several years ago, after seeing a painted chest she liked at the Metropolitan Museum of Art. She bought an unfinished piece of furniture, took classes in faux finishing and got hooked on stenciling.

These days, she designs many of her company's stencils and offers stenciling tips to customers. Her company also offers custom stencils, on-site stencil installation and stenciling classes. Ms. Smith particularly likes stenciling "little surprise areas," she said, holding a stencil that looked like a plaster ceiling cornice. "Stencil a cat so you see it when the bathroom door closes.

"Stenciling is simply pushing paint through a hole," she added. The stenciler secures the mylar design to the wall with masking tape, then applies paint in circular strokes using a round, flat-tipped brush. "The only mistake you can make is using too much paint," she said.

Ms. Smith recommends quick-drying stenciling paint, available in dozens of colors. Stencils range from $7 to $60. Her catalog costs $3.50.   STENCIL WORLD, P.O. Box 1112, Newport, RI 02840; (401) 847-0870.   ✉

STENCILER'S EMPORIUM, Jane Gauss's eight-and-a-half-year-old mail order company in Ohio, offers more than 2,000 stencil designs as well as paint, brushes and books. But if a customer still doesn't find a favorite, Ms. Gauss, a stencil artist for over 20 years, can provide custom designs.

Some stencils are simple, like precut border patterns that cost $6 to $10. Others are extremely complex and can cost over $100. Cut with laser computers, trompe l'oeil wall designs can require overlays in seven or eight different colors, each adding shading and depth.

Ms. Gauss, author of *Stenciling Your Walls* (Plaid Enterprises, $7.50), sells an array of early American folk designs, including flowers and starbursts. But interest in these is waning. "Everyone wants ivy," she said.

Stenciler's Emporium offers two design catalogs, a sampler for $8.50 containing over 700 designs and a loose-leaf notebook for designers containing over 3,500 designs for $30.   STENCILER'S EMPORIUM, P.O. Box 536, Twinsburg, OH 44087; (800) 229-1761 or (216) 425-1766.   ✉

DEE KELLER LIKES TO THINK BIG when she stencils. A custom designer, she stenciled a bookshelf onto a kitchen wall for a client who didn't have room for the real thing. And for a Philadelphia show house, she stenciled a fourposter canopy bed onto a wall in an alcove. "There's no limit to what you can do," she said.

Though she has a catalog of 300 designs ($5), Ms. Keller does on-site work in the Atlanta area, traveling from her shop in Newnan, Georgia. She often does floral designs, including elaborate vines and bouquets. (One customer stenciled her rosebud and ribbon design onto the hem of a wedding gown.) But trompe l'oeil designs are her favorites. "I can stencil an oriental rug onto your floor," she said. Catalog stencils range from $3 to $150.   DEE-SIGNS LTD, P.O. Box 960, Newnan, GA 30264, (404) 253-6444;  **DEE-SIGNS SHOWROOM,** 147 Jackson Street, Newnan, GA 30263; (404) 253-6444.  ✉

## STORAGE SUPPLIES (CONSERVATIONALLY CORRECT)

WHEN STORING DELICATE ITEMS, from photograph negatives to old prom gowns, good intentions are rarely enough. "Damage can occur precisely when you think you've got something safely stored away," said Bruce Hutchison, former head of the Textile Conservation Laboratory at the Cathedral of St. John the Divine in Manhattan.

Some wrapping materials stain, while others trap moisture and attract dust. And glues, paints and foams can leech out formaldehyde, which often distorts colors and corrodes metals.

Fortunately, a variety of conservationally correct storage supplies are currently available, including acid-free boxes, tissue paper and adhesives. And a handful of specialty companies, including mail order houses, stock the latest archival materials.

Talas, or Technical Library Services, owned by Jake and Marjorie Salik, specialized in bookbinding supplies when it opened more than 30 years ago. The company, which accepts mail orders, still stocks hand-made marble endpapers, bookbinding paints and leather for book covers.

But a big part of Talas's business is acid-free materials, including boxes in a variety of sizes. Priced from $5, the gray or beige boxes come with flaps or removable tops. Costume boxes, 18 inches wide and either 30, 40 or 60 inches long, are ideal for storing wedding gowns. Instead of glue, metal edges secure the sides, making the boxes strong enough to stack.

Talas also sells two types of acid-free tissue paper. The Saliks recommend buffered paper, buttressed with calcium carbonate and with an alkaline pH of 8, for cottons and linens (15 cents for a 20-inch by 30-inch sheet). For acidic fabrics, such as silk and wool, they suggest unbuffered tissue with a neutral pH (85 cents for a 24-inch by 36-inch sheet). Quantity discounts are available.

Most acid-free boxes and papers are actually lignin-free, which means the lignin content may not exceed 3 percent. Lignin, a natural element in wood pulp, eventually breaks down and forms acid.

A number of universities now require doctoral candidates to submit dissertations on acid-free paper. Mr. Salik also suggests photocopying important documents on acid-free paper. TECHNICAL LIBRARY SERVICES (TALAS), 568 Broadway (at Prince Street), New York, NY 10012; (212) 219-0770.

EVEN ITEMS IN ACID-FREE WRAPPINGS will eventually be vulnerable if stored in a humid basement or attic. But Light Impressions, a nearly 30-year-old mail order archival supply company, offers a number of items for testing and combating humidity levels.

Serious art collectors often use a recording thermometer/hygrometer, a battery-driven device that lists temperatures and humidity over a seven-day period. Light Impressions sells the Abbeon Cal model for $918.16. A cheaper alternative is Hydrion Humidicator Paper, which comes in a tape dispenser and changes color to indicate humidity levels ($7.50 for a 200-foot roll).

Light Impressions also sells a reusable desiccant canister filled with silica gel, which absorbs moisture. "You can dry it out in an oven and reuse it," said Dennis Inch, vice-president of Light Impressions.

The company offers a number of photographic storage supplies, as well, including polypropylene sleeves for protecting negatives, lignin-free envelopes for color prints and acid-free slide boxes. "Impure cardboards will eventually send out gases that can affect photographic images," said Mr. Inch. LIGHT IMPRESSIONS, P.O. Box 940, Rochester, NY 14603; (800) 828-6216. ✉

A CUSTOMER RECENTLY ASKED UNIVERSITY PRODUCTS, INC., to create special acid-free boxes for displaying popcorn kernels. "He said no two kernels are alike," said owner John Magoon, whose nearly 30-year-old mail order archival supply company devised custom kernel boxes with transparent mylar tops. (Similar boxes can display butterflies, leaves and other bugs and fauna.)

Besides a variety of matting materials and adhesives, University sells special storage containers for phonograph records, stamps and other collectibles. Mylar envelopes are specially sized to shield comic books, as are acid-free comic book boxes in silver or gold. And an acid-free three-ring binder for up to 675 baseball cards comes with a dignified maroon cover.

University Products also sells Wei T'o, a deacidification spray for paper ($41.15 a can). It can extend the life of paper by removing acid, but users must be careful. "Some inks may be soluble in that solution," Mr. Magoon warned. **UNIVERSITY PRODUCTS INC.,** P.O. Box 101, Holyoke, MA 01041, (800) 628-1912; in Massachusetts, call (800) 336-4847. ✉

# STOVES (VINTAGE), SOLD AND RESTORED

To SOME PEOPLE, they are just old stoves, a prosaic kitchen accoutrement at best. But not to David Erickson, who restores and sells vintage cookers at Erickson's Antique Stoves. "These things are mechanical works of art," he said. "They're gorgeous."

The old stoves in question range from nickel-plated Victorian coal-burners to huge, white 1950s models, loaded with chrome. Cast-iron gas ranges from the 1920s are particularly distinctive, with an exposed, nickel-plated gas pipe on the front and stately Queen Anne legs. Stoves from the '30s are more streamlined and, with fewer surface details, easier to keep clean. And boxy '40s stoves look more like today's models.

In recent years, old-fangled stoves have become increasingly popular in new-fangled kitchens, notably in older houses and apartments where a retro kitchen looks comfortable. But the stove rehabilitation business extends to recent restaurant models, which have sleek, contemporary lines and are designed for durability.

Even '60s stoves in harvest green and yellow are being restored by their owners and, occasionally, selling to collectors. "Many people are distressed by the quality of new stoves," said Mr. Erickson, a stove restorer since 1980. "The old ones have a unique style and heavy-duty construction. They just need a good, solid tune-up every 40 to 50 years."

A properly rehabilitated gas stove is essentially a new stove in an old body. Mr. Erickson, who completely dismantles each old stove, installs an automatic safety pilot; in bygone times, owners struck a match to light the oven. He also rebuilds old thermostats. If the original thermostat is still not reliable, he installs new components.

Mr. Erickson, who handles stoves from the 1870s to the 1950s, became a stove enthusiast—and restorer—by chance. A former industrial arts instructor, he bought an old Victorian train depot, then fixed up a vintage stove to heat it.

These days, the depot is his workshop and showroom, where he has about 200 stoves. He can pick up and deliver stoves nearly anywhere in New England, New York or New Jersey. Major repairs cost $500 to $3,000. Stoves rehabilitated by Mr. Erickson start at around $1,700.  ERICKSON'S ANTIQUE STOVES, 2 Taylor Street, Box 2275, Littleton, MA 01460; (508) 486-3589.

BEA BRYANT REHABILITATES ANTIQUE STOVES in the tiny town of Thorndike, Maine. But her old stoves have been shipped all over the world. (Her company, Bryant Stoves/Music Inc., once sent a vintage kitchen stove to the new Euro Disneyland outside Paris.)

Mrs. Bryant, a stove collector for over 40 years, deals mainly in stoves from the 1880s to 1930s. She also rehabilitates gas and wood combination stoves. Business took off in the early '70s when the energy crisis made the old models more cost effective, she said. "People needed cheap heat."

Mrs. Bryant, a past president of the Antique Stove Association, personally prefers very old models, including those from the 18th century. "The newer the stove, the plainer they got," she said. "People spent a lot of time designing the older ones."

Her company, in business since the late 1960s, specializes in restorations of the stoves of Clarion, Atlantic and Kineo, old Maine companies founded around 1839. Though the company takes trade-ins, it does not repair stoves it has not sold. Rehabilitated kitchen stoves start at $1,000. A free catalog is available.  BRYANT STOVES/MUSIC INC. Box 2048, Thorndike, ME 04986; (207) 568-3665.  ⊠

. . .

ANTIQUE STOVE HEAVEN, which rehabilitates and sells vintage stoves, requires three showrooms to display its full stock of antique cookwear. The Los Angeles company, in business since 1983, carries stoves ranging from turn-of-the-century woodburning models to 1950s models by Wedgwood.

Though the company stocks plenty of rank and file stoves from the '20s, '30s and '40s, the house specialty is the unusual, such as a 1920s Standard Electric, one of the first electric stoves ever made, and the 1923 Roper, a gas model outfitted with three ovens, six burners *and* a warming oven. Stove Heaven also stocks the O'Keefe & Merit Town & Country, a gigantic monster similar to a restaurant stove.

Most of the company's stoves run on gas. "We don't change the way they're made," said Dell Williams, whose son, Winsor Williams, owns the company. "But we do outfit them with automatic pilots."

The company stocks both rehabilited models and stoves in the rough. The company will restore the latter to meet the specifications of the customer, Mrs. Williams said. Stoves range from $895 to $12,000 for an elaborate Magic Chef from the '20s or '30s with lots of chrome. ANTIQUE STOVE HEAVEN, 5414 South Western Avenue, Los Angeles, CA 90062; (213) 298-5581.  ✉

## STRINGED INSTRUMENTS, REPAIRED AND RESTORED

DAVID GAGE'S TRIBECA WORKSHOP smells of wood and contains many of the varnishes and tools seen in a cabinetmaker's shop. But there's a big difference between repairing a bookcase and repairing a bass. Mr. Gage and his four associates, all trained musicians, restore stringed instruments—cellos, violins, violas and, the house specialty, basses. And though appearance is important, "The sound is what matters," said Mr. Gage, inspecting a wounded bass.

Like anything made of wood, stringed instruments are vulnerable to changes in temperature and humidity. But basses, with more wood than most instruments, are particularly susceptible to cracks and splits. Because of their size, they get bumped and nicked. "We get a lot of airplane damage," said Mr. Gage, whose customers include classical, country, jazz and amateur musicians.

Stringed instruments also need adjustments from time to time. The thickness and curve of the ebony fingerboard, for example, helps determine timbre.

Much of Mr. Gage's work is on older instruments. "A 150-year-old bass has a richer, more sophisticated sound than a new one," he explained. Most old instruments can be be repaired and adjusted. Cracks can be fixed and worn-out parts, such as bridges, soundposts and ebony fingerboards, repaired. "We try to keep as much of the original as we can, including the varnish," added Mr. Gage, an instrument restorer for over 15 years.

The company also makes cases so stringed instruments can travel on airplanes. "Cases are a necessity," Mr. Gage said. "Even if you buy a first-class seat for your bass, the airlines won't let it on unless it's in a case."

Mr. Gage charges $65 an hour, $30 minimum.  DAVID GAGE STRING INSTRUMENT REPAIR, 36 Walker Street, New York, NY 10013; (212) 274-1322.

PHILLIP INJEIAN HAS BUILT, restored and repaired violins for over 25 years. But some of his work is seasonal. Summer humidity, for example, can warp wood, which drops the violin's neck and raises string height. "The bridge needs to be adjusted a few millimeters," he said. Dampness also can swell the pegs, which hold the strings. Swollen pegs don't turn properly. The solution? A professional greasing. "Never leave an instrument in a basement," he cautioned.

Like most wood objects, violins, violas and cellos show wear with use. Bridges, which suspend the strings, wear down. Fingerboards become grooved and require replaning and sanding. And seams can split. Older instruments, in particular, are problematic. They are particularly susceptible to atmospheric change. "And most have gone through many repairs already," Mr. Injeian said. "It's a challenge to make the repairs look invisible."

Mr. Injeian also rehairs bows ($40, including cleaning), and again, weather is a consideration. Dry weather will tighten bows, so strings must be a bit loose. But for high humidity, which loosens bows, strings should be tight.

Mr. Injeian charges $75 an hour and up.   **PHILLIP INJEIAN LTD.**, 850 Seventh Avenue, Suite 1002 (near 55th Street), New York, NY 10019; (212) 397-1310 or (203) 834-0595.

ACOUSTIC GUITARS ARE SURPRISINGLY COMPLEX. They typically contain 60 to 70 pieces of wood. And inside, they're a maze of wood reinforcements. But properly cared for, they can last for years, says Matt Umanov, who has sold, repaired and restored acoustic and electric guitars for over 30 years. "A lot of problems we see come from neglect," he explained. Guitars get left in car trunks or damp basements. "Or you loan it to a friend who whacks it into a wall," he added.

Electric guitars aren't as delicate or vulnerable to climatic changes. "They're more subject to wear and tear from enthusiastic playing," Mr. Umanov said. The wiring in an electric guitar is about as complicated as that of a toaster, he added. But tiny wire coils can break; jacks can also cause trouble.

Mr. Umanov, an authorized repair shop for guitars by Martin, Gibson and Fender, also fixes banjos and mandolins. It costs $25 to change a set of strings, plus the cost of the strings.   **MATT UMANOV GUITARS,** 273 Bleecker Street, New York, NY 10014; (212) 675-2157.

MUSIC AND SCULPTURE are Rick Kelly's two main interests. And as a maker of custom guitars, he gets the best of both worlds. Mr. Kelly, a partner in Carmine Street Guitars, a Greenwich Village shop, has made both acoustic and electric guitars for 25 years. "A custom guitar can be designed to fit your particular playing style," he said. Some people like guitars with wide necks; some want the instrument built to fit their hand size.

A choice of wood is also available. Typically, Mr. Kelly uses ash, alder, walnut or mahogany for the body, which needs to resonate, and ebony and rosewood for the fingerboard, where a dense wood works best.

Mr. Kelly also repairs ailing guitars, which is more challenging than creating a new guitar from scratch. "You have to work from the inside out," he explained. "You can't take the top off like lifting the hood of a car." Much of his repair work is done using dental mirrors and tiny light bulbs.

Repairs start at $35 for a cleaning, new strings and a neck adjustment. Custom guitars start at $850 for a solid-body electric and go to $2,500 and up for an acoustic model. **CARMINE STREET GUITARS,** 42 Carmine Street, New York, NY 10014; (212) 691-8400.

## TABLE LEAVES

Almost no one ever loses a dining-room table. But table leaves are another matter. They languish in attics, get forgotten in closets and can easily be misplaced during moves.

Most cabinetmakers should have the skills needed to make a table leaf, says Joseph Biunno, whose woodworking shop specializes in furniture restorations and antique reproductions. "The hard part is to match the wood to the existing table and give it the same finish," he said.

The leaves must also be aged for a seamless match. "In the course of two weeks, you've got to give those leaves the appearance and flavor of an old table," Mr. Biunno said.

Table leaves fall into two categories. Some are replacements built for tables that can already accommodate leaves. Others are made for tables that must be rigged with an expanding device to accept the leaves. Various methods of table expansion exist. Some leaves can be removed and stored in a closet. Some fold into a compartment under the middle of the table. And some fold out at the ends, supported by wings.

While expansion devices can be fitted to most tables, the enlarged table must balance properly, Mr. Biunno said. Few tables can accept an unlimited number of leaves.

Mr. Biunno also makes customized boxes for storing and protecting table leaves. The felt-lined boxes, set on wheels, cost from $250 to $750. Customized table leaves for both new and antique tables start from $600 for a simple leaf.   JOSEPH BIUNNO LTD., 129 West 29th St., New York, NY 10001; (212) 629-5630.

IF A TABLE WAS MADE SOMETIME IN THE 20TH CENTURY, it should be fairly easy to match the wood for table leaves, says William A. Olsen, owner of Antique Furniture Workroom, which restores antique furniture, gold leaf, leather and lamps.

It's the older woods that pose problems. "Mahoganies from the 18th and 19th centuries no longer exist," Mr. Olsen said. Similar vintage chestnuts, rosewoods and big swirled walnuts are also hard to duplicate. And a perfect match is a must, "unless you plan to use a tablecloth," Mr. Olsen said.

The more-than-80-year-old company makes table leaves and expansion devices for both new and antique tables. The concern can also repair cracks in tabletops and bases. Table leaves are priced from around $800 to $1,500 apiece.   ANTIQUE FURNITURE WORKROOM, INC., 225 East 24th St., New York, NY 10010.

CUSTOMERS WANT TABLE LEAVES FOR LOTS OF REASONS, says Adel Tamer, whose father Mohammed started Tamer Fine Furniture more than 20 years ago. The Brooklyn woodworking concern recently made leaves for a customer who decided to save money by expanding his 42-inch cherrywood table instead of buying a new one.

If a table has never been expanded, Tamer will cut the top and fit the table with an expansion device to accommodate the new leaves.

Leaves one inch thick start at $125 and go up depending on wood, thickness and difficulty of matching the original table.   TAMER FINE FURNITURE CO., 465 Baltic St., Brooklyn, NY 11217; (718) 522-6427.

# TASSELS

IN 18TH-CENTURY EUROPE, well-dressed curtains, sofas and armoires were often garnished with decorative bundles of cotton, wool or silk yarn. These tassels could be large or small, elaborate or plain. Their main purpose was to add a whimsical dash of color.

Traditional silk tassels with corded tops and fringed skirts are still made by such companies as Scalamandré, which supplies decorators with custom work. But tassels are also available at retail shops like the following.

The elaborate tassels at Le Décor Français come from a workshop in Paris. "They're made in either wool or shiny cotton, exactly the same way they were made 100 years ago," said Jacqueline Coumans, the shop's owner.

The shop, which opened on Lexington Avenue in 1989, has a selection of ready-made tassels and tie-backs, from tiny three-inch tassels that can embellish pillows to heavy tassels connected with cord to hold curtains. The shop also sells custom-made tassels in a variety of sizes, colors and styles.

"There is no end to the kinds of tassels we can make," said Ms. Coumans, flipping through a catalog of styles. Customers can design their own tassels, choosing from tops and skirts that can be mixed and matched, or they can have tassels copied.

Prices start at $30 for a tassel meant to hang from the key on an armoire, and from $75 for a corded tie-back with large twin tassels. LE DECOR FRANCAIS, 1006 Lexington Avenue (near East 73rd Street), New York, NY 10021; (212) 734-0032. ✉

"WHEN CHOOSING TASSELS, the most important thing for most people is color, followed by style," said Samual Cohen, the owner of M & J Trimming Company.

The bright showroom, which opened in 1990, stocks more than 100 styles in a rainbow of colors, including hard-to-find dark hues, such as purple. The tassels and tie-backs, made mainly of rayon viscose or cotton in Italy, France or Spain, can also be custom-made.

Unusual models include key tassels with gold-trimmed brocade tops, large black Chinese tassels with fringed skirts and antique tassels in jet beads or metallic gold.

Prices range from $3 for a three-inch tassel to around $100 for a tasseled tie-back. **M & J TRIMMING COMPANY,** 1008 Sixth Avenue (near West 37th Street), New York, NY 10018; (212) 391-9072. ✉

HYMAN HENDLER & SONS is known for its enormous stock of ribbons, braids and decorative trimmings. But the company, in business for more than 85 years, also carries a large selection of rayon viscose tassels and tie-backs made in Spain. Prices start at $5.50 for a tassel.

Styles include tassels suspended from yarn rosettes, a popular embellishment for sofa arms. The tassels are designed in such color combinations as rose and green or navy and cream.

Tassels can last for years, and shop personnel usually recommend that customers buy tassels in colors they can live with easily. If a tassel loses its shape, it should be steamed or revived with a dab of water. **HYMAN HENDLER & SONS,** 67 West 38th Street, New York, NY 10018; (212) 840-8393. ✉

## TELEPHONES (VINTAGE), SOLD AND RESTORED

THOUGH HE SET OUT to revolutionize the world of communication, Alexander Graham Bell also had a lasting impact on interior design when he invented the telephone in 1876. "There were periods when hundreds of companies were making phones," said Richard Marsh, president of the Chicago Old Telephone Company, a mail order concern that restores and sells vintage phones.

Mr. Marsh estimates that more than a thousand different styles of phones have appeared worldwide during the past 117 years. And since the 1970s or so, vintage phones, from the 1960s Princess to 19th-century crank-up models, have grown increasingly popular with both serious collectors and those simply amused by the look of unusual old phones. "French phones had a third-party listening receiver," said Mr. Marsh. "In war movies, you always see the Gestapo listening in."

Telephone connoisseurs, in fact, often consult old movies when seeking a vintage phone. Mr. Marsh, in business since 1969, bought his first telephone, a classic 1920s candlestick, because it reminded him of one he had seen in a gangster film. In a famous publicity shot, Joan Crawford sits in a bubble bath talking on an Automatic Electric 40, a Deco-style phone, circa 1930 (from $269.95 for a restored model). The Stromberg Carlson 1191, a 1920s oval with a barbell-shaped receiver, was even dubbed the movie star's telephone because so many were used in Hollywood (from $299.95).

Besides selling old phones, the company does mail order repairs. Antique phones can be outfitted with parts cannibalized from old phones or reproduction parts. "We usually put new parts in garden-variety phones," said Mr. Marsh, who recommends old parts for valuable phones. "There's a big difference between a phone worth $100 and $1,000," he said. Repairs start at $50. A free catalog is available. CHICAGO OLD TELEPHONE COMPANY, 327 Carthage Street, Sanford, NC 27330; (800) 843-1320 or (919) 774-6625. ✉

PEOPLE WHO PICK UP OLD PHONES at flea markets or unearth them in an attic are usually in luck, according to Mary Knappen, whose 25-year-old mail order concern, Phoneco, restores and sells vintage telephones. "Most old phones can be repaired," she said. Besides outfitting phones with old or reproduction parts, Phoneco repaints old phones, polishes corroded brass and outfits phones with cloth, rubber or vinyl cords that clip into contemporary jacks. The company also sells phone parts and diagrams for do-it-yourselfers.

In addition to restored vintage phones, Phoneco offers reproduction candlestick phones in kits, $83 unassembled, $125 assembled in polished brass, $155 in black brass. A catalog costs $3. PHONECO, INC., 207 East Mill Road, P.O. Box 70, Galesville, WI 54630; (608) 582-4124. ✉

YASH JESRANI'S VINTAGE PHONES range from 1920s candlesticks, in black metal and brass, to the plastic question-mark-shaped Erica phone from the late 1950s. But his most popular item at his shop, Phone Boutique, is the Western Electric 302, a rectangular desktop phone, in black steel, from the 1930s. (Models from 1938 through the 1950s were of plastic.)

"It's a classic vintage phone," he said. "And it sounds good when it rings."

Audio qualities are one of the key attractions of vintage telephones, according to Mr. Jesrani, in business since 1971. "This dial has a clicking sound," he explained, holding up a black 1940s desktop phone from India ($110).

Mr. Jesrani modifies old phones as necessary, affixing dials to old phones that do not have them. For customers who want to keep the original appearance of a dial-less phone, he can discreetly attach a box hiding a touch-tone pad. Restorations start at $45.   PHONE BOUTIQUE, 828 Lexington Avenue (near 63rd Street), New York, NY 10021; (212) 319-9650.   ✉

THE 25-YEAR-OLD ANTIQUE Telephone Collectors Association publishes a monthly newsletter and sponsors shows, open to the public, where enthusiasts can buy, sell and trade phones and parts. Dues are $30. ANTIQUE TELEPHONE COLLECTORS ASSOCIATION, P.O. Box 94, Abilene, KS 67410; (913) 263-1757.   ✉

## TEXTILE CONSERVATORS

AS A TEXTILE CONSERVATOR, Judith Eisenberg works on all sorts of fragile fabrics, from shredded samplers to quilts riddled with holes. "They're usually flat textiles, like Asian embroideries, wall hangings, Torah curtains or lace," she said.

Not always, however. Several years ago, Ms. Eisenberg, a textile conservator for more than 15 years, was asked to help revive the original Winnie the Pooh. (The famous stuffed bear had a torn foot.) She also gently repaired his cohorts, Kanga, Piglet and Eeyore, the stuffed animals that inspired A. A. Milne's famous Pooh stories. All are now on view, behind glass, at New York's Donnell Library Center, 20 West 53rd Street.

Were Pooh just any old toy bear, he could have been repaired by a parent or, for a more professional touch, a textile restorer. "A restorer tries to make something look as much like the original as possible," Ms. Eisenberg said.

A conservator, in contrast, accepts that the object can't—and for historical reasons shouldn't—look as it did when it was first made. "You try to stabilize it to keep it from further deteriorating," she said. Aggressive alterations, such as ripping out stitching or replacing worn fabric, are avoided.

If there's a hole in a piece of fabric, for example, a restorer may reweave it. But a conservator is more likely to back it with fabric of the same color, which leaves the original undisturbed but takes attention away from the imperfection.

Occasionally, the lines between conservation and restoration blur a bit. Ms. Eisenberg, who charges $60 an hour for conservation work, recalled an antique crazy quilt in which bits of silk had deteriorated so much the lining showed. Rather than stabilize the shredded silk with a sheer overlay, she replaced the original fabric with silk specially dyed to match.

Once employed almost exclusively by museums, such textile conservators as Ms. Eisenberg now work for private clients as well, from full-scale collectors to individuals with a beloved snippet of heirloom lace. Besides treating objects to halt deterioration, conservators advise on the proper cleaning, storage and display of delicate textiles.

Ms. Eisenberg, who teaches textile conservation at the Fashion Institute of Technology, recently hand-stitched four antique needlelace panels onto sheer fabric so they could be framed. And since buckling causes fabrics to tear, she sews Velcro onto hangings and quilts to keep them flat against a wall.   **JUDITH EISENBERG;** (212) 691-2638.   ✉

MOST TEXTILE CONSERVATORS mount objects so they can lie flat in a frame. Joell Kunath specializes in three-dimensional mounting, so the object can be seen from all sides.

Much of her work, not surprisingly, is done for museums, including the Metropolitan Museum. But she also works for private clients, mounting such objects as antique waistcoats and wedding veils in the round.

"Clothes can be mounted as the Victorians mounted a suit of armor," said Ms. Kunath.

Before mounting, Ms. Kunath provides treatment for the object as needed, from wet cleaning to slight mending. She charges $250 a day; travel and supplies are additional.   JOELL KUNATH; (914) 235-0870.

# TILES (HANDMADE)

IN RECENT YEARS, the design world has embraced things hand-made, from wood furniture to decorative tiles. Indeed, after years of largely functional use, tiles are increasingly appearing as design elements on everything from fireplaces and floors to swimming pools and walls.

Though hand-made tiles have an obvious audience with those restoring historic houses or buildings, their appeal extends to anyone intrigued by the distinctive look of a hand-crafted product, with its individuality, color and, in many cases, patina of history.

Many hand-crafted tiles employ the methods, materials and designs popular during the Arts & Crafts movement, when individuality was also prized. Others evoke the Victorian era or beyond. And, of course, no two are alike.

"With hand-made tiles, you can get richer, more unusual colors than with most factory tiles," said Brenda Bertin, a tilemaker for more than 15 years. Hand-made glazes that contain classic ingredients, such as tin, copper, cobalt and iron, can result in warmer, older-looking tiles, she explained.

Ms. Bertin also strengthens her glazes with feldspar, which melts only at high temperatures. "If tiles are fired at very high temperatures, the clay and glaze fuse," she said. The resulting water repellant tiles can be used outdoors.

Ms. Bertin's pressed-tilemaking method, in fact, is not too different from that used since the Middle Ages. She starts with a drawing, transfers it to wax, carves the wax, then pours plaster molds, which are filled with stoneware clay. But instead of a hand-operated press, she uses a modern 5,000-ton hydraulic press.

Besides stock relief designs that include stars, flowers and geometrics, Ms. Bertin accepts commissions. For a Manhattan client who wished to be reminded of her house in Southampton, Ms. Bertin created tiles with pastoral scenes against a dark blue background. She also produced an encaustic frieze for the snack stand behind Heckscher Field in Central Park.

Plain glaze four-inch tiles cost $28 a square foot; decorative relief tiles cost $12 to $15 each. **BERTIN STUDIO TILES,** 476 Chemin Des Patriotes Nord, Mont St. Hilaire, Quebec, Canada J3H 3H9; (514) 536-0056. ✉

HISTORIC TILES ALWAYS APPEALED to tilemaker Linda Ellett, a co-owner of L'Espérance Tile Works in Albany, New York. And though she designs handmade tiles, much of her business is reproducing intricate Victorian designs in relief, in which the design projects from a flat background, and encaustics, in which different-colored clays fill grooves carved onto the tile surface.

Besides her collection of old tiles, Ms. Ellett often consults a library of catalogs from important 19th-century tilemakers. When the Mark Twain House in Hartford, Connecticut, needed tiles to restore a fireplace, only two tiles existed. Ms. Ellett hunted down designs for the rest in an old catalog from Low Art Tiles, a New England fabricator.

Ms. Ellett also can match vintage glazes from the 1860s to the 1960s. "If you have an old bathroom and only need a few tiles, it can be cheaper to have tiles made to match the existing ones than to rip out the entire bathroom," said co-owner Donald Shore, Ms. Ellett's husband.

Using a hand-press, Ms. Ellett works with traditional glaze recipes whenever possible. "A lot of old recipes used pure lead, so I do recipes that mimic the color and sheen," she said.

Six-by-six-inch decorative tiles cost $8 to $10 each. Decorative encaustics cost $110 a square foot. **L'ESPERANCE TILE WORKS,** 237 Sheridan Avenue, Albany, NY 12210; (518) 465-5586. ✉

A VISIT TO MEXICO YEARS AGO LEFT ANN SACKS with a keen interest in tile. So in 1980, Ms. Sacks, a Portland, Oregon, schoolteacher, entered the tile business. Ann Sacks Tile & Stone, eventually sold to Kolher Plumbing, now has seven showrooms throughout the United States, including New York.

Besides a selection of machine-made tiles in unusual shapes and colors, the company offers a range of hand-made art tiles, including tiles adapted from Arts & Crafts designs. The Moore-Merkowitz line, for example, features rustic pressed tiles infuenced by Moravian tile from the early 1920s. Six-inch-square decorative tiles range from $19.36 to $22.99 each.Catalogs cost $10. To order, call (800) 488-8453. ANN SACKS TILE & STONE, 5 East 16th Street, New York, NY 10003; (212) 463-8400. ✉

A SPECIALTY AT STELLAR CERAMICS in California is the Ancient Sands series. After an application of three or four different glazes, sand is thrown onto the tile. The tile is glazed again and then fired, resulting in misty colors and a slightly rough feel. "The look is natural and rustic," said Debbie Russell, the company's president.

Besides doing custom designs, Stellar has stock relief images including leaves, fruit and architectural motifs, several taken from Art Deco buildings in New York. Customers can choose from 117 glazes, which are mostly clear, and from white or red clay tiles. Plain tiles four inches square cost $14 to $18 a square foot. STELLAR CERAMICS, P.O. Box 1321, Healdsburg, CA 95448; (707) 433-8166. ✉ New York distributors: TILES, A REFINED SELECTION, 42 West 15th Street, New York, NY 10011, (212) 255-4450; WATERWORKS, 237 East 58th Street, New York, NY 10022, (212) 371-9266.

PEWABIC POTTERY USES the glaze recipes and tile-making techniques of Mary Stratton, who founded the company in 1903. Both new and historic designs are available, as are 500 different glazes. Four-inch-square tiles cost about $69 a square foot. PEWABIC POTTERY, 10125 East Jefferson, Detroit, MI 48214; (313) 822-0954. ✉ New York distributor: DESIGN SUPPLY/STONE SOURCE, 215 Park Avenue South (near 17th Street), New York, NY 10003; (212) 979-6400.

FULPER POTTERY OF FLEMINGTON, New Jersey, produced art pottery in crystalline and mottled glazes and colors that ranged from cat's-eye to violet wisteria. It closed after its factory burned in 1929. But the company started again in 1974, after Rada Fulper and her three sisters found 13 glaze formulas that had belonged to their grandfather, William Fulper III.

The company, now known as Fulper Glazes, produces hand-made tiles from those historic recipes. Fulper tiles are fired just once. During firing, the glaze breaks down, creating a multicolored effect, most notable in relief tiles. Four-inch-square tiles cost about $60 a square foot. FULPER GLAZES INC., P.O. Box 373, Yardley, PA 19067; (215) 736-8512. ✉

MICHAEL PRATT AND RETA LARSON, a husband and wife pottery team, designed their first hand-made tiles in 1980 while living in a cabin near Mount Hood in Oregon. The resulting tiles, rich in Arts & Crafts–style patterns, featured northwestern images, such as pine cones and bears.

Their tiles are still rich in botanical images, "historical but with a modern twist," Mr. Pratt said. A square foot of four-inch-square plain tiles costs $25.75. PRATT & LARSON, 1201 Southeast Third Avenue, Portland, OR 97214; (503) 231-9464. ✉ New York distributor: COUNTRY FLOORS, 15 East 16th Street, New York, NY 10003; (212) 627-8300.

BARDELLI, AN ITALIAN TILE MANUFACTURER, has a line of machine-made ceramic tile that uses designs by the late artist Piero Fornasetti. They include his whimsical sun and moon motifs on black-and-white five-inch-square tiles ($325 for a 24-tile set), a 24-tile frieze of multicolored hot-air balloons ($350) and a design that resembles shelves of leather-bound books (about $460 for a 16-piece set). HASTINGS TILES, 230 Park Avenue South (19th Street), New York, NY 10003; (212) 674-9700. ✉

# TIN CEILINGS

A CENTURY AGO tin ceilings were extremely popular, gracing countless restaurants, shops and kitchens all over the United States. They disappeared in World War II, when metal grew scarce.

But in recent years, interest in these elaborately patterned ceilings has returned on a more modest scale, said John Shanker, president of Shanker Industries, manufacturers of metal ceilings since 1912.

These days, pressed-metal ceilings with classic lines and curlicues can be seen in restaurants, bars, billiard halls, kitchens and bathrooms. The embellished panels, either painted or left tin-tone gray, can also line fireplaces, cover walls and, when perforated, even serve as radiator covers.

Tin ceilings are said to have originated in New York in the late 1860s, when enterprising shopkeepers used tin sheets to cover cracked plaster ceilings. Rope was added to hide seams, and carved rosettes masked rope joinings. Decorative metal sheets with images, often of Greek, Roman or Victorian origin, transferred onto metal dies from wood carvings were soon widely available.

"It was a way for middle-class homeowners to get the look of expensive hand-carved plaster at a fraction of the cost," said Fran Shanker, executive vice-president of the company.

Many of today's metal ceilings are actually steel. Shanker, of Oceanside, New York, offers 37 vintage ceiling and cornice patterns stamped in 30-gauge steel by a 65-ton press built in 1928. Panels can be colored with oil-based paint or left steel gray, protected by a coat of clear polyurethane. Copper and brass plating are also available, as are color coatings baked onto the metal.

Shanker Industries does not take retail orders but will provide a list of its distributors throughout the country. A free catalog is available. SHANKER INDUSTRIES, 3435 Lawson Boulevard, Oceanside, NY 11572; (516) 766-4477. ✉

METAL CEILINGS ARE QUINTESSENTIALLY AMERICAN, said Mark Quinto, vice-president of W.F. Norman Corporation, which manufactures metal panels, cornices and ornaments. Indeed, the Nevada, Missouri, company made an elaborate brass ceiling for a room in the Taj Mahal Casino in Atlantic City.

"We can do a subtle ceiling or a bold ceiling," Mr. Quinto said. Panels range from relatively flat three-inch patterns that repeat like wallpaper to elaborate patterns two inches deep that repeat every eight feet.

The nearly century-old company, which still uses designs from its 1902 catalogue, also uses its original production tools, including drop hammers and cast-iron dies. Most normal ceiling panels are made of tin-plated 30-gauge steel; copper and brass sheet are also available. Tin-plated steel panels two feet by four feet start at $19.

W.F. Norman also has a wide range of outdoor architectural embellishments, including urns, friezes, garlands, lion heads and weathervanes. Outdoor ornaments are available in sheet zinc, copper, bronze and other alloys. The company offers over 140 items. A catalog is available for three dollars. **W.F. NORMAN CORPORATION,** P.O. Box 323, Nevada, MO 64772; (800) 641-4038 or (417) 667-5552. ✉

A METAL CEILING, PROPERLY CARED FOR, will last for decades, said Charles Gruber of A.A. Abbingdon Affiliates Inc., the Brooklyn distributor for Shanker Industries. "You have places in Mercer Street in SoHo that have had the same ceiling for 120 years," he said.

Mr. Gruber, whose family has sold tin ceilings for more than 70 years, also recommends special cone-head nails, which enhance the panels' relief if they are nailed to a ceiling. There are also lay-in metal panels that fit into ceiling grids as acoustical ceiling squares do. Installation instructions are available.

Steel lay-in panels and nail-up panels, two feet by four feet, cost $20.30 each for orders under 200, $1,835 for more than 200. A.A. Abbingdon has a free catalog. **A.A. ABBINGDON AFFILIATES INC.,** 2149-51 Utica Avenue, Brooklyn, NY 11234; (718) 258-8333. ✉

# TOPIARY

*T*HEY DIDN'T GET TOP BILLING, but to garden enthusiasts, the real stars of the 1991 film *Edward Scissorhands* were the shrubs coaxed into whimsical shapes, such as leaping dolphins and graceful swans.

Topiary, the art of pruning and training plants into witty forms, was invented by Cnaius Matius, gardener to Julius Caesar, in the first century B.C. And after veering in and out of fashion over the centuries, it has become popular again, says Mia Hardcastle, co-owner of Topiary Inc. and designer of several gigantic toparies seen in *Edward Scissorhands.*

Several types of plantings qualify as topiary these days, including frames stuffed with sphagnum moss and covered with ivy or creeping fig, large, plant-covered frames and trained trees, plants and shrubs.

Mrs. Hardcastle, a former mechanical engineer, and her partner Carole Guyton, a long-time gardener, began designing and selling galvanized-steel topiary frames by mail order more than 20 years ago, when Mrs. Guyton was inspired by Disney World's flamboyant topiary. Frames can be ordered alone or planted.

Aided by books and visits to the zoo, Mrs. Hardcastle has created more than 80 shaped frames ranging from a tabletop turtle, five inches tall ($7.50 for frame alone; $22 planted) to a four-foot giraffe ($90 frame alone; $150 planted). Geometric and customized shapes, including spheres on stems, are also available. Free brochure with SASE. TOPIARY INC., 41 Bering Street, Tampa, FL 33606; (813) 254-3229. ✉

TOPIARY'S CURRENT POPULARITY is no mystery, says Deborah Reich, a topiary designer since 1987. Topiary complements postmodern architecture, appeals to the growing number of sophisticated gardeners and works well in city gardens. "You can have a trained herb in a pot or a small animal shape on a windowsill," said Ms. Reich, author of *The Complete Book of Topiary* (Workman, 1988). And espaliers, ideal for terraces, take no floor space.

Ms. Reich has created many customized pieces, including an eight-foot hemlock dinosaur for a lakeside house and a pair of condors once exhibited at the San Diego Zoo. These days she specializes in large frames for outdoor topiaries, which start at $250. "Seahorses are popular for seaside homes," she said. "But I've done just about any animal you can think of." A free brochure is available. DEBORAH REICH & ASSOCIATES LTD., 466 Washington Street, Suite 8E, New York, NY 10013; (212) 219-0873. ✉

LOGEE'S GREENHOUSE LISTS 2,400 INDOOR PLANTS in a three-dollar color brochure. Not surprisingly, a number of these can be trained for topiaries, including poodles, as topiary spheres are known. Myrtles, boxwood, rosemary and scented geraniums are a few of the most popular topiary varieties, says owner Joy Logee Martin.

Logee's, founded more than 100 years ago, also sells three types of creeping fig and has six strains of small-leaf ivy. Plants come in 2½-inch plastic pots and start at $2.75, minimum order $20.  **LOGEE'S GREEN-HOUSE,** 141 North Street, Danielson, CT 06239; (860) 774-8038.  ✉

# TV HIDEAWAYS

A SLEEK NEW TELEVISION in black or gray can look like a piece of sculpture in the right room. But it's often a lot more attractive to hide the television when it's not in use, particular in a traditional setting.

Most manufacturers of ready-made furniture offer cabinets and shelf units designed to conceal televisions, as well as VCRs and tapes. But an increasing number of carpenters and custom cabinetmakers, large and small, will create one-of-a-kind television enclosures or refit existing cabinets to accommodate a TV.

A variety of options exist if you're looking for a customized TV hideaway, according to Basil Walter, an architect who has designed custom television enclosures for over a decade.

For a restored 1880s home in New Jersey, for example, Mr. Walter, a partner in the firm Sweeny Walter Associates, designed an enclosure with paneling to match the existing woodwork. The new, thinner televisions also mean cumbersome, super-deep cabinets are not always necessary.

The most common enclosure is a cabinet with flipper doors that open out and push back into side chambers. The TV sits on a swivel platform that can pull out.

Remote control pop-up units, with the television hidden in a specially built cabinet, are also popular. With the push of a button, the cabinet top opens and the TV, set on a metal frame, is elevated for viewing.

With projection televisions, the screen can be lowered from its hiding place in a specially built drop ceiling. The image is projected on the screen from machinery concealed in "something that looks like a coffee table," Mr. Walter explained.

And a very large television can sit on a specially made cart with castors, hidden inside a cabinet. The cabinet doors can swing open to display the set. Or, for maximum viewing, the cart can be pulled out of the cabinet and set in the middle of the room.

Mr. Walter, who teaches custom cabinetry at Parsons School of Continuing Education, designs television enclosures according to client specifications, take bids from cabinetmakers and oversees the object's creation. He charges $100 an hour or a percentage of the total cost of the finished object.　SWEENY WALTER ASSOCIATES, 611 Broadway (at Houston Street), New York, NY 10012; (212) 505-1955.

CUSTOMIZED TELEVISION ENCLOSURES are a sizeable chunk of business at Antique Furniture Workshop, an 80-year-old custom cabinetry shop. But over half of the company's jobs entail converting antique cabinets into home entertainment centers, according to owner William Olsen.

Antique armoires usually require a specially built shelf to hold the television. Holes can be drilled to accommodate wires. And if the set is too deep for the cabinet, a hole can be cut in back. "We're seeing a lot of Edwardian pieces for television enclosures these days," Mr. Olsen said.

The firm recently converted an 18th-century inlaid bachelor's chest a client purchased at Sotheby's. "It worked nicely since the top doors opened like an armoire," Mr. Olsen said. "You could admire the wood drawers below while you watched TV."

Antique Furniture Workshop will also design and build enclosures according to customer specifications. A recent oak creation was made to look like a Mission table, 30 inches tall, with a bookcase beneath. Two panel doors hid the set. "A lot of people like low televisions," Mr. Olsen said. New enclosures start at around $1,000, conversions at around $300.　ANTIQUE FURNITURE WORKSHOP, 225 East 24th Street, New York, NY 10010; (212) 683-0551.

ALMOST ANY TYPE OF CHEST CAN BE CONVERTED to accommodate a pop-up television, according to Joseph Biunno, owner of Joseph Biunno Ltd., a custom cabinetry shop. The company once fitted a 24-inch-tall Chinese blanket cabinet with a pop-up TV unit and a six-inch base, so it could stand at the foot of the owner's bed. The television was flanked by shelves to hold the VCR and tapes.

Pop-up television mechanisms have been available for nearly 20 years, according to Mr. Biunno. But their popularity has grown in recent years as the price has dropped. Auton mechanisms, which Mr. Biunno's company uses, start at around $850, and work by remote control.

Good candidates for pop-up televisions are round tables, wood cubes and dressers with false drawerfronts. Woodwork starts at around $800 for something simple.  **JOSEPH BIUNNO LTD.,** 129 West 29th Street, New York, NY 10001; (212) 629-5630.

# TVs (VINTAGE), SOLD AND REPAIRED

$O$NE FOOLPROOF WAY to avoid seeing colorized versions of *It's a Wonderful Life* and other holiday classics is to watch them on an old black-and-white television. And most vintage sets from the postwar 1940s to early 1970s can still work when properly repaired.

The problem is finding someone to do the job. "Television repair is difficult," said antiques dealer Harry Poster, who has sold and repaired old televisions for about eight years. "They have hundreds of parts and pieces." While old radios usually used six or seven tubes, televisions had at least 20. And if a glass picture tube comes loose, it can explode. Early televisions are also heavy; consoles can weigh up to 200 pounds, while 50-pound "portables" were the norm.

Yet in recent years, collectors have started snapping up vintage televisions, which generally cost $300 and $400 in working order. Most collectors are choosy. "They want the weird, strange and unusual," Mr. Poster said. "A pretty wood cabinet from the '60s? Forget it."

Purists go for postwar sets, which usually had seven-inch screens set in elaborate, often amusing, cabinets. Many look like radios or mad scientist equipment. Connoisseurs of 1950s nostalgia also collect, though the big, boxy '50s sets aren't as esthetically pleasing, Mr. Poster said. Collectors assiduously avoid color televisions. Exception: early color tube sets from around 1953. Also in demand: very early transistor sets, such as the primitive-looking Philco Safari and sleek Sonys.

Mr. Poster charges from $100 to $200 to get a television in working order. He is also author of *Poster's Radio and Television Price Guide*

(Wallace-Homestead; $17.95). **HARRY POSTER**, P.O. Box 1883, South Hackensack, NJ 07606; (201) 794-9606. ✉

VINTAGE TELEVISIONS USUALLY wound up in an attic because they were broken or because the family got a newer model, said Steve Conklin, who has repaired tube televisions and radios for 21 years. In both instances, the set will need extensive repairs. Old foil capacitors had wax insulators, which absorb moisture. With age, they will cause any set to break down.

In contrast, today's mylar capacitors last for years. Tubes are also relatively easy to replace, Mr. Conklin said.

Still, vintage sets are fragile, even when reconditioned. "I wouldn't leave an old set on for hours," Mr. Conklin said. On the other hand, most people don't want to watch hours of black-and-white TV, he added. Television repairs start at $75. **STEVE CONKLIN**; (516) 324-3012.

TO REPAIR A VINTAGE TELEVISION, a schematic, or map of the set's inner workings, is needed. And Alton Bowman, a radio and television hobbyist, sells schematics for dozens of TV models from the late 1940s to the 1970s.

For do-it-yourself TV repairs, a tube tester is also needed, along with a knowledge of electronics. "You can get a shock off a TV set even if it's not turned on," Mr. Bowman said. Schematics cost six dollars, with SASE. **ALTON BOWMAN**, 4172 East Avenue, Canandaigua, NY 14424. ✉

## TYPEWRITERS, CLEANED, REPAIRED AND SOLD

MOST PEOPLE WHO OWN TYPEWRITERS agree that the machines are dinosaurs. But they're not extinct quite yet, and a handful of companies, such as Osner Business Machines, still sell, service and repair aging manual and electric typewriters.

Some people, notably professors, journalists and playwrights, like to think on typewriters. Others use them for addressing envelopes or dashing off a note. The tactile side of typewriters also has a sort of Rube Goldbergian appeal; lots of things happen, and it's all cause and effect.

Neglect is at the root of most typewriter problems. Inky grime builds up when machines aren't cleaned regularly. Keys get sticky. Letters blur. But most machines can be revived. Keys can be resoldered. And letter buttons can usually be replaced.

Aging manual typewriters fall into two categories—prewar antiques and functional oldies, from the 1950s and '60s. These can usually be restored to work, but they aren't working typewriters. Attractive antiques can cost several hundred dollars. Functional oldies can cost less than $100.

Osner has been in business since 1941. So, not surprisingly, the shop has a floor-to-ceiling inventory of hard-to-get parts—keys, letter buttons, levers. Though desirable, exact replacement parts are not always available since the machines are no longer manufactured. "But parts have to come from the same typewriter family, or there's no fit," said owner Mary Adelman.

Some repairs are simple. With wear, platens become hard and shiny, but they are easily re-covered with rubber. In fact, most old typewriters can last for years with regular cleanings and adjustments. Exceptions are machines with badly damaged carriages that can no longer be bent back into shape.

Cleaning and minor repairs start at $38.50 for manual typewriters and $58.50 for electric models. **OSNER BUSINESS MACHINES,** 393 Amsterdam Avenue (at 79th Street), New York, NY 10024; (212) 873-8734.

LEV SHAPIRO'S CROWDED TYPEWRITER SHOP is not far from Lincoln Center, and a number of his repairs are on music typewriters. Mr. Shapiro, who has repaired typewriters for 20 years, also services electric typewriters, manual typewriters, antique typewriters and a variety of much newer machines, such as laser printers.

A worn-out drive belt is a common complaint with electrics. But a big problem for typewriter users is finding the right ribbon. So Mr. Shapiro and his son, Boris, keep a large inventory in the shop.

Minor repairs from $39.50; complete overhauls from $59.50. **LINCOLN BUSINESS MACHINES,** 111 West 68th Street, New York, NY 10023; (212) 787-9397.

## UMBRELLAS,
## SOLD AND REPAIRED

*F*OR GILBERT CENTER, manager of the Uncle Sam Umbrella Shop, bad weather means brisk business.

For over 120 years, Uncle Sam, which occupies a bright, street level shop on West 57th Street, has sold and repaired umbrellas and canes. The shop has rain umbrellas in all sizes, colors and prices, from an $8.95 folding model to a $275 English brolly with a cherrywood handle. In the repair area in the back, Mr. Center and his staff can often revive wounded umbrellas while the customer waits.

It costs $2 to sew fabric to an umbrella's tip, from $5 for a new handle and from $6 for a new metal point. Broken ribs take longer to replace, as the entire umbrella needs to be taken apart, and cost $10 and up. Even cheap umbrellas can be fixed, though repairs may cost more than the original.

Historians trace the umbrella to ancient Egypt and Africa. Rain umbrellas, heavily waxed in the days before water repellants, are thought to be an 18th-century European invention, as are collapsible umbrellas.

"But it took years to refine them," said Mr. Center, who has repaired umbrellas nearly all his life.

Dozens of umbrella repair shops once dotted the New York area, "before the advent of Taiwan and cheap umbrellas," said Mr. Center. At one time, the United States boasted seven manufacturers of rain umbrella frames. Now there are none, and the frames, handles and fabrics Uncle Sam uses come almost exclusively from the Far East, Italy and England.

Still, Uncle Sam, which made umbrellas for the musical *My Fair Lady*, can customize umbrellas in various fabrics and colors, using sturdy, round-ribbed English frames for $65. And for customers who want to use an umbrella in lieu of a cane, the shop will affix a rubber tip to the sturdier models. UNCLE SAM UMBRELLA SHOP, 161 West 57th Street, New York, NY 10019; (212) 582-1977.

BOB STORY, MANAGER OF ZIP JACK CUSTOM Umbrella in Elmsford, New York, once made a huge yellow umbrella, 16 feet in diameter, that was placed atop a float in the Cotton Bowl Parade.

Zip Jack, in business since 1950, assembles and repairs almost any kind of umbrella, from huge patio umbrellas to delicate antique umbrellas, according to Manny Dubinsky, the company's founder. Zip Jack will fix broken rain umbrellas, often while the customer waits, charging $4.70 for new tension springs and $1.25 for sewing a tip.

The company, which sells a wide range of rain and novelty umbrellas, will also personalize umbrellas with hand-painted lettering. And umbrellas can be custom covered in a variety of fabrics and colors.

Zip Jack's specialty is the so-called market umbrella, a large wood-frame umbrella covered in unbleached canvas that is popular on decks and patios, and is on view in the Hyatt Regency Hotel atrium.

Manufactured in Elmsford, market umbrellas start at around $375; Zip Jack will repair broken ribs for $31 and up. The company, which has a showroom and a brochure, also sells, and repairs, the huge Cinzano and Perrier umbrellas seen in dozens of outdoor cafés.

Zip Jack has a messenger service for pick-ups and deliveries in Manhattan and will mail umbrellas it repairs all over the country. ZIP JACK CUSTOM UMBRELLA, 141 South Central Avenue (Route 9-A), Elmsford, NY 10523; (914) 592-2000. ✉

# Upholstery Cleaners

Most upholstery cleaners also clean carpets, but it doesn't always work the other way around.

"Upholstery is harder to clean than carpets," said Barry Swidler, a partner in Long Island Carpet Cleaners, a nearly 80-year-old Brooklyn concern that cleans both upholstery *and* carpets. Carpets usually have a straightforward, easily identifiable fiber composition, be it wool or synthetic. "With upholstery, you need to know all kinds of fabrics," he said.

Certain fabrics, such as wool, can be cleaned with water and detergent, the most effective cleaning method. But wet cleaning ruins such fabrics as crushed velvet and silk; these can require dry cleaning with solvents. Fabric cleaning is, in fact, somewhat subjective. Some fabrics clean beautifully, others do not. Prints, for example, usually clean better than solid colors. And Haitian cotton, a fabric that contains bits of seed, is notoriously hard to clean.

A professional upholstery cleaning can prolong the life of a chair or sofa, improve its appearance and remove accumulations of unhealthy bacteria. Fabrics that require dry cleaning in particular usually need to be cleaned more frequently than heavy duty wools and synthetics. "The solvent won't work if the fabric is too dirty," said Mr. Swidler.

Fortunately, most upholstery cleaners work on site, so owners don't need to part even temporarily with much-used furniture. It takes approximately 20 to 30 minutes to clean a typical six-foot sofa.

Mr. Swidler's firm usually uses an extractor to clean upholstery. The extractor consists of two tanks, containing cleaning solution mixed with hot water and waste water. Using a wand attachment, the cleaner sprays on the solution, then vacuums it back into the machine. Extraction is effective because it removes both dirt and water. (Too much water turns some fabrics brown.)

Long Island Carpet Cleaners charges $16 a foot for wet cleaning, $22 for dry cleaning and $20 to clean Haitian cotton. **LONG ISLAND CARPET CLEANERS, INC.,** 301 Norman Avenue, Brooklyn, NY 11222; (718) 383-7000.

SAM KORNET, WHO OPENED FABRA-CLEEN in Queens more than 45 years ago, says vacuuming is the best way to maintain upholstery between cleanings. "Vacuum patiently, thoroughly and frequently," he said. Before vacuuming, run a soft brush over your upholstery to bring dirt to the surface. Rotate cushions and pillows regularly. And use a fabric guard to prevent stains. "But only when your furniture is freshly cleaned," he added. "Otherwise you're sealing in the dirt."

Mr. Kornet, who runs his business with his son, Brian, specializes in hard-to-clean fabrics, such as silks and Haitian cotton. For polished cotton, another cleaning toughie, he recommends wet cleaning with a mild solution so the shine won't come off. And he cautions against letting polished cotton go too long between cleanings. "Dirt is abrasive and wears off the finish," he said.

Fabra-Cleen charges $15 a square foot for upholstery. FABRA-CLEEN, INC., 222-28 95th Avenue, Queens, NY 11429; (212) 777-4040 or (718) 776-3565.

DAVE BARKSTEDT PREFERS WET CLEANING to dry cleaning, even though his firm, Elite Carpet and Upholstery Cleaning, does both. "With wet cleaning, you can get the water really hot, up to 212 degrees," he said. Solvents also are heated, but only up to 108 degrees. "Besides, the best cleaner in the world is water," he added.

Carpet and upholstery cleaners for more than 15 years, Mr. Barkstedt and his wife opened their business in East Rockaway six years ago. Elite charges $18 a foot for wet cleaning, $20 a foot for dry cleaning. ELITE CARPET AND UPHOLSTERY CLEANING, INC., 23 Adams Street, East Rockaway, NY 11518; (516) 887-5437.

A GOOD WAY TO SELECT AN UPHOLSTERY CLEANER is to contact a large trade organization, such as the Association of Specialists in Cleaning & Restoration. Among ASCR's amenities is a lab to help members deal with problem fabrics. ASCR, 10830 Annapolis Junction Road, Suite 312, Annapolis Junction, MD 10701; (301) 604-4411.

## Vacuum Cleaners, Cleaned and Repaired

HERE ARE SOME THINGS that should never, ever find their way into a vacuum cleaner: stockings, rope, underwear, toys, tacks, nails, coins and big bunches of pine needles.

But most vacuum cleaners can be repaired, says Richard W. De-Silva, whose grandfather started Desco Vacuum Sales & Service nearly 40 years ago. "People don't always realize that," he said. "They usually just throw them away."

Burnt-out motors, broken switches and cracked hoses are among the most common repairs. And as long as the parts aren't obsolete, repairs are not usually a problem, said Mr. DeSilva, who also sells new vacuum cleaners.

Desco, which has a large inventory of discontinued machines, can often locate necessary brushes, motors and other parts for obsolete vacuums. The company also rebuilds and sells vintage Electrolux canister-style vacuum cleaners. The original metal canisters are cleaned and painted either aqua or gray. Motors are reconditioned. And new parts are added. "You can throw these old metal machines against a wall and you may get a dent," Mr. DeSilva said. "With the new plastic ones, they'd crack." Rebuilt machines, which start at $139, are also cheaper than new ones, which cost around $700 to $800.

Repairs at Desco start at about $6.95 for a new plug, including labor. DESCO VACUUM SALES & SERVICE, 131 W. 14th Street (near Seventh Avenue), New York, NY 10011, (212) 989-1800; 1236 Lexington Avenue (near 83rd Street), New York, NY 10028, (212) 879-1980.

MANY VACUUM CLEANER REPAIRS could be avoided if owners would simply read the user's manual, says Jack Fried, who owns Active Sew & Vac, a family business for more than 60 years. For instance, upright machines, which use rotating brushes to pick up dust, come with a rubber belt that should be changed every four months.

A big misconception is that vacuum cleaners can pick up anything, Mr. Fried added. "First pick up anything you can see, then use your vacuum cleaner to get the dirt and dust."

Mr. Fried, who also sells new vacuum cleaners and parts, suggests that machines be serviced every four years. The process, $39.95 and up, includes a complete cleaning and examination, motor overhaul, new filters, new bags and a little oil for the wheels. ACTIVE SEW & VAC INC., 735 Amsterdam Avenue (near 96th Street), New York, NY 10025; (212) 663-1600.

# VCRs, TVs AND CAMCORDERS, CLEANED AND REPAIRED

WHEN THE TV GOES DEAD, the audiocassette player eats tape and the camcorder fails to work after you drop it, the next step is usually to buy a replacement. But in some instances, it pays to have an item repaired.

Once a warranty is gone, customers usually have more expensive items repaired, said Joseph Passaretti, president of Pyramid Electronics, a nearly 50-year-old service center that repairs VCRs, TVs, audio equipment and other consumer electronics. "We repair all kinds of Walkmans, but we usually advise to only have the top-of-the-line units serviced if the warranty is out," he said.

Exceptions occur, of course. The picture tube, the heaviest, and most costly, item in a TV set, usually costs $250 to $350 to replace in a 19-inch set, Mr. Passaretti said. "But sometimes a specific set fits a certain cabinet," he explained. "Or there's sentiment attached. The TV was the last thing the husband gave the wife before he died and she wants it fixed."

For items under warranty, repairs can often be cheaper than replacement even if the customer winds up paying labor costs. As proof of a warranty, all the owner needs at an authorized service center, such as Pyramid, is the bill of sale. "It doesn't matter whether you've mailed the card back to the manufacturer," said Mr. Passaretti, whose company is authorized to repair 28 brands, including Sony, Panasonic, JVC, Magnavox and Kenwood.

Before bringing in an item, Mr. Passaretti suggests making certain it is broken. A damp tape, moistened by humidity in the air, is often to blame when VCRs won't rewind or fast forward. "Try a different tape or leave the machine alone a day or two to dry out," he advised. And if the TV screen goes snowy or plain blue when the VCR is played, try inserting an unused tape in the machine. "Brand new tape is very abrasive and takes dirt off the heads," Mr. Passaretti said.

Repairs range from $35 an hour for Walkmans to $85 an hour for camcorders. Estimates, deducted from the cost of the repair, are from $20 for Walkmans to $50 for camcorders.   PYRAMID ELECTRONICS, LTD., 353 East 76th Street, New York, NY 10021; (212) 628-6500.

PEOPLE TAKE CAMCORDERS TO THE BEACH, but sand and salt water can ruin the machines, according to Elbert Chan, president of E C Electronics, a 17-year-old authorized service center. "Salt water corrodes the circuit boards," he explained. "And we can never get all the sand out." In contrast, replacing a cracked camcorder case is a snap. "The components are more expensive," Mr. Chan said.

Mr. Chan suggests camcorder owners avoid using 120-minute tape, which is thinner than 60-minute tape and more likely to clog the machine's heads. Old tape, used for two or three years, can clog the heads as well.

E C Electronics, an authorized service center for 15 brands, including Sony, Aiwa, Fuji, Marantz and Scott, charges $89 to repair VCRs. Camcorder estimates are $40, deducted from the cost of the repair, $150 maximum for labor.  **E C ELECTRONICS,** 253 West 51st Street, New York, NY 10019; (212) 586-6156.

## VIDEOS MADE FROM OLD MOVIES OR SLIDES

W HEN PEOPLE ASK ALEX SHAHGHOLI what he does for a living, he can show them a video of his daughter Tina's third birthday party. Mr. Shahgholi's video-photo album, compiled by his company, International Video Services, features family slides and photographs punctuated by special effects and a soundtrack. There's also a title page, with whimsical letters shaped like crayons.

For years, videotape and film-editing companies, such as Mr. Shahgholi's, dealt mainly with professional clients in television and advertising. But as the use of VCRs, camcorders and other home video tools has increased, more nonprofessionals are requesting the services of studios to compile and edit home videos, transfer vintage eight-millimeter movies to video and create video-photo albums.

"People are becoming little Steven Spielbergs," said Mr. Shahgholi.

Do-it-yourself enthusiasts can rent an editing room at I.V.S., which features either the simplest equipment to cut and edit videotape ($15 an hour) or more sophisticated special effects equipment to create fade-outs, freezes and slow motion ($35 an hour). Editing lessons are available ($20 plus room fee). It usually takes a day to edit a wedding video.

"One customer recently made a 15-minute This is Your Life–type video using old home movie footage, stills, all sorts of stuff," Mr. Shahgholi said.

Clients who want I.V.S. to compile a video-photo album can drop off the necessary slides and photographs. Most want albums to revolve around a theme, such as a wedding, anniversary or vacation. Each image usually appears on the tape for no more than 10 seconds. "Otherwise it gets boring," Mr. Shahgholi explained. Music can be added if the customer provides an audiocassette or CD. A 50-image video-photo album with simple cuts costs $39.95; albums with special effects cost $59.95.

Though transferring old 8-millimeter, Super 8 or 16-millimeter home movies to video accounts for a chunk of Mr. Shahgholi's business, he warns customers to keep the original film. "Videos are for convenience, but they don't last as well as film," he said.

For customers who don't want to travel to I.V.S.'s Times Square studio, the company has drop-off centers, called Video Perfect, throughout the metropolitan area. For center locations, call (800) 426-7437. INTERNATIONAL VIDEO SERVICES, 1501 Broadway (43rd Street), New York, NY 10036; (212) 730-1411.

SOME CUSTOMERS HAVE NO IDEA what their films contain when they ask to have old home movies transferred onto videocassettes. "Their projector may have broken years ago," said Keith Eland, an account executive at USA Studios, a videotape editing company.

Most old home movies transfer easily to videotape, provided the original film is in decent shape. "The exception is when someone sends in a bag of film in 100 pieces," said Mr. Eland, whose company transfers 8-millimeter, Super 8 and 16-millimeter film onto tape. USA Studios charges approximately 10 cents a foot to transfer 8-millimeter and Super 8 tape. The company also rents editing studios. USA STUDIOS, 15 West 20th Street, New York, NY 10011; (212) 229-9898.

BESIDES TRANSFERRING OLD HOME MOVIES onto videotape, ANS, a company that edits videotape, transfers slides to videotape. But slides should be in good condition, said Elif Bilgin, an ANS salesperson. "We can't do much to improve them," she said.

Old 8-millimeter, Super 8 and 16-millimeter film, in contrast, can be put through a machine that adjusts color, light and other variables as it goes onto videotape. "We can't create miracles, but usually it looks better," she said. ANS, 91 Fifth Avenue (17th Street), New York, NY 10003; (212) 366-1733.

## WALLPAPERS
## (HISTORIC DESIGNS)

*F*OR YEARS, Bruce Bradbury was fascinated by anything Victorian, especially wallpaper. So in 1979, Mr. Bradbury, a printer in Benicia, California, began making his own, copying Victorian wallpaper patterns and creating new designs with a 19th-century feeling.

"I started very small," he said. "I used to write poetry on the selvages when I shipped off a roll."

Interest in wallpapers that flaunt the Victorian era's decorative images and flamboyant colors has grown in recent years, as more and more historic buildings and homes are restored to their original style.

These days, Bradbury & Bradbury Art Wallpapers, a mail order company, offers more than 100 hand-printed patterns, with an assortment of designs for walls, borders and the fanciful paper ceiling panels Victorians loved. "I look at a white room as a blank canvas," Mr. Bradbury said.

The Victorian fascination for elaborate wall and ceiling papers was rooted in philosophy. "They believed if you could make the world a more beautiful place, the world would be better," Mr. Bradbury said.

The company's catalog is $10 and includes a dizzying mix of Victorian prints, borders and panels. Among them are intricate patterns in the style of the English designer William Morris and boldly colored Moorish patterns. The company also offers a "heavy metal" collection, with designs in silver or gold. And a collection of early 20th-century American patterns is available as well.

Hand-printed paper starts at $40 a roll. Borders and friezes start at $12 a linear foot.    BRADBURY & BRADBURY ART WALLPAPERS, P.O. Box 155, Benicia, CA 94510; (707) 746-1900.   ✉

"EVERYTHING IS SO STANDARDIZED, but at home you can let your fancy go," said Tania Bobrinskoy, who with her husband, Nicholas, owns Zina Studio, custom wallpaper and fabric makers.

Designs by the tiny company in Mount Vernon, New York, are anything but standardized. Begun in 1929, Zina Studio produced wallpapers, often embellished with flowers and butterflies, for Elsie de Wolfe, Nancy McClelland and other well-known interior designers. The company still carries these classic designs as well as Mr. Bobrinskoy's more modern creations, which include bold florals and intricate geometric patterns.

Much of Zina Studio's business is in exacting wallpaper and fabric reproductions for museums and historic houses. The company has reproduced wallpaper for the Washington Irving House in Irvington, New York, and several historic mansions in Newport, Rhode Island, including the Elms. The company sells many of these designs.

Clients commissioning reproductions usually send crumbling wallpaper swatches, photographs and samples from the room's original colors.

Historic wallpapers at Zina Studio start at $45 a roll, 20th-century designs at $33 a roll. A swatch selection is available for $15.   ZINA STUDIO, 45 South Third Avenue, Mount Vernon, NY 10550; (914) 667-6004.   ✉

FOR YEARS, THIBAUT WALLCOVERINGS and Fabrics in Newark, New Jersey, specialized in contemporary wallpaper and fabric designs. But in the early 1980s, the 110-year-old concern began producing historic wallpapers in conjunction with the National Preservation Institute in Washington.

Thibaut's historic papers and fabrics are careful copies of wallpapers in historic American buildings and homes, including Oak Hill, the one-time home of President James Monroe, in Aldie, Virginia. Wall designs, borders and screen-printed fabrics are available, detailed in a two-dollar brochure.

The company also offers wallpapers based on china designs by the Royal Limoges company in France.

The company's historic papers are printed on prepainted vinyl-coated paper, priced from $20.99 a roll. Hand-screened painted borders, which are not prepasted, start at $23.99 for five yards. Fabric, 54 inches wide, comes in 100 percent cotton, is treated with Dupont Teflon, and starts at $39.99 a yard.   **THIBAUT WALLCOVERINGS AND FABRICS,** 480 Frelinghuysen Avenue, Newark, NJ 07114; (201) 643-3777.
✉

## WASTEBASKETS

PEOPLE KICK THEM, throw things at them and fill them with whatever they don't want. But Brooke Loening, who has a shop in Salisbury, Connecticut, thinks the wastebasket should be functional and attractive.

Mr. Loening found it a bit odd that people would spend thousands of dollars to decorate a room, then install a tacky plastic wastebasket right next to the antique desk. So in 1989, he and his business partner John Zabriskie decided to design wastebaskets with a little style.

The Loening/Zabriskie litter bins are fashioned from wood and come in several different styles. The basic model is a tapered octagon in mahogany, embellished with brass lion-head handles.

The company also makes a mahogany Chippendale-style basket, with four tapered sides and cut-out handles.

The baskets are lacquered on the inside. But the baskets will last longer if no one tosses in cola cans or banana peels, Mr. Loening said.

Before making their wastebaskets, the two men made cardboard prototypes of 60 different shapes, then pitched papers to see how much each could hold. "A wastebasket should look nice, but it's got to be utilitarian," said Mr. Zabriskie.

The baskets, made from reforested Indonesian mahogany, did so well they became a key item in Amandari, the shop the partners opened several years ago in Salisbury, Connecticut. Besides wastebaskets, Amandari also sells bowls, trays, jewelry boxes and other items, many embellished with polished pewter, designed by the partners.

A free catalog is available.   AMANDARI, 9 Academy Lane, Salisbury, CT 06068; (800) 449-7844.   ✉

ATTRACTIVE WASTEBASKETS were one of the items Harriet Boileau had difficulty finding during her years as an interior decorator. So in 1989, Ms. Boileau, who is based in Dorchester, England, designed a line of customized wastebaskets, marketed through her company, Cubbins & Company.

The Cubbins & Company wastepaper bins have wood bodies that can be painted, lacquered or covered with a rich selection of fabrics, including velvet, suede, silk, chintz and brocade. Inspiration for the line came from a pair of upholstered Edwardian wastebaskets with fluted tops that Ms. Boileau discovered in her grandmother's house, Wallingford Castle in Berkshire. One of the four-sided bins stood on brass feet, which Cubbins & Company copied as well.

The company's upholstered wastebaskets come with braid finishing and silk or chintz interiors, which can be protected by a removable plastic liner or with a plastic coating, which is invisible, Ms. Boileau says. Cubbins & Company, which accepts mail orders, also does custom jobs and will work with fabric supplied by the client. Upholstered wastebaskets start at about $230. Packing, postage and insurance is an additional $45.   CUBBINS & COMPANY, Rampisham Manor, Dorchester, Dorset, England DT2 OPT; 011-44-1-935-83060.   ✉

# WATCHES (WIND-UP), CLEANED AND REPAIRED

"IT'S THE SENTIMENTAL ATTACHMENT," said Stewart Unger, explaining why most people bring old watches to his 12-year-old Manhattan shop, Time Will Tell, for repairs. "People inherit them."

But old-fashioned pocket watches and wristwatches with old-fangled mechanical movements are popular with collectors as well as those who like the idea of a owning a timepiece not operated by a battery. Some people like watches that tick. Some like classic watch faces from the 1920s and 1940s. Some simply enjoy having a watch that winds.

Watches with traditional mechanical movements require more care and expense than today's battery-operated Quartz models. And, like traditional wind-up watches, the people who repair them are increasingly hard to find. "It's time-consuming work," Mr. Unger said, who also sells antique timepieces.

Many of his repairs are on American pocket watches by Elgin, Waltham and Hamilton, manufactured from 1880 to 1930, the heyday of the American pocket watch industry. "They were timepieces and fashion items," said Mr. Unger, who, with Edward Faber, coauthored the book *American Wristwatches* (Schiffer, $79.95). "When men stopped wearing vests, the wristwatch became prominent."

Some of the most distinctive pocket watches were manufactured for railroad conductors. These traditionally had stark white faces with bold, easy-to-read numbers and, sometimes, a red 12.

American pocket watches are fairly easy to repair since parts are usually available. "Elgin and Waltham made 50 million wrist and pocket watches between the 1860s and 1950s," Mr. Unger said.

Quality also was high. Some pocket watches had as many as 21 jewels. Jewels are the tiny concave glass bearings that suspend oil in the mechanism. Though brass bearings can be used instead of jewels, glass can take more wear; pocket watches usually have between 7 and 23 jewels, the more the better.

An overhaul for both pocket and wrist watches entails cleaning, reoiling and replacing the mainspring when necessary (from $190).

New crystals cost $50 to $60, and dial refinishing ranges from $55 to $100, though Mr. Unger often recommends some dials be left alone. "You can lose the feeling of the period with a cleaning," he said. Mr. Unger does not repair Quartz movements or sell batteries. TIME WILL TELL, 962 Madison Avenue (near East 75th Street), New York, NY 10021; (212) 861-2663. ✉

IT IS TIME FOR AN OVERHAUL WHEN A MECHANICAL watch begins to lose time, says Grace Szuwala, who owns Grace Time Service. To prolong the life of a mechanical watch, she suggests keeping the watch away from moisture. "Most old watches are not waterproof," she said. "And don't drop it," she added.

Ms. Szuwala, who learned watch repair in her native Poland, fixes all types of old watches, including Rolex, Patek Philippe, International and Bulova. Winding parts often need replacement, she said. "But mainly, the watches are worn out because they're old." Cleanings start at $40.

She also cleans and repairs Quartz watches, which are far less complex than traditional mechanical watches, and can replace a mechanical movement with a Quartz movement ($40 to $65). GRACE TIME SERVICE, 115 Greenwich Avenue (near East 13th Street), New York, NY 10014; (212) 929-8011. ✉

MOST MECHANICAL WATCHES need to be repaired because the oil has grown dirty and sludgy, says Tony Di Leonardo, who has repaired watches for over 40 years. "And the balance staff can break if a watch is dropped," he added.

Mr. Di Leonardo, whose Falt Watch Service is in Grand Central Station, repairs both wrist and pocket watches. For years, he serviced pocket watches carried by conductors.

Cleaning prices depend on the type of watch (Omega cleanings from $75, Rolex from $125). He also replaces crystals ($10 and up for plastic, $100 and up for sapphire, which doesn't scratch.) FALT WATCH SERVICE, 15 Vanderbilt Avenue, New York, NY 10017; (212) 697-6380.

# WEATHER VANES

LONG BEFORE THE ADVENT of meteorologists, newspaper weather maps and the Weather Channel, people consulted weather vanes to see which way the wind was blowing. "Many still do," said Ron Cabral, a partner in Crosswinds Gallery in Portsmouth, Rhode Island, a weather vane shop and mail order concern not far from Newport.

A well-balanced weather vane will turn with the slightest breeze. A cupola is the preferred perch, whether atop a garage or, for true traditionalists, a barn or shed. But many people set weather vanes in a garden, near a window. Others display them indoors to admire the craftsmanship.

Weather vanes, which date back to the ancient Greeks, arrived in America with New England's earliest settlers. Paul Revere made weather vanes; his apprentice, Shem Drowne, sculpted the fanciful grasshopper atop Boston's Faneuil Hall.

Balance is the key to a good weather vane. Even a 65-pound stainless-steel weather vane will turn if it's properly balanced. Improperly balanced, the weather vane's pin eventually wears down. The weather vane won't topple. But it won't turn as easily as it should.

Crosswinds, which represents 15 New England craftspeople, offers a range of prices, materials and styles, from cast aluminum ($50 and up) and imported, machine-made copper ($75 to $200) to molded copper ($225 to $1,000) and custom free-hand designs ($250 to over $1,000). A catalog is available free of charge. CROSSWINDS GALLERY, 15 Francis Street, Bristol, RI 02809; (800) 638-8263 or (401) 253-0344. ✉

MANY ANTIQUE WEATHER VANES can still do their job atop a cupola. But vintage vanes belong indoors, according to Marilyn Strauss, whose 18-year-old shop, Salt & Chestnut Weathervanes, on Massachusetts's Cape Cod offers old and new weather vanes.

"The old ones are so beautifully made you want to see them up close," she explained. And a weather vane displayed outside can get stolen. "It's best to have a copy made for the outdoors," Ms. Strauss said. Antique weather vanes need their original patina to maintain top value, she added. The auction record for an antique vane was $770,000 for an 1840s jockey and horse at Sotheby's in 1990.

Ms. Strauss, who represents 32 weather vane makers, specializes in commissioned hand-made vanes, from sailing ships to business logos. Antique weather vanes start at $500, new models from $80; most cost from $480 to $780. A catalog is available for $2. **SALT & CHESTNUT WEATHERVANES,** 651 Route 6A, P.O. Box 41, West Barnstable, MA 02688; (508) 362-6085. ✉

COPPER IS THE CLASSIC WEATHER VANE MATERIAL, said J. Donald Felix, a weather vane maker for over 20 years. "It's light, easy to work with and doesn't rust," he explained. It *does* turn greenish when left outdoors, an effect he likes. "New copper looks manufactured," said Mr. Felix, who prefers an aged finish. "And it collects fingerprints."

To create a freehand weather vane, Mr. Felix makes a paper pattern, traces it, then pounds it out in copper. "No two are alike," he said. Weather vanes from $200. A catalog is available for $1. **J. DONALD FELIX,** P.O. Box 995, Hampton, NH 03842; (603) 474-2225. ✉

## WEDDING DETAILS, SMALL AND LARGE

IF THE 1980s WAS THE DECADE of the Big Wedding, the early 1990s qualifies as the era of the personalized wedding, ultrapersonalized in some cases.

"It's not so much the grand party as it's something unique to the couple," said Nancy Davis, author of *Bridal Style,* (Hugh Lauter Levin Associates; $60), a new illustrated book of wedding ideas. "If you met at the seaside, you might want shells on your cake."

Or if you're fond of Harley Davidsons, like one bride pictured in Ms. Davis's book, you might ride your bike to your wedding wearing a black miniskirt and flowered boa (it's hard to carry a bouquet and steer a Harley). Indeed, it isn't always necessary to spend a lot of money to make a wedding personal.

Details are, of course, the basic element of a personal wedding.

And the following New York–area businesses all specialize in wedding details.

Like gowns, bridal headpieces blend fashion and tradition. And the latest headgear is "very plain," according to Marina Biagioli, a co-owner of Wedding Belles, a bridal headwear store in Oceanside, Long Island. "Not too many sequins, not too many pearls. Last year's brides wanted lots of shine."

Mrs. Biagioli and her partner, Marie Butchen, designed all 150 headpieces in their shop—rose-covered headbands, lace Juliet caps, crystal tiaras, pillbox hats and big bows for the back of the head, among others. Big for the early 1990s were cathedral-length veils (three yards by three yards). Bejeweled Indian-style headbands, beloved in the '80s, were out.

The two milliners, who customize each headpiece down to the lace, flowers and beads, recently fashioned a headpiece from a bow a bride wanted removed from her gown. They also restore and repair heirloom headgear for brides eager to wed in a mother's, or grandmother's, veil. Headpieces start at $150 and usually take six to eight weeks. WEDDING BELLES, 2848 Long Beach Road, Oceanside, NY 11572; (516) 764-1390. ✉

EVENING SHOE DESIGNER VANESSA NOEL, who started fashioning white silk wedding shoes nearly three years ago, devotes an entire room of her shop to down-the-aisle footwear. And through her catalog, she also provides wedding shoes by mail. The $7 catalog illustrates a range of hand-made shoes, from high tradition (Heart and Sole is a classic pump with a heart hiding the toes, $365) to high tops (the white silk wedding cowboy boot has silver tips and heels, $465).

Though backless shoes with jeweled buckles are hot sellers this season, Ms. Noel said nervous brides often want shoes with straps "so they won't fall out of their heels when they dance." Silk shoes can be dyed after the big event, she added. VANESSA NOEL, 26 East 66th Street, New York, NY 10021; (212) 737-0115. ✉

COUPLES CHOOSING WEDDING RINGS are often indecisive, according to Herman Rotenberg, whose business, 1,873 Unusual Wedding Bands, offers plenty of choice. His stall at the National Jewelers Exchange, opened over 40 years ago by his father-in-law Bill Schifrin, actually stocks more than 4,000 wedding bands in gold, platinum, diamonds and other stones.

Popular at the moment are bands in 22-karat gold, which looks yellow, and so-called artistic bands, often with a hand-crafted, individualized look. "They're not for everyone," he admitted.

Rings are also available in so-called pink gold, with a touch of copper added, and in green gold, devised by adding silver. Very few couples order identical rings, he added. Rings can be widened, narrowed and otherwise customized, a process that usually takes a day to a week, though not all couples are willing to wait. "One woman bought a ring, asked for the ladies' room key and came out wearing her gown," Mr. Rotenberg recalled.

Rings start at $40 for 14-karat gold and at about $250 for 22-karat gold. **1,873 UNUSUAL WEDDING BANDS,** National Jewelers Exchange, Booth 86, 4 West 47th Street, New York, NY 10036; (212) 944-1713.

BRUCE HINTON, OWNER OF ELAN FLOWERS IN SoHo, calls his latest creation the calorieless wedding cake. And from a distance it looks like a classic cake, with cream-colored layers supported by plastic columns and a bride and groom on top. But Mr. Hinton's cakes are fashioned entirely from roses and other wedding flowers, and garnished with seed pearls, ribbons and bows. "Brides kept asking for high-rise centerpieces," he said.

Floral wedding cakes can be designed to fit the wedding's colors and themes. "Brides usually want them for the head table," Mr. Hinton said. Some might even use them in lieu of a traditonal cake. "You can satisfy your visual appetite for wedding cake with these, then serve something other than cake for dessert," he added. Floral cakes, also available in pink cakeboxes for birthdays, cost $100 a layer. **ELAN FLOWERS,** 108 Wooster Street (near Spring Street), New York, NY 10012; (212) 343-2426.

ANNE NOONAN, A PARTNER IN SoHo LETTERPRESS, started her printing business a year and a half ago to print artists' books. But along the way, she and her husband, Joe Elliot, got requests for one-of-a-kind party invitations. Come spring, Ms. Noonan is busy printing unusual wedding announcements, often on hand-made paper. (For a preppy couple, Ms. Noonan created paper from madras shirts owned by the bride and groom.)

Using an old proof press from the 1960s, Ms. Noonan is able to print invitations individually. She even printed one invitation on sand-paper. One couple of Irish descent asked an artist friend to design a stylized border, part Celtic, part psychedelic, for their invitation.

Another bride used floral imagery borrowed from the invitation to her great-grandmother's 25th wedding party in turn-of-the-century Sweden. Invitations range from about $600 to $1,200. SOHO LETTER-PRESS, 69 Greene Street (near Spring Street), New York, NY 10012; (212) 925-7575.

FOR BRIDES WHO RELISH DETAILS, a decorative garter garnished with lace, rosettes and pearls is high on the list of must-have wedding items. And for six years, Maria Diamondopoulos, a costume designer from Garden City, New York, has designed devastatingly pretty ones fashioned in everything from venetian lace to reembroidered lace. "No blue ribbons," said Ms. Diamondopoulos, who got into the garter business by outfitting her six sisters when each got married.

Brides often buy two garters, she said. They choose something inexpensive, such as a crocheted lace garter, for the groom to toss to the available men in the audience ($12 to $18). But they invest $20 to $35 in a more elaborate keepsake garter in silk chiffon with rosebuds and appliqué or schiffli lace with rosebuds and bows. All garters are made of cotton elastic, which Ms. Diamondopoulos said stretches better than polyester lace.

Her garters are sold at Berdgorf Goodman, Neiman Marcus stores and Manhattan specialty shops, such as Only Hearts, 386 Columbus Avenue at West 79th Street, ([212] 724-5608) and most branches of Legroom. The designer can also provide names of additional vendors. MARIA DIAMONDOPOULOS; (212) 802-7103.

FOR BRIDES AND GROOMS with less than perfect smiles, two New York–area dentists offer Bride-smile and Groom-grin—cosmetic porcelain bonding to correct problems with tooth color, shape and position. Though anyone can, of course, order up cosmetic dental work, the dentists suggest having it done before a wedding.

"You'll be living with the wedding photos and videos for the rest of your life," said Dr. Alan Goldstein, a Manhattan dentist, who devised the service with Dr. Eugene Seidner, a New Jersey dentist. During the process, which can be accomplished in two days, problem teeth are repaired, then porcelain laminates are bonded onto the tooth. Laminates last at least five years, Dr. Goldstein added, and cost about $2,500 for four to six teeth.   DR. ALAN GOLDSTEIN, 3 West 71st Street, New York, NY 10023, (212) 580-8100;   DR. EUGENE SEIDNER, 29 Smull Avenue, Caldwell, NJ 07006, (201) 228-2233.

## WEDDING GOWNS, ALTERED, CLEANED AND RESTORED

*F*OR SOME, it's sentiment. For others, it's esthetics. And for a few, it's a clever way to save money. "Brides get married in antique wedding gowns for all sorts of reasons," said Marguerite Morgan, a textile conservator whose specialty is reviving—and resizing—old wedding gowns for new brides.

For years brides have married in classic gowns worn by their mothers, grandmothers and even great-grandmothers. But the practice became particularly strong in the late 1980s, said Mrs. Morgan, who has restored antique clothing for over a decade. "It's since fancy weddings became popular again," she said.

Spring is high season for wedding gown restorers, but demand is strong year round. "I've worked on some lovely gowns for winter weddings, too," Mrs. Morgan recalled. Most of the gowns brides bring her these days were originally worn by brides in the 1940s, '50s and '60s, but Mrs. Morgan works on older gowns, too.

She once restored a magnificent 1910 gown that belonged to the grandmother of the bride-to-be. The original hand-made bobbin lace and satin remained, though Mrs. Morgan had to replace the disintegrated silk sections with ivory brocade.

Age usually has less to do with the condition of a used wedding gown than the way the dress was stored over the years. "Some survive, even if they were rolled in a ball and thrown in the attic," Mrs. Morgan said. But even a relatively new gown can be a wreck if it was kept in air-tight plastic, which can create an acidic environment by sealing in moisture.

"This gown was practically in smithereens," she added, holding a recent snapshot of a smiling bride who insisted on wearing her mother's Liz Taylor–style dress, circa 1955. So Mrs. Morgan, who charges $300 and up to revive old gowns, restored the tattered garment with two new Chantilly lace panels that matched the old.

Mrs. Morgan also takes in or lets out seams where appropriate. In most cases, the latter is required. "The older gowns are usually a little snug across the back," she said. "It's vitamins and different lifestyles. Girls today exercise more than their mothers did." MARGUERITE MORGAN, 6 Highland Cross, Rutherford, NJ 07070; (201) 939-7222.

DISCOLORATION IS A BIG PROBLEM with antique wedding gowns. But sometimes a professional washing in cold water is all that's needed to whiten a gown, says Viola Lappe, whose Museum Quality Storage Box Company and Preservation Service cleans and packages wedding gowns in acid-free wrappings.

Dry cleaning is needed if there's a chance the gown will shrink. Otherwise, wet cleaning will wash away considerable acidity and dirt. A little bleach, carefully applied, also helps in some cases.

Brides often ship gowns to Mrs. Lappe after the wedding. Her company, in business since 1978, returns each gown, cleaned and pressed, in a 40-inch-long acid-free storage box that's lined with cotton muslin. Each box comes with a white cotton cover, decorated with a little pink bow.

Cleaning and boxing starts at $170. MUSEUM QUALITY STORAGE BOX COMPANY AND PRESERVATION SERVICE, 9 Laurel Lane, Pleasantville, NY 10570; (800) 937-2693. ✉

"I WAS VERY SKEPTICAL," declared Jerry Leibowitz. But as it turned out, his company, Fashion Award Cleaners, was able to clean and restore a 150-year-old heirloom wedding gown brought in by a young bride-to-be. "It looked like a dress from Tara," he said.

For delicate fabrics, it is necessary to test the gown in several places before beginning a full-scale cleaning. "We have to see if it will withstand a normal cleaning, a light cleaning or a hand cleaning," said Mr. Leibowitz, whose 30-year-old company frequently cleans beaded garments. But there is still an element of risk as the gown may have oxidized—and consequently be weaker—in different places. "You can't test the whole garment," he said.

Beads must be tested before a cleaning can commence, as well. "Sometimes the bead's surface disappears or peels away in a cleaning," Mr. Leibowitz said. "And sometimes the plastic simply dissolves and disappears."

Fashion Award Cleaners charges $150 and up to dry clean wedding gowns, and $100 to prepare garments for storage in acid-free wrappings. Alterations start at $25. **FASHION AWARD CLEANERS,** 1462 Lexington Avenue (near 94th Street), New York, NY 10128; (212) 289-5623. ✉

# WINDOWS (STEEL CASEMENT), REPAIRED

WHEN JOHN SEEKIRCHER began repairing steel casement windows in 1977, he could only find part-time work. Homeowners and co-ops routinely replaced old steel-frame windows with aluminum or vinyl frames. But these days restoring old steel window frames is a full-time job.

"A lot of people buying Westchester Tudors are repairing the old windows instead of installing aluminum replacement windows," said Mr. Seekircher, who recently repaired 160 steel-frame windows on a huge Westchester house.

And most landmark buildings with steel casement windows, including many Central Park West co-ops, are required either to restore existing frames or to find identical steel replacements. "These windows have a distinctive look," said Mr. Seekircher.

Steel casement windows, popular in late-19th-century Europe, were installed in countless New York–area homes and apartment buildings before World War II. They can last for decades when cared for properly.

Old windows can often be revived with minimal repairs. A professional cleaning can open windows sealed shut with age. Hinges can be repaired. Cranks can be replaced. And frames can be realigned so windows close tight. Storm windows and retractable screens can also be installed inside the windows.

Rotting steel sections can be repaired as well. Mr. Seekircher recently rebuilt the bottom of a steel-frame door for a Park Avenue apartment, doing on-site welding and fitting. "It's a lot cheaper than buying a new window," Mr. Seekircher said. Basic adjustment and service starts at about $30 a window.   SEEKIRCHER STEEL WINDOW REPAIR CORP., 630 Saw Mill River Road, Ardsley, NY 10502; (914) 693-1920.

AMERICAN STEEL WINDOW SERVICE CO., a nearly 80-year-old family-run business, specializes in altering and repairing steel windows, including casement windows, factory-style windows and old-style metal windows with side chains. But a big part of their business is supplying handles, hinges and other hard-to-find parts. "Hardware breaks," said owner Peter Weinberger. Some years back, his father, Dan, purchased large amounts of hardware from several manufacturers going out of business.

Though they usually predate air conditioners, steel casement windows can be adapted to accommodate most cooling units, Mr. Weinberger said. Basic repairs start at around $30 a window.   AMERICAN STEEL WINDOW SERVICE CO., 108 West 17th St., New York, NY 10011; (212) 242-8131.

ARCHITECTS ARE DESIGNING BUILDINGS with steel windows again, said Louis Lehrbaum, whose nearly 40-year-old company, A & S Windows, manufactures steel window frames for both residential and industrial use. Aluminum frames tend to be thick. Steel, in contrast, "makes a nice narrow sideline for a different look," he said. "They're putting them in new schools and factories."

A & S manufactures steel windows and doors and does customized work. Finished windows are also available.   A & S WINDOWS, 88-19 76th Avenue, Glendale, NY 11385; (718) 275-7900.

# WINDOWS (WOOD), REPAIRED AND CUSTOM-BUILT

*T*HE 1980S WERE BIG YEARS for aluminum, at least where window frames were concerned. Hundreds of worn-out wood-frame windows were discarded, notably in large apartment buildings and brownstones. The popular replacement was the double-hung aluminum-frame window that swings up for easy cleaning.

But custom-made wood-frame windows are hardly obsolete. They are the required replacement in official Landmark buildings, where the new windows need to look like the old. They can also be the replacement of choice. "Wood has a look and richness that some people love," said Joe Doherty, owner of Precision Windows, a wood-frame window manufacturer in the Bronx. "Some people also like the fact that you can change the color any time."

Twenty years ago, there were 20 wood-frame window manufacturers in the New York area. These days there are fewer than 10. But the choice of styles, woods, hardware and even glass has probably never been greater.

Mr. Doherty, in business since 1981, specializes in what he calls combination windows, or WVAs, which stands for wood, vinyl and aluminum. Sashes are customized in wood. But the frame holding the window into the wall is aluminum. Weatherstripping is pile-edged vinyl. Double-hung combination windows can swing out for cleaning.

The benefit, according to Mr. Doherty, is that the aluminum extrusions can be installed into existing frames, which can keep costs down.

Precision Windows also fabricates casement windows and installs German-made tilt-and-turn windows, which open like a door or tilt up to let air in. Windows can be created in pine or more costly woods, such as mahogany.

Windows start from around $350 for single-pane glass and can go into the thousands, minimum order three. PRECISION WINDOWS, 2980 Webster Avenue, Bronx, NY 10458; (718) 733-0517.

"IN THE LATE 1800s, THESE ARCHITECTS did nothing but put in oval windows," said Cosmo Cotroneo, a partner in Millwork Specialties, wood window manufacturers since 1966. Millwork Specialties has created dozens of oval and circular replacement windows for Landmark buildings, as well as more conventional double-hung wood windows.

The company in Brooklyn frequently makes frames and sashes for bent-glass windows. And Millwork, which uses pine or more costly woods, such as mahogany, can install old-fashioned weights and chain devices when necessary.

A benefit of wood is that it doesn't conduct heat or cold, like metal, Mr. Cotroneo said. But wood needs to be painted regularly.

The company also offers a variety of insulated panes, though these work best in newer buildings with insulated walls. "A brick wall is like a sieve," Mr. Cotroneo said. "Energy conservation was the last thing they thought of 150 years ago."

Prices start at around $100 for a small, single-pane window without installation, and can go into the thousands. **MILLWORK SPECIALTIES,** 189 Prospect Avenue, Brooklyn, NY 11215; (718) 768-8308.


MORRIS ZELUCK, PRESIDENT OF J. ZELUCK INCORPORATED, calls his customized wood-frame creations the Rolls Royce of windows. And they're priced accordingly, ranging from around $500 to over $10,000, per window.

What kind of window costs $10,000? A magnificent wood window, 10 feet tall, motorized to disappear into the floor by remote control. (Several of these windows were installed recently around an indoor pool.)

J. Zeluck, in business since 1921, manufactures everything from casement windows for Landmark townhouses to Palladian windows for postmodern mansions. Windows are made from mahogany, teak, cherry, walnut and other costly woods.

Various types of glass are available, including restoration and bulletproof. All work is done in an immaculate Brooklyn factory, both by hand and with a new computerized tool system.

The company also offers specialty items, such as windows that close automatically when it rains. A built-in photo-cell alarm system, nearly invisible, is also available. "If somebody wants toys, we can offer them," Mr. Zeluck said.   J. ZELUCK INC., 5300 Kings Highway, Brooklyn, NY 11234; (718) 251-8060.

## YARD PLANTERS AND WINDOW BOXES, UNUSUAL AND CUSTOM-MADE

In the city, where gardens are small, planters take on added importance. Versailles boxes stand like sentinels at the doorways of countless apartment buildings. And the window herb garden seems more appealing when it's planted in an attractive window box.

Since 1986, Tim Brown, president of Cedar Corps., has designed and built custom accessories for city gardens, from bull-nose planter boxes to benches and decks. He designs most of his work, though he has worked with architects and can build to specs.

Mr. Brown works mostly with wood—cedar, redwood and Philippine mahogany—and usually recommends solid stains for his outdoor creations. But he generally paints his Versailles boxes, with a decorative X on each side, in high-gloss enamel. His 24-inch wood cubes in clear redwood range from $115 to $180. Versailles boxes, which are a bit larger, start at around $300. **CEDAR CORPS.,** 152 Myrtle Avenue, Jersey City, NJ 07302; (201) 432-2522 or (212) 826-8665.

LEXINGTON GARDENS, a garden accessory shop that opened in 1989, offers a range of customized planters and window boxes in wood, stone and terracotta. And recently, the company has added lightweight fiberglass planters to its inventory. "A number of co-ops have weight restrictions for terraces," said Bob DiNapoli, a partner in the concern.

At the top of the line are classic molded English stone planters from Haddonstone. Less costly is a line of terracotta planters that look aged and a line of glazed Chinese ceramic planters. The shop also stocks antique one-of-a-kind planters. Planters start at $90. **LEXINGTON GARDENS,** 1011 Lexington Avenue (near East 72nd Street), New York, NY 10021; (212) 861-4390.

## ZIPPERS
## (HARD-TO-FIND)

"I RETIRED 10 YEARS AGO," says Herbert Stiefel, sounding somewhat unconvincing. Small surprise. On weekdays, Mr. Stiefel, aka the Zipperman, can be found at his desk in a windowless upstairs stockroom at Harry Kantrowitz Co., a Garment District trimmings shop. There he sells, adjusts and, occasionally, repairs zippers, much as he has since 1938.

For customers in search of zippers in hard-to-find colors, sizes and styles, Mr. Stiefel, a former zipper wholesaler, is an extraordinary resource. His stock, amassed over his 50-plus years in the Garment District, is enormous and, in zipper terms, priceless, with countless styles and colors no longer manufactured, such as black metal corset zippers or old green maternity zippers.

"I like the old metal Talon zippers," he said.

Despite a stock of more than 3,000 long, seemingly identical cream-colored cardboard boxes, Mr. Stiefel knows precisely where to look when a customer asks for a 14-inch dress zipper in salmon pink or a metal windbreaker zipper in apple green.

"That's the last one I have," he told a customer who needed a pale blue 22-inch jacket zipper with metal teeth. The price: one dollar.

If the zipper is too long, Mr. Stiefel shortens it, deftly snipping off a length and adding new end teeth with zipper pliers. And if the size still isn't right, he sells zippers by the yard in such basic colors as brown, black and navy, adding sliders as needed.

He also replaces broken sliders, choosing the proper size from a wall of anonymous-looking boxes.

Mr. Stiefel, who deals only with walk-in customers, does not install or replace zippers, though he occasionally makes limping zippers zip smoothly again by pressing them with his fingers.   **HARRY KANTROWITZ CO.**, 555 Eighth Avenue (near West 38th Street), New York, NY 10018; (212) 563-1610.

# Index

custom designs, 45–46
paint for, 305
Bookcases
lighting for, 177, 179
radiator covers with, 250, 251
resizing, 256
Book covers, leather, 305
Bookends, blackened steel, 157
Books
conservation of, 222, 223
decorating and design, 47–48
embroidery, 48
for inventing games, 132
hideaway, 44
on magic, 192, 193
rare, 48
stencil design, 304
Bottles, perfume, 225–27
Bowls, resilvered, 201
Bows, stringed-instrument, rehaired
and tightened, 310–11
Bowties, cleaned and customized,
208
Boxes
acid-free, 305–7
organizers to unpack, 213
Bracelets, repaired, 159
Brackets, 24–25
Braided rugs, 263–66
do-it-yourself, 265–66
Brass
electroplating, 285
replating, 253, 254
Bridal gowns
altered, cleaned and restored,
354–56
embroidered, 105
repairing lace, 260
storing, 305
Bridal registry, 60
Brief cases, repaired, 174, 175, 188,
189
Broadloom rugs, 261, 262
Bugs, *see* Insects
Bulletproof glass windows, 359
Business cards, custom-made, 301
Butterflies, display boxes for, 306

Cabinetmakers, 68, 327–29
for resizing wood furniture, 255–57
Cabinets, 25
designed to conceal TVs, 327–29
murphy bed, 203–4
paint jobs for, 219, 221, 296, 297
resized, 255
Cakes, floral wedding and birthday,
352
Calligraphy, 299, 300
Camcorders, cleaned and repaired,
338–40
Cameras, repaired, 49–51
Camping equipment, cleaned and re-
paired, 216–18
Candlestick phones, 317
Candlesticks, repaired, 283
Cane furniture, repaired, 51–52, 202
Canes, sold and repaired, 333
Canister-style vacuum cleaners,
337–38
Canopy beds, resizing, 256–57
Canvas reweaving, 263
Capitals, 25, 27
Carbon paper with attached pages,
302
Card games, vintage, 131–32
Card tricks, 191–92
Cards, custom-made, 299–301
Carpeting
cleaners, 63, 335, 336
*see also* Flooring; Rugs
Casement windows, 358
resizing, 256
steel, repaired, 356–57
CD-ROMs, installed, 70
CDs, old recordings transferred to,
290–91
Cedar closets, 53–54
do-it-yourself, 54
Ceiling medallions, restoration and
repair of, 237
Ceiling papers, 343–44
Ceiling roundels, 25
Ceilings, tin, 323–25
Cellos, repaired and restored, 309,
310